Social Development and High Technology Industries:

Strategies and Applications

Ahmet Cakir
ERGONOMIC Institute, Germany

Patricia Ordóñez de Pablos
University of Oviedo, Spain

Senior Editorial Director:	Kristin Klinger
Director of Book Publications:	Julia Mosemann
Editorial Director:	Lindsay Johnston
Acquisitions Editor:	Erika Carter
Development Editor:	Myla Harty
Production Editor:	Sean Woznicki
Typesetters:	Mackenzie Snader, Milan Vracarich, Jr.
Print Coordinator:	Jamie Snavely
Cover Design:	Nick Newcomer

Published in the United States of America by
Information Science Reference (an imprint of IGI Global)
701 E. Chocolate Avenue
Hershey PA 17033
Tel: 717-533-8845
Fax: 717-533-8661
E-mail: cust@igi-global.com
Web site: http://www.igi-global.com

Library of Congress Cataloging-in-Publication Data

Social development and high technology industries: strategies and applications / Ahmet Cakir and Patricia Ordonez de Pablos, editors.
    p. cm.
  Includes bibliographical references and index.
  Summary: "This book highlights the relationships between contemporary high technology and social development, the development and application of high technology, high technology competition, and economic development as it pertains to high technology"--Provided by publisher.
  ISBN 978-1-61350-192-4 (hardcover) -- ISBN 978-1-61350-193-1 (ebook) -- ISBN 978-1-61350-194-8 (print & perpetual access) 1. High technology industries--Social aspects. 2. Social planning. I. Cakir, Ahmet, 1943- II. Ordsqez de Pablos, Patricia, 1975-
  HC79.H53S63 2010
  303.48'3--dc23
                          2011029150

British Cataloguing in Publication Data
A Cataloguing in Publication record for this book is available from the British Library.

All work contributed to this book is new, previously-unpublished material. The views expressed in this book are those of the authors, but not necessarily of the publisher.

List of Reviewers

Ahmet Cakir, *Ergonomic Institute, Germany*
Patricia Ordóñez de Pablos, *The University of Oviedo, Spain*
Aliana MW Leong, *Macau University of Science and Technology, Macao SAR*
Ciro Campos Christo Fernandes, *Getulio Vargas Foundation, Brazil*
Jose Emilio Labra Gayo, *The University of Oviedo, Spain*
Leong Chan, *Portland State University, USA*
Lluís Jovell Turró, *Autonomous University of Barcelona, Spain*
Luiz Antonio Joia, *Getulio Vargas Foundation, Brazil*
Przemysław Kazienko, *Wroclaw University of Technology, Poland*
Radosław Michalski, *Wroclaw University of Technology, Poland*
Robert D. Tennyson, *University of Minnesota, USA*
Rossano Eusebio, *Autonomous University of Barcelona, Spain*
Sebastian Palus, *Wroclaw University of Technology, Poland*
Tugrul Daim, *Portland State University, USA*
Xi Li, *Macau University of Science and Technology, Macao SAR*

Table of Contents

Preface..vii

Chapter 1
Model Analysis and Development Strategy on Building an Industrial Research and Development
(R&D) Centre: Shanghai's Practice and Inspiration.. 1
    Xi Li, Macau University of Science and Technology, China
    Aliana MW Leong, Macau University of Science and Technology, China

Chapter 2
LoTour: Using Technology to Provide Competitive Advantage in Local Tourism Industries.............. 15
    Marcos Ruano-Mayoral, Egeo IT, Spain
    Ricardo Colomo-Palacios, Universidad Carlos III de Madrid, Spain
    Pedro Soto-Acosta, University of Murcia, Spain
    Ángel García-Crespo, Universidad Carlos III de Madrid, Spain

Chapter 3
Emergent Technologies and Social Connectedness in Learning... 25
    Kumar Laxman, Nanyang Technological University, Singapore
    Yap Kueh Chin, Nanyang Technological University,Singapore

Chapter 4
Internal Key Factor in the Export Performance of Spanish SMEs.. 38
    Lluís Jovell Turró, Autonomous University of Barcelona, Spain
    Rossano Eusebio, Autonomous University of Barcelona, Spain

Chapter 5
Evaluation of Corporate Structure Based on Social Network Analysis.................................. 58
    Sebastian Palus, Wroclaw University of Technology, Poland
    Przemysław Kazienko, Wroclaw University of Technology, Poland
    Radosław Michalski, Wroclaw University of Technology, Poland

Chapter 6

High Technology Industrialization and Internationalization: Exploring International
Technology Transfer 70
> *Leong Chan, Portland State University, USA*
> *Tugrul Daim, Portland State University, USA*

Chapter 7

E-Governance Adoption: Identification of Success Factors from Teachers' Perspectives in Greece 99
> *Ioannis Karavasilis, University of Macedonia,Greece*
> *Kostas Zafiropoulos, University of Macedonia, Greece*
> *Vasiliki Vrana, Technological Education Institute of Serres, Greece*

Chapter 8

E-Government Maturity Levels in Brazil: Lessons Drawn from Several Brazilian States 118
> *Ciro Campos Christo Fernandes, Getulio Vargas Foundation, Brazil*
> *Luiz Antonio Joia, Getulio Vargas Foundation, Brazil*

Chapter 9

Digital Transition in Alaska 136
> *Ping Lan, University of Alaska Fairbanks, USA*

Chapter 10

Pressures or Weapons? Applying Information Technologies to Innovate Organizational Structures
win the Information Age 151
> *Liang-Hung Lin, National Kaohsiung University of Applied Sciences, Taiwan*

Chapter 11

Improving Cognitive Load on Students with Disabilities Through Software Aids 163
> *Rubén González Crespo, Universidad Pontificia de Salamanca, Spain*
> *Oscar Sanjuán Martíne, Universidad de Oviedo, Spain*
> *Juan Manuel Cueva Lovelle, Universidad de Oviedo, Spain*
> *B. Cristina Pelayo García-Bustelo, Universidad de Oviedo, Spain*
> *Vicente García Díaz, Universidad de Oviedo, Spain*
> *Patricia Ordoñez de Pablos, Universidad de Oviedo, Spain*

Chapter 12

Reviewing the European Innovation Activities and Industrial Competitiveness................................ 176
> *George M. Korres, University of Newcastle, UK & University of the Aegean, Greece*
> *Aikaterini Kokkinou, University of Glasgow, UK*

Chapter 13

City Structure in Transition: A Conceptual Discourse on the Impact of Information and
Communication Technology (ICT)... 187
> *Kh. Md. Nahiduzzaman, King Fahd University of Petroleum and Minerals, Saudi Arabia*
> *Adel S. Aldosary, King Fahd University of Petroleum and Minerals, Saudi Arabia*

Chapter 14
European Learning Resource Exchange: A Platform for Collaboration of Researchers,
Policy Makers, Practitioners, and Publishers to Share Digital Learning Resources and
New E-Learning Practices 200
    Eugenijus Kurilovas, Vilnius University, Lithuania; Ministry of Education and Science, Lithuania
    & Vilnius Gediminas Technical University, Lithuania

Compilation of References 244

About the Contributors 276

Index 283

Preface

High technology, the fastest growing and the most active field which produces a significant impact on human society deserves a high degree of study and attention, and also scientific recognition. With this book,we highlight the relationships between contemporary high technology and social development, the development and application of high technology, the competition of high technology and coping strategies, the economic development relying on high technology industrial growth.

The intention of the editors of this book is to provide an international platform that brings together academics, researchers, lecturers, and persons in decision making positions, policy makers and practitioners from different backgrounds to share new theories, research findings and case studies, by enhancing understanding and collaboration in issues of social development and information technologies in recent developments in theory and practice.

The high technology refers to current rapidly developing technologies, including electronic technology, new material technology, new energy technology, bioengineering technology and communication technology. With the development and needs of scientific technologies and production practices, the emerging industries have achieved spectacular results in various fields, forming the features of high technology, in general terms, the prominent characteristics of high technology industries are high density on knowledge, information, technology and funds; special emphasis on knowledge, talent, and R&D foundation; breakthrough and creativity; and important impacts on the economy and society.

This book serves to address the growing need of our society to adopt emerging technologies into all aspects of business and economic activity, moving towards innovative solutions to research problems, and thus resulting in high performance systems. The key characteristic of this book is that it brings together the experts of the IT industry, both practitioners and researchers alike, in a high tech research arena, with academia promoting a sound contribution to IT literacy, as demanded by real users.

The book follows a clear strategy to be the reference edition for all those interested on the strategic role of IT and Management towards sustainable development (with main emphasis to be paid on practical aspects), the reference edition for all those (policy makers, government officers, academics and practitioners) interested in understanding Social Development and High Technology Industries and to become a reference edition for people thirsty for knowledge on social development and information technologies.

Social Development and High Technology Industries: Strategies and Applications aims to be a reference for politicians, students and government articles alike. The book is divided into 14 chapters and provides insight on social development and technology industries.

Ahmet Cakir
ERGONOMIC Institute, Germany

Patricia Ordóñez de Pablos
University of Oviedo, Spain

Chapter 1
Model Analysis and Development Strategy on Building an Industrial Research and Development (R&D) Centre:
Shanghai's Practice and Inspiration

Xi Li
Macau University of Science and Technology, China

Aliana MW Leong
Macau University of Science and Technology, China

ABSTRACT

The globalization of the market, production and technology, research and development (R&D) will be the inevitable path of economic growth (Du Debin, 2005). A city as an important pole of regional economic development has a concentration and radiation on its surrounding areas. Its effect mainly depends on the size of the city's competitiveness. Generally speaking, production is relatively limited in urban competitiveness; service-oriented urban competitiveness is slightly stronger, while innovative cities will have the strongest competitive edge, the region's core cities.

Therefore, innovativeness becomes one of the strategic development directions of cities and regions. The globalization of multinational corporation research and investment, the continuous development of local R&D institutions, along with the industrial R&D center cluster allow the enhancement of innovative capabilities and competitiveness. International Industrial R&D center is an R&D institution in a city or region, which gathers global and regional Multinational Corporation. It is becoming the world's newest product especially in technology innovation and orientation locations, such as the U.S. Silicon Valley, Singapore, Bangalore in India, Hsinchu and Shanghai in China.

DOI: 10.4018/978-1-61350-192-4.ch001

This chapter defines the concept of industrial R&D center in order to explore the industrial R&D impact upon the host country. On this basis, R&D center on the concept of the international industry is defined; interviews with experts as well as empirical studies on the development of industrial R&D centers are classified. Based on the above definition, this chapter will focus on building for the Shanghai R&D centers of global industry and practice related initiatives described and provide reference and guidance based on the proposed Shanghai foster industry related countermeasures R&D center for other cities by emphasizing on industrial R&D institutions.

INTRODUCTION: FOREIGN DIRECT INVESTMENT (FDI) AND INTERNATIONAL R&D INVESTMENT

Foreign Direct Investment (FDI) is one of the more popular issues in international economics. It means to control the business part of the property investors to directly participate in management for profit capital exporting activity. According to the World Investment Report 2007, direct investment outflows from developed countries increased by 56% over the previous year, amounting to 169.2 billion U.S. dollars. Despite the international financial crisis since 2008, and the global slowing down this new feature has manifested itself. FDI in developing countries in Asia reached a more robust foreign investment momentum. The output from developing countries rose 3% than the previous year (UNCTAD, 2008). It can be seen in the field of FDI, both developed and developing countries are actively expanding their market space.

In the traditional international investment field, scholars' researches mainly focus on production within the field of property investment. In recent years, more and more industrial R&D investments have continuously come into the researchers' perspective; along with the related research is the increasing concern for the community. In the current view, industrial R&D is no longer a novelty. With the development of economic globalization and the economy, there is a gradual increase in the dependence of the knowledge economy, industrial development, especially multinational corporations in the industry. The huge R&D in-

vestment has become an important driving force for socio-economic development. Development strategy from the perspective of transnational corporations, with increasingly fierce market competition, shows that the field of competition has been extended from traditional product sales to product research and development phase (Wang Chunfa, 2003). Therefore, it can be said that industrial R&D investment is the development of FDI in the advanced stage. Its purpose is to better utilize all types of R&D resources of the enterprise's core competitiveness.

At present, enterprises of transnational R&D investment can be divided into two types: one for the applied R&D center also known as Development Center, whose main task is the core technology in some countries and regions, thereby developing products to suit local needs. Second, is the research centre based on research and studies. Its main task is to engage in basic technical and theoretical research, and the long-term development for the company's strategic technology reserve resources.

In fact, from a time perspective, the industry R&D capabilities are constantly undergoing evolution. Industrial R&D functions such as multinational corporations shift their trajectory from the initial transfer of technology - for local product development - developing products for the global market - for the enterprises engaged in basic research (Li Rui, 2004). Currently, the main function of industrial research has become the global market product development, technical support, and implementation of basic research.

Multinational R&D progress in the industry, not only changed the shape of international economic operation, but it also has had a profound impact on the host country to attract investment in the development model. In recent years, many domestic and foreign cities have proposed to develop an R&D center to attract multinational companies to achieve strong R&D investment, further strengthening local innovation. This research can be the basis of related studies on industrial R&D impact on the host country and the intention of related industry.

INDUSTRIAL R&D IMPACT OF GLOBALIZATION ON HOST COUNTRY

Most scholars divide multinational industrial R&D investment on the impact mechanism of the host country into three areas: the demonstration effect, spillover effect and crowding-out effect.

The Demonstration Effect

The meaning of the original demonstration effect for the consumer behavior and consumption not only relates to its self-factors but also to its immediate environs. The impact of the surrounding environment brings about the exemplary role of individuals. For industrial R&D, the demonstration effect of its main industries, are more local companies beginning to realize the importance of innovation on R&D and thus, following the R&D centers, they set up their own R&D centre. Currently, Shanghai has grown into a leading multinational and domestic R&D center followed by many cities in China. Shanghai set up its own R&D institutions, such as China Telecommunications Company-Zhongxing Corporation. In addition, 60 multinational companies had moved their R&D center from Taizhou to Shanghai, indicating a typical result of the demonstrational effect.

This demonstration effect is not entirely a form of imitation. It can be further subdivided into business innovation awareness, innovation and management innovation and corporate internal mechanisms of the three levels of imitation. A local business that enhances its awareness of scientific innovation efficiency is a result of these three levels of development. It is thus obvious that Industrial R&D is important to demonstrate the effect of growth for local businesses. The era of knowledge economy, technology and innovation to become competitive and monopolistic enterprises have become the main source of high profits. Therefore, the globalization of industrial research draws host mode on the development of enterprises.

The Spillover Effect

Concept and Connotation Evolution of the Spillover Effect

According to Mike Dogger (1960), the concept of foreign investment in the economic welfare affects the host country. He defined 'the spillover effect' as when: technology providers supply technology to involuntary transferees and technology providers do not comfort anything in refund behavior (Blomström, 2003).

Before the 1970s, many researchers believed that technology 'spillover effects' is weak and is not conducive to the development of the transnational corporations in host countries, especially developing countries. Hymer (1970) proposed that foreign direct investment in transnational corporations are its domestic monopoly power in the international expansion of its performance. Monopoly power will directly lead to market distortions and poor anti-competitive effect, whereby the situation is not conducive to the growth of the host country's technology and development. Moran (1970), Lall and Streeten (1977), pointed out that because multinational companies do not generally use the most advanced technology used in subsidiaries of developing countries, the development in the host country is often utilized in lower levels of production technology. Therefore, multinational direct investment into the country can only lead the market in the country it occupies, while the growth of technology is impeded.

Later studies became a mainstream view of transnational corporations in host countries, which stressed the positive effect of technological growth. They believe that multinational corporations are the owners of advanced technology, and through technology transfer are dispersing leadership. Direct investment from multinationals and research and development activities in the host country have some positive effects, producing externalities and spillover. Therefore, the entry of multinational companies and their technology plays a great role in promoting growth towards the host country (Caves, 1974).

Researchers tend to compromise the view that transnational corporations and the relationship between technology transfer and diffusion of multinational companies did not deny the entry of the host country's technological growth, but also stressed that the technology diffusion and transfer were not automatic with the entry of FDI. It can be achieved with hard work and the support of the host country.

The entry of transnational corporations can create some spillover, but there may be local enterprises that might feel certain 'crowding out effects' and 'displacement effects'. This requires the host country to manage a tradeoff, effective management and control, and the positive effect will be amplified as much as possible, to curb the negative effects (Du Debin 2001; Sheng Lei, 2008).

An economist, Caves (1974), assessed the earliest form of technology spillovers involving multinational corporations.' He divided the entry of Transnational Corporation (TNC) into 'productivity spillover' and 'technology spillover'. 'Productivity spillover' refers to the entry of multinational companies that will lead to in-

creased competition in local markets. As increased competition inevitably eliminated less efficient enterprises, the efficiency of resource allocation is enhanced. The 'technology spillover' refers to the transfer of a certain technology of the subsidiaries and affiliates of transnational corporations to local companies.

Many researchers have put forward their views for technology spillovers and diffusion. Tommaso Perez (1997) pointed out that for the host country, TNCs can be classified into those that bring about direct transfer of technology spillover effects and indirect spillover effects. As long as multinational corporations build factories in other countries, there must be some technology transfers to the host country enterprises and individuals. 'Indirect Spillover' refers to the indirect result of the host companies to access the productivity improvements and innovation capabilities. Further, from the industrial point of view, multinational spillover is reflected in two forms: 'technology spillovers between different industries' and 'technology spillovers within the same industry'.

Blomstrom (1989, 1991) and Kokko (1992) divided the transnational corporations in the form of technology spillovers into four categories: First, competition due to technological upgrading of local enterprises as multinational corporations increased the technological innovation of local enterprises and R&D efforts, and technology and management with multinational companies are similar under the pressure of market competition. Second, spillovers generated by cooperation between subsidiaries or affiliates of transnational corporations and local enterprises in the fields of technology and management. Third, human capital spillovers, as multinational companies provided training to improve employees' technical and management competence. If the employee were employed by local enterprises in the future, he/she could improve the level of technology and management of local enterprises. Fourth, the demonstration effect or demonstration-type spillovers effect, the entry of multinational corporations to local businesses to show the production and management technologies, in which both take the initiative to local businesses with their own presentation, the related management and technical knowledge transfer also includes its own operating activities as a non-voluntary display and demonstration effect.

In addition, some scholars created another category of technology spillovers: convergence spillovers and competition spillovers. The convergence-based spillover is the technical standard of the host country enterprises to multinational corporations and the convergence trend. The competitive spillovers refers to host country enterprises continued adoption of more technology to narrow the gap between transnational corporations (Wang, 1992)

Sheng Lei (2009) studied the spillovers effect by quantifying the technical efficiency of China's industrial R&D and believed that foreign R&D into China for the improvement of technical efficiency of Chinese enterprises means more investment into the current performance for technical inefficiency and cannot be completed in the short term. Nevertheless, in the long run, the entry of foreign R&D institutions can indeed enhance the innovation of Chinese enterprises and R&D efficiency. Spillover effects where the current major Chinese companies' access to technology through the competitive effect of the revenue overrun, the demonstration effect in the development of Chinese enterprises is more limited influence. In addition, 'the degree of spatial concentration' shows a positive correlation in R&D spillover effects. It is obvious that many cities that build strong industrial R&D center can really improve the regional R&D and introduce more innovation to a certain extent.

Industrial R&D Crowding-Out Effect

Industrial R&D crowding-out effect is a negative effect of industrial R&D investment. The main meaning of transnational corporations in host countries and the establishment of R&D center will further enhance competition in the host countries, which lead to its market share being gradually diverted, and eventually out of the local market.

Therefore, crowding-out effect has a certain negative effect for multinational R&D products in the process of globalization. The host country should develop the demonstration effect and enhance the spillover effects of multinational R&D investment to proceed, through the awareness of local business R&D training, capacity enhancement and access to technology to defend against and counter the possible crowding-out effect.

INTERNATIONAL INDUSTRIAL R&D CENTRE

The Concept of the International Industrial R&D Centre

The Spatial Scale of the International Industrial R&D Centre

Spatial scale has an important role in the qualification in terms of its scope and content of the object space. In accordance with the space span, spatial scales from big to small can usually be divided into the following five types: the regional scale, community scale, neighborhood scale, site scale, space scale and detail scales. Detailed spatial scale is the smallest scale, where the research is extremely in-depth, often for the most basic elements of space research of R&D activities in detail. Spatial scale and site scale refers to the macro level activities of individual enterprises. Neighborhood scale is the spatial extent of the business enterprise together with its surrounding neighbors. Community scale is the object of study on a valid number of the group enterprises. Regional scale is the most macro-scale concept, either refers to a city study, and may also be composed of several cities in a common area.

International Industrial R&D Center as a social objective has its time, space, relationships and three-dimensional attributes. As a study of geography, it must first determine its spatial characteristics. As mentioned earlier, research in this article differs from the international industrial R&D center; research and development institutions, such as General Electric Research and Development Center and the China Software R&D Center-Hewlett-Packard, also from the rapid development of the city Class Technology Development Zone, as the former object of study is detailed scale, the latter is a neighborhood scale or plot scale of study. Spatial scales refers to the international industrial R&D center where the scope of urban space is more similar to cell-scale or regional-scale concept, from the perspective of the city or region to study the industry R&D activities.

International industrial R&D center in spatial scale as described by (Huang Lucheng, Li Yang 2004) are different concepts, the former refers to the activities of international R&D resources and a cluster of the latter is an enterprise specialized in research and development activities of institutions. More typical of the international R&D centers are the international industry in Silicon Valley, London, Shanghai, Bangalore that belong to the concept of cities and regions.

Organization Essence of the International Industrial R&D Center

Currently, clusters are more concerned about the regional economic study of a phenomenon, which refers to a particular field (usually a leading industry as the core). A large number of companies closely linked and related support organizations gathered in space, and the formation of strong, sustainable competitive advantage phenomenon. International Industrial R&D center from the organizational form and development point of view is process from an industry cluster to cluster development, but this industry R&D industry is not simply the production industry. Du Debin (2004) first proposed the international industrial R&D center with the concept and its definition of a city or region to gather a large number of multinational companies of global and regional research institutions, and thus become the world's new products and new sources of technological innovation. Therefore, the international nature of industrial R&D organization is a gathering or clusters.

The developing speed of science and technology research can be more understood according to the development and concentration of national and regional R&D industry. Multinational R&D institutions are gradually gathering China and India by examining the development of industries in the development of the two countries in recent years. In the 1990s, multinational companies like Fortune 1000 have entered India in 203 established research institutions. According to Asia Times Online on February 20, 2003, there were more than 70 multinational corporations setting up R&D institutions in India, including Delphi, Eli Lilly, HP, Heinz, Honeywell, and Daimler Chrysler. When coupled with those established before 1997, then India's total foreign R&D should be more than 100 locations. Turning to China, according to statistics in 2004, the United States Business Week & Global 1000 companies selected, only 33 R&D centers set up in China. At the end of 2006, a total of 196 foreign research and development institutions were set up in Shanghai with 2-3 institutions each month.

Definition of International Industrial R&D Center

Through the above analysis, it can be gleaned that a city favorably suitable for industrial R&D resources has more concentrated space, possesses extensive sources with strong radiation influences. According to the author, within the actual in-depth research and development center research results, are various types of R&D resources, with some interrelated and interdependent relationship, therefore, R&D resources have internal relations existing between the network and its features in the industry cluster. In conclusion, the author of the international industrial research and development center defined (International R&D Hub) as: research and development resources from domestic and international researches into the formation of industrial clusters and regional cities, with a strong product and technology innovation, is global R&D network nodes with regional and global influences. Typical international industrial R&D centers are: Silicon Valley, Detroit, Paris, Singapore, Hsinchu, Shanghai and Beijing. It is worth mentioning that this refers to the wider meaning of R&D resources, both corporate R&D also includes: R&D personnel, educational institutions, research institutes, scientific research and management institutions, industrial R&D and all related elements.

Developing Model of International Industrial R&D Center

Design of Developing Model

Concerning the individual of Industrial R&D, there is a huge gap between its development and leading factor.

The development model of international industrial R&D mainly through the study of world industrial R&D development process and power systems, identifies some common features with the developing pattern, is classified and summarized. As the world's industrial R&D function with a very large number of cities, cities and regions around the world have not yet established standardized and systematic statistics inasmuch as most of the information is not available. Concept and meaning in urban areas are different between countries as well. This difference in the international industrial R&D center of the development model caused certain difficulties.

The researcher collected information based on comparative analysis of cases since there is not enough data to overcome the bottleneck. The Delphi method was also used to bring about an analysis of typical urban and regional development process of dynamic system as a basis so as to explore the regular features on the developing progress of the international industrial R&D centre.

Selection of Research Target

As the definition of the international industrial R&D center on the large differences still exists in the current domestic and international academics, the subjects the United Nations "Human Development Report (2002)" reprinted, with global influence of the 46 international innovations in main urban centers.

First, "Wired" magazine published a global innovation hub of 46 cities, combined with elements of their environment and special characteristics, divided into four categories: traditional cities in developed countries, emerging cities in economically developed countries/regions, the core city of newly industrialized countries/regions, new cities of developing countries/regions.

A Google search of the key words "names + Global + Innovation + Hub", gives the corresponding frequency of feedback recorded as:

In each type cities, according to the corresponding frequency of feedback record, the results can be concluded as Table 1.

In these types of international industrial R&D center, New York, Silicon Valley, Singapore, Bangalore won the highest frequencies of the query in the network. This also shows that one of these cities attract more attention both domestic and overseas; on the other hand, these cities also show that pertinent information is relatively more abundant. Therefore, from typical urban and regional data and the principle of data availability, New York, Silicon Valley, Singapore, and Bangalore respectively are the four typical representatives of international industrial R&D centers,

Table 1. Type and web search frequency of international industrial R&D centre

Type	City	Frequency	Type	City	Frequency
Traditional cities of developed countries/ regions	New York City	453,000	Newly developing cities of developed countries/regions	Silicon Valley	1,960,000
	London	391,000		Boston	232,000
	Paris	243,000		San Francisco	199,000
	Chicago	226,000		Virginia	170,000
	Cambridge	204,000		Austin	139,000
	Los Angeles	174,000		Dublin	89,000
	Tokyo	151,000		Kyoto	79,200
	Seattle	141,000		Queensland	71,400
	Melbourne	109,000		Albuquerque	32,700
	Montreal	99,600		Flanders	18,500
	Helsinki	60,400		Gauteng	10,900
	Thames Valley	21,400		Oulu	948
	Bavaria	13,700		Malmo	551
	Saxony	9,120		Glasgow-Edinburgh	233
	Baden-Wurttemberg	224		Raleigh-Durham-Chapel Hill	157
Core city of newly in-dustrialized countries/ regions	Singapore	229,000	New cities of de-veloping countries/ regions	Bangalore	50,300
	Hong Kong	196,000		Hsinchu	787
	Taipei	46,700		Campinas	555
	Kuala Lumpur	40,200		El Ghazala	116
	Saint Paul	25,800			
	Inchon	367			

established through interviews with experts and the application of the Delphi method of research and development centers of international industry development pattern. To better complete the expert evaluation, the author collected, reviewed, completed and analyzed these cities and regional R&D investment in the development process respectively, from the social environment, industry, economy, and governmental management.

There is a slightly different way in the development of the four cities and regions development process: for example, New York, from being a high-tech industry has become highly influential in domestic and international arena with many multinational companies setting up global headquarters there; Bangalore, India, flourished from

being a poor city. Five experts and scholars from the United States, India and Taiwan-China and other regions were interviewed in order to bring about a more objective perspective of the cities. Background information was provided as well. Based on interviews with feedback information, the above areas of development in research and development impact of factors in the evaluation results, as shown in Table 2: the "+" indicates the factor for the importance of development on urban and regional, "+++" shows the most important, "- " means less relationship.

From the research results, in these promotion factors of International Industrial R&D center, human resources, tertiary institutes are the most important essential factors. In the above four

Table 2. Importance Survey on influence factors of R&D towards 4 cities

	New York	Silicon Valley	Singapore	Bangalore
Law system	+++	+++	+	+
Location transportation	+++	++	+++	+
Culturally inclusive	+++	+++	+	+
Marketing competition	+++	+	+	+
Global Strategy	+	+	++	++
Infrastructure	+++	+	++	++
Human resources	+++	+++	+++	+++
Government promotion	+	+	+++	+++
Enterprise participation	+++	+++	+	+
Tertiary institutes	+++	+++	+++	+++
Research institution	+	+	-	++
Service organization	++	++	+	+
Related industries	+++	++	+	-

areas, both human resources and development of higher education are the important elements of correlation. The most relevant results achieving twice the number of factors, including the legal system, regional transportation, culture and government to promote such an inclusive, indicating respondents are the environmental factors and the role of government; the impact of industrial R&D activities constitute the second most important factor; market competition, infrastructure, corporate participation and development of relevant industries in the development of certain cities and regions played influential roles.

The above differentiation between regions in the economically developed countries (regions) of New York and Silicon Valley has advantages. New York is essentially a comprehensive lead-based, and other elements of urban and regional importance of the three enjoys a "++" elements are mainly related industries, enterprises involved in research and development, infrastructure, market competition and culturally inclusive. This shows in New York, during the development of industrial R&D, business and industry participation and improving its infrastructure constitute the core of its development momentum.

For the development of Silicon Valley, the dominant factors of legal system, culturally inclusive and participation of its individual business indicate that Silicon Valley companies are actively involved in the development as the driving force for R&D activities.

The survey shows: Singapore's development is mainly due to its good location and strong government support. Similarly, the Bangalore evaluation result indicates there is a unique index on the government vigorously promoting the development of the industry.

It can be seen from the examples of New York, Silicon Valley, Singapore, and Bangalore that business and industry are gradually reduced from being the initial force and the government's role is growing. The development of Bangalore, apart from higher education and human resources, is because of the promotion by its government.

The development perspective of the above four cities and regions can be divided into two types: the development of business and industry as the main driving force in the New York and Silicon Valley, and the Government as the main driving force in Singapore and Bangalore. Enterprise and industry development of industrial research and development as the main driver of the region with economic strength, and the development of more powerful high-tech industrial base, such as Silicon Valley in the Development Office is a gathering place for the defense industry. Substituting the leading force in the regional government, its economic development or economic strength, and more or less problems, such as economic development is lagging as in India, a lower level structure, technical content is not higher (in Singapore). Therefore, in the government-led international industrial R&D center, the choice of its development strategy is to introduce foreign advanced production technology and R&D. Such region in the government's efforts to promote next the creation of suitable human resources, research and development environment and policies and regulations and other flexible elements.

CONSTRUCTION CHOICE OF SHANGHAI INTERNATIONAL INDUSTRY R&D CENTER

Advantage on the Construction of Shanghai International Industry R&D Center

Shanghai is one of China's most economically developed cities. It is one of the earliest port cities in the Orient along with a powerful economic structure, a strong industrial base, and hardworking people. Shanghai International Industry R&D center in the building has a rare advantage that can be summarized in the following four aspects:

Regional Advantages

Shanghai International Industry R&D in the development of regional advantages has an excellent geographical location. Its favorable economic position in two aspects:

First, in terms of geographical location, Shanghai is the largest economic center of China. Lo-

cated at the estuary of the Yangtze River, China's central coast, the Yangtze River Delta economic zone, makes it geographically unique. Yangtze River Delta Economic Zone has a broad support of the hinterlands.

Second, after years of development and construction, Shanghai has evolved a successful manufacturing industry. At present, Shanghai is the center of electronic information manufacturing, automobile manufacturing, petrochemicals and fine chemicals, fine steel, equipment manufacturing, bio-pharmaceutical manufacturing key development sectors, and has a number of powerful manufacturing enterprises. In Shanghai, a tertiary industry is developing as its industrial structure upgrades and its economy increasing substantially.

From the cultural location perspective, Shanghai is the intersection of Western culture; with strong diversity of cultural environment, and a strong culture of inclusiveness. International Industrial R&D centers from other development, the diversity of culture and environment to attract a global scale for R&D institutions and R&D personnel have greater advantages. Thus, Shanghai's unique Eastern and Western cultural background is beneficial for its international industrial R&D development.

Resource Advantage

At present, communications, transportation and other areas of infrastructure construction of Shanghai is superior compared to other cities in China. Good infrastructure, smooth flow of information, with scientific research institutes having a lot of qualified talents, makes it a preferred city of transnational corporations R&D institutions. R&D human resources in science and technology, the existence of a large number of high-quality labor force is an important condition for multinational companies to settle in Shanghai as quality human resources for multinational companies to support technical innovation are available.

Institutional Advantage

In institutional system, the Shanghai R&D of technology gets more attention as formulated a series on foreign R&D and domestic R&D companies related policies and regulations, greatly enhancing Shanghai R&D for domestic and foreign enterprises and to attract creative talents. To encourage and support the growth of modern industries, the Shanghai government has launched a special high-tech achievement transformation projects discount loans to finance pilot schemes, "in Shanghai for high-tech achievements into a number of provisions," "research projects of Shanghai Science and Technology Commission research project Intellectual Property Management (tentative)" and a series of policies and regulations.

Focusing Advantage

The establishment of multinational R&D institutions focuses on features and potential inertia; that is, a host of multinational corporations setting up R&D institutions, can bring a greater number of multinational R&D institutions in the gathering, while the more the number of multinational R&D institutions are gathered. The larger effect and the potential energy generated by focusing the greater the inertia for other multinational companies, the higher the attractiveness of R&D institutions. World economic integration, technological R&D globalization and international wave of Shanghai as China's largest economic center and most prominent in absorbing foreign capital, one of the cities are all kinds of investors into the world and expand the bridgehead of China's investment. Related statistics show that world-renowned multinational companies are very positive about Shanghai. Shanghai became the headquarters of the world's leading multinational organizations. The headquarters organization here includes headquarters, regional headquarters and regional branches and other types.

The Shortcomings as an International Industrial R&D Centre

In recent years, although attracting foreign investment and economic development has made considerable progress, many multinational companies have set up in Shanghai industrial R&D, yet not known as the Shanghai International Industrial R&D center. There is a certain gap between it and "wired" magazine selection from among the international industrial R&D center. According to data collected by the Shanghai Science and Technology Commission in a series of research results, international industrial R&D center in Shanghai and the gaps between the main three points can be summarized as follows:

First, as the main international industrial R&D center, there is absence of observable facts.

International industrial R&D center within the main body can generally be divided into R&D institutions, universities, research institutions, technology industry of the manufacturing enterprise, the relevant R&D services and R&D management departments. Only with these elements and the initial line of the city as an international industry, the basic requirements of research and development center yet, current research in the Shanghai R&D services in relevant training institutions are flawed. The specific performance of the enterprise innovation and research and development playing a direct role in boosting the risk of investment (Venture Capital) mechanism is still irrational, and lacks international integration, thus greatly restricting strong support of the domestic venture capital companies in Shanghai R&D development.

Second, related subject and the resources industry R&D institutions and transnational corporations lack specific docking.

At present, Shanghai R&D subjects in the promotion of cooperation and exchanges is also weak, with some of the multinationals research and development are conducted for their own interest. Some of the universities and research institutions in cooperation such as joint technology R&D research projects each year conduct over 60% of joint research by outsourcing it with local universities. General Electric Research and Development Centre and training projects has signed contracts with the Zhejiang University, the Shanghai Jiaotong University and the Shanghai Institute of Silicate Rocks for clean energy and the development and promotion of electric vehicle use.

Industrial R&D as a main core of the domestic R&D companies have little in R&D cooperation with multinational typical research projects. Currently, in addition to individual, foreign R&D institutions have been in contact with domestic enterprises or cooperation, the majority of foreign research institutions and domestic companies without any form of cooperation, which shows that Taiwan's R&D capability of domestic enterprises is currently low, and lacks the conditions for foreign R&D cooperation.

In the past, Shanghai has been referred to as the "paradise of adventurers," because Shanghai local entrepreneurs are rare. Shanghai is not a production of local entrepreneurs, but of mature companies and entrepreneurs. The city is not conducive for people who are just starting. One of the main factors of innovation is "too standard." Shanghai, the government, the enterprises or universities, have always been known to abide by the "rules." When the "natural order" is challenged, status quo conditions prevail and the innovative challenger faces extreme difficulty. Thus, a weak innovative enterprise in Shanghai is the lack of appropriate environment and incentives.

Route Choice on the Construction of R&D Center Shanghai International Industry

To sum up, Shanghai has built an international industrial R&D center in the road and the government should play a major role: to guide the quality of overseas R&D institutions in Shanghai, the Shanghai Industrial R&D driving force; on the other hand, Shanghai will have to work to achieve the government-driven industrial research and development center and corporate-driven industry R&D centers across the industry to create a globally competitive independent research, development and innovation. To this end, the researcher believes that the future development of the Shanghai Municipal Government should take more effort in the following measures to build the international industrial R&D Center.

Strengthen the Environment of Shanghai Industrial R&D

Industrial R&D environment, including the contents of a broader environment in both direct R&D personnel living there and indirectly related to the environment, the main consideration and direct R&D environment directly related to the risk of industrial R&D investment and intellectual property protection environment. Furthermore, it should fundamentally change the city innovation system; make enterprises the main body of innovation, creating business-bases, other research institutions and tertiary institutions to participate in the structural optimization of the innovation system.

Formulate Principle Policy Control on Foreign Research

On the set up purpose of R&D institutions, multinational companies in Shanghai R&D institutions can be divided into two categories: support the company's production needs in the host country based on scientific research efforts to explore the host country, especially competition for talent. Government support should be reduced based on the production of R&D institutions, and increase the host country to attract human resources that can be tapped for the purpose of R&D institutions. There is a large aid for such high-quality industrial R&D institutions into the local R&D personnel to upgrade the quality of Shanghai and accelerate integration into the global industrial R&D network.

Promote Research and Exchange on the Principal Part of R&D

First and foremost, consider the establishment of personnel training system between universities and multinational cooperation in research. Secondly, promote Chinese and foreign enterprises through the establishment of professional R&D campus, and R&D institutions together. Thirdly, the government can set up a fund to promote national research institutes and multinational R&D exchanges and cooperation in production of innovative new enterprises.

Encourage Mature Enterprises to Conduct R&D Overseas

Shanghai should encourage local enterprises to set up overseas R&D institutions. As Chinese enterprises are lagging behind in technological innovation, it is necessary to establish its own R&D institutions to track and monitor new trends in product development as the parent to obtain technical information with technologically advanced countries. Most especially, technology-intensive enterprises should take into account similar overseas industries, and technologically advanced country competitors to benefit the local R&D institutions.

REFERENCES

Blomstrom, M. (1991). Host country benefit of foreign investment. In McFetridge, D. (Ed.), *Foreign Investment Technology and Economic Growth*. Calgary, Canada: University of Calgary Press.

Blomström, M., & Kokko, A. (2003). *The economics of foreign direct investment incentives*. Foreign direct investment in the real and financial sector of industrial countries, pp. 37-56.

Cantwell, J. A., & Dunning, J. H. (1991). MNEs technology and competitiveness of European industry. *Aussnwirtschaft, 46*, 45–65.

Caves, R. E. (1974). Multinational firms, competition and productivity in host country market. *Economic, 41*, 176–193.

Cheng, H. L., & Yang, L. (2004). Analysis on the Status of Beijing as International R&D Center. *Science of Science and Management of S.& T., 25*(7), 25–29.

Du De bin, (2001). *The Research on the Multinational R & D globalization Location Model*. Shanghai: Fudan University Press.

Hymer, S. H. (1970). The efficiency (contradictions) of Multinational corporations. *The American Economic Review, 60*, 441–448.

Kokko, A. (1992). *Foreign direct investment, host country characteristics, and spillovers. Economic Research Institute, Stockholm School of Economics* [Ekonomiska forskningsinstitutet vid Handelshögsk.]. EFI.

Lall, S., & Streenten, P. (1977). *Foreign Investment, Transnational and developing countries*. London: Macmillan.

Lei, S. (2009). *Spatial Agglomeration and Knowledge Spillover of Foreign R&D in China*. Unpublished Doctoral Dissertation, East China Normal University.

Lei, Sheng, & Yong, Ma & Du De bin. (2008). Research on Reasonable Scale of Foreign R & D in China, Asia-pacific. *Economic Review, 4*, 27–35.

Moran, T. H. (1970). Multinational corporations and dependency: a dialogue for dependentistas and non-dependentistas. *International Organization, 32*, 79–100. doi:10.1017/S0020818300003878

Rui, L. (2004). *Multinational R & D investment and leap-forward development of technology in China*. Beijing: Economic Science Press.

Tommaso, P. (1997). Multinational enterprises and technological spillovers: An evolutionary model. *Journal of Evolutionary Economics, 7*, 169–192. doi:10.1007/s001910050040

UNCTAD. V. (2008). *World Investment Report*. United Nations Conference on Trade and Development New York and Geneva.

Wang, Y., & Blomstrom, M. (1992). Foreign investment and technology transfer: a simple model. *European Economic Review, 36*, 137–155. doi:10.1016/0014-2921(92)90021-N

Wang Chun Fa. (2003). *The historical evolution of national innovation systems and development trend in Major Developed Countries*. Beijing: Economic Science Press.

Ying, Zhu & Du De bin. (2005). Organization patterns and evolution of R&D globalization of multinational corporations. *Science and Technology Management Research, 25*(8), 56–60.

Chapter 2
LoTour:
Using Technology to Provide Competitive Advantage in Local Tourism Industries

Marcos Ruano-Mayoral
Egeo IT, Spain

Ricardo Colomo-Palacios
Universidad Carlos III de Madrid, Spain

Pedro Soto-Acosta
University of Murcia, Spain

Ángel García-Crespo
Universidad Carlos III de Madrid, Spain

ABSTRACT

The Internet has brought a radical change in the way tourism services are conceived. In this new scenario, not only has attracting tourists been modified over the Internet, but the provision of tourism services have been altered. Thus, the different factors of tourist services are in a new environment and they should operate in a coordinated manner to increase the value of tourism, to keep current tourists and attract new ones. With this aim, LoTour, the architecture presented in this chapter provides a platform for the integration of different services, provides comprehensive information on the tourist destination from the context (location, time of day, season, weather, etc) and the profile of the tourist.

INTRODUCTION

The convergence of IT and communications technologies and the rapid evolution of the Internet has been one of the most influential tourism factors that have changed travelers' behavior (Kenteris, Gavalas & Economou, 2009). Moreover, as discussed in Hui, Wanand & Alvin(2007), the suitable finding of tourism services is one of the main challenges when people travel. In this context, "Mobile tourism" represents a relatively new trend in the field of tourism and involves the use of mobile devices as electronic tourist guides (Kenteris, Gavalas & Economou, 2009). This new way of tourism has been facilitated by the rapid

DOI: 10.4018/978-1-61350-192-4.ch002

growth of mobile devices (mobile phones, palm-tops, PDAs…). The evolution of these devices in recent years has meant that these mobile devices have advanced computing capabilities and connectivity that enable them as valid solutions for mobile work.

Additionally, the tourism industry is demanding an ever-increasing level of value- added services in technologically complete environments, which are integrated and highly dynamic. As a consequence of this circumstance, administrative and corporate bodies in the tourism industry now have to focus on the development of new infrastructures, providing citizens with access to cultural content and tourism services. This focus on the development of new services is the primary objective of Tour. LoTour is a system that prosecutesthe concern with major or minor radicalizations to the relevant agents involved in the tourist activity in a certain geographical area. LoTour has to stimulate the economic relations of these business entities, since the tourist is going to contribute to this by literally handing in detailed, exhaustive information that will permanently update his or her tourist offer in the area, eliminating all the impediments that the ignorance of the language, the void familiarity with the environment or other reasons that impose to a desirable dynamics of expense. LoTour is a platform which more significant prop constitutes the integration between technologies of location and those of communications. The combination of both technologies will allow adequate the positioning of the tourist and will be able to have access to descriptive contents of the environment that the tourist makes a detour.

STATE OF THE ART

Because tourism is an information intensive business, there are opportunities to apply information technology to support tourism and tourists (Watson et al., 2004). The integration of tourism with the technology is an indisputable fact in the twenty-first century. Information and Communication Technologies (ICT) crucially impact travelers' knowledge, attitudes and behavior. Thus, the interaction of technology in tourism is reflected in different phases: before, during, and after the visit. LoTour is conceived as a solution capable of providing added value to the tourist experience through the combination of three distinct technologies or philosophies: Customer Relationship Management, Mobile Computation and Context Aware Systems. In this section we deal with each in relation to integration with tourism. The goal is to place LoTour from previous efforts and define this new platform from the analysis of the opportunities that research has not yet covered satisfactorily.

Customer Relationship Management

Tourism destinations are probably one of the most difficult products to market (Palmer, 2005). This has allowed the integration of tourism with the Customer Relationship Management has been very extensive, and, according to (Coltman, 2007), one of the traditional markets for these solutions. Customer relationship management (CRM) has become a research focus in the academic field since Ives and Learmonth (1984) put forward customer relationship life cycle concept. CRM refers to a customer-focused business strategy. There are several definitions of CRM in the literature, for example the one provided by Dyché (2002) who defines the concept as "The infrastructure that enables the delineation of and increase in customer value, and the correct means by which to motivate customers to remain loyal, indeed to buy again". CRM is an active, participatory and interactive relationship between business and customer (Özgenera & İrazb, 2006). The objective is to achieve a comprehensive view of customers, and be able to consistently anticipate and react to their needs with targeted and effective activities at every customer touch point (Piccoli et al., 2003).

Buhalis (1998) pointed out that the use of Internet in the tourism industry gives access to a great number of people, as well as offers the opportunity to develop closer relationships with customers. Internet enables consumers to communicate with organizations on a 24 h, 365 days a year basis and also it enables organizations to implement CRM programs enhancing the opportunities for interaction and a better understanding of both sides.

This vision of CRM is an enabler for any interaction with tourism. The first attempts to bring the two worlds are produced from the standpoint of integration between Web platforms and legacy systems such as CRM and back-office Enterprise resource planning (ERP) (Joo, 2002). Thus, according to Beldona, Morrison and O'Leary (2005), for the managers of airlines and car rentals is a necessary integration of customer relationship management tools on their websites. This is a new integration opportunity. That's why, according to Buhalis (2004), airlines have been investing in Customer Relationship Management programs in order to improve their direct communication and to manage their loyalty clubs. There have been several studies that employ cutting-edge technologies in areas relating to the use of CRM in the airline market, to prevent customer churn in the airline markets (Liou, 2009).

Hotels are also investing in the implementation of CRM (Sigala, 2005). This author states that CRM is a crucial strategy for sustaining competitive advantage in the current hotel marketplace. But she also pointed out that ICT is not the panacea and the exclusive CRM determinant factor. Other organizational and managerial factors such as culture, staff motivation and development also play a vital role on CRM's success. In the field of Online Travel Agencies, in recent years a boom in the capabilities of the agencies has been occurred, and their combination with low cost flights and hotels has meant another prolific research area with relevant work in relation to the use of CRM capabilities in this kind of organizations (Cho &

Agrusa, 2006). Finally, works on the investigation of the consequences of the introduction of CRM in Tourist Organizations sites also support the theory of the universality of the use of CRM in the tourism sector (Maswere, Dawson & Edwards, 2006).

Mobile Computation

In recent years two unrelated trends have stood at the forefront of technology. First are the great improvements in the accessibility of information which, driven by the Internet revolution, have made it possible to access huge amounts of information using a traditional PC and a simple browser. Second are the advancements in computer technologies which reach beyond the traditional desktop environment to areas such as mobile, or even wearable, computing (Carmeli & Cohen, 2001). Mobile computing has the potential to radically transform the way people interact with computers. It is motivated by the observation that computing and networking technologies are becoming increasingly powerful and affordable (Grimm, 2004).

Mobile Computing is an umbrella term and describes any technology that enables people to access information and which supports them in daily workflows independent of location (Holzinger & Errath, 2007).

Mobile computing systems range from wearable computing to car computing, from personal digital assistants to smartphones. Such mobile devices can transfer data in two ways - by transmitting over a wireless (or wired) network interface, and by taking advantage of user's mobility (Chaintreau et al., 2007). In LoTour, these two ways of communication are used in the ways of location based services and context aware technologies and by the use of several net protocols to connect the user and the information. The area of mobile computing in general and LoTour in particular is a good example of the "New Computing" in the sense indicated by Shneiderman (2002): the new computing technologies must enable end-users to accomplish their tasks and to relax, enjoy, and explore.

LBS and Context Aware

The term "location-based services" (LBS) is a rather recent concept that integrates geographic location with the general notion of services (Schiller & Voisard, 2004). With the development of mobile communication, these applications represent a novel challenge both conceptually and technically (Schiller & Voisard, 2004).

Furthermore, advances in ubiquitous computing have contributed to the development of specific needs related to context aware systems designed to exploit information from the environment to adapt it to several applications. Context-awareness is often seen as recently emerged research field within information technology, and in particular within the domain of the Web (Ceri et al., 2007). The origin of the context-aware computing dates back to 1994. Schilit and Heimer (1994) suggested the three parameters that determine a context: the location at which the software is used, the collection of nearby people and objects to it and changes of these objects in time. Some years later, Dey and Abowd (2000) proposed a more generic definition: Context is any information that can be used to characterize the situation of an entity. An entity is defined as a person, place or object that is considered relevant for the interaction between a user and an application or between users and applications.

Context-aware systems are able to tailor its operation to the current context without explicit user intervention. In particular, for mobile devices, it is desirable that programs and services specifically react to the current location at the time and other attributes of the environment and adapt its behavior according to any changes of information of context.

The possibility of offering contextual tourist information in a pervasive environment is a broad research field. There are examples of using LBS in the context of tourism (e.g. Abowd et al., 1997; Pashtan et al., 2003; Cheverst et al., 2000; Corallo et al., 2005; García-Crespo et al., 2009; García-Crespo et al., 2010).

LOTOUR

LoTour stems from the belief that sustainable growth in current patterns of tourism activity in Europe should rely not only on quantitative growth in the number of tourists in the proliferation of new destinations, but the emergence and development of models business based on innovative new products and services to be debtors to a large extent on technological innovation. Following this approach have been established three strategic objectives that support for the conceptual development of the platform.

Objective 1. Provide value added services to tourists at the destination by designing and implementing an ICT platform for innovative management.

Objective 2. Designing and implementing an ICT platform that enables the conceptualization and planning of tourism strategies developed by the Destination Management Office (DMO) in their area of influence.

Objective 3. Enable a tool which can become a benchmark for developing innovative business models that extend the value chain of tourism activities by tourists when visiting an area

To achieve these objectives, LoTour will therefore define an ICT platform whose pillar is integration of location technology (which we will refer indistinctly technologies as Geographic Information Systems or Location-Based Services, LBS technologies), and communication (GPS, localization in micro Bluetooth, RFID, WiFi, etc.).

The combination of both technologies enable the system to know the proper positioning of the tourist and then permit the access to content related to the environment around and to transact with the purchase of certain goods or services through the appropriate payment gateway.

Last but not least, a CRM tier, acts as an integrator of the different technological elements of the platform, optimizing his or her management in order that the tourist obtains a maximum of services and the public administrations have the aptitude to register, to support and analyze all the flows of information that the system is generating.

Description

Tourists can access and receive comprehensive and descriptive information of the environment in which they find themselves. The contents of this information shall be determined by LoTour from the context (location, time of day, season, weather, etc) and the profile of the tourist. The information is expressed in several languages and will cover the whole spectrum that may be of interest for tourists (leisure, culture, accommodation, catering, etc.).

The system incorporates a distinctive feature that will compromise the tourist not only to identify significant information and services in its vicinity, but to purchase using the same peripheral used to receive the tourist information.

Suppliers of tourism services will be encouraged to maintain economic relations with tourists. This is possible because LoTour can bring detailed, comprehensive and continually updated information within a given area of influence, removing all impediments to the ignorance of the language, the lack of familiarity with the environment or other reasons to impose a dynamic desirable expenditure.

DMOs will enjoy an integrated global view of the tourist taken from the exhaustive record of the interactions made by tourists to the system (both transactional and simple request for information). There will be like that the most obvious users of the analytical components of the structure CRM that agglutinates to the system, having an exceptional richness of information that constructed since

datamarts/datawarehouses will allow to design and to plan later the strategies of tourist action in the above mentioned region.

Architecture

In Figure 1 there is included a graph of context of the principal components and agents foreseen for LoTour:

The provision of services based on the dynamic position of the tourist implies, inevitably, as a first step, locating the tourist. LoTour integrates various positioning systems such as GPS, GPRS, WiFi and Bluetooth. This platform creates a virtual network of intelligent system capable of determining what network is suitable for tourists in terms of device used and demand for content and / or services. This network consists of a modular set of nodes capable of processing information, storing or transmitting it according to specific needs. The operation of the network is governed by a specific protocol that enables communication between devices, the passage of information through the nodes and that allows the dynamic creation and management of the network. This proprietary network will be supplemented with existing networks deployed by various communications providers that also will provide services to the user when there is no proprietary network available.

The virtual intelligent network is structured according to a modular design in three layers, namely processing layer, power supply layer and communication layer.

Processing layer brings intelligence to every node within the network. Moreover, this layer performs the tasks of communications control through the management of the establishment and the breaking of links and administration of all tasks related to network. The processing layer is also responsible for controlling the operating modes of power saving mechanisms of the nodes, which is of vital importance in wireless networks,

Figure 1. LoTour architecture

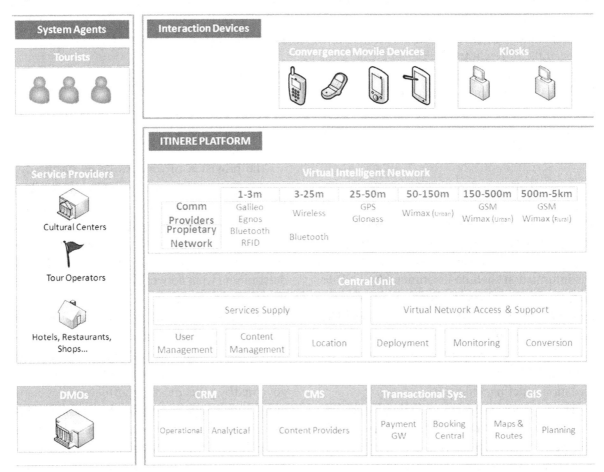

which need to operate autonomously for long periods of time.

Power supply layer brings power supply to the node and its components. The choice of power supply type depends on the particular characteristics of each node and the location of them. Communication layer is responsible of the wireless transmission of information. Nodes support different wireless communication standards, as well as cellular (GSM / GPRS / UMTS-HDSPA), personal area (PAN / Bluetooth), local area (802.11 a / b / g Wi-Fi) or metropolitan area (802.16 a / b Wi-Max).

The central unit acts as an integrator of the different technological elements of the platform. Thus, anticipating the needs of tourists, the central

unit can send updated and accurate information to the tourist. The central unit serves two main functions. On the one hand is responsible for providing value added services for tourists and, for the management of the virtual communication network, which allows LoTour to locate and deliver accurate information at all times. To carry out these functions, the central unit is built into the modules and components which are detailed below:

- **Content management.** Allows the access to outer systems that store information about points of interest. It also allows the administration of the contents stored in the system. Moreover it ensures that the content is always accessible and updated.

- **Deployment.** Allows downloading of content, different routes, signals of the exits, information kiosks for application downloads, webs, etc, and provides mechanisms for downloading applications to tourist's mobile devices.
- **Conversion.** It provides functions to convert images, text video and audio associated with each point of interest to the format best suited to the tourist's mobile device, taking into account standard formats. Besides supporting text to speech conversion.
- **User Management.** End users management including identification, preferences, session management and other common services.
- **Monitoring.** This component allows checking the operation of the system components, as well as knowing the status of the battery, the existing coverage and the communication protocols supported by each node.
- **Location.** Integrates mechanisms to transform and expand the geographic location data returned by the various nodes of the virtual network, using information provided by an external GIS server.

The platform presents a GIS to be funded by the geo-information available in public institutions. Thus, given the dispersal of geospatial data in various levels (local, regional, national and international), will be necessary to establish mechanisms to incorporate the data generated by each institution according to their competence in order to facilitate uniformity among official data, allowing a seamless exchange and integration. The GIS module is in charge of unambiguously locating the user's physical position and translating it into a logical position over a map, used to look for surrounding services. Maps are downloaded from the internet; therefore they give the user a visual output of his surroundings, indicating possible tourism services the user could be interested in.

The CRM component serves as the integrator of all data and user interactions, optimizing their management with the aim to let the tourist to get a maximum of benefits and services. Their functions range from the registration and identification of tourists up the processing of the interactions of tourists with the platform to extract patterns of behavior. These patterns are then analyzed to generate profiles of underlying preferences. Mentioned profiles are used to adjust the response of the platform and the behavior of different services to each tourist. The study of all this information through analytical CRM component also allow the derivation of valuation models and segmentation of tourists, along with the differentiation and selection of groups of tourists based on personal preferences. From the viewpoint of relationship marketing, the information will contribute to improved design of tourist facilities and the development of campaigns and offers tailored to the profiles of the target visitor.

The transactional services component encompasses all functionality related to the interaction between LoTour and other transactional systems (payment gateways, reservation agencies...). The CMS will provide an enabling environment for information update and expansion of the platform with the help of tourists, tourism service providers and DMO managers. The features that reside in this component can be grouped into four categories: content creation, content management, publishing and presentation. One key aspect to using a CMS is the need to bring new assets to the platform in a swift way. LoTour will be continuously updated: adding new content and services and updating existing ones on a continuous basis, responding to the requirements of tourists, sponsoring DMO promotional strategies and marketing campaigns and reflecting the supply of tourist services in a given area. Moreover, the contribution of the CMS is to bear a simple and integrated way the operations described. Those operations involve the review of many documentaries and the active generation of new ones.

Except for tourists' access to services of the platform will be implemented using personal computers. Tourists will be able to access the platform through dedicated kiosks and convergent mobile devices. The kiosks will be located at strategic points (bus and train stations, airports, tourist information offices, points of interest...) within the geographical area to which the platform coverage. In these kiosks, visitors can view descriptive information via multimedia presentations about the platform.

Additionally, tourists may register themselves as users and download the application for convergent mobile devices, enabling them to access the wide range of LBS y context aware services provided by LoTour. The key aspect is that the tourists use their own convergent mobile device, because they are already familiar with its use, thereby reducing the learning curve for access to the platform. However, it is also considered the possibility that certain DMOs hire suitable and configured devices to provide access to LoTour.

The overall operation of the platform LoTour is based on the coordinated cooperation of all the components described above to serve as providers and consumers of services as required. The provision of each of these services should be subject to a service level agreement in which each set of operations implemented in the service and the results thereof. This fact has two immediate advantages. Firstly, identify and decouple the functionality of the components to build an open and flexible platform, and secondly bring technology independence to component construction.

CONCLUSION AND FUTURE WORK

Bigger than in any other Top-5 European economies, the tourism industry is responsible for almost 12% of Gross National Product in Spain,

and in several areas of this country more than a third of regional jobs and incomes stem from this activity. LoTour platform is designed to become a significant tool for all tourism value chain agents in any particular area (individual tourists, tourism enterprises and public organizations), but is specially intended for public authorities due to the possibility to distribute and disseminate all kinds of tourism content, from more static environmental or cultural heritage related content to actively updated data about specific touristic offerings in the area (shopping, eating out, hospitality, etc.).

To sum up, Public Authorities responsible for managing tourism policies in a particular area can use LoTour when selling any particular project to design, develop, implement and maintain LoTour platform with technical and functional features defined in this document. LoTour is intended to be a focus point for touristic information in a given area. In one hand, it stores and sends touristic information to the users based on user preferences and context, and in the other hand it forwards this information using the most suitable network available.

REFERENCES

Abowd, G. D., Atkeson, C. G., Hong, J., Long, S., Kooper, R., & Pinkerton, M. (1997). Cyberguide: A mobile context-aware tour guide. *ACM Wireless Networks*, *3*(5), 421–433. doi:10.1023/A:1019194325861

Beldona, S., Morrison, A. M., & O'Leary, J. (2005). Online shopping motivations and pleasure travel products: a correspondence analysis. *Tourism Management*, *26*(4), 561–570. doi:10.1016/j.tourman.2004.03.008

Buhalis, D. (1998). Strategic use of information technologies in the tourism industry. *Tourism Management*, *19*(5), 409–421. doi:10.1016/S0261-5177(98)00038-7

Buhalis, D. (2004). eAirlines: strategic and tactical use of ICTs in the airline industry. *Information & Management, 41*(7), 805–825. doi:10.1016/j.im.2003.08.015

Carmeli, B., & Cohen, B. (2001). PiNet: Wireless Connectivity for Organizational Information Access Using Lightweight Handheld Devices. *IEEE Personal Communications, 8*(4), 18–23. doi:10.1109/98.943999

Ceri, S., Daniel, F., Matera, M., & Facca, F.M. (2007). Model-driven development of context-aware Web applications. *ACM Transactions on Internet Technology, 7* (1), article no. 2.

Chaintreau, A., Hui, P., Diot, C., Gass, R., & Scott, J. (2007). Impact of Human Mobility on Opportunistic Forwarding Algorithms. *IEEE Transactions on Mobile Computing, 6*(6), 606–620. doi:10.1109/TMC.2007.1060

Cheverst, K., Davies, N., Mitchell, K., Friday, A., & Efstratiou, F. (2000). *Developing a context-aware electronic tourist guide: some issues and experiences.* In Proceedings of the SIGCHI conference on Human factors in computing systems, p.17-24, April 01-06, The Hague, The Netherlands.

Cho, Y. C., & Agrusa, J. (2006). Assessing use acceptance and satisfaction Toward online travel agencies. *Information Technology & Tourism, 8*(3/4), 179–195. doi:10.3727/109830506778690795

Coltman, T. (2007). Why build a customer relationship management capability? *The Journal of Strategic Information Systems, 16*(3), 301–320. doi:10.1016/j.jsis.2007.05.001

Corallo, A., Elia, G., Lorenzo, G., & Solazzo, G. (2005). *A semantic recommender engine enabling an etourism scenario.* ISWC2005 International Semantic Web Conference 2005, 6-10 November, Galway, Ireland.

Dey, A. K., & Abowd, G. D. (2000). *Towards a Better Understanding of Context and Context-Awareness.* In CHI 2000 Workshop on the What, Who, Where, When, and How of Context-Awareness.

Dyche, J. (2002). *The CRM handbook: A Business Guide to Customer Relationship Management.* Boston: Addison-Wesley.

García-Crespo, A., Chamizo, J., Rivera, I., Mencke, M., Colomo-Palacios, R., & Gómez-Berbís, J. M. (2009). SPETA: Social pervasive e-Tourism advisor. *Telematics and Informatics, 26*(3), 306–315. doi:10.1016/j.tele.2008.11.008

García-Crespo, A., Colomo-Palacios, R., Gómez-Berbís, J. M., Chamizo, J., & Rivera, I. (2010). Intelligent Decision-Support Systems for e-Tourism: Using SPETA II as a Knowledge Management Platform for DMOs and e-Tourism Service Providers. *International Journal of Decision Support System Technology, 2*(1), 36–48. doi:10.4018/jdsst.2010101603

Grimm, R. (2004). System Support for Pervasive Applications. *ACM Transactions on Computer Systems, 22*(4), 421–486. doi:10.1145/1035582.1035584

Holzinger, A., & Errath, M. (2007). Mobile computer Web-application design in medicine: some research based guidelines. *Universal Access in the Information Society, 6*(1), 31–41. doi:10.1007/s10209-007-0074-z

Hui, T. K., Wanand, D., & Alvin, H. (2007). Tourists' satisfaction, recommendation and revisiting Singapore. *Tourism Management, 28*(4), 965–975. doi:10.1016/j.tourman.2006.08.008

Ives, B., & Learmonth, G. P. (1984). The information system as a compete it vie weapon. *Communications of the ACM, 27*(12), 1193–1201. doi:10.1145/2135.2137

Joo, J. (2002). A business model and its development strategies for electronic tourism markets. *Information Systems Management, 19*(5), 58–69. doi:10.1201/1078/43201.19.3.20020601/37171.8

Kenteris, M., Gavalas, D., & Economou, D. (2009). An innovative mobile electronic tourist guide application. *Personal and Ubiquitous Computing, 13*(2), 103–118. doi:10.1007/s00779-007-0191-y

Liou, J. H. (2009). A novel decision rules approach for customer relationship management of the airline market. *Expert Systems with Applications, 36*(3), 4374–4381. doi:10.1016/j.eswa.2008.05.002

Maswere, T., Dawson, R., & Edwards, J. (2006). Assessing the Levels of Knowledge Transfer within e-Commerce Websites of Tourist Organisations in Africa. *Electronic Journal of Knowledge Management, 4*(1), 59–66.

Özgenera, Ş., & İrazb, R. (2006). Customer relationship management in small–medium enterprises: The case of Turkish tourism industry. *Tourism Management, 27*(6), 1356–1363. doi:10.1016/j.tourman.2005.06.011

Palmer, A. (2005). The internet challenge for destination marketing. In Morgan, N., Pritchard, A., & Pride, R. (Eds.), *Destination Branding: Creating the unique destination proposition* (pp. 128–140). Oxford, UK: Elsevier.

Pashtan, A., Blattler, R., Heusser, A., & Scheuermann, P. (2003). *CATIS: A Context-Aware Tourist Information System.* In Proceedings of IMC 2003, 4th International Workshop of Mobile Computing, Rostock, Germany

Piccoli, G., O'Connor, P., Capaccioli, C., & Álvarez, R. (2003). Customer relationship management a driver for change in the structure of the US lodging industry. *The Cornell Hotel and Restaurant Administration Quarterly, 44*(4), 61–73.

Schilit, B. N., & Heimer, M. M. (1994). Disseminating Active Map Information to Mobile Hosts. *IEEE Network, 8*(5), 22–32. doi:10.1109/65.313011

Schiller, J., & Voisard, A. (2004). *Location-based services.* Amsterdam: Elsevier.

Shneiderman, B. (2002). *Leonardo's Laptop: Human Needs and the New Computing Technologies.* Boston: MIT Press.

Sigala, M. (2005). Integrating customer relationship management in hotel operations: managerial and operational implications. *Hospital Management, 24*(3), 391–413. doi:10.1016/j.ijhm.2004.08.008

Watson, R. T., Akselsen, S., Monod, E., & Pitt, L. F. (2004). The Open Tourism Consortium: Laying The Foundations for the Future of Tourism. *European Management Journal, 22*(3), 315–326. doi:10.1016/j.emj.2004.04.014

Chapter 3
Emergent Technologies and Social Connectedness in Learning

Kumar Laxman
Nanyang Technological University, Singapore

Yap Kueh Chin
Nanyang Technological University,Singapore

ABSTRACT

The judicious embedment of technologies in educational contexts can foster learning environments that encourage thoughtful reflections and support deeper learning to occur. Emergent technologies has the capacity to foster effective online learning environments where social processes of learning involving collaboration can be facilitated. Social construction of knowledge facilitated by virtual collaborative platforms can generate a community of learners where the more knowledgeable members share their expertise with their peers. In this chapter, the authors explore the affordances of emergent technologies such as asynchronous discussion forums, synchronous computer mediated communications and 3-D virtual realities in educational contexts. Such technologies can be harnessed to support the paradigmatic shift in instruction to foster more socially-mediated collaborative learning environments.

INTRODUCTION

The recent advances in the domain of communication technologies have afforded a growing number of cutting-edge applications that educators can leverage upon to build multimodal classroom ecologies that are socially oriented in nature (Chen et al., 2005). Embedding socially-mediated learning structures within a classroom community enables learners to construct knowledge through interpersonal interactions and collaborative communications (Slagter van Tryon & Bishop, 2006). The collective knowledge capital built by the community of learning serves serve as the shared

DOI: 10.4018/978-1-61350-192-4.ch003

context for the intellectual pursuits and academic excellence of its members. Effective learning can be accomplished when it involves interactions with peer learners in the creation of knowledge discourses based upon common epistemic goals (Zhu & Baylen, 2005). The judicious embedment of technologies in educational contexts can foster learning environments that encourage thoughtful cogitations, allowing deeper learning to occur (Maushak & Ou, 2007). And these reflections should not only be limited to discussions on subject content in academic areas but also cover socially related issues for learning to be truly experienced in a holistic manner (Dede, 1996). Research shows that technology has the capacity to foster effective online learning environments where social processes of learning involving collaboration can be facilitated (Russo & Benson, 2005; Ouzts, 2006). However, media alone doesn't influence successful online collaborations - the instructor is the key determinant to motivating collaborations.

Social constructivism as advocated by the Russian psychologist Lev Vygotsky posits that new knowledge is generated when there are social interactions within a community of students where the more knowledgeable members share their expertise with their peers. These socialization processes used in social constructivism embody reciprocal interactions creating a shared construction of meaning making by the members of an educational community (Sivan, 1986). The sharing of ideas and perspectives encourages deeper thinking and learning to be accomplished. Vygtosky called this approach to knowledge attainment as the "Zone of Proximal Development." In his own words, Zone of Proximal Development (ZPD) can be defined as "the distance between the actual developmental level as determined by independent problem solving and the level of potential development as determined through problem solving under adult guidance or in collaboration with more capable peers" (p. 86).

Wenger (1998) defines a learning community of practice as one that includes joint enterprise, mu-

tual engagement, and shared repertoire. Members who mutually share these three attributes develop unique ways of talking about meaning, practice, community, and identity of the knowledge valued amongst the group members. Wenger further asserts that our existence as social beings is central to the ways we learn, that knowledge gathering is our ability to experience the world and engagement with the world in meaningful ways is the product of learning. Information stored in explicit ways is only a small part of knowing, and knowing involves primarily active participation in social communities and internalization of knowledge. Wenger feels that traditional formats of schooling, in that sense, seem limited in providing the necessary access to conditions and tools that enhance students' participation within social structures of learning and open up their thinking horizons.

Technology has the capacity to extend learning beyond classroom boundaries and create electronic educational spaces that connect students in a network of applied learning. Harnessing the participative nature of technology-supported interactions situates learning in communities of practice sharing a repertoire of knowledge resources.

ASYNCHRONOUS DISCUSSION FORUMS

The integration of asynchronous discussion forums in education has the potential to cover most of the communication tasks between students and teachers: debate about controversial topics, brainstorming, questioning, homework submission queries, news dissemination, etc (Ponnusawmy, & Santally, 2008). Moreover, learners can also use forum discussion space as an online socializing zone. Discussion forums are good for extended discussions and wide information dissemination but require motivation or structure. Discussion forums create a virtual environment similar to face-to-face classroom environments where knowledge could be critically constructed, validated and shared. An important characteristic of asynchronous discussion forums is that students dominate the discussions, not the facilitator. The facilitator creates a learning environment where students are responsible for their own learning. From the students' point of views, Murphy and Manzanares (2005) reported evidences of individual increasing awareness of the different perspectives of a discussed problem. Learners also commented on their interest in sharing and collaborating in relation to the knowledge building process and to expand and further knowledge acquisition. They not only stressed how they had personally become more aware of different viewpoints and expanded their knowledge, but they also described the various ways they intended to expose other participants to different perspectives. Ponnusawmy and Santally (2008), echoing the same views, reported that support for the use of discussion forums in distance education was widespread. Discussion forums provided platforms for students to see different perspectives, which could help to foster new meaning construction and encouraged student ownership of learning and collaborative problem-solving skills. They encouraged participants to put their thoughts into writing in a way that others could understand, promoting self-reflective dialogue and dialogue with others. In addition, discussion forums had the potential to expose students to a broader range of views as compared to face-to-face talk, and hence enabled them to develop more complex perspectives on a topic. The research done by Frey, Sass and Arman (2006) produced evidence that online discussions benefited shy or international students by providing them with more time to clarify and develop their opinions. However, simply requiring students to post messages to address the instructors' questions might not result in effective learning. Effective discussions require thoughtful design, facilitation and assessment.

An inherent characteristic of asynchronous discussion forum is its ability to promote social construction of knowledge among student par-

ticipants. Waters and Gasson (2007) were of the view that individuals only possessed a partial understanding of the problem, so group problem solving was akin to assembling a jigsaw puzzle. Every participant must contribute his part of the picture without initially being able to comprehend the whole, which was then gradually constructed through sustained online debates. In this way, a community of inquiry built a joint, yet distributed understanding of their domain of practice. Students were expected to share their experiences, negotiate meanings and construct subject matter knowledge through discussion. Constructivist educators generally agree that discussions in communities of inquiry contribute to higher order thinking and helped learners in their knowledge creation-students are stimulated to engage actively in their own learning processes (Stein et al, 2006). In addition, working in collaborative groups provides opportunities for students to be engaged in knowledge building where knowledge is constructed. As meaning making is a dialogic and mediated process through the agency of language, individuals construct knowledge when they are engaged socially and actively in solving shared problems or tasks (Chin & Chia, 2002). Arvaja, Salovaara, Hakkinen and Jarvela (2007) put forward the idea that the function of communication is in promoting students' reasoning and negotiation skills through suggestions, clarifications, counter arguments and questions asking. In addition, students build their reasoning on one another's messages with the other person's message serving in part as a resource for one's own interpretations. Research by Weinberger and Fischer (2006) revealed that argumentative knowledge construction is based on the assumption that learners need to be engaged in specific discourse activities and the frequency of these discourse activities is related to the extent of knowledge acquisition. Learners constructed arguments in interaction with their learning partners in order to acquire knowledge about argumentation, as well as knowledge of content subject matter. In argumentative knowledge construction, there is a need for students to inquire about complex problems, construct and balance arguments and counter- arguments in order to prove possible resolutions to these problems. Learners thus continuously warrant, qualify or argue against solutions to the problems until they converge towards a joint solution. By balancing arguments and counter-arguments in order to solve complex problems, participants learn how to argue within a domain and acquire content knowledge. With the construction of sequences of argumentation, students may acquire multiple perspectives upon a problem. The acquisition of multiple perspectives on a problem facilitates students to flexibly apply the newly acquired knowledge to solve future problems. Pena-Schaff and Nicholls (2004) reported that knowledge construction should be seen as a social, dialogical process in which different perspectives were incorporated. This exchange of ideas and negotiation of meaning affected not only the individual's cognition but also the group's "distributed cognition" as participants transmitted, negotiated and transformed their ideas in the creation of new knowledge. In the process of articulation, reflection and negotiation, students engaged in meaning making knowledge construction processes. These processes could become even more powerful when communications among peers was done in written form, because writing done without the immediate feedback of another person through oral communications and body language required further elaboration in order to convey the right meanings.

SYNCHRONOUS COMPUTER-MEDIATED COMMUNICATIONS

Synchronous communications foster networked social interactions that generate camaraderie, connectedness, and a sense of accomplishment amongst its learners (Liu et al., 2007). Synchronous communications achieve these social interactions by allowing immediate feedback and responses, enabling learners to simultaneously interact in a collaborative environment (Johnson, 2006). Mirroring face-to-face interactions, synchronous communications facilitate communications by bringing together geographically dispersed students within a web of learning influenced by the dimension of real-time immediacy (Liu et al., 2007). Educational research shows that the use of synchronous communications by simulating face-to-face communications afford real-time collaborations (Yamada & Akahori, 2007). Synchronous communication tools include chat, web-conferencing, audio-conferencing and video-conferencing. The immediacy and promptness of feedback can help replicate face-to-face collaborations (Maushak & Ou, 2007). Such online collaborations provide opportunities for students to discuss on a variety of issues, ask questions, share different perspectives, debate and elaborate on the merits of others' opinions. By actively taking part in the learning transactions students negotiate and construct meaning making. In addition, online interactions induce a higher level of learner motivation due to the influence of social presence created by prompt responsiveness.

Nevertheless, though synchronous communications try to simulate face-to-face interactions between instructors and students, there is a lack of natural social interactions that can possibly cause feelings of isolation (Weller, 2007). McMillan and Chavis (1986) define the notion of a sense of community as having a sense of belonging - a feeling that members matter to one another and to the group with a shared faith of commitment to be together. Educators have been exploring ways to establish this type of atmosphere in online-learning environments to overcome learners' feelings of isolation. A strong sense of online community can strengthen information exchange, learning support, commitment to group goals and collaboration (Rovai & Wighting, 2005).

In some ways, learning facilitated by synchronous communication tools such as chat have been found to yield better outcomes than face-to-face classroom interactions. For example, Lobel et al. (2002) found that online synchronous interactions in an inquiry based learning context were parallel in nature, whereas face-to-face interactions were typically viewed as serial events. Parallel communications are observed when online discussion participants post their individual messages simultaneously with a given time and date stamp. Researchers found that parallel communications enhanced the perceived worth of the group to be many times the sum of the worth of its individuals and it is this synergy that made collaborative learning both attractive and effective. Seventy percent of discussion participants in a synchronous learning situation were found to be actively participating in the discussions within five-minutes of the one-hour discussion period. The researchers felt that the high percentage of participation could be attributed to the dynamic nature of interactions in terms of trust formation and information flow than that seen in a face-to-face similar situation. Wang and Newlin (2001) also discussed the use of synchronous communications in the facilitation of online courses and the impact they can have on the social interactions of students. They believe that online chats fulfil the promise of computer mediated communications by offering the opportunity for people who are geographically distant to feel interpersonally close to one another.

Amongst the advantages of synchronous interactions, teacher immediacy and dynamic interactions have been highly emphasized by many researchers. As Nipper (1989) pointed out, "The primary aim of implementing computer conferencing in adult learning is to overcome the problem of social distance between learners and teachers, not just geographical distance" (p. 71). This is key to building up a greater sense of bonding and trust amongst learners participating in an educational initiative. As Clifton (1999) pointed out, the level of trust between all involved in the educational process has to be high if a sense of community is to develop.

...when people do not trust each other, and when they do not share norms, obligations, and expectations, as is presently the case in many universities, the community is not likely to develop, and the self-interest of people in their status is likely to predominate. (Clifton, 1999)

WEB SIMULATIONS

Day and Reibstein (1997) defined simulations as a facsimile of reality, which is intended to display "what would transpire if the assumed conditions were to occur in reality". They argued that simulations offer a more effective way to understand the future. Simulations would therefore be useful to learn about complex situations (where data is incomplete, unreliable or unavailable), where the problems are unfamiliar, and where the cost of errors in making decisions is likely to be high. The potential for combining sophisticated visual and graphics display with other features of the microcomputers has been recognized as very promising by educators for some time. For example, when combined with the interactive capability of the microcomputer, good simulations may provide students with meaningful opportunities for thinking, problem solving and decision making. Students could be actively involved in identifying variables, defining hypotheses, and determining methods of measurement, treatments, procedures, and proposed techniques of data analyses. Such simulations can also allow students to examine models and relationships of the real world under controlled conditions.

Initial internet-based simulations were mainly created by programmers or those who took great pride in their own programming prowess. They may have a background in their fields of discipline but were not necessarily good teachers themselves. They found great satisfaction in their creations and were happy to share with those who appreciated their work. In recent years more educators have begun to recognize the potential of such simulations in teaching and learning. While interactive simulations cannot replace actual classroom face-to-face learning experiences, they could complement classroom instructional activities. These simulations together with appropriate instructional mediation allow students to construct and codify their own knowledge schemas. This is what Redish (1999) meant when he coined the term "scientific constructivism", A dose of social constructivism can also easily be injected by having students working on the simulation-related task together. By working together collaboratively, students can build up a shared repertoire of knowledge resources through collective synergy. Simulations could also help address and assess potential alternative conceptions among respondents who are beginning to study a particular topic. Deep processing and rich-associative lateral thinking skills could be developed in working on tasks that involve the manipulation of interactive simulations to develop sound conceptual understandings.

Simulations have been found to be effective in motivating students to learn and those that encourage exploration may be particularly engaging to students, especially girls (Kinzie & Joseph, 2008). Students are usually more engaged when they face a challenge that they feel they can meet to be able to learn at higher levels of efficiency. However, the level of challenge should match the student's skill levels. If the task is too hard, the student will give up easily, and if it is too easy, the student may become bored. To promote learning, simulations must encourage students to reflect on and explain what is happening. To internalize learning, students need to be given opportunities to reflect upon their online interactions. Several simulation programs use animated pedagogical agents to help students reflect on what they are learning by providing explanations to questions students ask.

THREE-DIMENSIONAL (3-D) VIRTUAL WORLDS

A virtual world is a computer-based simulated environment: a synchronous, persistent network of people, represented as avatars, facilitated by networked computers (Bell, 2008). Virtual worlds are embedded with both immersive and social media environments. They may not always have specific rules and goals as they allow for user-created content, user-defined purposes and a sense of presence with others at the same time and place. They create new dynamic opportunities for learning, innovation, and collaboration that go beyond the physical and geographical limitations of the physical world.

3D virtual worlds are increasingly receiving greater attention by educators due to their potential in delivering immersive, authentic learning experiences in socially situated contexts (Kluge & Riley, 2008). Shroeder (2008) explained that 3-D virtual worlds offer online social spaces that exist over time after the user has left the virtual environment, and they are synchronous, immersive worlds facilitating social interactions. 3D virtual worlds are increasingly becoming popular as engaging instructional spaces since they can accommodate a large number of users and combine many interactive elements such as social networking, seamless sharing of rich media, real-time online presence and connectivity to enhance the quality of learning. The latest developments in 3-D virtual worlds provide a new level of immersive experience, incorporating rich visual elements and animations that provide efficacious social learning environments (Carter & Click, 2006).

As an innovative learning technology, 3-D virtual worlds have the potential to significantly enhance learning experiences and facilitate transfer of knowledge by providing immersive virtual environments for social and collaborative learning in a context that closely mimics real-world scenarios (Cross, O'Driscoll & Trondsen, 2007). Situated learning theory suggests that knowledge must be socially situated in an authentic context for learning to occur (Lave & Wenger 1991). Situated learning theory is relevant for learning in virtual worlds since emphasis is placed on development of cognition through socially situating learning set in authentic contexts.

3-D virtual worlds such as Active Worlds and Second Life offer multimodal data rich environments that allow students to manipulate accessible data, role-play and engage in problem-solving activities. Dede (2004) mentioned that 3D virtual worlds combine action along with symbolic and sensory factors that induce a "psychological sense of sensory and physical immersion" that makes the learner feel that s/he is inside the virtual environment. 3-D virtual worlds support formal and informal learning and support self-directed learning. They are rich experiential learning environments that support learning interactions through user created content. As collaborative, learner-centered environments, the design of these multi-user social virtual spaces supports diverse learning styles.

The use of virtual learning environments can facilitate critical reflection and communications between online learners, which can lead towards better building of communities of practice. Tools available in virtual learning environments that support the reflective process include chat and voice discussion with interaction taking place in synchronous real-time (Boulos et al., 2007). Second Life is a popular example of a 3-D virtual world that can appropriately be leveraged for educational purposes. Second Life boasts the ability to go beyond simply being a method of distance learning to becoming a tool that has reached both formal instruction and informal knowledge-sharing in communities of practice (Ondrejka, 2007). It has over 150 different virtual worlds in existence today and was released to the public in 2003 by Linden Lab (2003), a San-Francisco-based company. Users, represented by digital avatars, are known as residents; function within Second Life by walking, flying, or teleporting. It is a real-time

dynamic distributed environment that enables users to build and create a uniquely customized, personalized environment suited for their specific purposes. Second Life has a high-level, built-in scripting language and building tools, making it extremely easy to build content and to create scripts. Residents can use Second Life to socialize, play, do business, and of course learn with the content and from one another.

ELECTRONIC GAMING

Games, though popular in the entertainment sector, is increasingly being used for non-entertainment purposes including education, corporate and military training, and health care (Scanlon, 2007). The development of gaming has involved a complex set of processes including interactions between entertainment gaming and educational-oriented gaming (Gee, 2005). The entertainment gaming market began to develop in the 1980s and it continues to thrive today (Levitan, 2010). Gee (2005) was the first educator to acknowledge that serious video games had elements that helped people learn and suggested integrating elements of these video games into educational contexts in classrooms. While old-fashioned edugames persist, the cutting edge of the fusion of video gaming and education is occurring within highly engaging and interactive gaming environments (Gee, 2005). By incorporating the learning advantages of immersive video games as opposed to traditional simulations, serious games can improve adult learning on the job (De Freitas, 2006). Although video gaming is being explored in educational contexts, the research into gaming in education is in its infancy stages and lack systematic evaluation. Educational games for learners are fast becoming an important and growing field of research study.

Online games offer limitless possibilities for training simulations, as they currently include multi-user dungeons (MUDs), multiplayer online role play games (MMORPs) and massively multiplayer online first-person shooter games (MMOF-PSs) (De Freitas, 2006). An important element of gaming being investigated for its instructional potential involves stealth teaching or guidance (Bopp, 2005). This occurs when designers attempt to camouflage the direct teaching aspects of games since gamers do not like being reminded of being taught or guided and the learning gains come from the enjoyment of gaming as embedded in the challenges of engaging in problem solving (Bopp, 2006). In a covered guided discovery, for example, a casual remark made by a character may provide a clue for solving a gaming situational problem. The remark "may not be remembered consciously, but it…primes the correct solutions for the problem (Bopp, 2005, p. 17). The gaming environment in serious games provides opportunities for players to engage in social activities that simulate the social interactions between people in real-time (Bopp, 2005). The adaptive nature of games requiring players to apply flexibility and reflexivity improves learner motivation and involvement (Burgos, Moreno, Sierra, Fernandez-Manjon, Specht, & Koper, 2008). These games are even more successful if agent characters are developed and utilized in the games since agents introduce a social element by enhancing conversational interactions through verbal and non-verbal communication modes (Muller & Weiss, 2008). The use of such agents creates an intelligent tutoring system involving elaborate planning and interactive story telling that could be highly beneficial to learning. Another major benefit of gaming is that it allows trainers to replace verbal explanations of how things work with actual experiences of the workings of the subject matter (Levitan, 2010). Gaming has been leveraged upon at several different levels of training since gaming provides the learners with more richer, robust learning environments with higher degrees of interactivity (Pellegrino & Scott, 2004). The player can experiment and try different creative ways to achieve his or her goal in a safe manner (Pellegrino & Scott, 2004). The extent to which

learning takes place is directly linked to the degree of emotional engagement in the functionalities of gameplay. Games invoke vibrant emotional responses and also demand more decision making, problem solving and rewards-based incentives. Good educational games don't necessarily call for sophisticated visual extravaganzas that can be found in commercial games. They can be simple games that put good gameplay around interactions helpful to learning (Pellegrino & Scott, 2004). A good game should not be able to be easily mastered and requires several practice sessions to master. In terms of structure, it should include multiple learning paths facilitating decision making and problem solving (Pellegrino & Scott, 2004). Being immersed in multiple scenarios and tackling them from multiple perspectives, forces players/learners to understand the dynamics of underlying strategies to play well (Squire, 2005). He found that students did develop new vocabularies and displayed enhanced complex thinking and negotiation skills while playing the games. He further argued that it is timely to develop better games-based pedagogical theories to improve the implementation of gaming in educational contexts. Another learning advantage of serious games is that they engender cognitive dissonance (Van Eck, 2006). Games can introduce contradictory ideas and so encourage players to accommodate new realities by modifying existing mental models of the world to encode new information. Interacting with a game situates a learner within a constant iterative cycle of formulation, testing, and revision of knowledge schemas.

MOBILE LEARNING

Mobile learning provides students with access to anytime, anywhere learning via handheld devices and wireless networks, etc., and makes the resulting content available to learners in non-traditional distant locations. Mobile learning has shattered the requirements for students to be seated for lengthy periods at a given time and place. It enables students to take courses at their convenience at a location they desire, and at a time they choose Mobile learning also has great potential in broadening the boundaries of the conventional classroom and elevating learning to a higher level of optimum performance. The widespread availability of wireless-fidelity (Wi-Fi) networks, the shrinking costs of data hosting/ storage solutions, and the availability of a variety of inexpensive small information appliances have enabled learners to be connected within an expansive web of learning globally linking learners in geographically distributed locations. Learners can now readily gain access to course content and socially be connected to engage in collaborative modes of learning. The ubiquity of mobile learning provides for economies of scale that afford low cost of ownership of mobile devices and increasing levels of educational quality (Williams, 2009).

In this technology-driven era, students need to develop key 21st century skills. These skills include critical thinking, problem solving, creativity, and effective communications. Students need to develop information, media, and technology skills that enable accessing, evaluating, and using information from multiple sources. Students also need to develop skills that focus on flexibility, adaptability, initiative, self-direction, productivity, and responsibility. Mobile devices present students with opportunities to develop 21st century skills. Research reveals that mobile devices can be used to enhance social skills such as student collaboration and groupwork (Zurita & Nussbaum, 2004). Students nowadays also need to be able to learn from multiple sources and recognize patterns within and between the sources (Siemens, 2007). Mobile devices can expand the context of formal and community learning environments (Kim, 2009). During their focus group discussions, Eteokleous and Ktoridou (2009) highlighted the various benefits associated with m-learning devices. Portability, cost effectiveness, accessibility, convenience, and student ownership

were considered the technological advantages related to mobile learning. Collaboration, student interaction, and increased students involvement were perceived to be the pedagogical benefits (Eteokleous & Ktoridou, 2009).

M-learning does not come without its limitations though. Limited screen size, lack of technological skills, and wireless connectivity are all disadvantages related to using mobile devices for learning (Shen, Wang, & Pan, 2008). However, as technological advancements occur, these limitations may be reduced. More research pertaining to the benefits and limitations associated with m-learning needs to be conducted at all levels of educational performance.

CONCLUSION

Learning has been argued to be a socially constructed process. The social context of the learner is a factor in determining the success of an instructional activity. For example, Matel & Ball-Rokeach (2001) argued that *'the social effects of the Internet should be placed in the framework of people's sociostructural connections, including cultural, ethnic, social, and local-physical circumstances.'* Hence, there has been increasing calls for the design of pedagogy to move away from its traditional focus on individual learning to collaborative learning. The affordances of emergent technologies can be harnessed to support this paradigmatic shift in instruction to foster more immersive and effective learning environments. Learning technologies can foster virtual worlds where information sharing, communications and collaborations can be facilitated, either synchronously or asynchronously. Through active participation, in-world residents begin to understand the cultural norms of community practices, gradually becoming a member of the growing learning community of practice and contributing to its shared knowledge capital. Technology mediated instructional environments provide students with opportunities to become fully immersed in an educational community of practice, thus extending learning beyond fixed classroom durations and boundaries. Social construction of knowledge through sharing and exchanging of perspectives, without being affected by spatial, physical and geographical constraints can be facilitated by emergent technologies. Careful design of the elements of the learning environment needs to be incorporated as an essential component of the effective development of an electronic courseware. This will ensure a greater degree of success in achieving deeper learning and greater learner satisfaction.

REFERENCES

Arvaja, M., Salovaara, H., Hakkinen, P., & Jarvela, S. (2007). Combining individual and group-level perspectives for studying collaborative knowledge construction in context. *Learning and Instruction, 17*, 448–459. doi:10.1016/j.learninstruc.2007.04.003

Bell, M. W. (2008). Toward a Definition of —Virtual Worlds‖. *Journal of Virtual Worlds Research, 1*(1).

Bopp, M. (2006). Didactic analysis of digital games and game-based learning. In M. Pivec (Ed.),*Affective and emotional aspects of human-computer interaction; Game-Based and Innovative Learning Approaches. Vol.1: The Future of Learning*. Amsterdam: IOS Press

Boulos, M. N., Hetherington, L., & Wheelert, S. (2007). Second life: An overview of the potential of 3-D virtual worlds in medical and health education. *Health Information and Libraries Journal, 24*(4), 233–245. doi:10.1111/j.1471-1842.2007.00733.x

Burgos, D., Moreno, P., Sierra, J. L., Fernandez-Manjon, B., Specht, M., & Koper, R. (2008). *Building adaptive game-based learning resources: The marriage of IMS learning design and <e-adventure>*. Retrieved from www.eucm/publications/articles.html.

Carter, B., & Click, A. (2006). *Imagine the real in the virtual: Experience your second life*. Paper presented at the 22nd Annual Conference on Distance Teaching and Learning, Wisconsin, Madison.

Chen, N., Ko, H., Kinshuk, K., & Lin, T. (2005, May). A model for synchronous learning using the Internet. *Innovations in Education and Teaching International, 42*(2), 181–194. doi:10.1080/14703290500062599

Chin, C., & Chia, L. G. (2002). *Problem-based learning: Using students' questions to drive knowledge construction*. New York: Wiley Interscience.

Clifton, R. A. (1999). The education of university students: A social capital perspective. *College Teaching, 47*(3), 114–118. doi:10.1080/87567559909595798

Cross, J., O'Driscoll, T., & Trondsen, E. (2007). Another life: Virtual worlds as tools for learning. *ELearn Magazine, (3)*.

Day, G. S., & Reibstein, D. J. (1997). *Wharton on dynamic competitive strategy*. New York: John Wiley & Sons.

De Freitas, S. (2006). *Learning in immersive worlds: A review of game-based learning*. Bristol, UK: Joint Information Systems Committee (JISC) E-Learning Programme. Retrieved from http://www.jisc.ac.uk/whatwedo/ programmes/elearning_innovation /eli_outcomes/GamingReport.aspx.

Dede, C. (1996). The evolution of distance education: Emerging technologies and distributed learning. *American Journal of Distance Education, 10*(2), 4–36. doi:10.1080/08923649609526919

Dede, C. (2004). Enabling distributed-learning communities via emerging technologies. *Proceedings of the 2004 Conference of the Society for Information Technology in Teacher Education (SITE),* Charlottesville, VA. 3-12.

Eteokleous, N., & Ktoridou, D. (2009). Investigating mobile devices integration in higher education in Cyprus: Faculty perspectives. *International Journal of Interactive Mobile Technologies, 3*(1), 38–48.

Frey, B. A., Sass, M. S., & Arman, S. W. (2006). Mapping MLIS asynchronous discussions. *International Journal of Instructional Technology & Distance Learning, 3*(1).

Gee, J. P. (2005). *Why are video games good for learning?* Retrieved from http://www.academic-colab.org/ resources/documents/ MacArthur.pdf.

Johnson, G. (2006). Synchronous and asynchronous text-based cmc in educational contexts: A review of recent research. *TechTrends: Linking Research & Practice to Improve Learning, 50*(4), 46–53.

Kim, P. (2009). Action research approach on mobile learning design for the underserved. *Educational Technology Research and Development, 57*(3), 415–435. doi:10.1007/s11423-008-9109-2

Kinzie, M., & Joseph, D. (2008). Gender differences in game activity preferences of middle school children: Implications for educational game design. *Educational Technology Research and Development, 56*(5/6), 643–663. doi:10.1007/s11423-007-9076-z

Kluge, S., & Riley, L. (2008). Teaching in virtual worlds: Opportunities and challenges. *Issues in Informing Science and Information Technology, 5,* 127–135.

Lajoie, S. P., Lavigne, N. C., Guerrera, C., & Munsie, S. D. (2001). Constructing Knowledge in the Context of BioWorld. *Instructional Science, 29*(2), 155–186. doi:10.1023/A:1003996000775

Lave, J., & Wenger, E. (1991). *Situated learning: Legitimate peripheral participation.* Cambridge, UK: Cambridge University Press.

Levitan, E. (2010). *Higher education administrators' perceptions of the use of simulation games for adult learners.* Argosy University.

Liu, X., Magjuka, R., Bonk, C., & Lee, S. (2007). Does sense of community matter? *Quarterly Review of Distance Education, 8*(1), 9–24.

Lobel, M., Neubauer, M., & Swedburg, R. (2002). Elements of group interaction in a real-time synchronous online learning-by-doing classroom without F2F participation. *USDLA Journal, 16*(4).

Matel, S., & Ball-Rokeach, S. J. (2001). Real and virtual social ties: Connections in the everyday lives of seven ethnic neighborhoods. *The American Behavioral Scientist, 45*(3), 550–564.

Maushak, N., & Ou, C. (2007r). Using synchronous communication to facilitate graduate students' online collaboration. *Quarterly Review of Distance Education, 8*(2), 161–16.

McMillan, D. W., & Chavis, D. M. (1986). Sense of community: a definition and theory. *Journal of Community Psychology, 14*(1), 6–23. doi:10.1002/1520-6629(198601)14:1<6::AID-JCOP2290140103>3.0.CO;2-I

Murphy, E., & Manzanares, M. A. R. (2005). Reading between the lines: Understanding the role of latent content in the analysis of online asynchronous discussions. *International Journal of Instructional Technology & Distance Learning, 2*(6).

Nipper, S. (1989). Third generation distance learning and computer conferencing. In Mason, R., & Kaye, A. (Eds.), *Mindweave: Communication, Computers and Distance Education.* Oxford, UK: Pergamon.

Ondrejka, C. (2007). Education unleashed: participatory culture, education, and innovation in second life. *The John D. and Catherine T. MacArthur Foundation Series on DigitalMedia and Learning*, 229-251.

Ouzts, K. (2006). Sense of community in online courses. *Quarterly Review of Distance Education, 7*(3), 285–296.

Pena-Schaff, J. B., & Nicholls, C. (2004). Analyzing student interactions and meaning constructions in computer bulletin board discussions. *Computers & Education, 42*, 243–265. doi:10.1016/j.compedu.2003.08.003

Ponnusawmy, H., & Santally, M. I. (2008). Promoting (quality) participation in online forums: A study of the use of forums in two online modules at the University of Mauritius. *International Journal of Instructional Technology & Distance Learning, 5*(4).

Redish, E. F. (1999). *Building a science of teaching physics [online].* Millikan Award Lecture (1998). Available http://www.physics.umd.edu/ rgroups/ ripe/papers /millikan.htm

Rovai, A. P., & Wighting, M. J. (2005). Feelings of alienation and community among higher education students in a virtual classroom. *The Internet and Higher Education, 8*, 97–110. doi:10.1016/j.iheduc.2005.03.001

Russo, T. C., & Benson, S. (2005). Learning with invisible others: Perceptions of online presence and their relationship to cognitive and affective learning. *Journal of Educational Technology & Society, 8*(1), 54–62.

Scanlon, J. (2007). Getting serious about gaming. *Business Week Online, 8-14, 1*–4.

Shen, R., Wang, M., & Pan, X. (2008). Increasing interactivity in blended classrooms through a cutting-edge mobile learning system. *British Journal of Educational Technology, 39*(6), 1073–1086. doi:10.1111/j.1467-8535.2007.00778.x

Shroeder, R. (2008). Defining virtual worlds and virtual environments. *Journal of Virtual Worlds Research, 1*(1), 2–3.

Siemens, G. (2003). *Learning ecology, communities, and networks: extending the classroom.* Elearnspace.

Sivan, E. (1986). Motivation in social constructivist theory. *Educational Psychologist, 21*(3), 209. doi:10.1207/s15326985ep2103_4

Slagter van Tryon, P., & Bishop, J. M. (2006, Spring). Identifying e-mmediacy strategies for web-based instruction. *Quarterly Review of Distance Education, 7*(1), 49–62.

Stein, D. S., Wanstreet, C. E., Engle, C. L., Glazer, H. R., Harns, R. A., Johnston, S. M., et al. (2006). *From personal meaning to shared understanding: The nature of discussion in a community of inquiry.* Midwest Research-to-Practice Conference in Adult, Continuing, and Community Education 2006.

Vygotsky, S. L. (1978). *Mind in society: The development of higher psychological process.* Cambridge, MA: Harvard University Press.

Wang, A. Y., & Newlin, M. H. (2001). Online Lectures: Benefits for the virtual classroom. *T.H.E. Journal, 29* (1), 17-24, Retrieved July 19, 2004 from http://www.thejournal.com/magazine/vault/A3562.cfm.

Waters, J., & Gasson, S. (2007). *Distributed knowledge construction in an online community of inquiry.* Proceedings of the 40th Hawaii International Conferences on System Sciences 2007.

Weinberger, A., & Fischer, F. (2006). A framework to analyze argumentative knowledge construction in computer-supported collaborative learning. *Computers & Education, 46,* 71–95. doi:10.1016/j.compedu.2005.04.003

Weller, M. (2007). The distance from isolation: Why communities are the logical conclusion in e-learning. *Computers & Education, 49,* 148–159. doi:10.1016/j.compedu.2005.04.015

Wenger, E. (1998). *Communities of practice: Learning, meaning and identity.* New York: Cambridge University Press.

Williams, P. (2009). *Assessing Mobile Learning Effectiveness and Acceptance.* George Washington University.

Yamada, M., & Akahori, K. (2007, February). Social presence in synchronous CMC based language learning: How does it affect the productive performance and consciousness of learning objectives? *Computer Assisted Language Learning, 20*(1), 37–65. doi:10.1080/09588220601118503

Zhu, E., & Baylen, D. (2005). From learning community to community learning: pedagogy, technology and interactivity. *Educational Media International, 42*(3), 251–268. doi:10.1080/09523980500161395

Zurita, G., & Nussbaum, M. (2004). A constructivist mobile learning environment supported by a wireless handheld network. *Journal of Computer Assisted Learning, 20*(4), 235–243. doi:10.1111/j.1365-2729.2004.00089.x

Chapter 4

Internal Key Factor in the Export Performance of Spanish SMEs

Lluís Jovell Turró
Autonomous University of Barcelona, Spain

Rossano Eusebio
Autonomous University of Barcelona, Spain

ABSTRACT

The internationalization is a complex process that requires a great effort, both financial and human, that some companies cannot spare, especially if they are medium or small companies. The authors' investigation is based upon these medium and small companies and the problems they face, and analyzes the issues that affect their export intensity. For this, a multidimensional model is proposed as a result of a deep research on literature on this field. The results of this study show how technological innovation is an important aspect when determining an effort for exportation in this kind of companies.

PROBLEM STATEMENT AND RESEARCH OBJECTIVES

There is a constant growth on the number of companies that look for opportunities in international markets as a strategy to keep or retain their position in the market. Medium and Small Companies (SMEs), due to their characteristics, find a hard way when they begin an internationalization process. In this aspect, exporting has been the most common way of internationalization because it

requires less financial and human resources and it carries lower risks (Leonidou et al., 2002). In sum, it's an internationalization process, defined as the development of a set of activities that lead to the establishment of somewhat stable links with international markets (Root, 1994; Rialp, 1999).

This paper focuses on the research realm of the companies' internationalization, which is characterized by a broad set of views, mainly from multiple disciplines, that derive from the numerous instruments that the enterprises use for entering foreign markets. Coviello & McAuley insist systematically on this matter (1999:243).

DOI: 10.4018/978-1-61350-192-4.ch004

Based on this, this paper wants to analyze one of the most important among the set of internationalization tools, which is exportation as a mode of entry in foreign markets.

Economic literature, which encompasses different theoretical currants, has dealt with the export phenomena either from a macroeconomic view or from a more business-based perspective. The former includes all the approaches that try to explain trade between different countries and/or productive sectors. The researches that analyze the export results from a macroeconomic perspective tend to conclude that the international activity of an enterprise would be conditioned by institutional actions and by the conditions offered by its country of origin (Porter, 1990).

There is no doubt that a macro vision offers a good explanation for international commerce and competence among countries, but it's not complete or it's limited for explaining the competitive issues of a company in a specific geographic zone or sector and especially to understand a company's role in an international projection.

Traditionally, researches concerning the examination of the export results of the enterprises based on their competitive capacities have focused on the identification of all the factors that explain why the company made the decision to export, as well as on the export effort, expressed normally by the percentage of the total sales that the company cashes in foreign markets. As indicated by a series of authors (Bilkey, 1978; Thomas & Araujo, 1986; Miesembock, 1988; Andersen, 1993; Leonidou & Katsikeas, 1996; Zou & Stan, 1998), the obtained results are characterized by a high fragmentation and in many cases by an important contradiction between them. This suggests that a more encompassing model that integrates different perspectives is necessary.

On the other hand, most of the research is based on the study of the determinants of export results of Anglo-Saxon enterprises –mainly north American-. Like Zou & Stan (1998, 353). In their work about the main and most recent empirical researches that focus on the analysis of the determinants of export results, studies that focus on non-Anglo-Saxon companies are scarce. Hence, the need to focus this research towards other geographic contexts, such as Europe and Asia.

These latter, even if they indicate some generic determinants of the export results of the enterprises, they are limited for explaining the results of Catalan or Spanish companies.

Today, the various studies that have been published about the Spanish enterprises are a proof of the growing interest for this topic. Due to the notability of enterprises' internationalization in general, and of their exports in particular, one can observe an important number of works focused on these subjects[1]. Some of them focus particularly on the case of one autonomous community[2]. Nonetheless, empirical evidence at the local levels is yet inexistent.

Analyzing the export results from the perspective of a concrete territory is in line with all those researches that consider it as a factor for the cohesion, the specialization, the diversification and the competitivity of companies. Moreover, even if the territorial factor is not the object of this research, we insist on the fact that when doing a research on a concrete territory, particularly in the business realm of Terrassa, it validates the obtained results. It is not in vain that the enterprises in a realm such as the indicated above reinforce their competitivity via externalities. There is enough empirical evidence that demonstrates that the links between the enterprises' system and their territory are accentuated and that they constitute the fertile soil for the frequent existence of external economies for the enterprises, but internal in the geographic area. This was shown by the pioneer work of Marshall (Marshall, 1890) and afterwards those of Arrow (Arrow, 1962), (Romer, 1986), (Porter, 1990) and (Krugman, 1995).

We will focus our research based upon this context. Our principal objective is to analyze the internal determinants of the export behaviour in small and medium-sized companies (SMEs) in an important local geographic zone of Spain. The reason why we are analyzing this kind of companies is because there is a lack of attention on this field (Karagozoglu and Lindell, 1998).

THEORETICAL MODEL

The internationalization phenomena has been studied for decades by a vast number of researchers, from various theoretical perspectives. In this sense, one may clearly observe that when explaining the internationalization process the academics have not yet come to an agreement on which are the most relevant characteristics of the phenomena[3].

Broadly, three distinct sets of researches or perspectives for the study of business internationalization can be distinguished. From the economic perspective or the theory of international Business, a group of works analyze the reach of a company's internationalization as a process that depends highly on the tradeoff between its advantages and its costs. This view is closely linked to what Rialp (1999) calls "the traditional explanations of Direct Foreign Investment" (DFI) which are built by various currants of thought:

- Contributions from industrial economics that explain internationalization based on monopolistic advantages.
- Others that issue from the "Theory of Internationalization" hold (based on the theory of transaction costs) that the companies choose direct foreign investment when the other options such as exports and licenses are much expensive due to market imperfections.
- Dunning's "eclectic paradigm" (1981) explains transnational companies' behavior parting from specific property and localization advantages. Finally,
- The called "Macroeconomic Model" integrates commerce theories with the direct foreign investment and holds that the DFI

has its origins in the activity of the investor country which has a comparative disadvantage, in a sector on which the receiver country has a comparative advantage.

Hence, the key to understanding foreign investment lies in the incensement of productivity in the receiver countries, due to the infusion of a set of resources linked to Japanese companies.

Secondly, the approaches that focus on the process analyze the internationalization parting from the growing compromise of the Enterprise with the foreign market. In this sense, uncertainty leads to a gradual increase of foreign operations, based on learning and the acquirement of knowledge (Johanson y Wiedersheim-Paul, 1975; Lee y Brasch, 1978). Within this group of theories, one may underline the "Uppsala Model", Vernon's "lifecycle model" (1966) and the "Model based on the adoption of innovation".

This way, beyond the approach to which these theories belong, while some authors explain internationalization parting from a series of localization and property advantages (for example Dunning 1988), other researchers see internationalization as a gradual process, incremental stage by stage, on which companies acquire knowledge and expertise and reduce their risks through time (Johanson & Wiedersheim-Paul, 1975; Bilkey & Tesar, 1977; Johanson & Vahlne, 1977, 1990; Cavusgil, 1980; Czinkota & Johnston, 1981; Reid, 1981).

Additionally, a third group of authors see internationalization as a variable that depends of the structural and organizational characteristics of the Enterprise, as well as of its competitive capacity and the management's characteristics (Welch & Loustarinen, 1988; Aaby & Slater, 1989; Katsikeas et al., 1995). In this context, internationalization may be channeled through the following modes of entry: exports, cooperation, alliances, and direct foreign investment. (Root, 1994; Durán, 1994; Plá, 2000).

The empirical research on this field tends to identify the reasons of the decision for exportation, and its effort expressed upon the company's sales percentage in the foreign markets. As several authors expose (Bilkey, 1978; Thomas & Arujo, 1986; Leonidou & Katsikeas, 1996; Zou & Stan, 1998), the results are characterized by high fragmentation and contradiction in some cases. Because of this, a second objective will be to establish a model of integrated characteristics that will adjust the different contributions on this matter.

According to these fields, we analyse these theories with the objective to obtain a final model of export performance.

Non-Gradualistic Models of Export

Authors like Bilkey (1978), Miesembock (1988), Aaby & Slater (1989), Ford & Leonidou (1991), Gemunden (1991), Chetty & Hamilton (1993), Leonidou (1998), Piercy et al. (1998) have focused on the study of structural and organizational characteristics that inhibit or facilitate exportation. We now describe the main variables that have been analyzed empirically, and their degree of influence on the success of the enterprises' export activities.

Size of the Enterprise and Development of Exportations

One of the key subjects that has dominated the researches, is the effect of the size of the company in its export performance (Fillis, 2001). Size of the company has been traditionally used as one of the main predictors of business internationalization. In this context, it is said that the relation between the company's size and its ability to export is important for understanding the degree and the form of its internationalization. However, the empirical evidence is not entirely conclusive (Culpan, 1989; Samiee & Walters, 1990; Bonaccorsi, 1992; Calof, 1994; Rynning & Anderson, 1994; Westhead, 1995 & Moen, 1999). On one hand, there are authors like Bonaccorsi (1992), Calof (1993,1994), Nakos et al. (1998), Dean et

al. (2000), Nassimbeni (2001), Melle & Raymond (2001) who proove that there's a positive relation between a company's size and its export activity. Johanson and Vahlne (1977) suggest that there is a critical size needed for the internationalization to occur. On the other hand, some researchers (Cavusgil & Nevin, 1981; Mc Guiness & Little, 1981; Czinkota & Johnston, 1983; Diamantopoulos & Inglis, 1988; Ali & Swiercz, 1991; Julien, Joyal & Deshaies, 1994), have prooved that a company's performance abroad is not affected by its size. Moreover, Calof (1993) indicates that SMEs may reach high levels of exportation because the difficulties they encounter in local markets lead them to enter international markets.

Beyond the amount an the origin of capital, Huerta and Labeaga (1992) suggest that, for the Spanish case, there would be a positive effect between the export results and the export experience. In this sense, although some authors suggest that there is a negative relation (Cavusgil, 1984; Diamantopolous & Inglis, 1988; Moon & Lee, 1990), or even the absence of relation at all (Katsikeas, Piercy & Ioannidis, 1996), other authors like Alonso & Donoso (2000) confirm the positive direction of the relation, suggesting that a major experience would reduce the learning costs.

Alonso & Donoso (2000) conclude that the existence of a foreign trade department (which entails the presence of workers specialized in export activities) affects positively the exportation intensity. In this sense, the reviewed literature suggests that the companies that commit strongly to export activities employ a big export team and have better organized departments, in contrast with companies that exhibit lower levels of exportation (Diamantopoulos & Inglis, 1988).

Management Characteristics

The directive function is one of the determinant factors (if not the main one) for competitivity in an economy (Andersson, 2000; Fillis, 2001). In this sense, the decisions made on the process of internationalization are linked to abilities and motivations of the directives implicated in the process (Reuber & Fischer, 1998). On this regard, the directors are capable of identifying the advantages of internationalization, nor to take advantage of them. He even affirms that more than the company size; the director is the one who determines the advance in the internationalization process of the Enterprise. Competencies such as creative and innovative thinking, acknowledging of opportunities, less risk aversion, and networking in the company may be determinant of the company's degree of internationalization (Fillis & McAuley, 2000).

Orientation to International Marketing

It seems clear that today the vigilance of the variables that compound the marketing mix is essential for the companies. Having a differentiated product, adapted to the market needs and with the adequate technologies constitutes the key to success in these markets. For example, a research based on case studies has demonstrated that the success of the new international companies depends, mostly, on their international projection from their starting point, together with innovative products or services and a strong management that focuses on the growth of international sales (Mc Dougall et al, 1994). We further explain the variables that are included in the model:

Product Adaptation

On their research about 65 Finnish exporting enterprises Laine and Kock have demonstrated that success in exportations depends on a good quality, good products, specialized personnel and know how. On the other hand, others researches identified as the cause for success the capacity of the enterprise to develop the product, which includes the modification of a preexistent product and the development of new products, which affects the effectiveness and efficiency in the delivery of a

superior value to the target markets. In this sense, he says that the enterprises that differentiate and adapt their products to the foreign demand have a more active export result (Kirpalani & Macintosh, 1980; McGuinnes & Little, 1981; Kleinschmidt & Cooper, 1984; Kedia & Chhokar, 491986; Burton & Schlegelmilch, 1987; Ryans, 1988; Louter et. al.,1991; Domínguez & Sequeira, 1993; Hitt & Kim, 1997, among others).

Price Policies Towards Foreign Markets

It is clear that the product's differentiation may affect the price policy of export enterprises. On general basis, Price discrimination in different markets is related to the export intensity of the companies. However, the research results are not very conclusive on this matter. Authors like Fenwick & Amine (1979), Kirpalani & McIntosh (1980) & Piercy (1981), Namiki (1994), Styles & Ambles (1994) and Samiee & Anckar (1994) advocate for a flexible Price strategy in different markets. But in the works by Cunningham & Spigel (1979), Bilkey (1982), these results do not tend to be confirmed.

Promotion Mix

Promotion activities are determinant in the export success of enterprises. Researchers identified the marketing differentiation through investments in promotion and brand development as an added value for export success. However, very few researches have studied this variable as a precedent for exportation. Authors like Kirpalani & McIntosh (1980), Yaprak (1985), Amine & Cavusgil (1986), Fraser & Hite (1990), Styles & Ambler (1994), Alonso (1994) and Alonso & Donoso (1994), Merino & Moreno (1996), Rialp (1997), and Moreno & Rodríguez (1998) tend to assign a bigger export success to the enterprises that use tha promotional tools on a more regular basis.

Distribution Strategy

Selecting a distribution channel for exportation and determining the extent of the enterprise's responsibilities in the distribution are very complex and difficult decisions. These have had a profound impact on the export success of the enterprises (Root, 1994). The most common distribution channels are: direct export, on which the producer has low or no control over the product distribution; and the property networks (generally through commercial subsidiaries), on which the producer has entire control over the activities that lead to the product's distribution in the foreign markets. In between these two there are other methods that range from independent but not integrated channels, through the use of commissioned agents and independent distributors, to more internalized forms on which various activities are controlled by the producer, while others are controlled by the intermediary. Other authors like Topritzhofer & Mozer (1979), Rabino (1980), Bilkey (1982), Rosson & Ford (1982), Yaprak (1985), Anderson & Coughlan (1987), Klein et al. (1990), Cavusgil et al. (1994) and Alonso (1994b), agree that a major control over the distribution activities is a determinant warrantee of a more active export result.

Gradualist Approaches of Exportation

According to the gradualist approaches, at the beginning the enterprises internationalize their activities in countries that are geographically and culturally close and only afterwards do they increase their international commitments, as they start accumulating international experience (Johanson & Vahlne, 1977:23). In this way, the internationalization process would obey well planned criteria. However, one may observe that in some cases the enterprises choose their markets based on the characteristics of demand, of the distribution channels, of the clients or, for example, on the existence of a legal frame that may favor their

entry. Moreover, in certain cases the selection of markets turns out to be more reactive because it doesn't depend directly on planned decisions made by the Direction. In these cases the enterprise exports to another country –in principle- to respond to concrete orders placed by a foreign importer (Bilkey & Tesar, 1977). Nevertheless, the reviewed literature suggests that a greater productivity in the development of foreign activities would have a positive impact on the export results (Cavusgil & Naor, 1987, Diamantopoulos & Inglis, 1988; Dichtl et al, 1990; Lee & Yang, 1990; Koh, 1991; Donthu & Kim, 1993; Evangelista, 1994; Dean et al., 2000).

International evidence suggests that strategic alliances have grown more important in the last decades. In this sense, the alliances as well as the networks may be linked to Research and development, marketing, joint materials supply or distribution cooperation. So, the strategic alliances and the cooperation agreements constitute a powerful tool for accessing markets and technologies in a rapid way, as well as for achieving scaled economies and knowledge, sharing risks and costs, adding up synergies and knowledge's and complying with certain prerequisites established by some governments.

In this sense, in the reviewed literature there's a high number of works that highlight an important number of advantages that come from international alliances (Hakansson & Johanson, 1988; Hamel, 1991; Lorange & Roos, 1992; Blodgett, 1992).

Technology and Innovation as Determinant of the Export Results

The way business take place is changing due to the shorter lifecycle of the products, the emphasis on innovation and the rapid development of information technologies (Jones, 1999; Crick & Jones, 2000; Andersson et al, 2004). For example, Lewit (1983) indicates that technology is a factor that contributes to a more homogeneous world and that the development of information technologies has made the distances between countries smaller and has allowed communications to flow more rapidly.

Cosh & Hughes (1996) argument that technology enterprises are the ones they found to be internationalizing faster and that their export performance is linked to investments on research and development and innovation. Additionally, Almor & Hashai (2004) affirm that the enterprises that are based on technology usually enjoy the advantages of being first. This unique know-how is a significative resource on which to create a competitive advantage.

Different academics have found that the level of technology may be an important factor in the explanation of the enterprises' internationalization. Likewise, the empirical evidence on the effect of innovative activities in the export results is very broad. Almost unanimously, the studies conclude that they have a significative effect. Moreover, Kohn (1997), Eusebio et al (2004) and Eusebio & Llonch (2005) indicate that the SMEs that invest abroad, tend to rely more on their technological advantages based on R&D, than on advantages base don advertisement.

As it may be seen, the relation between technology and export performance is yet ambiguous. However, there is one aspect that holds more conclusive consistency. This way, the evidence shows that there's a positive influence of the product quality on the export performance, even if research on this topic is yet limited (Aaby & Slater, 1988). In this sense, both Daniels & Robles (1982) for the Peruvian case, like Joynt (1982) for Norway, conclude that the quality of the product is perceived as one of the most relevant competencies.

AN INTEGRATIVE MODEL OF STUDY

As it was observed in the literature review presented on the previous section, the different research lines that have focused on the export results from different perspectives (microeconomic and gradualist) could as well complement each other. Apparently, certain discrepancies in the obtained results would be due to the study of the phenomena from different perspectives, which would provocate the existence of partial and incongruent results (Rialp & Rialp, 2001). In this respect, the little clarity in the founding's due to the lack of a model that was able to assimilate and synthetize the different approaches of the literature (Zou & Stan, 1998). So this is why the present research wants to contribute with a model that explains the export results, integrating recommendations issued from all the previous studies.

In accordance with the previous literature review and given the abundance of literature regarding this topic, we suggest that the exportation effort is placed in a multidimensional framework, in which we have identified four determinant factors: (1) CAC (*Company and Activity Characteristics*), those factors derivate of the characteristics of the company and the export activity, (2) ES (*Export Strategy*), gathering the determinants of the export strategy, (3) IMS (*International Marketing Strategy*) formed by elements of the marketing strategy, (4) The dimension that is denominated IIS (*Innovation an Implementation Strategy*).

Figure 1 displays the four dimensions of determinants of export intensity and the sign of established hypothesis.

RESEARCH METHODOLOGY

This data was obtained from a mail survey dated February 2003, addressed to a total of 640 registered SMEs in the Terrasa Chamber of Commerce[4]. After two postal mails and a telephonic reminder, 164 valid answers were obtained. The measure for export intensity was calculated as the sales percentage that came from foreign markets (Germuden, 1991).

In view of this high number of available variables, and to avoid similar results, we performed a factorial analysis. The method for extracting the

Figure 1. General Model. Source: Own version based onAaby & Slater (1989)and Leonidou &Katsikeas (1996).

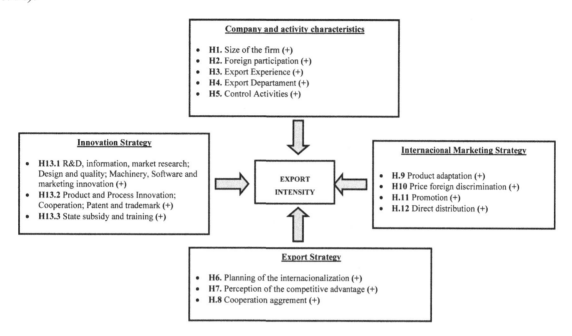

factors has been by principal components and, considering the number of variables, we have applied a Varimax rotation in order to facilitate the interpretation of the results. On the realization of the analysis, we were able to extract 8 factors with an explained variance of 70%. The obtained results are correct if one attains to the values in the Kaiser-Meyer-Olkin Test (equal to 0,913) and to Bartllet's sphericity proof (with an approximate Chi-square approximate of 1440,08 with a signification, 000).

The main results from the factorial analysis are shown in Table 1.

RESULTS AND CONCLUSION

In order to value and confirm the suggested relationships in the theoretical framework (Figure 1) a regression analysis was performed in order to analyze the firm's export intensity and identify its key factors. Table 2 displays the results of this analysis.

As Table 2 shows, the results of the regression analysis were satisfactory, if we consider the variability percentage that the model exhibits. The determination coefficient (R^2) of 0.77 indicates that 77% in the overall export intensity is explained by the eight factors. The F-value was 25.197 a statistic significance. Table 2 shows that all factors have statistical significance with positive signs. Although they indicate that these factors have a positive effect on the company's export intensity, this positive effect is higher with innovation factors and competitive prices. The coefficients for the export commitment factor and the training factor have obtained the lowest value.

Regarding the export commitment, the signification is too low, and that means that the export department does no longer constitute a prioritary competitive aspect. This is due to the fact that today most of the enterprises have an export department with highly qualified personnel to develop the tasks involved in the internationalization process. In all cases, despite the non elevated signification, we recognize the positive effect of these variables

Table 1. Results Factor Analysis

Factor	Factor Denomination	Variables Included
Factor 1 17,601	*Innovation Inputs*	-R&D investments -Hire technical information services -Hire design -Hire quality services -Software and hardware investments -Machinery and installations investments -Hire marketing research- customer's profile -Creativity reward mechanism -Technological advisors -Product development planning -Innovation activities planning -Collaboration with innovating companies
Factor 2 31,578	*Innovation Outputs*	-Product innovation -Process innovation -Patent and brand registry in Spain -Patent and brand registry abroad -Technological agreements -Numeric control machinery -Robotized production process -CAD assisted design -Innovation support -Quality control
Factor 3 43,554	Communication Strategy	-Promotional activities -Web page -Annual actions -Stands and trade fairs -Promotions and discounts, advertising, catalogs
Factor 4 51,683	Innovation Competitiveness	-Innovation competitiveness -Quality competitiveness -Image competitiveness -Design competitiveness
Factor 5 58,932	Strategic Vocation	-Company's dimension -Exterior strategy -Product differentiation -Price strategy -Subsidiary disposal -Capital possession
Factor 6 63,138	Export Commitment	-Workers of export department -Languages in export department -Existence of export department -Cooperation
Factor 7 67,243	Training/Education	-Workers with training and educational degrees in international commerce received on 2002 - R&D area
Factor 8 70,133	Price Competitiveness	-Price Competitiveness

in the exportation intensity. The obtained results confirm the findings made in other researches: Madsen, 1989, Leonidou et al, 1998, Suárez & Álamo (2005) and Eusebio & Llonch (2005), among others. At the same time, the factor covers

also the effect of the cooperation variable. In this case, cooperation with other enterprises for the development of export activities tends to have positive effects in the export results of the enterprises of Terrassa, according to the results obtained by

Table 2. Determinants of export intensity in SMEs

Independent variable	Standardized Coefficients
Export commitment	.174 *
Strategic vocation	.310 **
Price competitiveness	.474 ***
Innovation competitiveness	.326 **
Innovation Inputs	.586***
Innovation outputs	.498 ***
Communication Strategy	.246 *
Training/ Education	.198 *
Constant	25,67***
N° Observ.= 161;	
R²: 0,77	
F value= 25,197***	

* $p<.10$; ** $p<.05$; *** $p<.01$

Hakansson & Johanson, (1988), Astley & Brahm, (1989), Hamel, (1991), Lorange & Roos, (1992).

Secondly, the elevated signification of the strategic vocation confirms that the enterprises with certain dimensions, with a well planned internationalization strategy and some control of the marketing mix variables tend to obtain more successful exterior results. One the one hand, the dimension that tends to be determinant for this collective of enterprises, confirming the results obtained by Yaprak, (1985); Cavusgil & Naor, (1987); Culpan, (1989); Calof, (1994); Nakos et al., (1998); Pedersen & Petersen, (1998); Dean et al., (2000); Melle & Raymond, (2001) and Nassimbeni, (2001). In the same way, the planning of the exterior strategy and the control over the marketing mix variables lead to the exportation of differentiated products at prices customized accordingly for each foreign market and to the increase of investments in the distribution channels. The obtained results match the researches undertaken by Koh, (1991); Donthu & Kim, (1993); Evangelista, (1994) and Dean et al., (2000) regarding the planning of foreign activities. Regarding the product differentiation in the

foreign markets we confirmed the findings of Ryans (1988), Louter et al. (1991), Domínguez & Sequeira (1993), Hitt & Kim (1997), Eusebio & Llonch (2005 and 2006) among others. Finally, the positive effect of the investments on the distribution channels is in line with the results of Yaprak (1985); Anderson & Coughlan, (1987), Klein et al, (1990), Beaimish et al., (1993), Cavusgil et al., (1994), Alonso, (1994a) among others.

When analyzing the Directors board's perception of their product's competitiveness abroad, the results are very suggestive. This result is very negative if one considers that in order to compete actively abroad one must have products with a high technological content to avoid competition of the developing countries that possess cheap labor. In all cases, trust in the technological content of the product, both in innovation, image, and design and quality is very significative. The obtained results highlight the positive effects of directive perceptions (even if price perception is superior than the others) and are in line with the results of other researches: Dichtl et al., 1990; Müller, 1991; Kumcu et al., 1995; Leonidou et al., 1998; Madsen, 1998. This confirms the 7th hypothesis: additionnally, the results proove that the directives of Terrassa's enterprises are undergoing a phase of important changes: on the one hand they trust the low Price of their products, but on the other hand, they start relying on other factors that are important in today's economy. This idea is very similar to the situation observed in other countries like Italy (Eusebio & Llonch, 2006), where product competitivity was based on low Prices for a long time. These results confirm a positive trend of change that replaces Price for more important variables like the technological content of the exported products.

On the other hand, the results of the regression analysis show the importance of technological innovation in the export results of the enterprises of Terrassa. As it follows from the results, the impact of the innovative activity on the export intensity is positive and the relation is very significative. The elevated signification of the input and the output of the innovative activity is an indicator that all the variables that are summed up in those two factors are very significative. This result is not surprising because the innovational technological effort that Terrassa's enterprises make is very reduced, both for innovation investments and for the innovation results, (for the time of generation of product and process innovations and for the registration of brands and patents). In all cases, the results show the importance of having a well planned innovative strategy, because it brings upon clear benefits in the export results. The results we obtained confirm those obtained by other national researches (Rodríguez, 1999; Alonso & Donoso, 1998; Lefebvre et al., 1998; Alonso, 1994a; Merino & Moreno, 1996; Merino, 1998; Moreno & Rodríguez, 1998; Rodríguez, 1999; Melle & Raymond, 2001; Eusebio et al, 2004) and international researches as well (Cavusgil, 1984; Cooper & Kleinschmidt, 1985; Daniels & Roberts, 1982; Aaby & Slater, 1989; Hirsch & Bijaoui, 1985; Eusebio & Llonch, 2005).

As follows from the regression analysis, even if the communication strategy has a positive effect over the export intensity, this effect is of little significance. The result is not surprising, less if we consider that the enterprises in the Terrassa demarcation are used to investing all their communication budgets in stands, fairs and catalogues, investing at the same time few resources in other communication instruments such as advertising, promotions, and other promotion actions. Consequently, if the efforts on these activities were increased, it is very probable that the signification of the factor would increase and so that the impact over export activity increases. The results are in line with those of Kirpalani & McIntosh (1980); Yaprak (1985); Amine & Cavusgil (1986); Fraser & Hite (1990); Styles & Ambler (1994); Alonso (1994A); Alonso & Donoso (1994); Rialp (1997) and Moreno & Rodríguez (1998) among others.

Finally, the analysis shows the positive effect of formation over the export result of the simple.

the obtained factor covers the current level of superior formation in the enterprise, the number of employees with specialized education on foreign trade, and specifical to the R&D area, over the total of the personnel. In this case, the results suggest that when the employees receive more education, the Enterprise is more active in the foreign markets. Just as it is demonstrated by the regression analysis results, the relation between the mentioned factor and the export intensity in the enterprises of Terrassa is very strong, thus confirming, in part, the 13.3th hypothesis, in line with the results obtained by Arcus, (1992) and Valos & Baker, (1996).

In summary, an analysis of the key factors of the export intensity for SMEs has been developed. The study suggests that the SMEs export effort can only be understood within a multidimensional framework. In this multidimensional framework, we have identified eight dimensions related with the company's innovative capacity, strategic criteria and export commitment. According to our expectations, the technological and innovation process are the key internal factors of the intensity export in the Spanish SMEs.

REFERENCES

Aaby, N. E., & Slater, S. T. (1989). Management Influences on Export Performance: A review of the Empirical Literature 1978-88. *International Marketing Review, 6*(4), 7–23. doi:10.1108/EUM0000000001516

Álamo-Vera, F. (2005). Internationalization: firms and managerial factors. *International Journal of Entrepreneurial Behaviour & Research SMES, 11*(4), 258–279. doi:10.1108/13552550510603298

Ali, A. & Swiercz. (1991). Firm size and export behaviour: Lessons from the Midwest. *Journal of Small Business Management*, 71–78.

Almor, T., & Hashai, N. (2004). The competitive advantage and strategic configuration of knowledge-intensive, small- and medium-sized multinationals: A modified resource-based view. *Journal of International Management, 10*(4), 479–500. doi:10.1016/j.intman.2004.08.002

Alonso, J.A. (1991/2). La Internacionalización de la Empresa Española. *Economistas, 52*, 76-86. Diciembre-Enero.

Amine, L., & Cavusgil, S. T. (1986). Export Marketing Strategies in the British Clothing Industries. *European Journal of Marketing, 20*(7), 21–33. doi:10.1108/EUM0000000004653

Andersen, O. (1993). On Internationalization Process of Firm: A Critical Analysis. *Journal of International Business Studies, 24*(2), 209–231. doi:10.1057/palgrave.jibs.8490230

Anderson, E., & Coughlan, A. (1987). International Marker Entry and Expansion Via Independent or Integrated Channel of Distribution. *Journal of Marketing, 51*(1), 71–82. doi:10.2307/1251145

Andersson, S. (2004). Internationalization in different industrial contexts. *Journal of Business Venturing, 19*(6), 851–875. doi:10.1016/j.jbusvent.2003.10.002

Arcus, T. P. (1992). *Australian Business in Asia: Climbing the Mountains*. Victoria: Business Council of Australia.

Arrow, K. J. (1962),Economic Welfare and the Allocation of Resources for Invention. In R. Nelson (ed.). *The Rate and Direction of Inventive Activity*.Princeton University Press, pp. 609–626. -- Collected papers of K.J. Arrow. Vol. 5, Harvard University Press.

Axinn, C. N. (1988). Export Performance: Do Managerial Perceptions Make a Difference? *International Marketing Review, 5*(2), 61–71. doi:10.1108/eb008353

Bagchi-sen, S. (1999). The Small and Medium Size Expoters' Problems: An Empirical Analysis of Canadian Manufacturers. *Regional Studies, 33*(3), 231–245. doi:10.1080/00343409950082427

Beaimish, P. W. (1990). The Internationalization Process for Smaller Ontario's Firms: A Reasearch Agenda. In Rugman, A. M. (Ed.), *Research in Global Strategic Management-International Business*.

Beccatini, G. (1975). *Lo sviluppo economico della Toscana, con particolare riguardo all'industrializzazione leggera. Florencia*. IRPET.

Bilkey, W. J. (1978). An Attempted Integration of the Literature on the Export Behaviour of Firms. *Journal of International Business Studies, 9*(1), 33–46. doi:10.1057/palgrave.jibs.8490649

Blodgett, L. L. (1992). Factors in the Instability of International Joint Ventures: An Event History Analysis. *Strategic Management Journal, 13*, 475–481. doi:10.1002/smj.4250130607

Bloodgood, J., & Sapienza, H.J. & ALMEIDA, J.G. (1996). The Internationalization of New High-Potential U.S. Ventures: Antecedents and Outcomes. *Entrepreneurship Theory and Practice, 20*(4), 61–76.

Bonaccorsi, A. (1992). Relantionship Between Firm Size and Export Intensity. *Journal of International Business Studies, 23*(4), 605–635. doi:10.1057/palgrave.jibs.8490280

Burton, F., & Schlegelmilch, B. (1987). Profile analyses of nonexporters versus exporters grouped by export involvement. *International Marketing Review, 1*(27), 38–49.

Calof, J. C. (1994). The Relationship Between Firm Size and Export Behaviour Revisated. *Journal of International Business Studies, 25*(2), 367–387. doi:10.1057/palgrave.jibs.8490205

Calvo, J. (1993). *La Internacionalización de las PME Manufactureras Españolas. Economía Industrial, 291* (pp. 66–75). Mayo Junio.

Campa, J.M. & Guillén, M.F. (1999). Internalization of exports: Firm- and location-specific factors in a middle-income country. *Management Science, 45*(11), 1463–1478. doi:10.1287/mnsc.45.11.1463

Capacidades Exportadoras y Estrategia Internacional de la Empresa. (1993). *Empresas y Empresarios Españoles en la Encrucijada de los '90*. Madrid: Civitas.

Cavusgil, S. T. (1980). On the Internationalization Process of Firm. *European Research, 8*(November), 273–281.

Chetty, S. (1999).Dimensions of Internationalisation of Manufacturing Firms in the Apparel Industry. *European Journal of Marketing, 33,* (½),121-142.

Christense, N, C.,Da Rocha, A. & Kerbel, R. (1987). An Empirical Investigation of the Factors Influencing Exporting Succes of Brazilian Firms. *Journal of International Business Studies, 18*(3), 61–77. doi:10.1057/palgrave.jibs.8490412

Cooper, R., & Kleinschmidt, E. (1985). The Impact of Export Strategy on Export Sales Performance. *Journal of International Business Studies, 16*(1), 37–56. doi:10.1057/palgrave.jibs.8490441

Cosh, A., & Hughes, A. (1996). International merger activity and the national regulation of mergers. a UK perspective. *Empirica, 23*(3), 279–302. doi:10.1007/BF00924974

Coviello, N., & McAuley, A. (1999). Internationalisation and the Smaller Firm: A Review of Contemporary Empirical Research. *Management International Review, 39*(3), 223–256.

Crick, D., & Jones, M. V. (2000). Small high-technology firms and international high-technology markets. *Journal of International Marketing, 8*(2), 63–85. doi:10.1509/jimk.8.2.63.19623

Culpan, R. (1989). Export Behavior of Firms: Relevance of Firm Size. *Journal of Business Research, 18,* 207–218. doi:10.1016/0148-2963(89)90045-3

Cunningham, M., & Spigel, R. (1971). A study in successful exporting. *European Journal of Marketing, 5*(1), 2–12. doi:10.1108/EUM0000000005176

Czinkota, M., & Johnston, W. J. (1981). Segmenting U.S. Firm for Export Development. *Journal of Business Research, 9*(4), 335–365. doi:10.1016/0148-2963(81)90012-6

Daniels, J., & Robles, F. (1982). The choice of technology and export commitment: the peruvian textile industry. *Journal of International Business Studies, 13*(Primavera/Verano), 67–87. doi:10.1057/palgrave.jibs.8490792

de Internacionalización de la Empresaa, E. P. (1994b)... *Información Comercial Española, 725*(Enero), 127–143.

Dean, D., Mengüç, B., & Myers, C. (2000). Revisiting Firms Characteristics, Strategy and Export Performance Relationship. *Industrial Marketing Management, 29,* 461–477. doi:10.1016/S0019-8501(99)00085-1

Diamantopoulos, A., & Inglis, K. (1988). Identifying Differences Between High-and-Low Involvement Exporters. *International Marketing Review,* (Fall): 5, 52–60.

Dichtl, E., Köglmayr, H., & Müller, S. (1990). nternational orientation as a precondition for export success. *Journal of International Business Studies, 21*(1), 23–41. doi:10.1057/palgrave.jibs.8490325

Domínguez, L., & Sequeira, C. (1993). Determinants of LDC Exporte's Performance: A Cross National Study. *Journal of International Business Studies. First Quarter, 24,* 19–40.

Donoso, V. (1989a). *Características y Estrategias de la Empresa Exportadora Española*. Madrid: Icex.

Donoso, V. (1989b). La Empresa Exportadora Española: Una Caracterización. *Papeles de Economía Española, 39*, 311–338.

Donoso, V. (1992). Mercado único y empresa exportadora. *Información Comercial Española, 705*, 153–167.

Donoso, V. (1993) Rasgos y Actitudes de la Empresa Exportadora Española. *Economistas, 55 Extr.*,134.143.

Donoso, V. (1994). *Competitividad de la Empresa Exportadora Española.* Madrid: Icex.

Donoso, V. (1995). La Internacionalización de la Empresa y el Apoyo Público.*Economistas, 64*, 194.204.

Donoso, V. (1996). Obstáculos a la Internacionalización y Políticas Públicas de Promoción. El caso de España. *Papeles de Economía Española, 66*, 124–143.

Donoso, V. (1998a). *Competir en el Exterior. La empresa Española y los Mercados Internacionales.* Madrid: Icex.

Donoso, V. (1998b). La empresa española en el final de los noventa. *Economistas, 77*, 131–139.

Donoso, V. (2000). Modelización del comportamiento de la empresa exportadora española·. *Información Comercial Española, 788*, 35–58.

Donthu, N., & Kim, S. H. (1993). Implication of Firms Controllable Factors on Export Growth. *Journal of Global Marketing, 7*(1), 47–63. doi:10.1300/J042v07n01_04

Dunning, J. (1988). The Eclectic Paradigm of International Production. *Journal of International Business Studies, 19*(1), 1–31. doi:10.1057/palgrave.jibs.8490372

Durán, J. (1994). Factores de competitividad en los procesos de internacionalización de la empresa. *Información Comercial Española, 735*, 21–41.

Eusebio, R. (2004). Innovación Tecnológica y Resultado Exportador: Un análisis empírico aplicado al sector textil-confección español. *Revista Europea de Dirección y Economía de la Empresa, 12*(2), 73–88.

Evangelista, U. (1994). Export Performance and Its Determinants: Some Empirical Evidence from Australian Manufacturing Firms. *Advances in International Marketing, 44*(2), 219–235.

Export performance revisited(1994). *International Small Business Journal, 18.*

Fagerberg, J. (1988). International Competitiveness. *The Economic Journal, 98*, 355–374. doi:10.2307/2233372

Fenwick, I., & Amine, L. (1979). Export Performance and Export Policy: Evidence from de UK Clothing Industry. *The Journal of the Operational Research Society, 30*(8), 747–755.

Fernández, E., & Vázquez, C. (1994). *La internacionalización de la empresa. Documento de Trabajo n° 75/94.* Universidad de Oviedo.

Fillis, I. (2000).Being creative at the marketing /entrepreneurship interface: lessons from the art industry. *Journal of Research in Marketing and Entrepreneurship.*

Fontrodona, J., & Hernádez, J. (2001). *Les multinacionals industrials catalanes.* Departament d'Indústria, Comerç i Turisme, Generalitat de Catalunya.

Ford, D., & Leonidou, L. (1991). Research Development in International Marketing: A European Perspective. In Plaiwoda, S. (Ed.), *New Perspectives on International Marketing.* London: Routledge.

Fraser, C., & Hite, R. (1990). Participation in the International Market Place by US Manufacturing Firms. *International Marketing Review, 7*(5), 63–71. doi:10.1108/EUM0000000001536

Gabrielsson, J., & Wictor, I. (2004). International activities in small firms: Examining factors influencing the internationalization and export growth of small firms. *Canadian Journal of Administrative Sciences*, *21*(1), 22–34.

García, J., Álamo, F., & Suárez, S. (2002). Determinantes organizativos y directivos de la actividad exportadora: evidencia empírica en el sector vitivinícola español. *Cuadernos de Economía y Dirección de la Empresa*, *13*, 519–544.

Gemunden, H. G. (1991). Success Factors of Export Marketing: A Meta-Analytic Critic of the Empirical Studies. In Paliwoda, S. J. (Ed.), *New Perspective on International Marketing*. London: Routledge.

Generalitat de Catalunya (1990-1999). *Informe anual de l'empresa catalane*. Departament d'Economia i Finances. Direcció General de Programació Econòmica.

Gutiérrez de Gandarilla, A., & Heras, L. (2000). La proyección exterior de las empresas españolas: Una contratsación empírica de la teoría gradualista de la internacionalización. *Información Comercial Española*, *788*, 7–18.

Håkansson, H., & Johanson, J. (1988).Formal and Informal Cooperation Strategies in International Industrial Networks. In Contractor & P. Lorange (eds). *Cooperative Strategies in International Business*. (pp.369-379)Lanham, MD: Lexington Books, F.J.

Hamel, G. (1991). Competition for competence and interpartner learning within international strategic alliances. *Strategic Management Journal*, *12*, 83–103. doi:10.1002/smj.4250120908

Hamilton, R. T. (1993). Firm Level Determinants of Export Performance: A Meta Analisys. *International Marketing Review*, *10*(3), 26–34.

Hirsch, S., & Bijaoui, I. (1985). R&D Intensity and Export Performance: a Micro View. *Weltwirtschaftliches Archiv*, *121*, 138–251. doi:10.1007/BF02705822

Hitt, M., & Kim, H. (1997). International Diversification: Effects of Innovation and Firm Performance in Product-Diversified Firms. *Academy of Management Journal*, *40*(4), 767–798. doi:10.2307/256948

Huerta, E., & Labeaga, J. M. (1992).Análisis de la decisión de exportar: una aproximación con datos macroeconómicos. *Investigaciones Económicas, suplemento*, pp. 41-47.

Internationalization and Market Entry Mode: A Review of Theories and Conceptual Framework. (1997). Management. *International Review (Steubenville, Ohio)*, *37*(2), 27–42.

Internationalization of the firm from an entrepreneurial perspective (2000). *Int. Stud. Manage. Organ, 30* (1), 3-92.

Johanson, J., & Vahlne, J. E. (1977). The Internationalization Process of the Firm: A Model of Knowledge Development and Increasing Foreign Market Commitments. *Journal of International Business*, *8*(1), 23–32. doi:10.1057/palgrave.jibs.8490676

Johanson, J., & Wiedersheim-Paul, F. (1975). The Internationalization of the Firm: Four Swedish Cases. *Journal of Management Studies*, *12*(2), 305–322. doi:10.1111/j.1467-6486.1975.tb00514.x

Johnston, W. J. (1983). Exporting: Does Sales Volume Make a Difference? *Journal of International Business Studies*, (Spring/Summer): 147–153.

Joint, P. (1982).An Empirical Study of Norwegian Export Behaviour. Czinkota, M. & Tesar, G. (Ed.), Export Management an International Context, pp. 55-69. New York: Praeger.

Jones, M.V. (1999).The internationalization of small high-technology firms. Journal of International Marketing. Journal of Marketing Theory and Practice, 8 (2), 8-17 & 7(4), pp. 15-41.

Joyal, A., & Deshaies, J. (1994). SMEs and International Competition. *Journal of Small Business Management, 32*(3).

Kaleka, A., & Katsikeas, C. (1998). Souces of Competitive Advantage in Hight Performing Export Company. *Journal of World Business, 33*(4), 378–393.

Karagozoglu, N. & Lindell, M. (1998).nternationalization of Small and Medium-Sized Technology-Based Firms: An Exploratory Study. *Journal of Small Business,*44.59.

Katsikeas, C. (1996). The export development process:an integrative review of empirical models. *Journal of International Business Studies, 27*(3), 517–551. doi:10.1057/palgrave.jibs.8490846

Katsikeas, C., & Piercy, N. (1998). Identifying Managerial Influences on Exporting: Past Research and Future Directions. *Journal of International Marketing, 6*(2), 74–102.

Katsikeas, C., Piercy, N., & Ioannidis, C. (1995). Determinants of Exports Performance in a European Context. *European Journal of Marketing, 30*(6), 6–35. doi:10.1108/03090569610121656

Katsikeas, C., & Samiee, S. (2002). Marketing strategy determinants of export performance: a meta-analysis. *Journal of Business Research, 55*, 51–67. doi:10.1016/S0148-2963(00)00133-8

Kedia, B., & Chocar, J. (1986). Factors Inhibiting Export Performance of Firms: An Empirical Investigation. *Management International Review, 26*(4), 33–44.

Kirpalani, V., & Mcintosh, N. (1980). International Marketing Effectiveness of Technology-Oriented Small Firm. *Journal of International Business Studies, 11*(Spring), 81–90. doi:10.1057/palgrave. jibs.8490625

Klein, S., Frazier, G. L., & Roth, V. J. (1990). A Transaction Cost Analysis Model of Channel Integration in International Market. *JMR, Journal of Marketing Research, 272*, 196–208. doi:10.2307/3172846

Kleinschmidt, E., & Cooper, R. G. (1984). A Typology of Export Strategies Applied to the Export Peformance of Industrial Firm. In *Kainak* (pp. 217–231). E, International Marketing Mangement.

Koh, A. (1991). Relationships Among Organizational Charateristics, Marketing Strategy and Export Performance. *International Marketing Review, 8*(3), 46–60. doi:10.1108/02651339110004906

Kohn, T. O. (1997).Small Firms as International Players. Small Business Economics, 9 (1), 45-51. In Krugman, P. (1991). Geography and Trade. Cambridge, MA: MIT Press.

Kumcu, E., Hancar, T., & Kumcu, E. (1995). Managerial Percepcions of the Adequacy of Export Incentive Programmes: Implications for Export-Led Economics Developments Policy. *Journal of Business Research, 32*, 163–174. doi:10.1016/0148-2963(94)00038-G

Laine, A., & Kock, S. A. (n.d.). Process model of internationalization. New times demands new patterns. *University of Bath.*

Lee, C., & Yang, Y. (1990). Impact of Export Market Expansion Strategy on Export Performance. *International Marketing Review, 7*(4), 41–51. doi:10.1108/02651339010000910

Lee, W., & Brasch, J. (1978). The Adoption of Export as an Innovative Strategy. *Journal of International Business Studies, 9*(1), 85–93. doi:10.1057/palgrave.jibs.8490653

Leonidou, L. (1998). Organizational Determinants od Exporting:Conceptual, Methodological and Empirical Insights. *Management International Review, Special Issue, 1998*(1), 7–52.

Leonidou, L., & Morgan, N. (2000). Firm-Level Export Performance Assessment: Review, Evaluation and Development. *Journal of the Academy management. Science, 28*(4), 493–511.

Levitt, T. (1983). The Globalization of Market. *Harvard Business Review, 61*(May-June), 92–102.

Llonch, J. (2005).Internal Key factor in Export Performance: A Comparative Analysis in Italian and Spanish textile-Clothing Firms. *Journal of Fashion Marketing Management.*

Lorange, P., & Roos, J. (1992). *Strategic Alliances: Formation, Implementation and Evolution.* Cambridge, MA: Blackwell Publishers.

Los enfoques micro-organizativos de la internacionalización de la empresa: Una revisión y síntesis de la literatura(1999)., *Información Comercial Española,* 781, 117-127.

Louter, P. J., Ouwerkerk, C., & Bakker, B. (1991). An Inquiry into Succesful Exporting. *European Journal of Marketing, 25*(6), 7–23. doi:10.1108/03090569110001429

Madsen, T. (1989). Successful Export Marketing Management: Some Empirical Evidence. *International Marketing Review, 6*(4), 41–57. doi:10.1108/EUM0000000001518

Marshall, A. (1930). *Principles of Economics: an introductory tex"t. 1.890,* Principles of Economics. London:Macmillan and Co., First

MC guinnes, N. & Little, B. (1981).The Influence of Product Characteristics on the Export Performance of New Industrial Products. *Journal of Marketing, 45,* spring, 110-122.

Mcauley (2000). *Modelling and measuring creativity at the interface.*

MCdougall, P. et al. (1994). Explaining the Formation of International New Ventures: The Limits of the Theories from International Business Research. *Journal of Business Venturing, 9,* 469–487. doi:10.1016/0883-9026(94)90017-5

Melin, L. (1992). Internationalization asa Strategy Process. *Strategic Management Journal, 13,* 99–118. doi:10.1002/smj.4250130908

Melle, M., & Raymond, J. (2001).Competitividad Internacional de las Pymes Industriales Españolas. *Ponencia presentatada al XI Congreso de ACED, Zaragoza,* 17-18 de setiembre de 2001.

Merino de Lucas, F. (1998). La salida al exterior de la Pyme manufacturera española. *Investigación Comercial Española, 773*(Septiembre-Octubre), 13–24.

Miesenbock, K. (1988). Small business and exporting: a literature review. *International Small Business Journal, 6*(2), 42–61. doi:10.1177/026624268800600204

Moen (1999).The relationship between firm size, competitive advantages.

Moon, J., & Lee, H. (1990). On the Internal Correlated of Export Stage Development: An Empirical Investigation in the Korean Electronics Industry. *International Marketing Review, 7*(5), 16–27. doi:10.1108/EUM0000000001532

Moreno, L. (1996). Actividad comercial en el exterior de las empresas manufactureras españolas, y estrategias de diferenciación de product. *Papeles de Economía Española, 66,* 107–123.

Moreno, L., & Rodríguez, D. (1998). Diferenciación de producto y actividad exportadora de las empresas manufactureras españolas, 1990-1996. *Investigación Comercial Española, 773*(Septiembre-Octubre), 25–35.

Müller, S. (1991). *Die psyche des managers als determinante des exporterfolges.* MP.

Nakos, G., Brouthers, K., & Brouthers, L. (1998). The Impact of Firm and Managerial Characteristics on Small and Medium. Sized Greek Firm's Export Performance. *Journal of Global Marketing*, *11*(4), 23–47. doi:10.1300/J042v11n04_03

Namiki, N. (1994). A Taxonomic Analysis of Export Marketing Strategy: An Exploratory Study of US Exporters of Electronic Products. *Journal of Global Marketing*, *8*(1), 27–50. doi:10.1300/J042v08n01_03

Naor, J. (1987). Firm and Managment Characteristic as Discriminators of Export Marketing Activity. *Journal of Business Research*, *15*(3), 221–235. doi:10.1016/0148-2963(87)90025-7

Nassimbeni, G. (2001). Technology, Innovation Capacity, and the Export Attitude of Small Manufaturing Firms: A Logit/Tobit Model. *Research Policy*, *30*, 245–262. doi:10.1016/S0048-7333(99)00114-6

Nevin, J. R. (1981). International Determinant of Export Marketing Behaviour: An Empirical Investigation. *JMR, Journal of Marketing Research*, *18*(1), 114–119. doi:10.2307/3151322

On the Internationalization Process of Firms. (1990). In Thorelli, B., & Cavusgil, S. T. (Eds.), *International Market Strategy* (pp. 3–32). Oxford, UK: Pergamon Press.

Pedersen, T., & Petersen, B. (1998). Explaining gradually increasing resource commitment to a foreign market. *International Business Review*, *7*, 483–501. doi:10.1016/S0969-5931(98)00012-2

Piercy, N. (1981). Company Internationalization: Active and Reactive Exporting. *European Journal of Marketing*, *15*(3), 26–40. doi:10.1108/EUM0000000004876

Pla, J. (2000). *La Estrategia Internacional de la Empresa Española*. Fundació Universitària Vall d'Albaida.

Porter, M. E. (1990). *The Competitive Advantages of Nation*. New York: The Free Press. Universidad de Stirling, Escocia.

Profitable Export Marketing Practices. (1987). An Exploratory Inquiry. In Rosson, P., & Reid, S. (Eds.), *Managing export entry and expansion*. New York: Praeger.

Rabino, S. (1980). An Examination of Barriers to Exporting Encountered by Small Manufacturing Companies. *Managment International Review*, *20*(1), 67–73.

Reid, S. (1981). The Decision-Maker and Export Entry and Expansion. *Journal of International Business Studies*, *12*(2), 101–112. doi:10.1057/palgrave.jibs.8490581

Rialp, A. (1997). *Las fases iniciales del proceso de internacionalización de las empresas industriales catalanas: una aproximación empírica. Tesis doctoral*. Universidad Autónoma de Barcelona.

Rialp, J. (1996). El papel de los acuerdos de cooperación en los procesos de internacionalización de la empresa española: un anàlisis empírico. *Papeles de Economía Española*, *66*, 248–266.

Rialp, J. (2001). Conceptual Framework on SMEs Internationalisation: Past, Present and Future Trend of Research. In ƒ Rodríguez, D. (1999). Relación entre innovación y exportaciones de las empresas: Un estudio empírico. *Papeles de Economía Española*, *81*, 167–180.

Rodríguez, D. (1999). Diversificación y tamaño en las empresas industriales españolas. *Papeles de Economía Española*, *78/79*, 236–249.

Root, F. (1994). Entry Strategies for International Market. Milan: Lexinton book Mc.

Rosson, P., & Ford, D. (1982). Manufacturer-Overseas Distributor Relations and Export Performance. *Journal of International Business Studies*, (Fall): 57–72. doi:10.1057/palgrave.jibs.8490550

Ryans, A. (1988). Marketing Strategy Factors and Market Share Achievement in Japan. *Journal of International Business Studies, 19*(3), 389–409. doi:10.1057/palgrave.jibs.8490393

Rynning, M., & Andersen, O. (1994). Structural and Behavioral Predictors of Exports Adoption: A Norwegian Study. *Journal of International Marketing, 2*(1), 73–89.

Samiee, S., & Anckar, P. (1998). Currency choice in industrial pricing: A cross-national evaluation. *Journal of Marketing, 62*(3), 112–127. doi:10.2307/1251747

Samiee, S., & Walters, P. G. P. (1990). Influence of Firm size on Export Planning and Performance. *Journal of Business Research, 20*(2), 325–342.

Schlegelmilch, E. (1987). Profile Analyses of Non-Exporters Versus Exporters Grouped by Export Involvement. *Marketing International Research, 27*(1), 38–49.

Sharma, D., & Johanson, J. (1987). Technical Consultancy in Internationalization. *International Marketing Review, 4*(4), 20–29. doi:10.1108/eb008339

Small firm internationalization: an investigative survey and future research directions(2001). *Management Decision, 39*(9), 767-783.

Styles, C., & Ambler, T. (1994). Export Performance Measures in Australia and the United Kingdom. *Journal of International Marketing, 6*(3), 12–36.

Suárez Ortega, S., Alamo Vera, F., & García Falcón, J. (2002). Determinantes organizativos y directivos de la actividad exportadora: evidencia empírica en el sector vitivinícola español. *Cuadernos de Economía y Dirección de la Empresa, 13*, 519–543.

Tesar, G. (1977). The Export Behaviour of Smaller Sized Winsconsin Manufacturin Firm. *Journal of International Business Studies, 8*(1), 93–98. doi:10.1057/palgrave.jibs.8490783

The Impact of Size on Internationalization. (1993)... *Journal of Small Business Management,* (Octubre): 50–56.

The Mechanism of Internationalization. (1990)... *International Marketing Review, 7*(4), 11–24.

Thomas, M. & Araujo, L. (1986). Theories of Export Behaviour: A Critical Analysis. *European Journal of Marketing, 19* (2), \42-52.

Topritzhofer, E., & Moser, R. (1979). Exploratorische LOGIT Analysen zur Empirischen Identifikation von Determinanten der Export Tüchigkeit von Unternehmen. *Zeitschrift für Betriebswirtschaft, 49*(10), 873–890.

Valos, M., & Baker, M. (1996). Developing an Australian model of export marketing performance determinants. *Marketing Intelligence & Planning, 14*(3), 11–20. doi:10.1108/02634509610117311

Variables Associated with Export Profitability. (1982)... *Journal of International Business Studies, 13*(2), 39–56. doi:10.1057/palgrave.jibs.8490549

Ventajas Comerciales y Competitividad: Aspectos Comerciales y Empíricos (1992*). Cuadernos del ICE*, 705, Mayo.

Welch, L. S., & Loustarinen, R. (1988). nternationalization: Evolution of a Concept. *Journal of General Managment, 14*(2), 34–55.

Westhead, P. (1995). Exporting and No-Exporting Small Firms in Great Britain: A Matched Pairs Comparison. *International Journal of Entrepreneurial Behaviour Research, 1*(2), 6–36. doi:10.1108/13552559510090604

Wiedersheim-Paul, F., Olson, H. C., & Welch, L. S. (1978). Pre-Export Activity: the First Step in Internationalization. *Journal of International Business Studies*, *9*(1), 47–58. doi:10.1057/palgrave.jibs.8490650

Yaprak, A. (1985).An Empirical Study of the Differences Between Small Exporting and No-Exporting Us Firm. *International marketing Review, spring, 2,* 72-83.

Zou, S., & Stan, S. (1998). The Determinants of Export Performance: A Review of the Empirical Literature Between 1987 and 1997. *International Marketing Review*, *15*(5), 333–356. doi:10.1108/02651339810236290

ENDNOTES

[1] In this sense, exists a large Lumber of research focused to the internationalization of spanish firms: Alonso (1991, 1992, 1993 y 1994b), Donoso (1992), Alonso & Donoso (1989a, 1989b; 1993; 1994, 1998a, 2000), Calvo (1993), Campa & Guillen (1995), Merino & Moreno (1996) Rialp & Rialp, (1996) Moreno & Rodríguez (1997), Merino (1998), Rodríguez (1999), Gutierrez & Heras, (2000), Alonso, Donoso (2000); Alonso & Donoso, (1998); Suárez Ortega, Álamo Vera & García Falcón, (2000); Rialp & Rialp, 2001; Melle & Raymond (2001).

[2] Like Catalunya (Alonso (1994) Rialp (1997); Fontrodona Francolí & Hernández Gascón,(2002).

[3] (Welch y Luostarinen, 1988; Melin, 1992; Andersen, 1997; Zou y Stan, 1998; Katsikeas et al., 2000)

[4] The Terrasa demarcation generates 3.5% of Cataluña's gross product income, and it is of significant importance in the exportation of electronic devices from Spain.

Chapter 5
Evaluation of Corporate Structure Based on Social Network Analysis

Sebastian Palus
Wroclaw University of Technology, Poland

Przemysław Kazienko
Wroclaw University of Technology, Poland

Radosław Michalski
Wroclaw University of Technology, Poland

ABSTRACT

Social network analysis provides helpful reports and comparisons, which may support the corporate human resources management. Several ideas, measurements, interpretations and evaluation methods are presented and discussed in the chapter, in particular group detection, centrality degree, location analysis, process management support, dynamic analysis, and social concept networks.

INTRODUCTION

Over the past few years, corporations have evolved from sets of individual units to collaborating social beings. Recent companies are implementing various ideas to help their employees to get known and co-operate with each other and therefore improve performance of their work. Some of them are company integration events, trips and more fresh as well as less expensive intranet social websites.

Hence, people get into various relationships due to their different job activities. Based on these relationships, a typical social network describing organizational connections can be created. These social connections between employees can be extracted from the data about pure communication like email exchange, phone calls, instant messengers or teleconferences. This paper describes a general social network approach to help analyzing the knowledge flow in the organization (Musiał, 2008) and therefore supporting corporate management.

DOI: 10.4018/978-1-61350-192-4.ch005

Figure 1. Social Network Analysis in Organization

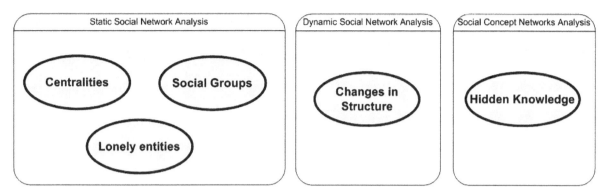

Each company or organization can be compared to a living organism (Gloor, 2004). Like in the nature, each unit is dependent on others and only altogether they really form a complete system. Nevertheless, the essential part of a human body is the nervous system which steers and supervises all other processes. The similar role plays the knowledge flow for the corporate lifecycle. Thus, analysis and optimization of communication efficiency within organization is very important. Such analysis can detect invisible anomalies and suggest some improvements in managing corporate policies, hierarchy structure and social approach to employees, which may result e.g. in achieving competitive edge, making the organization more flexible. or friendlier to its employees.

SOCIAL NETWORK APPROACH TO CORPORATE ASSESSMENT

Social Network Extraction

A corporate social network can be extracted from various IT systems utilized in the organization, in particular from internal communication like email logs, phone billings and from common activities, e.g. events, meetings, projects, etc. Some other sources for the social network extraction may be intranet community forums and physical location of workplaces, i.e. fact of sitting in the same office room.

A process of generating social network requires to determine the objects connecting people – concentrating humans activities. These can be an email message, for which two roles of users can be distinguished: email sender and email recipient. Some additional recipients extracted from fields 'To', 'Cc', 'Bcc' can, in turn, effect relationship

Figure 2. System architecture overview

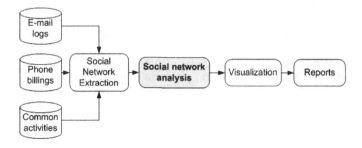

Figure 3. Social Network vs. Corporate Hierarchy

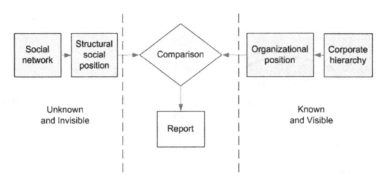

strengths. A phone call object can be treated similarly with roles of caller and receiver. These two object types (email and calls) are an example of direct relationships where actors through their mutual communication directly know about their connections.

In specific cases, there may be a need to perform additional preliminary processing on social network members. For example, if most of CEO's correspondence is sent by the secretary using secretary's own email address, both the secretary and CEO may be treated as a single social entity – one network node depending on general analysis requirements. Another example is the automatic correspondence sent by different kinds of applications, which has no important meaning in social network – those entities (nodes) may be removed from further analysis, because they even do not exist in the corporate hierarchy as well.

Some other objects are container type. People are connected indirectly through them by being a part of an activity and it is not certain that they communicated directly at all. These objects are common events/meetings/projects in which some employees can participate in. For example, if two employees are both the team members in the same project, they are thought to be in common social relationship. The same approach can apply to Active Directory or ERP system group memberships, forum discussions and even office room co-workers.

Comparison with Corporate Hierarchy

In most corporate information system structures, directory services are used to reflect internal hierarchy (Carter, 2003). These directory services allow the administrator to build a hierarchy tree of organization units, departments, teams and individuals; leafs in this tree are single employees. The most common implementation of LDAP/X.500 directory services is Microsoft Active Directory (Iseminger, 2000). Assuming that information contained within directory structure is correct and up-to-date, the organizational hierarchy derived from Microsoft Active Directory can be directly used in structural comparisons, Figure 3. This comparison confronts the known and visible organizational structure (extracted e.g. from Microsoft Active Directory) against the real but invisible social relationships computed from communication and common activities (structure of the social network).

If the organization maintains no directory service (or it is outdated), there are also other options available: extracting this structure from HR system or even manual import of the corporate hierarchy from organizational documents.

Having both the formal structure of the organization and the structure of the social network we can estimate their equivalence. To be more accurate, we would like to know whether the positions and roles of actors in the network structure correspond to their official roles and positions. Summing up, all needed data can be divided into two groups: a) the data necessary to build the social network, b) the additional data for comparative analyses. Note that both source types can be automatically processed using data available in appropriate IT systems.

Equivalence Measurement Methods

Two main approaches to measurements of equivalence between corporate structure (hierarchy) and social network (graph): comparison by pairs or by ranks of employees.

Instead of considering the whole network, the first method focuses on comparing employees pairwise. People in a pair must be very close in the organizational hierarchy and are either in the direct relation superior-inferior (Pair 2 and 3 in Figure 4) or are at the same level and have the same direct supervisor (Pair 1 in Figure 4). Then, for both pair members, we analyze the difference between their social measures, e.g. centrality degree, clustering coefficient, etc. These measures can be compared separately or weighted and combined as proposed in (Rowe, 2007) (Figure 5). Pairs where social metrics differ more than a given threshold are supposed to be at different levels of the hierarchy. Otherwise, if the social score is similar, it means they are even in the terms of organizational structure. Comparing these to the real hierarchy will point out anomalies e.g.

Figure 4. Extracting of pairs from the organizational hierarchy for comparison

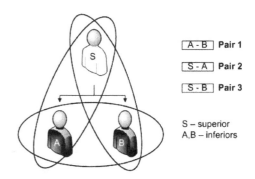

when a superior is at the level of his/her inferior or even below.

Second proposal compares two ranks, e.g. using well-established comparison methods (Fagin, 2003): Kendall's coefficient of concordance (Kendall, 1948) or Spearman's rank correlation (Spearman, 1904/1987). These rank correlation measures answer the question how similar the corporate hierarchy (the first rank) and the social network (the second rank) are in the organization. The first rank is derived directly from the corporate hierarchy – each level of the hierarchy should have weights assigned, starting from the top level (tree root) to the lowest one (leaves). Later, these weights are assigned to all employees working on the particular levels. So, probably, on the top of the first rank will be CEO, then directors, managers and regular employees at the bottom. The second rank is built by using social network analysis (SNA) and one or more structural metrics

Figure 5. Difference between social measures – centrality degree (1), clustering coefficient (2) and combined (3)

$$(1) \quad Diff_{Cen\,A\text{-}B} = Cen_A - Cen_B$$
$$(2) \quad Diff_{Clu\,A\text{-}B} = Clu_A - Clu_B$$
$$(3) \quad Diff_{Comb\,A\text{-}B} = Cen_A \cdot w_{Cen} + Clu_A \cdot w_{Clu} - Cen_B \cdot w_{Cen} + Clu_B \cdot w_{Clu}$$

Cen_X – centrality degree for node X;
Clu_X – clustering coefficient for node X;
w_y – weight for measure y.

Figure 6. Comparison between two structures: an organizational hierarchy and a social network graph (employee B has higher centrality measure than his superior S)

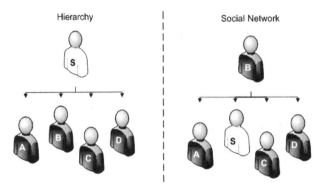

regarding the node importance. An exemplary combined and normalized metric (Social Score) is proposed in (Rowe, 2007), and can be used to build social network rank. If the rank comparison result (Kendall's or Spearman's coefficient) is close to 1, both ranks appears to be very similar. It means that the corporate structure and social network well correspond with each other. If the result is near 0, there is almost no similarity between both structures.

However, as noted in the Conclusions section, the decision about changes in the corporate structure should not be automatically made based only on the proposed equivalence metric results.

STATIC ANALYSIS OF SOCIAL NETWORKS

Centralities

There are several structural measures which can be applied to static social network analysis (SNA). Primary benefit from applying graph theory analysis to social networks is the identification of most important actors (Kazienko, 2009; Musiał, 2009; Wasserman, 1994). In one measure, a central node of the graph is the one with the greatest number of connections to other nodes. Therefore, a central person in the social network is the most popular person in the certain community (local centrality) or in the whole network (global centrality) (Klein, 2004; Scott, 2000). However, the main goal of the concept presented in this paper is not to detect such actors, but to point out differences between the invisible social position (extracted from the social network in the analytical way) and the official, visible position in the organizational structure. It is suspected that the most important people in the corporation should probably be the department directors or team leaders. What happens if there are some other people with the higher centrality degree than them? Conclusions can be ambiguous. It could mean that there are some "hidden natural leaders" who may not fulfill their potential and their role in the official hierarchy may be too low (Balkundi, 2005). However, it may also mean the opposite; the real leader position is too high for his abilities. It depends on the scale of difference between centrality degree of the real leader and the potential one. If this difference is small, there is probably no reason to apply any changes into organizational structure. For example, there can be a secretary who manages most of the business cases for the leader. Nevertheless, if the difference is high, it is highly probable that some serious changes in the hierarchy structure need to be performed to optimize team's performance. (Figure 6)

Figure 7. An illustration of group comparison shows anomalies (B4 has stronger relationship with Department A)

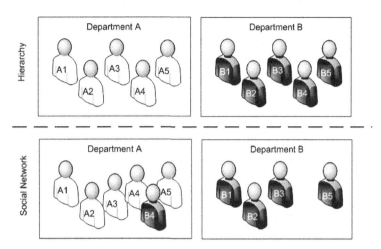

Social Groups

A social network can be divided into smaller groups (subgraphs, communities). The equivalent structures in the corporate hierarchy are subtrees of teams and departments. As a result, corporate analysis of groups includes comparison of social network groups and hierarchy subtrees to detect differences. One of the possible scenario in such case is when a person is more connected to the other team members in the social network than it comes from the organizational hierarchy. As in the example in previous section, the possible set of actions for the management depends on the difference between link strengths to the own group in opposite to strengths of the links to other groups. If this difference is significant, then the system may suggest to move this employee to another department/team in order to improve his or her efficiency. (Figure 7)

Other scenario is linked to the idea of developing swarm intelligence in the form of Collaborative Innovation Networks (Gloor, 2004; Gloor, 2006). The groups, which are not present in the corporate hierarchy can be recognized as independent collaborative initiatives and, if given a free hand and the friendly environment, may lead

to creation of new, fresh ideas. A perfect example of such structure is the Linux kernel developers community, where members of different corporations in the whole world are working together on new ideas and taking knowledge development to the higher level based on their interests (Lee, 2000).

Lonely Entities

In each society, there are "outliers" - people who are not fitting well into their group. Such actors can be easily detected in the social network. Because of their weak ties to other people, they usually far from the centres of the network (Musiał, 2009). According to psychological studies, it is obvious that teamwork is not performing well because of them. Unless they are real geniuses, it is required to find out reasons of this behavior by doing internal investigation and take steps to deal with it, e.g. move them to another team or dismiss. (Figure 8)

Process Management Support

These days, more and more companies are transforming their own management style in order to be more process-oriented. To achieve it, the

Figure 8. A lonely entity E in the social network

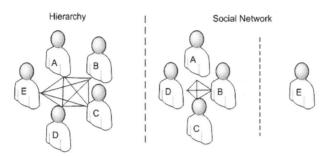

knowledge gained through the static analysis of social networks may be very helpful for the management staff. If a company does already have its own processes defined in some formal way and these processes may correspond to different layers of social network, an analysis may show whether they are really used. For example, if a process should be carried out in the group of three employees on some chosen layer, the existence of the ordered path between these employees may confirm (but not definitely) that this process does work. However, if there is no such path, the company management needs to perform some steps to find out why the process fails and to fix this problem: to redesign the process or to enforce employees to follow the procedures.

Location Analysis

Apart from the hierarchy structure management and proper employees' selection, companies have to deal with yet another problem. If we would consider the organizations bigger than small family businesses, where employees are counted in hundreds or thousands, the optimal office allocation arises as a significant issue. It is very important to establish effective communication between two closely collaborating departments as easy as possible by placing their offices next to each other. While the close relationships between e.g. sales and finance departments are fairly obvious, some other inter-department links may not be so clear. This is where the analysis of the social network can be very helpful. A frequent communication between two social groups indicates that they have got many things in common. They may work on the same project, discuss some financial issues or plan ahead future marketing moves. However, the distant collaboration can be less effective if their offices are far away from each other, even in different buildings. The detailed SNA report may point out the strength of relationships between entire departments and, after confronting it with the physical locations, may facilitate some adjustments. Department A can be moved closer to department B to improve their communication. Department C, in turn, whose link to A is much weaker, can be placed in the location where its members can easily discuss project details with departments D and E using a new conference room in another part of the building. Possibilities are only limited by the infrastructure.

DYNAMIC SOCIAL NETWORK ANALYSIS

Studying dynamics of changes in social networks over time is currently one of the most interesting research topics (Wasserman, 1994). Even in stable environments, social networks evolve. People establish new friendships as well as break others. Anyway, this paper focuses on changes caused by HR management. Moving employees to other teams/departments, hiring new workers, dismissing others, promoting, relegating – all of these actions have a huge direct impact on social network structure. It usually requires some time to gather the appropriate data but after it happens, managers have a very powerful knowledge of rules linking HR management with corporate social structure. The analysis of dynamics in the social network, which is extracted from the long term data about user activities and communication, provides the answers to some tough questions. Which employees should be promoted? Which ones should be relegated? Which people should be fired to strengthen the others and their social ties? Which workers should be assigned to a new project? The more and diverse data is available for analysis the better prediction accuracy.

However, the length of analyzed period is crucial for final results due to internal or external factors. It should be noted that there may be some departments not so active within specific periods, increasing their interactions in some other time. For example, controlling department might be in intensive contact with almost all departments while creating the next year budget whereas for the rest of the year, it might communicate only with a few key company persons. The same situation can be observed in the quality department, that maintains connections periodically in order to perform internal or external audits. Thus, the window of analysis in that case should be big enough to gather such activity irregularities or to find out if long-lasting processes are carried out properly. On the other hand, such big window may discard dynamic recent changes, which are not desired either. One of the proposed approaches is weighting of social connection with time factor so that the recent activities are weighted higher than the older ones (Kazienko, 2009).

SOCIAL CONCEPT NETWORKS (SCN)

Concept maps are structures showing which terms are connected with each other by co-occurrence in the same object such as email message (Cañas, 2005; Novak, 2008). Social concept networks is an idea of joining concept maps with social networks where the relationship between actors is based on email messages and common activities. Relationship strength is computed from the usage frequency of given terms/phrases in the linking objects. Actually, all SN-specific analysis can be applied to social concept networks. Interpretation of them is slightly different, though. For example, in this kind of social network, centrality degree identifies actors with the highest knowledge on given topic, experts.

Once keywords specific for a given project are declared, the social concept network immediately shows people with the expertise relevant to it. After comparing them to the group of people officially assigned to the project, it is possible to reveal actors with a "hidden knowledge", i.e. people who are not formally part of the project but are socially considered to be helpful. It can be a sign for the management to add these experts to this project and the future ones. Same analysis will also expose project members who are, in fact, not involved in discussions on project-specific topics.

EXPERIMENTAL STUDIES

Introduction

To test the idea of matching corporate structure and social network presented in this chapter, two networks have been build and analyzed (Michalski, 2011). One is based on mid-size manufacturing company located in Poland source data and the other one uses data gathered from Enron corporation.

The process of building social network consists of choosing the graph type (directed or undirected) and weight calculation method between nodes. The authors decided to build directed graph with the weight of an edge between node i and j is as follows:

$$w_{ij} = \frac{\sum e_{ij}}{\sum e_i} \quad w_{ij} = \frac{\sum e_{ij}}{\sum w_{ij} = \frac{\sum e_{ij}}{\sum e_i} e_i} \quad (1)$$

where $\sum e_{ij}$ is the number of e-mails sent by node i to node j and $\sum e_i$ is a total number of e-mails sent by member i. It means that weight w_{ij} focuses on local neighborhood of an employee rather than on global network characteristic.

The next step is to calculate social network metrics used in comparison. It has been shown that some metrics are more suitable in matching social network to corporate hierarchy.

Final step of the process consists of comparison of social network and corporate hierarchy. It is accomplished by answering the question how many employees in social network rank are a good fit for certain level in corporate hierarchy. The basic result is made up of percentage coverage of each management level by correspondent social network rank employees. If a significant differences are found, more detailed analysis may be performed, even focusing on each employee when needed.

Companies Description

The first analyzed company is a manufacturing company located in Poland. The company employs 300 persons, whereas 1/3 are clerical workers, the rest - laborers. The period analyzed was half a year. The type of organizational structure is functional (Daft, 2009). However, due to organization operating model and its consequences to organizational structure clarity as well as logs interpretation possibility, only a subset of organization have been chosen for current analysis: 49 clerical employees not directly related to manufacturing process. Three-level management structure exists in the selected company part: management board (2 persons), managers (11 persons) and regular

employees (36 persons) and they work in twelve different departments. There were no organizational changes during the analyzed period.

Enron, the another analyzed company, was one of the largest energy corporation around the world. It become especially famous worldwide in 2001 due to financial manipulation scandal. The Enron email dataset was made public by the Federal Energy Regulatory Commission during its investigation. The email dataset had a number of integrity problems which were corrected by researchers at MIT and SRI International (Cohen, 2009). The Enron hierarchy structure is still not publicly available. However, there are sources which can provide information concerning plenty of job positions of given employees and their department or division (Rowe, 2007). Because only some of employees existed in email corpus, authors have decided to analyze social network building only within limited set of managers and employees which positions - with high probability – were known.

Results

As stated before, the graphs built were directed with weight defined in Equation 1. The authors have decided to calculate most popular metrics used in social network analysis within each network their built: in-degree centrality, out-degree centrality, centrality beetweenness, centrality closeness, clustering coefficient Watts-Strogatz and centrality eigenvector (Musiał, 2009). Ranks of social network position using above metrics have been compared to organization structure to gain information how well the organization levels had been matched. Because it has been found that none of the used metric and tested metric combinations were able to make the clear distinction between the first (management board) and the second management level (managers and directors), further analysis has focused on distinction management as a whole from regular employees. The results are presented in Table 1.

Table 1. Accuracy of management level matching while using various social network metrics

	Percentage of the first and the second management level matched		Percentage of regular employees matched	
	Manuf. comp.	Enron	Manuf. comp.	Enron
In-degree centrality	85	67	94	85
Out-degree centrality	62	50	86	77
Centrality beetweenness	38	33	78	69
Centrality closeness	46	33	81	69
Clustering coefficient	15	17	69	62
Centrality eigenvector	77	67	92	85

The results show that only some metrics are capable to make good distinction between management and employees. The best of them are: in-degree centrality and centrality eigenvector. It proves that the basic distinction between managers and others is based not on outgoing relations rather than on incoming relations (in-degree centrality) and the importance of employees contacting with us (eigenvector centrality).

DISCUSSION

Profile of Relationships

Throughout the process of building and analyzing the social network only the existence of mutual communication of common activities has been considered so far. However, the fact that email message sent from person *A* to person *B* does not determine itself the nature of the relationship between *A* and *B*, e.g. whether it is rather positive or negative. The emotional character of the single message should also effect relationship strength. Nevertheless, sophisticated and powerful text recognition tools would be required to examine the profile of the messages, not mentioning the advanced forms of expression like irony, sarcasm or even the meaning of the attached images or videos. There are no effective methods for these

purposes yet (Krippendorff, 2004; Wiebe, 2005). This is just to point out that even a strong relationship between two people not necessarily means that they like each other. We should always be aware that connections in the artificially extracted social network do not completely reflect the complex nature of human relationships.

Decision Making

All presented analysis methods should focus on two general evaluation rates: similarity of the structural position and the role both in the social network and in the official organizational hierarchy.

Having the differences between the social network and hierarchy recognized, the management of the organization can undertake appropriate decisions to decrease these differences. For example, the position in the structure can be affected by moving employees to other teams/departments. Changes of roles in the hierarchy are achieved by promoting/relegating.

Moreover, new positions and roles can be discovered in the social network which do not exist in the corporate hierarchy structure. As a result, the managers can create new positions in the organization.

CONCLUSION

Social network approach to manage problems is capable to significantly improve the Human Resources efficiency by either detection of hidden anomalies in the corporate hierarchy or making communication between employees more effective and easier. By analyzing semantics of email messages exchanged within the corporate network we are able to identify individuals with "the hidden knowledge".

Overall, social network approach to the problem of corporate management appears to be very helpful, however, all analysis need to be well interpreted to improve performance and social health of the company. This is only a tool. Still, human resources have to be managed by humans.

ACKNOWLEDGMENT

This work was supported by The Polish Ministry of Science and Higher Education, the development project, 2009-11.

REFERENCES

Balkundi, P., & Kilduff, M. (2005). The ties that lead: A social network approach to leadership. *The Leadership Quarterly, 16*, 941–961. doi:10.1016/j.leaqua.2005.09.004

Cañas, A. J., Carff, R., Hill, G., Carvalho, M., Arguedas, M., & Eskridge, T. (2005). Concept maps: Integrating knowledge and information visualization. In Tergan, S.-O., & Keller, T. (Eds.), *Knowledge and information visualization: Searching for synergies* (pp. 205–219). Heidelberg, NY: Springer Lecture Notes in Computer Science. doi:10.1007/11510154_11

Carter, G. (2003). *LDAP System Administration*. New York: O'Reilly Media.

Cohen, W. (2009). Enron Email Dataset. Retrieved from http://www.cs.cmu.edu/~enron/

Daft, R. L. (2009). *Organization Theory and Design* (10th ed.). Cincinnati, OH: Engage Learning.

Fagin, R., Kumar, R., & Sivakumar, D. (2003). Comparing top k lists. *SIAM Journal on Discrete Mathematics, 17*(1), 134–160. doi:10.1137/S0895480102412856

Gloor, P. (2004). *Net.Creators. Unlocking the Swarm Creativity of Cyberteams through Collaborative Innovation Networks*. Retrieved from http://www.swarmcreativity.net/ html/book_swarmcrea.htm

Gloor, P. (2006). *Swarm Creativity, Competitive advantage through collaborative innovation networks*. Oxford, UK: Oxford University Press.

Iseminger, D. (2000). *Active Directory Service for Microsoft Windows 2000 Technical Reference*. Redmond: Microsoft Press.

Kascarone, R., Paauwe, J., & Zupan, N. (2009). HR practices, interpersonal relations, and intrafirm knowledge transfer in knowledge-intensive firms: a social network perspective. *Human Resource Management, 48*(4), 615–639. doi:10.1002/hrm.20301

Kazienko, P., Musiał, K., & Zgrzywa, A. (2009). Evaluation of Node Position Based on Email Communication. *Control and Cybernetics, 38*(1), 67–86.

Kendall, M. G. (1948). *Rank Correlation Methods*. Oxford, UK: Oxford

Klein, K. J., Lim, B., Saltz, J. L., & Mayer, D. M. (2004). How do they get there? An examination of the antecedents of centrality in team networks. *Academy of Management Journal, 47*, 952–963. doi:10.2307/20159634

Krippendorff, K. (2004). *Content Analysis: An Introduction to Its Methodology* (2nd ed.). Thousand Oaks, CA: Sage.

Lee, G. K., & Cole, R. E. (2000). *The Linux Kernel Development as a Model of Knowledge Development.* Working Paper, October 25, 2000, Haas School of Business, University of California, Berkeley.

Michalski, R., Palus, S., & Kazienko, P. (2011). *Matching Organizational Structure and Social Network Extracted from Email Communication.* BIS 2011, 14th International Conference on Business Information Systems. Lecture Notes in Business Information Processing LNBIP, Springer, Berlin Heidelberg.

Musiał, K., & Juszczyszyn, K. (2008). A method for evaluating organizational structure on the basis of social network analysis. *Foundations of Control and Management Sciences, 9,* 97–108.

Musial, K., & Juszczyszyn, K. (2009). *Properties of Bridge Nodes in Social Networks, 1st International Conference on Computational Collective Intelligence - Semantic Web.* Social Networks & Multiagent Systems, Springer-Verlag, Lecture Notes in Artificial Intelligence 5796, 2009, pp. 357-364.

Musiał, K., Kazienko, P., & Bródka, P. (2009). *User Position Measures in Social Networks.* The third SNA-KDD Workshop on Social Network Mining and Analysis held in conjunction with The 13th ACM SIGKDD International Conference on Knowledge Discovery and Data Mining, KDD 2009, June 28, 2009, Paris France, ACM Press, Article no. 6.

Novak, J. D., & Cañas, A. J. (2008). *The Theory Underlying Concept Maps and How to Construct Them. Technical Report IHMC CmapTools 2006-01 Rev 01-2008.* Florida Institute for Human and Machine Cognition.

Rowe, R., Creamer, G., Hershkop, S., & Stolfo, S. J. (2007). *Automated Social Hierarchy Detection through Email Network Analysis.* Proceedings of the 9th WebKDD and 1st SNA-KDD 2007 workshop on Web mining and social network analysis, pp. 109-117

Scott, J. (2000). *Social network analysis: A handbook* (2nd ed.). London: Sage.

Spearman, C. (1904. (1987). The proof and measurement of association between two things. *The American Journal of Psychology, 15,* 72–101. doi:10.2307/1412159

Wasserman, S., & Faust, K. (1994). *Social network analysis: Methods and applications.* New York: Cambridge University Press.

White, D. R. (2004). Network Analysis and Social Dynamics. *Cybernetics and Systems, 35,* 173–192. doi:10.1080/01969720490426858

Wiebe J., Wilson T., Cardie C. (2005). Annotating Expressions of Opinions and Emotions in Language. *Language Resources and Evaluation, 1*(2). (2005), pp. 0-0.

Chapter 6
High Technology Industrialization and Internationalization:
Exploring International Technology Transfer

Leong Chan
Portland State University, USA

Tugrul Daim
Portland State University, USA

ABSTRACT

Through exploring high technology industrialization and internationalization, the chapter reviews related issues from three interconnected levels: national, enterprise, and technology level. Part 1 gives a detailed discussion on technology transfer policy in different countries. Part 2 focuses on the issues of international technology transfer at enterprise level. Part 3 explores how technology characteristics can influence international technology transfer. The following parts review the methodologies and research gaps. Lastly, the chapter summarizes some key questions for future research.

DOI: 10.4018/978-1-61350-192-4.ch006

1. INTRODUCTION

1.1 Backgrounds of Research

International technology transfer is a direct approach to improve national technology level and strengthen national competence. Introducing advanced technologies from foreign countries can boost the speed of technology development in the host country. Through technology import, host countries can often shorten the learning time, enjoy the latecomer advantage, and achieve technology leapfrogging. However, international technology transfer is not an easy process. Barriers existed because of huge gaps among countries in terms of social values, economic development, and technology level. There are more complicated issues if technology exporters belong to the developed world, while the technology importers come from developing world. Technology policies vary significantly due to the difference of conditions between developed and developing countries.

Since most technology exporters are companies from developed countries and most technology importers are from developing countries, this chapter will focus on technological transactions between developed and developing countries. Also due to the large policy differences between the two sides, typical countries will be selected for detailed discussions. As the largest developed country, United States is also the largest technology exporter in the world. This is because its unparallel global technological leadership built from the last century. Policy measures in United States can typically represent the interests of many other developed countries such as Europe Union, Japan, etc. From the perspective of developing countries, China and India have the largest market potential in the world. China is also the largest technology importer globally. It generates many business opportunities and attracts a lot of investments from developed countries. Therefore, technology policy of these countries will be discussed in this chapter.

1.2 Levels of Technology Transfer

This chapter focuses on the research of government's technology policy and its influence on international technology transfer. Technology policies have been a focal point for a long time. Due to the ever changing environment of world politics and economy, there are too many uncertainties in policy-making for every country. It is not uncommon some policies cannot meet government's original requirement as they were legislated. The rapid development of high technology has made stable technology policy a difficult task. Therefore, it is necessary to study the causal factors and intrinsic relationship of issues involved. It is also meaningful to evaluate the effect of current technology policies, so we can learn valuable lessons.

International technology transfer can be studied from different perspectives. One approach is to focus on the entities involved in the process, i.e. technology exporter, technology importer, and technology itself. A new approach is to explore the growing trends of international technology transfer from different perspectives of various levels. Through comprehensive literature review, this chapter investigates the mechanisms of international technology transfer from three interrelated levels:

1. National level;
2. Enterprise level;
3. Technology level.

Detailed discussions will be given to explore the problem areas in each level, and also to discover the intrinsic connections among these aspects. High-tech industries are emphasized due to their fast changing nature and growing impact on policy-making.

1.2.1 National Level

From a macro perspective, there are many environmental factors affecting international technology transfer, which may include innovation policy, capital investment, and market trend. Technology transfer is directly influenced by market need and technology push. The government can enhance law enforcement through legislation or offer incentives to support and regulate international technology transfer. For example, technology transfer activities are affected by technology export control and intellectual property protection. Such measures can protect the interests of stakeholders. Technology policy is the key to establish connections between international technology transfer and innovations. Technology policy measures should be emphasized to guide various innovators in their innovation process.

1.2.2 Enterprise Level

From a meso perspective, stakeholders of international technology transfer mainly include domestic enterprises, foreign enterprises, intermediary agents, research institutes, and industrial associations, etc. In the process of technical transactions, the strategies of enterprises are the determinants for the success of international technology transfer. Their innovative capability is an important factor affecting technology transfer. This includes enterprises' cumulative technology capacity, learning capability, and organizational culture. Since most innovations are cooperative efforts among enterprises and other actors, the issues faced by host government are to adjust related policies, provide an innovative environment, thus to promote industrial innovation capability.

1.2.3 Technological Level

From a micro perspective, the characteristics of technology include technology status, adaptability, and availability, etc. Technology transfer strategy is closely related to technological in-novation mechanisms, which include market pull, technology push, and innovation systems. The technological characteristics play important roles because they decide the viability of specific transfer objects between the provider and receiver. We will focus the discussion on several of these technological features including: technology trajectory, technology distance, and technology adaptability.

In summary, decision makers should consider the above three levels to promote international technology transfer. In the following sections, each level will be studied in details.

2. NATIONAL LEVEL INFLUENCING FACTORS

Government interference on international technology transfer is very common worldwide. High technology has become the key factor of promoting regional economy and realizing sustainable development. It is high technology that builds the core competence of nations. Improving technology level and enhancing regional innovation capability have been the principal goal for all countries in the world. Rapid development and intense competition on high technology have significant impact on policy-making. Not only countries invest heavily to develop new technologies, but also they apply various measures to protect their high-tech competitive edge.

International technology transfer as a major means of advancing national technology level has long been influenced by government. Policy factors include national security, foreign affairs, economic environment, etc. With the deepening trend of globalization, it is natural to see an increasing need of internationalized technology collaboration. However, different strategies between developed and developing countries have made the topic more complicated to study. Here we examine government policy related to high-tech industries from the perspectives of both sides.

2.1 Technology Export Control in Developed Countries

Technology policy has the goal of making the best use of technology to achieve the national goals of improved quality of life for all citizens, continued competitive economic growth, and national security (Bromley, 2004). Therefore, developed countries invest huge amount of capital in R&D to maintain their technology competitive edge. For example, United States introduced the American Competitiveness Initiative (ACI) in 2006, a major policy initiative to ensure that the US continues to be the world's leader in science and technology (Hemphill, 2006). The ACI plans to commit $50 billion to increase funding for R&D and $86 billion for R&D tax incentives in ten years (Bush, 2006). High-tech industries have been proved to be the most important growing force in US economy. In the past two decades, America's research-intensive industries - aerospace, chemicals, pharmaceuticals, communications equipment, computers and office equipment, scientific instruments, semiconductors, and software - have been growing at about twice the rate of the economy as a whole (Clinton, 1997). However, United States faces tough technology competitors worldwide. Policy support for technological R&D is also strong in many other advanced industrial nations, such as Japan and EU countries.

The transfers of technology, including technology exports and imports, have to strictly conform to government's regulations. Different countries have issued numerous law terms and regulations regarding to cross-border technical transactions. These regulations are updated frequently to strengthen government's control of international technology transfer. Many technology exporting countries, especially developed countries, have strict censorship over high-tech transactions with foreign countries to prevent technology leakage which may potentially damage national interest. Many technology importing countries, mostly developing countries, require technology trans-

fer deals to be registered in government agency. These restrictions will serve to protect domestic infant industries and decrease reliance on foreign technology.

2.1.1 Technology Export Control of United States

United States have very strict but systematic control on technology exports. The Export Administration Act (EAA) and Export Administration Regulations (EAR) build the foundation of America's legislation on commodity and technology export (Reynolds, 2002). According to these regulations, technology export must be approved by the federal government through licensing. The licenses are divided into General License and Validated License. The later has more restrictions that will take longer time to process. The Department of Commerce maintains a Commodity Control List (Corr, 2003), which includes all sensitive commodity or technologies that need special censorship. All items on the list are coded and manifested with export criteria. The list is an important component of EAR, and its contents are frequently updated by government. Another important aspect is the destination or end user of the export. Foreign countries except Canada are divided into seven categories: Z, S, Y, W, Q, T, and V. Each category represents different controls on exports. For example, countries belong to Z category is under complete embargo.

According to various regulations, United States has restricted technology transfer to China in many high-tech areas, which includes: Information and communications technologies (ICT), shipbuilding, aviation, space & satellite, nuclear power, etc (Erickson & Walsh, 2008). Moreover, the American Congress passed the Exon-Florio Amendment (EFA) to the 1988 Omnibus Trade and Competitiveness Act (Byrne, 2006). EFA aimed to prohibit any foreign acquisition, merger, or takeover that might impair U.S. national security. It is for sure that the concept of national security includes both traditional foreign policy criteria and defense issues. However, it is controversial whether economic considerations should be included. Indeed, there are inherent links among national security, industrial security, free trade, and the free flow of capital across borders. From the applications of EFA in recent years, it can be inferred that the term "national security" be interpreted broadly to include economic considerations. Many cross-border economic and technological activities are restricted by these regulations (Stagg, 2007).

2.1.2 Impacts on Lenovo's Technology Acquisition

Here we explore an example that demonstrates the negative effect of above regulations. In late 2004, China's largest computer manufacturer - Lenovo acquired IBM's PC business unit. The deal worth $ 1.75 billion (including $ 0.5 billion assumed debt), which consists: $ 650 million in cash, $ 600 million in securities, and an 18.9 percent stake for IBM in Lenovo (Antkiewicz & Whalley, 2007; Biediger, et al., 2005). Lenovo's acquisition was motivated by many reasons: 1. Have access to IBM's global sales channel and distribution network; 2. Obtain IBM's brand and assets for sustainable competitive advantage in global markets; 3. Obtain IBM PC's technology and R&D capability for making high end computers (Rui & Yip, 2008). On the other hand, the deal also satisfied IBM's corporate strategy of transforming from a hardware manufacturing company to a global service provider and software company (Dittrich, Duysters, & Man, 2007). However, the deal aroused the attention from American federal government. One thing worth notice here is that the acquisition includes IBM's R&D labs, which located in both United States (North Carolina) and Japan (Yamato). These new facilities will improve Lenovo's R&D capability into world class standard (Altenburg, Schmitz, & Stamm, 2008). However, in January 2005, according to EFA regulations, the Commit-

tee on Foreign Investment in the United States (CFIUS) started a lengthy process to review the acquisition due to the concerns that the deal could compromise national security (He & Lyles, 2008). The concerns include possibility of transferring sensitive technology from IBM to Lenovo. During the investigation, Lenovo conceded on various terms in the contract. The most important issue is that Lenovo lost its access to IBM's original R&D facilities in the North Carolina Research Triangle Park. Lenovo have to build a new R&D center in another location. Three month later, the final decision from CFIUS conclude that the merge posed no threat to national security, and the deal was completed in May 2005. Although this is a successful cross-border M&A case, we can see the importance of policy influence on international technical transactions. The EFA regulations effectively limited foreign company's access to American R&D facility and technology.

2.2 Technology Import Strategy in Developing Countries

While the developed nations try to maintain their technology advantage by tightening export control measures, many industrializing countries are trying to increase technology inputs, modernizing key manufacturing sectors, and establishing key technology programs. Examples of these countries include China, India, Brazil, etc. However, international technology transfer is still an important method for them to acquire advanced technologies. Here we discuss related technology policies in developing countries.

2.2.1 Latecomer Advantage of Technology Development

Uneven development is a common phenomenon in the world, and technology gap vastly exists among different countries. These gaps can provide latecomer countries distinctive advantage in technology development, which is so called "the latecomer advantage of technology" (K. Lee & Lim, 2001). Many scholars have carried out research on latecomer advantage in the last two decades, and the debates between latecomer advantage and disadvantage has not been stopped. Meanwhile, similar concept of technology leapfrogging was brought forward from the researches of miracle in East Asia, especially from the experience of Japan and South Korea (Hobday, Rush, & Bessant, 2004; Narin & Frame, 1989). It has been proved in many researches that, industrializing countries may not necessarily follow the same technology paths formed by the developed countries. They may leapfrog some steps and develop different or unique progress paths of themselves. For example, scholar (Hobday, 1994) argued that it is possible for developing country to catch up with developed country directly, bypassing huge investment on technological accumulation.

International technology transfer is the most important method for developing countries to realize the latecomer advantage and achieve technology leapfrogging. Foreign investment can bring in both capital and advanced technology, thus it is a preferred channel for most developing countries since they are in short of both. Investments from the Multinational Companies (MNCs) are extremely important for the latecomers to acquire foreign technologies, but there are many factors to consider such as technology assessment, transfer cost, and absorption capability, etc. Technology learning also exists in some non-formal channels which may include academic communication, flow of scientists and engineers, etc. These channels have been playing a more important role along with the growing trend of technological internationalization.

The mechanism of latecomer advantage of technology is straightforward. Technology innovation can be a risky and expensive investment, but it is much safer and cheaper to learn from available foreign technologies. Moreover, technology life cycle curves have determined technology diffusion and spillover. Path dependency in technol-

ogy development can assist latecomers to trace success in developed countries. The technology gap is a prerequisite for the latecomer advantage. However, this kind of advantage is relative and conditional because it depends on various factors such technology trajectory, technology distance, technology adaptability, correct timing, etc. The technology gap can also be a trap and result to further disadvantages. In order to realize the advantages and eliminate the disadvantages, technology policy in developing countries should try to improve absorptive capability and innovative capacity.

The trend of globalization has significantly improved the condition for latecomers' catching-up process. Innovation resources are allocated more diversely around the world, especially, fast-growing and geographically dispersed corporate networks are formed in both developing and developed countries. International technology transfer can exist in many new channels including R&D collaboration, cross border M&A, outsourcing, etc. These channels are new opportunities for the emerging economies. However, companies in the developed countries usually want to keep their technology edge as well as leading position. These factors have produced new challenges for developing countries to catch-up and realize the latecomer advantage of technology. Not only they need to accumulate technology learning capabilities, but also they need to select the right technological direction that fit into the global innovation networks.

2.2.2 Technology Import Strategy in China

China is the largest technology importer in the world. Therefore, technology policy of China will highlight a typical picture of international technology transfer issues from the perspective of developing countries. China adopted an open door policy in the early 1980s, and Foreign Direct Investment (FDI) has become the driving force for economic development since then. Due to historical reasons, the technological gap is huge between China and the developed world. International technology transfer through FDI is a dominant strategy in policy level. This strategy has largely raised the country's production capability and technology level. However, there are some negative effects because most policy measures focus on the improvement of production efficiency and capability rather than innovation capacity. Here we take a deeper look in China's technology import strategy.

"Trading of domestic market for foreign technology" has been a major strategy of China's technology policy to attract FDI and promote technology transfer since the 1980s. In a broader sense, this policy covers all measures that acquire foreign technology through granting foreign companies free access to domestic market. There have been many disputes on the effect of this policy in China, and the topic has aroused wide attention in academia. The main argument is that "Can technology be exchanged for by market share?" The rationale of this strategy assumes that China could use the latecomer advantages to upgrade its industrial structure and technology level. At the mean time, China can save lots of foreign exchange on technology by just giving away some market share. However, in some high-tech industries, the advantage of latecomers has scarcely been realized, domestic innovation capacity makes little improvement, and technological gap is further widened. In some extreme cases, such as the automobile industry, local enterprises have even fallen into the trap of reliance on import of core technologies. In recent years, similar technology policy has been applied again on technology transfer deals in the high-speed rail industry. As China introduced Electric Multiple Units technology from four different countries (Japan, Germany, France, and Canada), but the core technologies are still controlled by the foreign side (Chan, 2009).

There are still many difficulties in China's industrial policy regarding to international technology transfer. These include how to jump out of the trap of technology transfer loop, how to convert the latecomer advantage into real benefit; how to make transition from labor-intensive industry to technology-intensive industry; how to transform resource advantage into technology edge; how to change from "manufactured in China" to "innovated in China". As China gained access into the WTO in late 2001, the country began to face even more challenges resulted from globalization. The latecomer advantage of technology can still play an important role in promoting domestic industries and technological development. However, in order to realize these advantages, host government should adjust its technology transfer policy, select appropriate technologies as break through point, and construct a sustainable national innovation system.

2.3 Policy on Intellectual Property Rights

Government policy on Intellectual Property Rights (IPR) has direct influence on international technology transfer. Developed and developing nations have drastic disputes on whether stronger IPR protection can foster technology transfer or not. Their needs and views on IPR differ widely. Here we analysis the causal factors of these issues.

IPR enforcement can be achieved through the use of patents, copyrights, trademarks, and trade secrets, etc. These measures serve to protect private innovations and creativity for a limited period of time. IPR protection of a country usually includes two aspects, i.e. internationally accepted agreements and regulations from domestic legal system. As an international initiative, the World Intellectual Property Organization (WIPO) was created as a division under the United Nations in 1967. Its purpose is to protect intellectual property and to resolve related IPR disputes (Okediji, 2008). However, WIPO has not been very effective at protecting IPR because its dispute resolution mechanism is not very strong. To further enhance

IPR protection, the Trade-Related Aspects of Intellectual Property Rights (TRIPs) Agreement was established during the Uruguay Round of the General Agreement on Tariffs and Trade (GATT) in 1994. Since TRIPs was adopted by World Trade Organization (WTO), all countries belong to or want to join WTO must fully comply with the agreement (Helfer, 2004). TRIPs include comprehensive IPR protection and provide a twenty year protection period for innovations in high technology areas such as pharmaceuticals, biotechnology, and software. The TRIPs agreement is much more effective in resolving IPR disputes than WIPO.

2.3.1 IPRs in Developed Countries

Domestic IPR protection legal systems vary from country to country, and these regulations can be stricter and override the above international agreements. The two most important U.S. legal instruments used for addressing foreign IPR infringement are Section 337 of the Tariff Act and Section 301 of the Trade Act. These regulations enabled the federal government to take a more aggressive stance in protecting US IPRs in overseas markets. The US government established a precedent of using unilateral threats of sanctions to deal with alleged intellectual property infringements no matter TRIPs terms are satisfied or not (Johnson & Walworth, 2003). The industrialized countries view IPR protection as a necessary means of incentivizing innovation. For instance, patents provide a guarantee of return for inventors on their invested time and capital during R&D process. Large number of research evidence showed that strong protection of IPRs are essential to international technology transfer because it may attract more FDI for developing countries (Nagaoka, 2009; Park & Lippoldt, 2008). Multinationals will hesitate to make investment in developing countries if their interests are not protected. This will influence their strategies of technology transfer, and lead to the transfer of low-tech products (Fosfuri, 2000).

2.3.2 IPRs in Developing Countries

Quite opposite with the view from the developed world, many developing countries treat IPR as potential barriers to international technology transfer. Strengthened IPR protection significantly increases the costs of transferring advanced technologies from foreign countries. Although international technology transfer is essential to all developing countries, they do not have enough capital investment and accumulated technology capability upon which they can innovate through independent R&D. To certain extant, overemphasize on IPR protection will hinder domestic industries to benefit from technology imitation (LaCroix & Konan, 2002). Therefore, strong IPR protection may not be a good strategy for a developing country to boost short-term technology development and foster domestic innovation. Moreover, with limited budgets, many developing countries are unwilling to invest extra resources and efforts on IPR enforcement.

2.3.3 IPRs as Development Instruments

Although the drastic differences among developed and developing countries seem contradicted, a deeper look into the industrial history can tell us the intrinsic connections on the topic. Empirical research (Higino, 2005) has shown that the relationship between IPR protection and innovation capability is positive in developed countries, but less effective in developing countries. This might be the reason why weak IPR protection has always been a strategy in developing countries. However, similar strategies have been adopted in many developed countries during their developing stages. A good example in case is Japan in the 1960's (Kiyota & Okazaki, 2005), when weak IPR protection had largely facilitated the imitative strategy in the country. As a second example, article from the New York Times (Lohr, 2002) revealed that the United States used to have weaker IPR protection during its early development stage. South Korea also adopted flexible policies during its developing periods to promote the learning of foreign technologies (W. Y. Lee, 2000). Nowadays IPR protections in all these countries are much strengthened, and they began to pressure current developing countries to improve related protections.

The Development of India's Pharmaceutical Industry in the last two decades can strengthen the above findings. Weak IPRs regime fostered the development of domestic technology capabilities in India's pharmaceutical industry since the 1970s. It is remarkable achievement that new drugs can be introduced domestically only within four to five years after their introduction in foreign countries (Kumar, 2002). If an Indian domestic company can modify the manufacturing process of a foreign medicine, they can produce the same product without patent infringement (Chaturvedi & Chataway, 2006). This has established low cost leadership advantage among local companies and increased domestic social welfare due to the lowered drug prices. As a large number of medicines went off its patent protection during the late 1980s, Indian generic drugs further experienced a rapid growth of exports to the world market. An interesting effect is that the increased technological capabilities of Indian pharmaceutical companies have brought in more FDI from MNCs. New joint ventures and R&D centers were setup mainly draw upon trained manpower and research infrastructure available in the country, despite the fact that Indian patent regime did not provide strong patent protection (Kumar, 2002). By introduction and assimilation of advanced technologies from abroad, Indian pharmaceutical companies have emerged as competitive suppliers in the world. This highlights the impact of IPR policy on technology development.

3. ENTERPRISE LEVEL INFLUENCING FACTORS

Domestic and foreign enterprises are the entities that carry out the international technology transfer process. Their investment and strategies have decisive impact on the success of the process. In this section, we explore the influencing factors and the behaviors of companies from the perspectives of both sides. FDI is the most common means for developing countries to acquire advanced technologies from developed countries (Liu & Wang, 2003). It has significant influence on the host country in many different levels and aspects. However, the outcome may either be positive or negative. On the one hand, FDI contributes to the host country in terms of capital investment, technology advancement, and employment. On the other hand, it increases the reliance on foreign technology, and intensifies competition for domestic company.

3.1 Technology Transfer from Multinational Companies

Multinational companies (MNCs) are the most important carriers of FDI, as well as advanced technologies. Researches in this field are focused on the issues and relationships between MNCs and local industries. From the perspective of MNCs, discussions can include investment motivations, governance modes, location selection, scale of investments, and related market behaviors. From the perspective of domestic industries, issues are mainly about the effects of FDI. Literature topics include technology spillover, technology adoption, innovation diffusion, and impact on industrial structure, etc. Traditionally, primary channels of FDI from MNCs are Greenfield investment, joint ventures, and original equipment manufacturer (OEM) production. New trends can include value chain optimization such as R&D collaboration, outsourcing, and cross-border merger and acquisition (M&A). Literatures on restructuring of MNCs' boundary bring different perspectives on international technology transfer (Samina & will, 2004).

There are several approaches that technology be transferred from MNCs to host countries, these including: selling of high-tech equipment, trade in knowledge and technology, joint ventures, and international movement of employees, etc (Hoekman, Maskus, & Saggi, 2005). The efficiency of international technology transfer highly relies on the macro political and economic environment, including market scale, tax incentives, labor availability, salary and wage. In this connection, it is natural to link these factors with the innovation systems of host country. Overall, technology transfer is an effective way for MNCs to expand market share and sales revenue in host countries. This also makes it possible for the host country to obtain advanced technology from abroad. Host country can benefit from technology spillover through demonstration effects, labor turnover, and industrial structure upgrading (E. X. Fan, 2003; Liu & Buck, 2007). First, domestic companies tend to adopt new production and management techniques introduced by MNCs through imitation or reverse engineering (Tidd & Izumimoto, 2002). Second, employees trained by MNCs may disseminate their technical knowledge when changing jobs or starting their own company (Driffield & Girma, 2002). Third, MNCs may transfer related technology to domestic companies to complement their product chain, i.e. upstream intermediate goods suppliers and downstream products purchasers (Javorcik, 2003).

Through careful examination of the international technology transfer process, we can learn that it is influenced by many institutional and environmental issues. These interconnected determinant factors form a complex technology transfer structure. First, market potential is an important factor for a company's to decide whether to make overseas investment or not. From a foreign perspective, technology transfer is the most effective approach to start and develop foreign market. The

larger the market potential, the more resources and technologies will be transferred. Second, better technology capacity of the host country would facilitate the transfer process. For example, a good vertical supply chain may reduce cost, enhance efficiency, and provide better support. These resources can help MNCs to realize their strategic goals in the domestic market. Third, MNCs tend to make use of their technology advantage to achieve a monopolistic status. If their leadership position was threatened by domestic players, they would introduce new technologies more frequently and reinforce the technology transfer process. Intensified competition may push both MNCs and domestic companies to develop new technologies, which can contribute to technological innovation of local industry. Lastly, international technology transfer deals are governed by the technology policies in the host country. The policy measures and related regulations toward FDI can have great impact on technology transfer behavior. For example, the effectiveness of IPR protection is a determinant factor whether technology transfers can take place or not. An important issue faced by the enterprises is to adjust their technology transfer strategies according to host country environment, thus to balance long-term technology advantage and market success.

3.2 Impact of Technology Transfer on Domestic Enterprise

From the perspective of local industries, there are more issues to consider about the negative effects brought by FDI. Although international technology transfer is a fast track in technology development, it may not naturally result in long-term innovation, or sustainable innovation. (Gao, Zhang, & Liu, 2007). It is widely accepted that the adoption of transferred or purchased technologies has both positive and negative impacts on Chinese firms. Technology transfer activities would generally improve production and market performance of many industrial firms, but it might also impede the innovation performance of high-tech firms. Many Chinese firms have been relying largely on costly generation technologies (e.g. key equipment and apparatuses), resulting in negative impacts of technology transfer on cultivating their core competence (Guan, Mok, Yam, Chin, & Pun, 2006). Moreover, MNCs tend to minimize spill-over effects to domestic companies, so they can maintain competitive advantages. Recent trend has shown that MNCs prefer to establish wholly owned subsidiaries in destination countries. As a result, knowledge transfers tend to be internalized between MNC and its wholly owned subsidiaries (Marin & Bell, 2006).

Although the demonstration effect may lead local companies to upgrade their technology level, it also intensifies market competition. With stronger technology edge and capital support, MNCs can easily rule out weaker local competitors and setup entry barriers to the market through technology lock-in. Technology absorptive capacity of local company is the primary factor whether they can take advantage from spillovers (Farris, 2007; Nieto & Quevedo, 2005). This will in turn depend on their strength of investment on R&D. However, R&D expenditures of domestic firms can rarely parallel with those of large MNCs. The advantage of labor turnover for local companies is largely influenced by the market strategy and R&D structure of MNCs. To restrain the flowing away of quality employees to domestic competitors, MNCs provide higher salary packages for human resources than that of local companies (Driffield & Girma, 2002). This further increases the burden of domestic companies on their R&D activities.

In recent years, MNCs are getting more involved in vertical technology transfer. The linkages between MNCs and local suppliers or buyers will reduce cost and improve efficiency (Saliola & Zanfei, 2009). However, the entrance of MNCs through FDI may deteriorate the industry infrastructure of developing countries. Most local companies of developing countries stay at the bottom segment of the "smiling curve" (Dedrick,

Kraemer, & Tsai, 1999). They earn marginal profit through supplying raw materials and labor force for the developed world. Although these companies can receive a certain degree of technology transfer through outsourcing, the high-tech core is always retained by MNCs in the developed countries. Research (Lemoine & Unal-Kesenci, 2004) has shown that many outward-oriented and highly competitive industries, which are based on imported technology and foreign affiliates, seem to have had limited impact on local production and on the diffusion of technology in domestic industry.

There are both strengths and weaknesses for domestic companies to compete in the local market. They have access to cheap but abundant resources for low-cost production. They have better understanding of market environment, consumer behaviors, cultures, etc. However, their disadvantages are obvious too. A major problem restricting the development of domestic companies is that they lack distinctive technology competence. Compared with their counterpart MNCs, domestic companies are weak in terms of advanced technology and knowledge accumulations. Due to intense market competition, these companies do not have enough resources for long-term R&D input. With the deepening trend of internationalization, domestic enterprises are eager to transfer better technology from foreign countries to increase market competency in a relative short amount of time. The goal is to leap forward into the technology frontier, thus engender a competitive status in the market. The ability of sustainable innovation has been the key of distinctive competence for companies. Therefore, it is important for domestic companies to choose appropriate technology to invest or transfer. It should be planned according to available resources, technology capacity, market orientation, and technology characteristics.

3.3 Policy Concerns at Enterprise Level

Many industrializing countries introduce policies to attract FDI and encourage transfer of advanced technology from abroad. These measures include: investment grants, taxes incentives, reduced tariffs, export subsidy, education and training, etc. These are very attractive terms for MNCs to invest in foreign countries. However, host countries also introduce many restrictive regulations toward FDI. These policies are often aimed for improvement of local competency and weakening the reliance on foreign technologies or products. Many developing countries require FDI in forms of joint ventures rather than wholly owned subsidiaries of MNCs. Take China as example, although wholly owned subsidiaries are allowed, the policy benefits are far from the same than that of joint ventures. In some other countries such as Japan and South Korea, during their developing stages, when policy gave priority to technology acquisition, MNCs were prohibited to establish wholly owned subsidiaries (Kiyota & Okazaki, 2005; Yun, 2007). Since FDI can either foster or restrain the development of domestic industries, it is the government's role to balance the interests of both local and foreign stakeholders, thus guide and regulate FDI.

4. TECHNOLOGY LEVEL INFLUENCING FACTORS

This section discusses the technological factors affecting international technology transfer. The characteristics of technology such as adaptability, maturity, and distance have significant impacts on the success of transaction.

4.1 Technology Adaptability

Technology adaptability in a foreign market is a vital factor for the success of international technology transfer. Much has been written in the literature about the need to transfer appropriate technology for developing countries. When compared to a domestic context, technology transfer in an international context is subjected to more diversified environmental conditions, such as cultural differences, thus creating greater challenges (Cui, Griffith, Cavusgil, & Dabic, 2006). The nature of the technology to be transferred is built intrinsically in the products, manufacturing processes, and management systems. There are numerous examples of unsuccessful launches of products in developing countries. Some are caused simply by marketing failures, while other examples which go beyond such simple failures are product designs which depart from local custom as regards tastes, habits, and preferences and thus may never be accepted (Bruun & Mefford, 1996). The adaptation and modification of technology should be viewed from a strategic and organizational perspective, as technical integration of the technology provider's process with the acquirer's system must make allowance for different operating contexts (Platt & Wilson, 1999). Study has shown that technology policy of developing country comprises more than choosing technology as a means to production, but includes the control of a broader selection of technical and non-technical items that link technology to strategy through capabilities of the host country (Hipkin, 2004).

Some of the primary objectives for importing foreign technology into developing economies are aimed at improving the industrial development bases in order to achieve technological advancement. However, many of these efforts by the governments of developing countries have failed because such technologies are not sustainable (Dunmade, 2002). The sustainability of a foreign technology in a developing economy depends on

Figure 1. Indices of foreign technology adaptability. Source: Dunmade (2002)

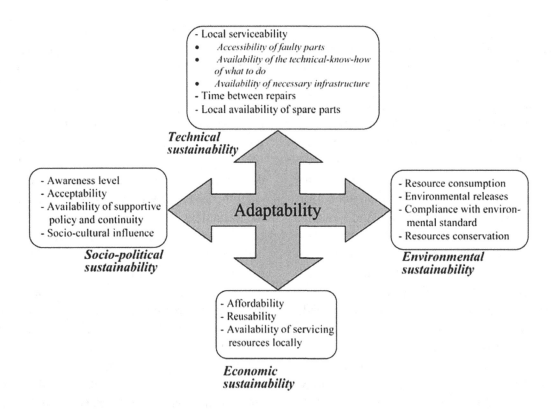

the adaptability of the technology to the society, while adaptability itself is determined by the complex interrelationships of the various factors as shown in Figure 1.

Scholars (Child, 1997; M. Tuominen, Rajala, & Moller, 2004) have argued that, in order to understand the complexity of adaptability, research should deal with all three intertwined dimensions of the construct, which include: technology, market, and organization-related factors. To this extant, successful international technology transfer must consider the nature of technology, market trend, and enterprise level capabilities. Literature has pointed out that international technology transfer, from the perspective of developing countries, technological novelty is sometimes far less important than relevance (Basch, 1993). For example, in the pharmaceutical industry, appropriate technology are more important to serve the

purpose of: direct application to reducing risk of infection and disease; affordability and cost-effectiveness; saving foreign exchange; satisfying public demand with political benefit to the government; and promotion of social equity.

4.2 Technology Trajectory

Both institutionalized regime practices and existing technological trajectories have an inherent advantage in determining the direction of socio-technical change (Rock, Murphy, Rasiah, van Seters, & Managi, 2009). In the process of international technology transfer, foreign providers and domestic receivers have different perspectives and strategies toward technology trajectory.

Technology trajectory can be illustrated by S-curves. Both the process of an emerging technology's evolvement and the pattern of its adoption in the market can be illustrated to conform to S-shaped curves. When compared with traditional technologies, emerging technologies may have market uncertainty and unknown impact on industrial development. These new technologies generate potential market opportunities for new investments, thus bring great challenges to decision makers. From the perspective of developing countries, emerging technology can further provide a window of opportunity for technology leapfrogging, which can trigger significant improvements to domestic industrial structure.

Technology transfer can take place at any stages of technology life cycle, but not all technologies can have the chance to reach its natural limit on the S-curve. A replacing technology may form another S-curve through establishing a brand new technology trajectory if it satisfies the same market need, and there will be a trend for companies to replace the incumbent technology with new technology. For many MNCs in the developed world, a better choice is to sell or transfer the current technology rather than completely abandon it. This process has been illustrated by the "Flying Geese" model proposed by Japanese scholars (Kojima, 2000). For new firms in the industrializing economies, they are more likely to choose the technology at an early stage on the S-curves. However, that may bring challenges for the MNCs since it raises new potential competitors (Lemoine & Unal-Kesenci, 2004).

Scholars proposed a reverse product life-cycle model (Figure 2) which explores this trend in technology transfer (Hayter & Edgington, 2004). The S-curve goes through three different stages and explains the relationship between foreign and local companies. In Stage I, foreign MNCs wish to relocate mature technologies in low cost developing countries, and the strategy catered the needs of technology receivers to attract investment and import technology. There are relatively few conflicts because the motivations of both sides coincide with each other. In Stage II, due to the fast growth and need of innovation in destination country, tensions begin to emerge due to a narrower technology gap. Lastly, in Stage III, the two sides have interest conflict in terms of R&D, investment, and other resources. The host country needs to upgrade its technological capabilities, but MNCs hesitate to transfer better technology for fear of losing their competitive advantage. From the perspective of fast industrializing counties such as China, the situation has evolved into Stage II & III, where conflicts emerged due to the need for innovation. Therefore, both sides need to make compromise on technology transfer.

4.3 Technology Gap and Distance

Scholars (Blalock & Gertler, 2009) define "technology gap" as the distance from a domestic firm's technical competency level to that of international best practice. Literatures studying institutions and technological development found technology gap is one of the determining factors of technology transfer. These studies claim that developing economies catch up only when they actively learn and adapt from leaders (Nelson, 2007). However, technology gaps exist because countries invest differently in education, R&D, and other inputs into technological change (Aghion & Howitt, 1992; Romer, 1986). Their choices about how to invest, as well as the productivity of these investments varied because of the differences in economic and social dimensions (Lundvall, 1992; Rodrik, Subramanian, & Trebbi, 2004). Technological unevenness endures primarily due to the spread of ideas is contingent on active attempts by firms to learn, imitate, and adapt existing technologies (Lall, 1992; Viotti, 2002).

Similar concept of technology distance proposed by another scholar (Griliches, 1979) postulated that knowledge stock levels of firms depend on not only their indigenous R&D investment but also knowledge stock developed by other firms. Following this idea, many other scholars (A. B. Jaffe, 1986; Watanabe, Matsumoto, & Hur, 2004) have developed new concepts such as

Figure 2. The reverse product cycle model and technology transfer. Source: Hayter and Edgington (2004)

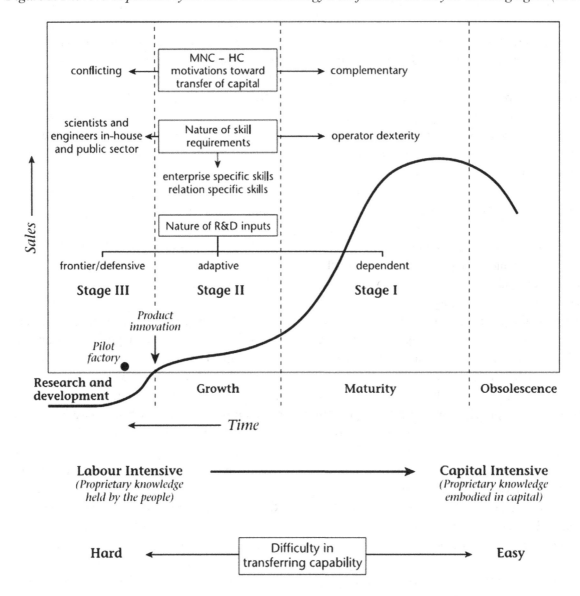

technological proximity, technological position, and technological diversification. Technology distance between partners can have an impact on their choice of the cooperation mode. A longer distance may lead to limited capability to learn, assimilate, and share knowledge, thus cause negative effect on innovation.

There are some unsolved disputes about the effect of technology distance. From one perspective, firms with a longer distance may be too far away from the best practice and unable to absorb quickly and efficiently. Firms with a smaller gap should have better technical competency and could easily catch up with the technology frontier. From another perspective, firms who lie far away from the technology frontier have the most space to gain higher returns from learning. Firms with a smaller technology gap may have already mastered similar technologies that have lower returns, but making further effort to alter existing practices are more

Table 1. Researches on impacts of technological gaps

Author	Year	Country	Results
Lai et al	2009	China	Nonlinear
Chudnovsky et al	2008	Argentina	Negative
Luckraz	2008	Australia	Positive
Girma and Gorg	2007	England	Nonlinear
Kohpaiboon	2006	Thailand	Negative
Oliveira et al	2006	Brazil	Negative
Alvarez and Molero	2005	Spain	Negative
Bjorn et al	2005	Eastern Europe	Positive

difficult. Scholars from different countries carried out many empirical researches showed that technology gap can result either positive (Bjorn, Johannes, & Ingmar, 2005; Luckraz, 2008) or negative (Alvarez & Molero, 2005; Chudnovsky, Lopez, & Rossi, 2008; Oliveira, Jayme, & Lemos, 2006) impacts to the learning process. Some other scholars found that the relationship can be nonlinear and U-shaped (Girma & Gorg, 2007; M. Lai, Wang, & Zhu, 2009). Table 1 shows some latest results of the impacts of technology gaps.

As a short summary of the above literatures, it is clear that technology gaps and distance have significant impacts on technology transfer and diffusion. However, the characteristics such as size and direction of the impact are still unclear. Scholars (Criscuolo & Narula, 2008; M. Lai, et al., 2009) claimed that absorptive capacity should be crucial for economies that have a sizeable distance from the technological frontier. Therefore, technology assessment is still necessary based on the technological capabilities of enterprises.

5. METHODOLOGY

As discussed in previous sections, the impacts on international technology transfer are complex and multi-leveled. Therefore, methodologies from different perspectives should be employed to carry out related research. Scholars (Salo & Salmenkaita, 2002) suggest that there are synergies between the three intelligence tools that serve to inform policy decisions, i.e., technology foresight, technology assessment, and research technological development (RTD) program evaluation. This section will summarize related methodologies to study technology transfer policy, enterprise strategy, and technology selection.

5.1 Technology Roadmapping

Technology roadmapping represents a powerful technique for supporting technology management and planning, especially for exploring and communicating the dynamic linkages between technological resources, organizational objectives and the changing environment (Phaal, Farrukh, & Probert, 2004). The roadmapping process contributes to the integration of business and technology and to the definition of technology strategy by displaying the interaction between products and technologies over time, taking both short- and long-terms product and technology aspects (Groenveld, 2007).

The value of technology roadmaps for technology planning, technology selection, and technological innovation has become widely recognized (Rinne, 2004). It is very flexible and has been widely used at industrial level to support strategic planning. Scholars (Petricka & Echols, 2004) suggest that firms concentrate on technological trajectories by combining technology roadmapping and other techniques to make more sustainable product development decisions.

In some recent studies, there has been a trend to apply technology roadmapping to governmental activities. For example, Japanese scholars (Yasunaga, Watanabe, & Korenaga, 2009) use roadmaps to develop governmental innovation policy for promoting technology convergence. European scholars (A. Tuominen & Ahlqvist, 2010) use socio-technical roadmapping as a tool for integrating the development of transport policies and intelligent transport systems and services in Finland.

5.2 Technology Foresight

Foresight has been defined as "the process involved in systematically attempting to look into the longer-term future of science, technology, the economy and society with the aim of identifying the areas of strategic research and the emerging generic technologies likely to yield the greatest economic and social benefits" (Martin, 1995). Foresight is a process involves consultative procedures to ensure feedback to and from relevant actors. The main aspects of this process can be summarized as 'the five Cs': 1. concentration on the longer term; 2. coordination between the stakeholders' visions, intentions and actions; 3. consensus on research areas that seem particularly promising; 4. communication; 5. commitment to the implementation of R&D policies (Martin, 1995; Salo & Salmenkaita, 2002).

Technology foresight was evolved from technology forecasting, but covered a broader scope. Foresight activities at national level have been used as policy instrument since the early 1970s in Japan (Georghiou, 2003). Many industrialized countries and several advanced developing countries have practiced some form of foresight exercise. At industry level, some scholars (Georghiou & Keenan, 2006) claim that foresight can be used in exploring future opportunities so

as to set priorities for investment in science and innovation activities, and building new networks and linkages across fields, sectors and markets, or around problems. These attributes also fit the requirement of analysis in international technology transfer. Foresight methodologies include both quantitative and qualitative tools. Some widely used methods are, for example, monitoring, trend analysis, modeling, scenario analysis, Delphi studies (Porter, 2004).

5.3 Technology Assessment

Technology assessment encompasses activities which analyze and evaluate the anticipated impacts of a given technology, examine areas of potential social conflict caused by its deployment, promote a constructive dialogue between the stakeholders, and produce recommendations for improving the technology and the terms of its application (Eijndhoven, 1997). Technology assessment has been widely applied in public policy-making and in business decision-making (Tran & Daim, 2008).

Many technology assessment approaches and tools have been identified to conduct related research, which include: structural modeling, scenario analysis, impact analysis, risk assessment, decision analysis, cost benefit analysis, Delphi, and evaluation of emerging technologies (Tran & Daim, 2008). Technology assessment techniques can be applied to international technology transfer at enterprise level for evaluation of technology alternatives, selection and acquisition of appropriate technologies, and strategic technological planning.

5.4 The Delphi Method

The Delphi method was originally developed for U.S. Air Force as a group decision method (Dalkey & Helmer, 1963). The technique uses a panel of experts who are not allowed to interact in order that their judgments will not be influenced by each other. The questionnaire survey usually takes several rounds before getting consensus from the participants. The Delphi method has four key features: 1. Anonymity; 2. Iteration; 3. Controlled feedback; and 4. Statistical aggregation of group response (Rowe & Wright, 1999).

The Delphi process requires experts repeatedly express their opinions through a series of linked questionnaires. The first round focuses on the exploration of the subject, and the participants will contribute additional information through answering open questions. The middle rounds involve the process of reaching a common understanding of how the group views the issues. The final results occur in the last round after analyzed all previous information (Doke & Swanson, 1995). During the consultation process, two types of information will flow among experts through the effort of coordinators: 1. available data previously requested by respondents; 2. considerations suggested as potentially relevant by other respondents (Dalkey & Helmer, 1963). To save researcher and participants' time and effort, the first round is sometimes substituted by deliberate literature review. The middle rounds could be combined due to time constrains and low response.

The Delphi method has been adopted in many countries and in a wide range of fields. National Delphi has been conducted in Japan for every 5 years to generate informative projections on potential technological advances. Many other countries such as Germany, Korea, and Britain have emulated similar efforts. The technique is applied to fields including project selection, operations management, drug policy, and administration management issues (V. S. Lai, Wong, & Cheung, 2002; Rayens & Hahn, 2000).

5.5 Analytic Hierarchy Process

The Analytic Hierarchy Process (AHP) is a quantitative decision-support method designed to deal with complex multi-criteria decisions. It can be applied for structuring, measurement and synthesis of factors or elements that affect decision-making. The process involves decomposition of a complex and unstructured research problem into an organized set of components (Saaty, 1980). The basic steps involved in the AHP process, regardless of the nature and scope of the research problem, are the following: 1. Construction of a hierarchical model; 2. Prioritization of elements; 3. Calculation of results.

The advantages of AHP include simplicity, ease of use, and flexibility. The method is designed to assist complex decision-making when a relatively large number of quantifiable and intangible criteria are to be tested. The method allows calculating priorities and weights for specific elements in a hierarchical structure in order to identify the most important elements (Saaty, 1980). AHP gives a clearer understanding of the situation through decision-making group, and leads to a higher degree of commitment to a chosen alternative (Harker & Vargas, 1987). AHP was successfully applied in many research areas of product and technology selection (Pandejpong & Kocaoglu, 2003; Taha, et al., 2007; Vaidya & Kumar, 2006).

6. GAP ANALYSES

By reviewing the literatures of international technology transfer and summarizing the discussions from the previous sections, this part of the chapter analyzes the research gaps in this field. Scholars (Rock, et al., 2009) suggest that a multi-level perspective is necessary for policy makers to consider the complex ways in which macro-scale economic, political, social, and environmental factors, meso-scale industrial networks and institutions, and micro-scale technological developments co-evolve and co-determine one another in ways that are difficult to control or predict. To this extent, the research gaps can be categorized into three interrelated levels, which include the policy level, industry level, and technology level.

6.1 Gaps at Policy level

At national level, technology transfer policy needs to promote industrial development and foster domestic innovation. For example, the Chinese government deliberately trades market access for technologies, obliging foreign investors to share technologies if they want to sell to the domestic market. German scholars (Altenburg, et al., 2008) found that the strategy is unique because only large economies with high potential market can apply it. They suggest further research to show whether this unique catch-up process (China and India) can promote sustained innovation. Literature (Hatani, 2009) found that China's FDI policy has not been very successful in the creation of linkages between MNCs and local firms, and in developing local firms' independent technological competence. The author suggests that emerging economies need a more comprehensive policy design to promote intimate interactions with MNCs and improve the conditions for technology transfer. Another literature (Bin, 2008) has urged that government regulations should be combined with commonly followed technological strategies in determining the relationship between domestic in-house R&D and foreign technology transfer. Some authors (P. Fan & Watanabe, 2006) highlight the need of balancing the import of foreign technology and indigenous development, and the engagement of business/private sector as a major force in improving technological capabilities.

Technology policy serves to maintain national security, social welfare, and economic benefit for host country. This is true no matter the host country belongs to the developed world or the developing world; no matter it is technology exporter or technology importer. From perspectives of both sides, technology policy faces the problem of making tradeoffs among interests. Fastening high-tech exports can ensure national interests, but may undermine international collaboration and foreign investment. Loosening FDI policy will boost economy growth, but may deteriorate

domestic industrial structure. IPR policy can provide a better competition environment, thus encouraging technology innovation, but it may either increase or decrease technology diffusion. Technology policy regarding to these aspects will significantly influence international technology transfer activities, thus impact the efficiency of National Innovation Systems.

Technology importing countries focus on technology catch-up by regulating local industry structure, promoting technological advancement, and fostering domestic innovation. Korean scholar (K. Lee, 2005) identified two catch-up modes in emerging countries: Taiwan followed the sequential steps of OEM, ODM and OBM, through technology transfer from foreign countries; Korea jumped from OEM directly to OBM by skipping some stages. He suggests that China might be a third mixing model which need further study. FDI policy serves the purpose of attracting foreign capitals and advanced technology. The government can favor some specific technologies or industries more than others. This is related to a nation's long-term strategic planning which can be reflected in their critical technology programs. Therefore, government will give priorities and benefits to transfer technology in these planned areas. From an opposite perspective, policy will also protect some important industries and restrict FDI to change domestic industrial structure. Generally speaking, a nation's technology policy is to balance the factors of attracting foreign investment, transferring appropriate technology, fostering innovation, and protecting local industry.

Technology exporting countries have various regulations to maintain competitive advantage. High-tech export control policy prohibits sensitive technologies to be transferred across borders. For those technologies that can be transferred, IPRs must be protected to safeguard national interest. In previous sections, we discussed that related regulations in the United States have significant impact on international trade and technology transfer. However, these policies have potential drawbacks and have already aroused wide concerns in the United States. Political opposition to foreign acquisitions can be driven not only by genuine national security concerns, but also by protectionist impulses. Regarding to these criticisms, the recent amendments to the Exon-Florio CFIUS framework introduced by the National Security Act of 2007 tried to strike a reasonable balance between national security concerns and promoting the inflow of foreign capital in the United States (Georgiev, 2008).

6.2 Gaps at Enterprise level

The rules that govern how industries develop technologies and solve technological problems, are characterized as meso-scale phenomena influenced from below by micro technological niches, and from above by macro features and factors embedded in the socio-technical landscapes constituting particular places, regions, or countries (Rock, et al., 2009). Building an enterprise-centered innovation system and enhancing the innovation performance at industry level remains a challenging task in China. Different strategies and interests between domestic companies and foreign MNCs have made international technology transfer hard to control and maneuver. Scholar (Castellacci, 2008) argued that competitiveness and cohesion should be regarded as two complementary policy objectives. Current literatures focus on both competition and collaboration mechanism between the two sides, but no consensus has been reached.

From the perspective of domestic companies, a major challenge is the selection of effective technology strategies to compete against or cooperate with MNCs in the era of globalization (E. D. Jaffe, Nebenzahl, & Schorr, 2005). Literature introduced two kinds of environmental factors, barriers to appropriability and opportunities for improvement, to study local firms' technology strategies. The barriers to appropriability include regulatory, information, resource, coordination, and commitment issues. Four kinds of opportunities for improvement in the development of emerging technologies include learning, cultural, incentive, and organizational opportunities (Gao, et al., 2007). The authors tried to explain the ineffectiveness of Chinese companies' technology strategy, and called for future research to further examine the impact of external resources on the selection of technology.

From the perspective of foreign MNCs, it is also a challenge to balance the collaboration and competition with domestic companies. On the one hand, they can have better access to market and resources if they cooperate and transfer technology to local firms. One the other hand, transferring advanced technology may threaten company's competitive advantage and raise potential competitors. It is not uncommon to see in a joint venture when the local side learned all core technologies and then the foreign side was sent away. Scholars (Un & Cuervo-Cazurra, 2008) suggest that studies of technology strategy in MNCs should not only analyze technology development in subsidiaries of MNCs, but also examine how such development differs from that of domestic firms. Future research should compare the investments and strategies adopted by subsidiaries of foreign MNCs and those undertaken by domestic firms.

As the largest developing country, China has been quite successful in low-tech sectors. However, in developing high-tech sectors, many predicaments still exist. Some policy-induced barriers often result to higher costs and technology internalization in MNCs. Even in recent years, companies in some sectors are still complaining of various official barriers for their access to the market despite the growing openness to foreign MNCs (Zhou, 2008). If China were to continue to leap ahead through international technology transfer, the major policy barriers and interest conflicts must be addressed. Further research is needed on how to improve international technology transfer policy that considering and balancing the interests between local and foreign companies.

6.3 Gaps at Technology Level

Characteristics of technologies should be taken into account in any technology selection model, which include the uncertainties of commercial and technical success, the development history of the technologies, the resource requirements to develop technologies, the degree to which the technologies contribute to established missions and the current life-cycle stage of the technologies (Torkkeli & Tuominen, 2002). Technological innovations are embodied in products and processes, so analyzing and comparing them remains a challenge, especially they are difficult to be measured across country and time.

Technology selection is closely related to business strategy. From the perspective of foreign companies, scholar (Tian, 2010) suggests that a combination between selection of entry modes, selection of technologies, and selection of investment priorities is a more promising approach to cross-border technology management. Especially, selection of technologies has been suggested as an important approach to minimize risks in international technology transfer. Western scholars (Cannice, Chen, & Daniels, 2003, 2004; Jordan & Lowe, 2004) argued that MNCs should choose to use periphery, dependent and tacit technologies in the affiliates they establish in emerging markets to minimize unwanted technology appropriation. However, this strategy gradually becomes not applicable in the case of Chinese market since MNCs often face pressing strategic issues of intense competition and fast-changing market needs, and have to compromise their interests over technology transfer issues. These concerns include: 1. MNCs may have to establish joint ventures to please the local government for possible support in a business project. 2. They may have to use core, independent and explicit technologies in local affiliates in exchange for market entry permission. 3. They may have to focus on production of locally sold products and promotion of traditional products in order to pre-empt the

market before their rivals. 4. They may have to invest in projects that hire unskilled local workers in order to establish good relationships with the government (Tian, 2010). Therefore, scholar called for further research to examine how MNCs may manage diffusion through technology selection to balance such strategic concerns.

From the perspective of domestic companies, Chinese scholars (Guan, et al., 2006) suggest that firms should acquire state-of-the-art technologies that lead to innovation and improvement. Local companies should formulate viable international technology transfer strategies for strengthening new product development and managing innovation process rather than simply attaining for production scale or speed. This idea suggests companies to consider the characteristics of technology when they make decisions on technology transfer. As illustrated in previous sections, technology trajectory, technology distance, and technology adaptability issues should be studied according to market situation. Scholars (Carayannopoulos & Auster, 2010) suggest further research on international expansion behaviors when a firm is sourcing knowledge that is outside of its domestic market. From the perspective of host government, technology transfer should be a combination of efforts by both domestic and foreign firms, aimed at increasing local competencies, on the one hand, and at adapting technology to host market conditions, on the other hand (Saliola & Zanfei, 2009).

Scholars (Nill & Kemp, 2009) suggest that the selection of technology is to be done in a combined top-down and bottom-up manner, based on visions for system innovation and local interest in the new technology or system. Another scholar (Nemet, 2009) focused on three factor on technical change: demand-pull, technology-push, and government-led, and argued that ex ante assessment of the relative technical opportunities between incremental and non-incremental technical change is difficult and fraught with uncertainty, thus requires governments have access to prodigious technical expertise. However, the Chinese government has primarily relied on a top-down approach, instructing large domestic companies to invest in innovation (Girma & Gong, 2008). This approach has not resulted in genuine improvements. Therefore, appropriate methods and approaches should be developed to support the selection of technology from a systematic perspective including all levels.

7. FUTURE RESEARCH

From the above discussion and analysis, we can conclude that many problems coexist in the process of international technology transfer, especially for emerging markets. Interrelated influencing factors at various levels have made the issue very complicated to study. Therefore, several important research questions are identified as guidelines for future research:

1. What to transfer?
2. How to transfer?
3. What policy measures to foster the transfer?

Question 1 explores what technology is appropriate for international technology transfer. The possible answers may depend on decision maker to judge from technology characteristics such as technology trajectory, technology distance, and technology adaptability. Question 2 indicates that companies have to select the most effective channels for international technology transfer. Question 3 needs adequate government policy to encourage and promote the efficient transfer of technology.

Future research can focus on the specific environment of emerging economies such as the BRICs (Brazil, Russia, India, and China). As Western scholars (Lloyd & Turkeltaub, 2006) have argued, China and India are the real golden bricks (BRICs) on the wall. These countries bring a lot of business opportunities for the rest of the world: large potential market, fast growing economy, etc.

The research can be very meaningful for policy makers, foreign investors, local enterprises, and whoever wants to better understand high-tech industrialization and internalization.

REFERENCES

Aghion, P., & Howitt, P. (1992). A model of growth through creative destruction. *Econometrica, 60*(2), 323–351. doi:10.2307/2951599

Altenburg, T., Schmitz, H., & Stamm, A. (2008). Breakthrough? China's and India's Transition from Production to Innovation. *World Development, 36*(2), 325–344. doi:10.1016/j.worlddev.2007.06.011

Alvarez, I., & Molero, J. (2005). Technology and the generation of international knowledge spillovers: An application to Spanish manufacturing firms. *Research Policy, 34*(9), 1440–1452. doi:10.1016/j.respol.2005.06.006

Antkiewicz, A., & Whalley, J. (2007). Recent Chinese Buyout Activity and the Implications for Wider Global Investment Rules. *Canadian Public Policy - Analyse De Politiques, XXXIII*(2), 207-226.

Basch, P. F. (1993). Technology transfer to the developing world: does new technology have any relevance for developing countries? *Tubercle and Lung Disease, 74*(6), 353–358. doi:10.1016/0962-8479(93)90077-B

Biediger, J., Decicco, T., Green, T., Hoffman, G., Lei, D., & Mahadevan, K. (2005). Strategic Action at Lenovo. *Organizational Dynamics, 34*(1), 89–102. doi:10.1016/j.orgdyn.2004.11.007

Bin, G. (2008). Technology acquisition channels and industry performance: An industry-level analysis of Chinese large- and medium-size manufacturing enterprises. *Research Policy, 37*(2), 194–209. doi:10.1016/j.respol.2007.11.004

Bjorn, J., Johannes, S., & Ingmar, K. (2005). Industry Level Technology Gaps and Complimentary Knowledge Stocks as Determinants of Intra-MNC Knowledge Flow. *Journal of Economics and Business, 8*(1&2), 137–156.

Blalock, G., & Gertler, P. J. (2009). How firm capabilities affect who benefits from foreign technology. *Journal of Development Economics, 90*, 192–199. doi:10.1016/j.jdeveco.2008.11.011

Bromley, D. A. (2004). Technology policy. *Technology in Society, 26*, 455–468. doi:10.1016/j.techsoc.2004.01.005

Bruun, P., & Mefford, R. N. (1996). A framework for selecting and introducing appropriate production technology in developing countries. *International Journal of Production Economics, 46-47*, 197–209. doi:10.1016/S0925-5273(96)00082-5

Bush, G. W. (2006). *American Competitiveness Initiative*. Domestic Policy Council Office of Science and Technology Policy.

Byrne, M. R. (2006). Protecting National Security and Promoting Foreign Investment: Maintaining the Exon-Florio Balance. *Ohio State Law Journal, 67*, 849.

Cannice, M. V., Chen, R., & Daniels, J. D. (2003). Managing international technology transfer risk: A case analysis of U.S. high-technology firms in Asia. *The Journal of High Technology Management Research, 14*, 171–187. doi:10.1016/S1047-8310(03)00020-8

Cannice, M. V., Chen, R., & Daniels, J. D. (2004). Managing international technology transfer risk: Alternatives and complements to ownership structure. *Management International Review, 4*(special issue 1), 178-189.

Carayannopoulos, S., & Auster, E. R. (2010). External knowledge sourcing in biotechnology through acquisition versus alliance: A KBV approach. *Research Policy, 39*, 254–267. doi:10.1016/j.respol.2009.12.005

Castellacci, F. (2008). Innovation and the competitiveness of industries: Comparing the mainstream and the evolutionary approaches. *Technological Forecasting and Social Change, 75*, 984–1006. doi:10.1016/j.techfore.2007.09.002

Chan, L. (2009). *Technology Transfer to China: Case of the High-speed Rail Industry*. Paper presented at the Portland International Conference on Management of Engineering and Technology.

Chaturvedi, K., & Chataway, J. (2006). Strategic integration of knowledge in Indian pharmaceutical firms: creating competencies for innovation. *International Journal of Business Innovation and Research, 1*(1/2), 27–50. doi:10.1504/IJBIR.2006.011087

Child, J. (1997). Strategic choice in the analysis of action, structure, organizations and environment: retrospect and prospect. *Organization Studies, 18*(1), 43–76. doi:10.1177/017084069701800104

Chudnovsky, D., Lopez, A., & Rossi, G. (2008). Foreign direct investment spillovers and the absorptive capabilities of domestic firms in the Argentine manufacturing sector (1992-2001). *The Journal of Development Studies, 44*(5), 645–677. doi:10.1080/00220380802009159

Clinton, W. J. (1997). *Science and Technology Shaping the Twenty-First Century*. Office of Science and Technology Policy.

Corr, C. F. (2003). The Wall Still Stands! Complying with Export Controls on Technology Transfers in the Post-Cold War, Post-9/11 Era. *Houston Journal of International Law, 25*(3), 441.

Criscuolo, P., & Narula, R. (2008). A novel approach to national technological accumulation and absorptive capacity: Aggregating Cohen and Levinthal. *European Journal of Development Research, 20*(1), 56–73. doi:10.1080/09578810701853181

Cui, A. S., Griffith, D. A., Cavusgil, S. T., & Dabic, M. (2006). The influence of market and cultural environmental factors on technology transfer between foreign MNCs and local subsidiaries: a Croatian illustration. *Journal of World Business,* (41): 100–111. doi:10.1016/j.jwb.2006.01.011

Dalkey, N., & Helmer, O. (1963). An experimental application of the Delphi method to the use of experts. *Management Science, 9,* 458–467. doi:10.1287/mnsc.9.3.458

Dedrick, J., Kraemer, K. L., & Tsai, T. (1999). *ACER: an IT Company Learning to Use Information Technology to Compete. IT in Business, Center for Research on Information Technology and Organization.* University of California.

Dittrich, K., Duysters, G., & Man, A.-P. d. (2007). Strategic repositioning by means of alliance networks: The case of IBM. *Research Policy, 36,* 1496–1511. doi:10.1016/j.respol.2007.07.002

Doke, E. R., & Swanson, N. E. (1995). Decision variables for selecting prototyping in information systems development: A Delphi study of MIS managers. *Information & Management, 29,* 173–182. doi:10.1016/0378-7206(95)00021-N

Driffield, N., & Girma, S. (2002). *Regional Foreign Direct Investment and Wage Spillovers: Plant level Evidence from the Electronics Industry.* University of Nottingham.

Dunmade, I. (2002). Indicators of sustainability: assessing the suitability of a foreign technology for a developing economy. *Technology in Society, 24*(4), 461–471. doi:10.1016/S0160-791X(02)00036-2

Eijndhoven, J. C. M. V. (1997). Technology assessment: product or process. *Technological Forecasting and Social Change, 54,* 269–286. doi:10.1016/S0040-1625(96)00210-7

Erickson, A. S., & Walsh, K. A. (2008). National security challenges and competition: Defense and space R&D in the Chinese strategic context. *Technology in Society, 30,* 349–361. doi:10.1016/j.techsoc.2008.04.001

Fan, E. X. (2003). Technological spillovers from foreign direct investment-a survey. *Asian Development Review, 20*(1), 34–56.

Fan, P., & Watanabe, C. (2006). Promoting industrial development through technology policy: Lessons from Japan and China. *Technology in Society, 28*(3), 303–320. doi:10.1016/j.techsoc.2006.06.002

Farris, G. F. (2007). Research on innovation management and technology transfer in China. *The Journal of Technology Transfer, 32,* 123–126. doi:10.1007/s10961-006-9003-1

Fosfuri, A. (2000). Patent protection, imitation and the mode of technology transfer. *International Journal of Industrial Organization, 18,* 1129–1149. doi:10.1016/S0167-7187(98)00056-3

Gao, X., Zhang, P., & Liu, X. (2007). Competing with MNEs: developing manufacturing capabilities or innovation capabilities. *The Journal of Technology Transfer, 32,* 87–107. doi:10.1007/s10961-006-9002-2

Georghiou, L. (2003). *Foresight: Concept and Practice as a Tool for Decision Making.* Expert Papers, Technology Foresight Summit Budapest.

Georghiou, L., & Keenan, M. (2006). Evaluation of national foresight activities: assessing rationale, process and impact. *Technological Forecasting and Social Change, 73,* 761–777. doi:10.1016/j.techfore.2005.08.003

Georgiev, G. S. (2008). The Reformed CFIUS Regulatory Framework: Mediating Between Continued Openness to Foreign Investment and National Security. *Yale Journal on Regulation*, 25.

Girma, S., & Gong, Y. D. (2008). FDI, linkages and the efficiency of state-owned enterprises in China. *The Journal of Development Studies*, *44*(5), 728–749. doi:10.1080/00220380802009233

Girma, S., & Gorg, H. (2007). The role of the efficiency gap for spillovers from FDI: Evidence from the UK electronics and engineering sectors. *Open Economies Review*, *18*(2), 215–232. doi:10.1007/s11079-007-9031-y

Griliches, Z. (1979). Issues in assessing the contribution of R&D to productivity growth. *The Bell Journal of Economics*, *10*, 92–116. doi:10.2307/3003321

Groenveld, P. (2007). Roadmapping Integrates Business and Technology. *Research-Technology Management*, *50*(6), 49–58.

Guan, J. C., Mok, C. K., Yam, R. C. M., Chin, K. S., & Pun, K. F. (2006). Technology transfer and innovation performance: Evidence from Chinese firms. *Technological Forecasting and Social Change*, *73*, 666–678. doi:10.1016/j.techfore.2005.05.009

Harker, P. T., & Vargas, L. G. (1987). The theory of ratio scale estimation: Saaty's Analytic Hierarchy Process. *Management Science*, *33*(11), 383–403. doi:10.1287/mnsc.33.11.1383

Hatani, F. (2009). The logic of spillover interception: The impact of global supply chains in China. *Journal of World Business*, *44*(2), 158–166. doi:10.1016/j.jwb.2008.05.005

Hayter, R., & Edgington, D. (2004). Flying Geese in Asia: The Impacts of Japanese MNCs as a Source of Industrial Learning. *Tijdschrift voor Economische en Sociale Geografie*, *95*, 3–26. doi:10.1111/j.0040-747X.2004.00290.x

He, W., & Lyles, M. A. (2008). China's outward foreign direct investment. *Business Horizons*, *51*, 485–491. doi:10.1016/j.bushor.2008.06.006

Helfer, L. R. (2004). Regime Shifting: The TRIPs Agreement and New Dynamics of International Intellectual Property Lawmaking. *Yale Journal of International Law, 29*.

Hemphill, T. A. (2006). US innovation policy: creating (and expanding) a national agenda for global competitiveness. *Innovation: Management, Policy, &. Practice*, 10.

Higino, S. P. (2005). International trade, economic growth and intellectual property rights: A panel data study of developed and developing countries. *Journal of Development Economics*, *78*, 529–547. doi:10.1016/j.jdeveco.2004.09.001

Hipkin, I. (2004). Determining technology strategy in developing countries. *Omega*, *32*(3), 245–260. doi:10.1016/j.omega.2003.11.004

Hobday, M. (1994). Technological Learning in Singapore: A Test Case of Leapfrogging. *The Journal of Development Studies*, *30*, 831–858. doi:10.1080/00220389408422340

Hobday, M., Rush, H., & Bessant, J. (2004). Approaching the innovation frontier in Korea: the transition phase to leadership. *Research Policy*, *33*, 1433–1457. doi:10.1016/j.respol.2004.05.005

Hoekman, B. M., Maskus, K. E., & Saggi, K. (2005). Transfer of technology to developing countries: Unilateral and multilateral policy options. *World Development*, *33*(10), 1587–1602. doi:10.1016/j.worlddev.2005.05.005

Jaffe, A. B. (1986). Technological Opportunity and Spillovers of R&D: Evidence from Firms' Patents, Profits, and Market Value. *The American Economic Review*, *76*(5), 984–1001.

Jaffe, E. D., Nebenzahl, I. D., & Schorr, I. (2005). Strategic Options of Home Country Firms Faced with MNC Entry. *Long Range Planning, 38,* 183–195. doi:10.1016/j.lrp.2004.11.013

Javorcik, B. S. (2003). *Search of Spillovers through Backward Linkages. World Bank WP.* Does Foreign Direct Investment Increase the Productivity of Domestic Firms.

Johnson, C., & Walworth, D. J. (2003). *Protecting U.S. intellectual property rights and the challenges of digital piracy.* U.S. International Trade Commission.

Jordan, J., & Lowe, J. (2004). Protecting strategic knowledge: Insights from collaborative agreements in the aerospace sector. *Technology Analysis and Strategic Management, 16,* 241–259. doi:10.1080/09537320410001682900

Kiyota, K., & Okazaki, T. (2005). *Foreign Technology Acquisition Policy and Firm Performance in Japan, 1957-1970: Macro-aspects of Industrial Policy.* CIRJE Discussion Papers.

Kojima, K. (2000). The "flying geese" model of Asian economic development: origin, theoretical extensions, and regional policy implications. *Journal of Asian Economics, 11,* 375–401. doi:10.1016/S1049-0078(00)00067-1

Kumar, N. (2002). Intellectual property rights, technology and economic development: experiences of Asian countries. *RIS Discussion Paper, 25.*

LaCroix, S. J., & Konan, D. E. (2002). Intellectual property rights in china: the changing political economy of Chinese-American interests. *World Economy, 25,* 759–788. doi:10.1111/1467-9701.00462

Lai, M., Wang, H., & Zhu, S. (2009). Double-edged effects of the technology gap and technology spillovers: Evidence from the Chinese industrial sector. *China Economic Review, 20,* 414–424. doi:10.1016/j.chieco.2009.06.007

Lai, V. S., Wong, B. K., & Cheung, W. (2002). Group decision making in a multiple criteria environment: A case using the AHP in software selection. *European Journal of Operational Research, 137,* 134–144. doi:10.1016/S0377-2217(01)00084-4

Lall, S. (1992). Technological capabilities and industrialization. *World Development, 20*(2), 165–186. doi:10.1016/0305-750X(92)90097-F

Lee, K. (2005). Making a Technological Catch-up: Barriers and Opportunities. *Asian Journal of Technology Innovation, 13,* 97–131. doi:10.1080/19761597.2005.9668610

Lee, K., & Lim, C. (2001). Technological Regimes, Catching-up and Leapfrogging: the Findings from the Korean Industries. *Research Policy, 30,* 459–483. doi:10.1016/S0048-7333(00)00088-3

Lee, W. Y. (2000). The Role of Science and Technology Policy in Korea's Industrial Development. In Kim, L., & Nelson, R. R. (Eds.), *Technology, Learning, & Innovation - Experiences of Newly Industrializing Economies* (pp. 269–280). Cambridge, UK: Cambridge University Press.

Lemoine, F., & Unal-Kesenci, D. (2004). Assembly Trade and Technology Transfer: The Case of China. *World Development, 32*(5), 829–850. doi:10.1016/j.worlddev.2004.01.001

Liu, X., & Buck, T. (2007). Innovation performance and channels for international technology spillovers: Evidence from Chinese high-tech industries. *Research Policy, 36,* 355–366. doi:10.1016/j.respol.2006.12.003

Liu, X., & Wang, C. (2003). Does Foreign Direct Investment Facilitate Technological Progress? Evidence from Chinese Industries. *Research Policy, 32,* 945–953. doi:10.1016/S0048-7333(02)00094-X

Lloyd, J., & Turkeltaub, A. (2006). India and China are the Only Real Brics in the Wall. *Financial Times (North American Edition)*, (Dec): 4.

Lohr, S. (2002). New Economy- The Intellectual Property Debate Takes a Page from 19th-Century America. *The New York Times*, (Oct. 14).

Luckraz, S. (2008). Process Spillovers and Growth. *Journal of Optimization Theory and Applications*, *139*(2), 315–335. doi:10.1007/s10957-008-9425-z

Lundvall, B. A. (1992). *Introduction. National Systems of Innovation - Toward a Theory of Innovation and Interactive Learning*. London: Pinter.

Marin, A., & Bell, M. (2006). Technology spillovers from foreign direct investment (FDI): The active role of MNC subsidiaries in Argentina in the 1990s. *The Journal of Development Studies*, *42*(4), 678–697. doi:10.1080/00220380600682298

Martin, B. R. (1995). Foresight in science and technology. *Technology Analysis and Strategic Management*, *7*(2), 139–168. doi:10.1080/09537329508524202

Nagaoka, S. (2009). Does strong patent protection facilitate international technology transfer? Some evidence from licensing contracts of Japanese firms. *The Journal of Technology Transfer*, *34*(2), 128–144. doi:10.1007/s10961-007-9071-x

Narin, F., & Frame, J. D. (1989). The growth of Japanese science and technology. *Science*, *245*, 600–605. doi:10.1126/science.245.4918.600

Nelson, R. R. (2007). The changing institutional requirements for technological and economic catch up. *International Journal of Technological Learning. Innovation and Development*, *1*(1), 4–12.

Nemet, G. F. (2009). Demand-pull, technology-push, and government-led incentives for non-incremental technical change. *Research Policy*, *38*, 700–709. doi:10.1016/j.respol.2009.01.004

Nieto, M., & Quevedo, P. (2005). Absorptive capacity, technological opportunity, knowledge spillovers, and innovative effort. *Technovation*, *25*, 1141–1157. doi:10.1016/j.technovation.2004.05.001

Nill, J., & Kemp, R. (2009). Evolutionary approaches for sustainable innovation policies: From niche to paradigm. *Research Policy*, *38*, 668–680. doi:10.1016/j.respol.2009.01.011

Okediji, R. (2008). WIPO-WTO Relations and the Future of Global Intellectual Property Norms. *Netherlands Yearbook of International Law, 39*.

Oliveira, F. H. P., Jayme, F. G., & Lemos, M. B. (2006). Increasing returns to scale and international diffusion of technology: An empirical study for Brazil (1976-2000). *World Development*, *34*(1), 75–88. doi:10.1016/j.worlddev.2005.07.011

Pandejpong, T., & Kocaoglu, D. F. (2003). *Strategic Decision: Process for Technology Selection in the Petrochemical Industry*. Paper presented at the Portland International Conference on Management of Engineering and Technology.

Park, W. G., & Lippoldt, D. C. (2008). Technology Transfer and the Economic Implications of the Strengthening of Intellectual Property Rights in Developing Countries. *OECD Trade Policy Working Papers*.

Petricka, I. J., & Echols, A. E. (2004). Technology roadmapping in review: A tool for making sustainable new product development "decisions". *Technological Forecasting and Social Change*, *71*, 81–100. doi:10.1016/S0040-1625(03)00064-7

Phaal, R., Farrukh, C., & Probert, D. (2004). Technology road mapping - A planning framework for evolution and revolution. *Technological Forecasting and Social Change*, *71*, 5–26. doi:10.1016/S0040-1625(03)00072-6

Platt, L., & Wilson, G. (1999). Technology development and the poor marginalized: context, intervention and participation. *Technovation,* (19): 393–401. doi:10.1016/S0166-4972(99)00030-9

Porter, A. (2004). Technology futures analysis: Toward integration of the field and new methods. *Technology Futures Analysis Working Group. Technological Forecasting and Social Change, 71,* 287–303. doi:10.1016/j.techfore.2003.11.004

Rayens, M. K., & Hahn, E. J. (2000). Building consensus using the policy Delphi method. *Policy, Politics & Nursing Practice, 4,* 308–315. doi:10.1177/152715440000100409

Reynolds, J. B. (2002). Export Controls and Economic Sanctions. *The International lawyer 36*(3).

Rinne, M. (2004). Technology roadmaps: Infrastructure for innovation. *Technological Forecasting and Social Change, 71,* 67–80. doi:10.1016/j.techfore.2003.10.002

Rock, M., Murphy, J. T., Rasiah, R., van Seters, P., & Managi, S. (2009). A hard slog, not a leap frog: Globalization and sustainability transitions in developing Asia. *Technological Forecasting and Social Change, 76*(2), 241–254. doi:10.1016/j.techfore.2007.11.014

Rodrik, D., Subramanian, A., & Trebbi, F. (2004). Institutions rule: The primacy of institutions over geography and integration in economic development. *Journal of Economic Growth, 9*(2), 131–165. doi:10.1023/B:JOEG.0000031425.72248.85

Romer, P. M. (1986). Increasing returns and long-run growth. *The Journal of Political Economy, 94*(5), 1002–1037. doi:10.1086/261420

Rowe, G., & Wright, G. (1999). The Delphi techniques as a forecasting tool: Issues and analysis. *International Journal of Forecasting, 15,* 353–375. doi:10.1016/S0169-2070(99)00018-7

Rui, H., & Yip, G. S. (2008). Foreign acquisitions by Chinese firms: A strategic intent perspective. *Journal of World Business, 43,* 213–226. doi:10.1016/j.jwb.2007.11.006

Saaty, T. (1980). *The Analytical Hierarchy Process: Planning, Priority Setting, Resource Allocation.* New York: McGraw-Hill.

Saliola, F., & Zanfei, A. (2009). Multinational firms, global value chains and the organization of knowledge transfer. *Research Policy, 38*(2), 369–381. doi:10.1016/j.respol.2008.11.003

Salo, A., & Salmenkaita, J.-P. (2002). Embedded foresight in RTD programs. *International Journal of Technology. Policy and Management, 2*(2), 167–193.

Samina, K., & will, M. (2004). Innovating through acquisition and internal development: A quarter-century of boundary evolution at Johnson & Johnson. *Long Range Planning, 37*(6), 525–547. doi:10.1016/j.lrp.2004.09.008

Stagg, J. C. (2007). Scrutinizing Foreign Investment: How Much Congressional Involvement Is Too Much. *Iowa Law Review, 93,* 325.

Taha, R. A., Choi, B. C., Chuengparsitporn, P., Cutar, A., Gu, Q., & Phan, K. (2007). *Application of Hierarchical Decision Modeling for Selection of Laptop.* Paper presented at the Portland International Conference on Management of Engineering and Technology.

Tian, X. (2010). Managing FDI technology spillovers: A challenge to TNCs in emerging markets. *Journal of World Business, 45*(3), 276–284. doi:10.1016/j.jwb.2009.09.001

Tidd, J., & Izumimoto, Y. (2002). Knowledge exchange and learning through international joint ventures. *Technovation, 22,* 137–145. doi:10.1016/S0166-4972(01)00006-2

Torkkeli, M., & Tuominen, M. (2002). The contribution of technology selection to core competencies. *International Journal of Production Economics, 77*(3), 271–284. doi:10.1016/S0925-5273(01)00227-4

Tran, T. A., & Daim, T. (2008). A taxonomic review of methods and tools applied in technology assessment. *Technological Forecasting and Social Change, 75*, 1396–1405. doi:10.1016/j.techfore.2008.04.004

Tuominen, A., & Ahlqvist, T. (2010). Is the transport system becoming ubiquitous? Socio-technical roadmapping as a tool for integrating the development of transport policies and intelligent transport systems and services in Finland. *Technological Forecasting and Social Change, 77*, 120–134. doi:10.1016/j.techfore.2009.06.001

Tuominen, M., Rajala, A., & Moller, K. (2004). How does adaptability drive firm innovativeness? *Journal of Business Research, 57*(5), 495–506. doi:10.1016/S0148-2963(02)00316-8

Un, C. A., & Cuervo-Cazurra, A. (2008). Do subsidiaries of foreign MNEs invest more in R&D than domestic firms? *Research Policy, 37*, 1812–1828. doi:10.1016/j.respol.2008.07.006

Vaidya, O. S., & Kumar, S. (2006). Analytic hierarchy process: An overview of applications. *European Journal of Operational Research, 169*(1), 1–29. doi:10.1016/j.ejor.2004.04.028

Viotti, E. B. (2002). National Learning Systems: A new approach on technological change in late industrializing economies and evidences from the cases of Brazil and Korea (R.O.). *Technological Forecasting and Social Change, 69*, 653–680. doi:10.1016/S0040-1625(01)00167-6

Watanabe, C., Matsumoto, K., & Hur, J. Y. (2004). Technological diversification and assimilation of spillover technology: Canon's scenario for sustainable growth. *Technological Forecasting and Social Change, 71*(9), 941–959. doi:10.1016/S0040-1625(03)00069-6

Yasunaga, Y., Watanabe, M., & Korenaga, M. (2009). Application of technology roadmaps to governmental innovation policy for promoting technology convergence. *Technological Forecasting and Social Change, 76*, 61–79. doi:10.1016/j.techfore.2008.06.004

Yun, J.-H. J. (2007). The Development of Technological Capability and the Transformation of Inward FDI in Korea from 1962 to 2000. *Innovation and Technology in Korea*, 33-54.

Zhou, Y. (2008). Synchronizing Export Orientation with Import Substitution: Creating Competitive Indigenous High-Tech Companies in China. *World Development, 36*(11), 2353–2370. doi:10.1016/j.worlddev.2007.11.013

Chapter 7
E–Governance Adoption:
Identification of Success Factors from Teachers' Perspectives in Greece

Ioannis Karavasilis
University of Macedonia, Greece

Kostas Zafiropoulos
University of Macedonia, Greece

Vasiliki Vrana
Technological Education Institute of Serres, Greece

ABSTRACT

This chapter introduces Technology Acceptance Model, the Diffusion of Innovation model and constructs of trust, risk and personal innovativeness as a means of studying e-governance adoption. As governments around the world are moving forward in e-governance development it is important to identify factors that determine acceptance under specific circumstances prevailing in each country and give strategic insight to increase the usage of e-governance services. Primary and secondary education teachers responded to an online survey resulting to 230 questionnaires. A SEM validation of the proposed model reveals that Personal Innovativeness, Compatibility and Relative advantage are stronger predictors of intention to use, compared to trust, and perceived risk. The findings give some clues and directions for planning effective e-governance practices and could assist policy-makers with the first guidelines about which areas should be improved in order to enhance e-governance services.

DOI: 10.4018/978-1-61350-192-4.ch007

INTRODUCTION

National and local governments as well as many international organizations across the world, under the pressure of globalization, the changes in technology and the de-regulation in economic and social life, have made significant investments in bringing better governance to the people through the use of improved information and communication technologies (ICT) (Gupta, 2004; Mistree, 2007; Panagis et al., 2008). Information and communication technologies not only have the potential to improve the quality of services, but also to produce cost savings, make government policies and programs more effective, become more transparent, reduce discretionary decision making and introduce simpler methods and procedures in order to address the expectations of the citizens (Singh, 2007). Moreover, they can help public administrations to cope with the many challenges (Commission of European Communities, 2003; Gil-Garcia & Pardo, 2006). However, governments need to understand that e-governance is much more than technical issues (Lau, 2004) and should not focus on ICT itself. A mix of technological, administrative, social, human, legal disciplines must be created (Biasiotti & Nannucci, 2004) and governments should use ICT combined with organizational change and new skills in order to improve public services, democratic processes and public policies (Commission of European Communities, 2003).

Governments have largely left out the most legitimate stakeholders of e-governance the public users, during the conceptualization, development and implementation of the e-governance programs (Jain & Patnayakuni, 2003) and up to now are driving the development agenda of e-governance and the investment in electronic services based on their understanding of what citizens need and without measuring what increases citizens' willingness to adopt e-governance services. Mofleh & Wanous (1999 p.1) wrote "Governments must first understand variables that influence citizens'

adoption of e-Government in order to take them into account when delivering services online".

In order to explain and analyze the factors influencing the adoption and use of computer technologies several models have been proposed. They take into consideration attitudes, beliefs and intentions as these are important factors in the adoption of computer technologies (Bagozzi et al., 1992). The theory of reasoned action (TRA) (Fishbein & Ajzen, 1975); the Technology Acceptance Model (TAM) (Bagozzi et al., 1992; Davis, 1980) the theoretical extension of the TAM (TAM2) (Venkatesh & Davis, 2000); the Diffusion of Innovation (DOI) (Rogers, 1995) the Unified Theory of Acceptance and Use of Technology (UTAUT) (Venkatesh et al., 2003); the Perceived Characteristics of Innovating (PCI) (Moore & Benbasat 1991); the Prior Experience Model (Taylor & Todd 1995a); the Personal Computing Model (Thompson et al., 1991); the Task-Technology Fit Model (Goodhue 1995; Goodhue & Thompson 1995); the D&M IS Success Model (DeLone & McLean, 1992) and the Updated D&M IS Success Model Model (DeLone & McLean, 2003), are models widely used, alone or in combinations among them or in combination with related theories, to study the users' acceptance of the new technologies from different perspectives.

The study investigates factors that determine the adoption of educational e-governance websites by teachers of primary and secondary education in Greece. The term "educational e-governance websites" refers to the webpages of Greek School Network, the Ministry of Education, Lifelong Learning and Religious affairs, websites of Regional Primary and Secondary Education Administrations, and websites of Primary and Secondary Education Administrations. It uses constructs from the Technology Acceptance Model (TAM) and Diffusion of Innovation (DOI) and integrates the constructs of trust and risk in the model as they are well accepted models and have also been used to predict user acceptance in the field of e-governance. It measures intention-to-use e-government websites. Intention to-use has been found to be a strong predictor of actual system usage in the IS literature (Colesca & Dobrica, 2008). The study uses an online survey to record teachers; opinions and attitudes. It analyzes the data using a refinement procedure, controlling reliability and validity, and validates the proposed model using Structural Equation Modeling.

E-GOVERNANCE IN GREECE

The Constitution of Greece (2008, article 5A, paragraph 2) provides that everyone has the right to participate in the Information Society. The facilitation of access in the information handled electronically, as well as their production, exchange and distribution constitutes obligation of the State.

The e-government readiness index was undertaken by the United Nations in 2001 and included 191 countries worldwide (Jain-Palvia & Sharma, 2007). The e-government readiness index is a composite index comprising the web measure index, the telecommunication infrastructure index and the human capital index. The United Nations e-government readiness report (2008) ranked Greece's e-government project as number 44 worldwide with an e-government readiness index 0.5718. Greece dropped from the 35 position in 2005, to the 44 in 2008. The United Nations (2010) e-government development index (EGDI) is a comprehensive scoring of the willingness and capacity of national administrations to use online and mobile technology in the execution of government functions. It is based on a comprehensive survey of the online presence of all 192 Member States, in 2010. Mathematically, the EDGI is a weighted average of three normalized scores on the most important dimensions of e-government, namely: scope and quality of online services, telecommunication connectivity, and human capacity. Each of these sets of indexes is itself a composite measure that can be extracted and analyzed independently: EGDI = (0.34 X online service index) + (0.33 X telecommunication index) + (0.33 X human capital index). In the United Nations E-Government Survey (2010) Greece is placed in the 41st position with an EGDI index of 0.5708 and lags behind other EU countries (United Nations, 2010).

The Observatory for the Greek Information Society is established by the Greek Law 3059/2002 and it constitutes the main point of reference for accurate and up to date information. According to the Observatory for the Greek Information Society (2009), 54% of households in Greece have a computer while corresponding percentage in EU27 is 68% and in EU15 72%. Households with Internet access is 39.4%, 60% and 64% in Greece, EU27 and EU15 respectively. Households without Internet access, mentioned as reasons: 17% don't want to, 16% lack of skills, 7% high cost of equipment, 6% don't need it and 5% high cost of access. Former Prime Minister Konstantinos Karamanlis (2009) declared 'With the new Operational Program "Digital Convergence", of National Strategic Reference Framework (ESPA) 2007-2013 we aspire to lead our country in an equal level with that of the other advanced EU countries the EU regarding digital services. Our objective is to cover over 2 million households and enterprises all over the country, in the next seven-year period". Regarding e-government adoption and the percentage of individuals using the Internet to interact with public authorities 19% make transactions with public authorities, 15% obtain information from public authorities' websites, 11% download forms and 6% submit forms online. Indicative of the obstacles for the adoption of e-governance in Greece is the declaration of the President of Panhellenic Socialist Movement (PASOK) and currently Prime Minister of Greece, George Papandreou (2009) "Greece experiences a crisis in economy, politics, institutions and values. All Greek citizens feel the impact of this crisis almost in every aspect of their everyday. Citizens feel intensely the corruptness, the non-transparency, the bureaucracy, the obstacles, the overspending and the social exclusions" and he continues "Our suggestion is to develop electronic governance progressively, however in a fast, effective and efficient manner, based on the principle that the all public administration procedures are open to public".

Greek education system is centralized, by means that the Ministry of National Education lifelong learning and Religious Affairs formulates and implements the educational policy (Giamouridis, 2006; Massialas, 1981). The education system is also characterized by "intense bureaucratization, strict hierarchical structures, extensive legislation (polynomy) and "formalism""(Koutouzis et al, 2008, p.1). According to the Ministry of Education lifelong learning and Religious Affairs (http://www.ypepth.gr) 150,798 teachers are permanent civil servants while according to Ministry of Interior (http://www.ypes.gr) in Greece there are 370,517 permanent civil servants and approximately 550,000 on specific term employment contracts. It is interesting to investigate attitudes of teachers as they represent a percentage of 40.69% of permanent civil servants and 16.38% of all civil servants in Greece. Also they are all holders of University degrees and a previous study (Vrana et al., 2007) has shown that they have positive attitude towards e-governance websites. Adoption of e-governance websites by teachers is voluntary and can be viewed as evidence that teachers perceive them as a superior choice, extracting value from them, to the traditional paper-based, face-to-face and phone consultation services.

TECHNOLOGY ACCEPTANCE MODEL

TAM is the most widely accepted model of technology acceptance behaviors' as it has been proved parsimonious and robust in a wide variety of IT and across countries (Gefen, 2002; Han & Jin, 2009; Taylor & Todd, 1995b). TAM intents

"to provide an explanation of the determinants of computer acceptance that is general, capable of explaining user behavior across a broad range of end-user computing technologies and user populations, while at the same time being both parsimonious and theoretically justified" (Davis et al, 1989, p.985).

TAM was developed by Davis (1980) and Bagozzi et al. (1992) and is an extension of the TRA. TRA is a model from social psychology which is concerned with the determinants of consciously intended behaviors (Malhotra & Galletta, 1999). According to TRA salient beliefs and their normative beliefs are important predictors of a person's behavioral intention. TAM has also strong behavioral elements (Bagozzi et al., 1992). A person's actual system usage is mostly influenced by his or her behavioral intentions toward usage and are influenced by the perceived usefulness and perceived ease of use of the system. Attitudes can be used to predict behavior with considerable success under appropriate conditions (Petty & Cacioppo, 1981).

Fundamental constructs in TAM are: Perceived ease of use and perceived usefulness. Perceived ease of use is defined as "the degree to which a person believes that using a particular system would be free of physical and mental effort" and perceived usefulness of the system as "the degree to which a person believes that using a particular system would enhance his or her job performance" (Davis 1980, p. 320).

The major advantage of TAM is that it can be extended when new technologies are introduced by using domain-specific constructs. In this vein, Moon & Kim (2001) used TAM to explain user's behavior toward the World-Wide-Web (WWW). In their study, they introduced playfulness as a new factor that reflects the user's intrinsic belief in WWW acceptance. Devaraj et al. (2002) found that TAM components—perceived ease of use and usefulness—are important in forming consumer attitudes and satisfaction with the e-commerce channel. Koufaris (2002) used TAM along with

Consumer Behavior, and Flow and Environmental Psychology to provide a better understanding of consumer behavior on the web. Besides ease of use and usefulness, compatibility, privacy, security, normative beliefs, and self- efficacy are included in an augmented TAM by Vijayasarath (2004) to investigate intention to use on line shopping. Yi et al. (2005) produced insights into the factors that influence technology acceptance decisions by professionals and provided new ideas in the understanding of user acceptance of technology. Lee et al., (2003) comparing TAM and TPB examined the role and location of exogenous variables in explaining user acceptance of object-oriented technology. Zain et al. (2005) attempted to identify the relationships between IT acceptance and organizational agility in order to see how the acceptance of technology contributes to a firm's ability to be an agile competitor and Saade & Bahli (2005) used an extended version of TAM, including cognitive absorption to explaining acceptance of an on-line learning system.

In this vein, previous studies have used TAM to investigate factor that affect citizens' adoption of e-governance services. However, TAM alone was not able to explain issues of technology adoption related to e-Government. Additional factors, such as costs and technology maturity were considered as well. Colesca & Dobrica (2008) analyzed the case of Romania using TAM and they argue for the inclusion of trust, quality and satisfaction as attitudinal constructs on the basis of the e-government context. Al-adawi et al. (2005) proposed a conceptual model of citizen adoption of e-government which integrates constructs from the TAM and trust and risk literature. Using a variation of TAM also, TAM, TAM2, and DOI theory, and trust were used by Sang et al.(2009) to build a parsimonious yet comprehensive model of user adoption of e-Government. The findings of the study have shown that the determinants of the research model, perceived usefulness, relative advantage, and trust were supported. Jaeger & Matteson (2009) examined the relevance of

the TAM for e-Government websites at federal government level in the United States through an exploratory research study.

TRUST AND RISK IN E-GOVERNANCE

Trust is defined as "an individual's (trustor, here is citizen) belief or expectation that another party (trustee, here e-government) will perform a particular action important to trustor in the absence of trustor's control over trustee's performance" (Alsaghier et al., 2009 p.298). Trust is the foundation of any transaction that takes place between two parties (Schaupp & Carter, 2008), is central to daily interactions, transactions, and practices and is considered as a crucial enabler in e-governance adoption (Al-adawi, et al., 2005; Belanger & Carter, 2008; Colesca, 2009; Huang et al., 2006). Trust is difficult to be observed and measured directly. Recent studies, regard trust as dynamic concept with different developmental stages or phases each with specific characteristics rather than a static phenomenon. This dynamic view of trust "has led to the development of different trust models that identify different relationships and actors" (Tassabehji & Elliman, 2006 p.3). "Trust makes citizens comfortable sharing personal information, make online government transaction, and acting on e-Government advices" mentioned Alsaghier (2009, p. 295). Citizens' trust should be established in order e-government to succeed (Warkentin, 2002). "Because governmental agencies may be required by law to share information with other agencies or with the citizenry, the need for trust in the maintenance of accurate citizen information will increase" (Horst et al., 2007). Yet, citizens do not trust e-governance. The trust problem could be due to many critical factors such as the impersonal nature of the online environment, the use of technology, security issues and the uncertainty and risk of using open infrastructures (Al-Awadhi & Morris, 2009; Browne, 2001).

Teo et al. (2009) examined the role of trust in e-government success. In their model there are two dimensions of citizen's trusting beliefs toward an e-government Web site—trust in government and trust in technology. Colesca (2009) identified age, perceived usefulness, perceived quality, perceived concerns, perceived organizational trustworthiness, trust in technology, propensity to trust and years of internet experience as the factors that affect citizens' trust in e-governance. Five constructs, namely, disposition to trust, familiarity, institution- based trust, perceived website quality, perceived usefulness and perceived ease of use were used by Alsaghier (2009) to conceptualize trust in e-government.

Previous researches have tried to found the connection between trust and TAM (Gefen et al., 2003a, 2003b; Pavlou, 2003; Wu & Chen, 2005). Gefen et al. (2003a) found out that trust is an antecedent of perceived ease of use and perceived usefulness and influences behavioral intention to use. Pavlou (2003) claimed that trust is one of the factors that influence perceived usefulness and Wu & Chen (2005) that trust is considered as an important antecedent of intention to use and attitude.

Perceived risk is defined as "the citizen's subjective expectation of suffering a loss in pursuit of a desired outcome" (Warkentin et al., 2002, p. 160) and gives the trust dilemma its basic character (Al-adawi et al., 2005). Trust is needed only when uncertain situations exist and the level of risk perception decreases when the individual trusts others that are involved in the transaction (Horst et al., 2007; Johnson-George & Swap, 1982). Perceived risk has the impact on electronic service acceptance (Rotchanakitumnuai, 2008). Previous studies in the context of e-commerce indicate that perceived risk is a main barrier towards acceptance (Bahli & Benslimane, 2004; Pavlou, 2003; Lim, 2003). According to Pavlou (2003), in e-commerce perceived risk is composed of behavioral and environmental uncertainty. Behavioral uncertainty arises because online service providers have the chance to behave in an opportunistic manner by taking advantage of the impersonal nature of the electronic environment. Environmental uncertainty exists mainly because of the unpredictable nature of the Internet. Belanger & Carter (2008) claimed that the same happens for e-government. Featherman & Pavlou (2002) identified five indicators of electronic service risk: psychological, financial, privacy, performance, and time risk. Rotchanakitumnuai (2008) based on the work of Featherman & Pavlou (2002) and relative literature review explored the importance of five risk facets that affect the e-government service value: performance risk (a risk that the service will not work as expected), privacy risk (a risk that user's personal information may be misused), financial risk (a risk that users may have to pay more money), time risk (a risk that wastes time of the user as a result of making a wrong decision), and social risk (the potential change of status in one's social group as the result of adopting a product or service). According to their findings the three perceived risk concerns are performance, privacy, and financial audit risk.

Previous research has discussed the role of trust in reducing the risk as well the role of perceived risk in reducing users' intentions to exchange information and complete transactions (Pavlou, 2003; Warkentin et al., 2002). E-governance websites are much more than an information technology interface and are open to the public and accessible from anywhere in the world. "Different types of risks and uncertainties prevail in online transactions" mentioned Teo et al. (2009). For these reasons Al-adawi et al. (2005) claimed that perceived risk must be considered to explain citizens' intention to use e-governance websites. Thus, trust and risk are significant notions that should be investigated to understand citizens' adoption of e-governance.

DIFFUSION OF INNOVATIONS THEORY

The Diffusion of Innovations (DOI) theory was developed by Rogers (1995) in order to explain how an innovation diffuses through a society. "An innovation is an idea, practice, or a phenomenon perceived to be novel by an individual or a community" (Singh, 2008 p.1227) and diffusion is defined "as the process by which an innovation is communicated through certain channels over time among the members of a social system" (Rogers 1995, p.10). E-governance services can be considered as an innovation as they are perceived to be novel by citizen, and are delivered via the Internet (communication channel) to citizens, a community of potential adopters (Singh, 2008). An innovation creates a kind of uncertainty which is important in the diffusion (Lehmann, 2004).

Rogers (1995) identified five attributes that affect the rate of diffusion namely relative advantage, compatibility, complexity, triability and observability. Relative advantage is defined as "the degree to which an innovation is perceived as better than the idea it supersedes". The greater the perceived relative advantage of an innovation, the more rapid its rate of adoption is likely to be. Compatibility, as "the degree to which an innovation is perceived as consistent with the existing values, past experiences, and needs of potential adopter". An idea that is incompatible with someone values, norms or practices will not be adopted as rapidly as an innovation that is compatible (Robinson, 2009). Complexity is the "degree to which an innovation is perceived as difficult to understand and use". Innovations that are simpler to understand are adopted more rapidly than innovations that require the adopter to develop new skills and understandings (Robinson, 2009). Triability is the "degree to which an innovation may be experimented with on a limited basis". An innovation that is trialable represents less uncertainty to the individual who is considering it (Robinson, 2009). Finally observability is the "degree to which the results of an innovation are visible to others". Visible results lower uncertainty and also stimulate peer discussion of a new idea, as friends and neighbors of an adopter often request information about it (Robinson, 2009).

Previous studies considered DOI for investigation of e-governance acceptance and integrated it with other models (Carter & Bélanger, 2005; Patel & Jacobson, 2008; Sang et al., 2009). Sang et al. (2009) based on previous researches (Agarwal & Prasad, 1998; Carter & Bélanger, 2005) claimed that relative advantage, compatibility and complexity are more important than others in predicting intention to use a technology. Moreover complexity construct in the DOI is often considered as perceived ease of use construct in the TAM and triability and observability have no strong correlations between them and users' attitude toward IT adoption. Therefore they included only relative advantage and compatibility constructs in their research model. Sang's et al. (2009) views were adopted in this paper.

THE STUDY

In order to explore the factors that determine the adoption of educational e-governance websites of teachers in primary and secondary education in Greece, based on the aforementioned literature TAM, DOI, trust and risk are integrated to propose a model of user adoption of e-governance. According to Huang's et al. (2006) research model personal innovativeness influences the attitude toward e-governance adoption. Agarwal & Prasad (1998) developed a modified TAM based on the idea that personal innovativeness positively moderates the relationship between the perceptions of relative advantage, ease of use, and compatibility and the decision to adopt an innovation. Construct of personal innovativeness is integrated to the proposed model.

Consequently in the unified model, the following hypotheses are tested (Figure 1):

H1. Trust in e-government websites has an effect on perceived Risk.

H2. Perceived ease of use has a direct positive effect on Perceived usefulness.

H3. Perceived risk has a direct effect on Attitude towards use.

H4. Perceived risk has a direct effect on Intention to use.

H5. Trust in e-government websites has a direct effect on Attitude towards use.

H6. Trust in e-government websites has a direct effect on Intention to use.

H7. Perceived ease of use has an effect on Attitude towards use.

H8. Perceived ease of use has an effect on Intention to use.

H9. Perceived usefulness has a direct effect on Attitude towards use.

H10. Perceived usefulness has a direct effect on intention to use.

H11. Personal innovativeness has an effect on Attitude towards use.

H12. Personal innovativeness has an effect on Attitude towards use on intention to use.

H13. Compatibility has an effect on Attitude towards use.

H14. Compatibility has an effect on intention to use.

H15. Relative advantage has an effect on Attitude towards use.

H16. Relative advantage has an effect on Intention to use.

H17. Attitude towards use has a direct effect on Intention to use.

METHODOLOGY

An empirical research study was conducted using an online survey. Internet users have been chosen to be surveyed. The reason is that lack of e-Government usage focus primarily on the "digital divide" (Mofleh & Wanous, M; 1999). Colesca (2009, p32) wrote: "nonusers haven't favorable attitudes towards the use of electronic

Figure 1. The research model

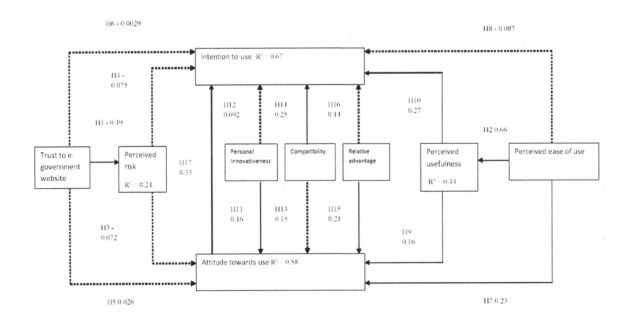

services in relation with the governmental agencies". Therefore, the research does not investigate people who are electronically incapable of accessing services.

A link to the main webpage of the Greek School Network (http://www.sch.gr) notified users of the website about the online questionnaire website. Users willing to participate visited a tailor made web site and responded to the questionnaire. The data were recorded to a database. The Greek School Network offers e-mail accounts (username@sch.gr form) and fully personalized access to education staff. In order to ensure that the responder was a teacher, the e-mail of the responder was recorded. From all questionnaires that were received only those of username@sch.gr form were admitted. Finally, 230 completed and usable questionnaires were received.

The questionnaire used in this study was adopted from previous studies. Five point Likert scales are used ranging from strongly disagree to strongly agree. The questionnaire consists of eight parts: 1)Trust in e-governance websites, 2) Perceived Risk, 3) Perceived Ease of Use, 4) Perceived Usefulness, 5) Innovativeness, 6) Compatibility, 7) Relative advantage, 8) Attitudes towards use, 9) Intention to use.

A pilot study using an extended questionnaire containing all the scales proposed in the literature review was conducted by administering the questionnaire to 50 primary and secondary education teachers. Finally, for each construct the scale presenting the largest Cronbach's alpha was decided to be included in the final questionnaire, since Cronbach's alpha provides the lower-bound estimate for the Composite Score Reliability, which is eventually used in the analysis of the resulting questionnaire (Table 1).

FINDINGS

Reliability and Validity of the Instrument

LISREL 8.8 was used to analyze the data using the maximum likelihood approach, with the item covariance matrix used as input.

Confirmatory Factor Analysis was used for model refinement. Testing the measurement model involves examining the convergent validity, discriminant validity, and internal consistency of the constructs. Reliability and convergent validity of the measurements are estimated by the item factor loadings, Composite Reliability, and Average Variance Extracted (Fornell & Larcker, 1981).

Convergent validity refers to the extent to which the items under each construct are actually measuring the same construct. Two methods were applied to assess convergent validity. First, item reliability was examined for each item, which suggested that the factor loading of each item on its corresponding construct must be higher than 0.55 (Teo et al., 2009). All items had a loading above the suggested threshold. Convergent validity was assessed by examining the average variance extracted (AVE) for each construct. The AVE for a construct reflects the ratio of the construct's variance to the total variances among the items of the construct. The average extracted variances are all above the recommended 0.50 level (Hair et al., 1998; Teo et al., 2009), Table 2.

Discriminant validity refers to the extent to which a given construct differs from other constructs. As all items loaded more heavily on their corresponding constructs rather than on other constructs, discriminant validity was satisfied. Further, the square roots of all AVEs were larger than correlations among constructs, thereby satisfying discriminant validity. Table 3 shows that all the inter-construct correlations are below 0.9. Also the estimated correlation between all construct pairs is below the suggested cutoff of 0.9 and this implies distinctness in construct content

Table 1. Items used

Trust in e-governance websites
adopted by Teo et al. (2009) Constructs also tested in pilot study: Colesca & Dobrica (2008); Sang et al.(2009)
1 e-government Web sites are trustworthy
2 e-government Web sites are seem to be honest and truthful to me
3 e-government Web sites can be trusted
Perceived Ease of Use
adopted from Carter & Bélanger (2005). Constructs also tested in pilot study: Colesca & Dobrica (2008); Sang et al.(2009) ; Shih (2004); Teo et al. (2009)
1 Learning to interact with a state government Website would be easy for me.
2 I believe interacting with a state government Website would be a clear and understandable process.
3 I would find most state government Websites to be flexible to interact with.
4 It would be easy for me to become skilful at using a state government Website.
Perceived Usefulness
adopted from Wangpipatwong et al. (2008). Constructs also tested in pilot study: Colesca & Dobrica (2008); Sang et al.(2009); Shih (2004); Teo et al. (2009)
1 Using e-Government websites enables me to do business with the government anytime not limited to regular business hours.
2 Using e-Government websites enables me to accomplish tasks more quickly.
3 The results of using e-Government websites are apparent to me.
4 Using e-Government websites can cut travelling expense.
5 Using e-Government websites can lower travelling and queuing time.
Risk
adopted from Belanger & Carter (2008)
1 The decision of whether to use a state e-government service is risky
2 In general, I believe using state government services over the Internet is risky
Attitudes towards use adapted from Shih (2004). Constructs also tested in pilot study: Huang et al. (2006)
1 I like to use government websites
2 It is pleasure for me to use government websites
3 It is desirable for me to learn how to use government Website
Intention to use adopted from Carter & Bélanger (2005). Constructs also tested in pilot study: Al-adawi et al. (2005) ; Belanger & Carter (2008); Huang et al. (2006); Sang et al.(2009)
1 I would use the Web for gathering state government information.
2 I would use state government services provided over the Web.
3 Interacting with the state government over the Web is something that I would do.
4 I would use the Web to inquire about state government services.
Personal innovativeness adapted from Huang et al. (2006),
1 I find it stimulating to be original in my thinking and behavior.
2 I am challenged by ambiguities and un-solved problems.
Compatibility Adopted from Sang et al. (2009). Constructs also tested in pilot study: Carter & Bélanger (2005)
1 I think using e-Government systems would fit well with the way that I like to gather information from government agencies.

continued on following page

Table 1. Continued

2 I think using e-Government systems would fit well with the way that I like to interact with government agencies.
3 Using e-Government systems to interact with government agencies would fit into my lifestyle.
4 Using e-Government systems to interact with government agencies would be compatible with how I like to do things.
Relative advantage adopted from Sang et al. (2009). Constructs also tested in pilot study: Carter & Bélanger (2005)
1 Using e-Government systems would enhance my efficiency in gathering information from government agencies.
2 Using e-Government systems would enhance my efficiency in interacting with government agencies.
3 Using e-Government systems would make it easier to interact with government agencies.
4 Using e-Government systems would give me greater control over my interaction with government agencies.

Table 2. Composite Reliability (CR), and Average Variance Extracted (AVE)

	Composite Reliability (CR)	**Average Variance Extracted (AVE)**
Personal Innovativeness	0.77	0.63
Trust in e-governance website	0.93	0.83
Perceived Risk	0.91	0.83
Perceived Ease of Use	0.87	0.64
Perceived Usefulness	0.93	0.74
Compatibility	0.91	0.74
Relative advantage	0.89	0.68
Attitudes towards use	0.89	0.75
Intention to use	0.92	0.76

Table 3. Inter-Construct Correlations

	Trust in e-governance website	**Perceived Risk**	**Perceived Ease of Use**	**Perceived Usefulness**	**Innovativeness**	**Compatibility**	**Relative advantage**	**Attitudes towards use**
Perceived Risk	0.36							
Perceived Ease of Use	-0.20	-0.49						
Perceived Usefulness	0.41	0.40	-0.30					
Innovativeness	0.41	0.39	-0.36	0.62				
Compatibility	0.41	0.51	-0.41	0.59	0.56			
Relative advantage	0.40	0.45	-0.32	0.64	0.55	0.71		
Attitudes towards use	0.49	0.44	-0.37	0.64	0.60	0.64	0.65	
Intention to use	0.48	0.46	-0.41	0.57	0.67	0.70	0.66	0.73

or discriminant validity (Gold et., 2001; Teo et al., 2009). As shown in Table 2, Composite Reliabilities are above the threshold of 0.7. Overall, the measures in this study are reliable and valid.

The Model Testing

Structural Equation Modeling (SEM) was used to test the hypotheses. The first step in model testing is to estimate the goodness-of-fit of the research model. Recommended fits are suggested from previous studies (Bagozzi & Yi 1988; Hair et al., 1998) goodness-of-fit index (GFI), Adjusted Goodness of Fit Index (AGFI), normed fit index (NFI), non-normed fit index (NNFI), comparative fit index (CFI), and the root-mean-square error of approximation (RMSEA) as the indices for evaluating the overall model fitness. The chi-square test provides a statistical test for the null hypothesis that the model fits the data, but it is too sensitive to sample size differences, especially where the sample sizes exceed 200 respondents (Fornell & Larcker, 1981). Bagozzi & Yi (1988) suggested a chi-square per degrees of freedom instead. All of the fit indexes indicate that the structural model has a good fit: Chi-square/d.f. ($\leq$ 3.0) = 2.39, GFI ($\geq$0.80) = 0.82, AGFI ($\geq$0.80) = 0.80, NFI ($\geq$0.90) = 0.96, NNFI ($\geq$0.90) = 0.97, RMSEA ($\leq$0.08) = 0.078, CFI ($\geq$0.90) = 0.98. The second step in model estimation is to examine the path significance of each hypothesized association in the research model and variance explained (R^2) by each path. The standardized path coefficients, and explained variances of the structure model are presented in Figure 1. In the presence of Personal Innovativeness, Compatibility, and Relative advantage, the findings reveal somewhat different properties compared to those reported in previous studies (Zafiropoulos et al., 2010).

While in Zafiropoulos et al. (2010) trust is found to have an effect on both the attitude towards use and the intention to use, findings from this study do not support the same properly (Figure 1). It seems that both Trust and Perceived Risk,

have no significant effect on either attitude towards use or to intention to use. Therefore, although hypothesis H1 is supported, hypotheses 3, 4, 5, and 6 are not supported. Regarding the negative effect γ=-0.49 of Trust to e-government websites on Perceived risk, a possible explanation would be that people, who trust governmental agencies, actually trust the employees who work there. Thus people who declare that they trust the government probably have high trust levels to the civil servants with whom they communicate and have good interpersonal relations. Using e-government practices, those people, might be afraid that they will lose this interpersonal relation with the civil servants, and this situation may increase perceived risk for the citizens. Dashti et al. (2009, p.3) mentioned: "A key distinction between public servants working in government and those working in e-government lies in their level of visibility and direct contact with the public, which in turn influences how much the public trusts them".

Further, concerning the effects originating from Perceived ease of use and Perceived Usefulness, the findings suggest that the original TAM model partially fits the data. Perceived ease of use affects Perceived usefulness (β=0.66) and has a direct effect on attitude towards use (β=0.23), but it does not have a significant direct effect on intention to use. Therefore, Perceived ease of use only has an indirect effect (β=0.1782) on intention to use, and H8 is partially supported. On the other hand, Perceived usefulness has direct effects on both attitude towards and Intention to use (β=0.16 and β=0.27 respectively). Finally, it seems that Personal innovativeness, Compatibility and Relative advantage have direct or indirect effects on attitude towards use or intention to use, but with only one of them each time. This means that when they have a direct effect on attitude they don't have an effect on intention and vice versa. In detail, Personal innovativeness has a direct effect on Attitude towards use (β=0.16), but not a significant effect on Intention to use. However, it does have a small indirect effect (β

=0.0528) to intention via the effect to Attitude towards use. Thus H11 and II12 are supported (the second through an indirect effect). Compatibility has only a direct effect to Intention to use (β=0.25) and has no effect on Attitude towards use (H13 not supported, H14 supported). Finally, Relative advantage has a direct effect on Attitude towards use (β=0.21), but not to Intention to use. The second is only indirectly affected by relative advantage through the effect of Attitude on Intention (β=0.0693). Thus H15 and H16 are supported, at least partially. Overall, considering direct and indirect effects of the variables and the sizes of the indirect effects, it seems that Compatibility is the most important predictor of Intention to use. Attitude towards use has a direct effect on Intention to use (β=0.33), supporting H17. This effect is larger than the effect of Compatibility but still it is comparable to it. Overall, first Attitude towards use, second Perceived usefulness and third compatibility are the three significant predictors of Intention to use.

CONCLUSION AND DISCUSSION

The findings show that in the presence of three new parameters (Personal Innovativeness, Compatibility and Relative advantage) Trust and Perceived Risk lose their predictive power. Considering the multidimensional properties of the model, this means that in the presence of the three variables, Trust to government websites and Perceived Risk predicted power is absorbed by the predictive power of the new variables. The three new key variables are constructs influencing directly or indirectly intention to use and attitudes towards use, but it is Compatibility that has an overall strong effect to intention to use. Personal innovativeness is the willingness of an individual to try out any new. Some teachers are more willing to take a risk by trying out innovation, whereas others are hesitant to change their practices. Highly innovative teachers are likely

to consider e-governance services as more favorable and its tangible results more demonstrable to them. So it is crucial to contact them first to try out e-governance services and then they can disseminate their positive experiences to others. Government can also train and educate teachers to increase their personal innovativeness. Teachers will use e-governance services more if they understand their value over the existing systems and will use them if it helps them to work more efficiently. The introduction of e-governance will not automatically create improved governance unless it is based on policies to promote the effective utilization of technology. Therefore governments should communicate to citizens the relative advantages of using online services from retrieving information to completing transactions. High levels of compatibility are also associated with increased intentions to adopt e-governance services that mean teachers who consider e-governance services compatible to their lifestyle intend to use e-governance services. This is a cultural theme and governments should invest in campaigning internet technologies at all stages of everyday life from business to leisure and emphasize work style compatibility. Moreover, government can classify civil servants into training groups, as to deliver different skills to different actors within the public administration arena.

Culture, welfare state, and political system influence the usage of e-governance (Patel & Jacobson, 2008) and citizens' behavior differs between countries (Colesca, 2009). For these reasons it is important to identify factors that determine acceptance under specific circumstances prevailing in each country and give strategic insight to increase the usage of e-governance. Additionally, the importance of measurement of e-governance is rooted in the contribution that the former can provide to monitor the efficiency and effectiveness of public spending. The findings give some clues and directions for planning effective e-government practices and could assist policy-makers with the first guidelines about which areas should be improved in order to enhance e-governance services.

Teachers in Greece represent a percentage of 40.69% of permanent civil servants and 16.38% of all civil servants in Greece (Ministry of Interior, http://www.ypes.gr). Adoption by them of e-governance has the potential to change the way that education administrations organizations carry out their tasks. Governments capitalize on the unique benefits of online services, explaining relative advantage to teachers work and promoting their use as a status of innovation, and indicating the services' congruence with a teachers' lifestyle. Further exploration and integration of additional adoption constructs is needed in order to develop a more comprehensive, yet parsimonious model of e-Governance adoption. Even though the study offers the first piece of evidence on e-governance website adoption by teachers, the recommendations would be helpful in developing and implementing new e-governance plans.

Although the original TAM fits the data fairly well, the findings suggest that by taking into account new variables, new conclusions arise that differ from previous ones. Further analysis is needed to clarify the interconnections among the variables.

REFERENCES

Agarwal, R., & Prasad, J. (1998). A Conceptual and Operational Definition of Personal Innovativeness in the Domain of Information Technology. *Information Systems Research*, 9(2), 204–215. doi:10.1287/isre.9.2.204

Al-adawi, Z., Yousafzai, Z., & Pallister, J. (2005). *Conceptual Model of citizen adoption of e-government*. Paper presented at The Second International Conference on Innovations in Information Technology.

AlAwadhi, S., & Morris, A. (2008). The Use of the UTAUT Model in the Adoption of E-government Services in Kuwait, In *Proceedings of the 41st Hawaii International Conference on System Sciences*, (pp. 1-11). Washington, DC, USA: IEEE Computer Society.

Alsaghier, H., Ford, M., Nguyen, A., & Hexel, R. (2009). Conceptualising Citizen's Trust in e-Government: Application of Q Methodology. *Electronic. Journal of E-Government*, 7(4), 295–310.

Bagozzi, R., Davi, F., & Warshaw, P. (1992). Development and Test of a Theory of Technological Learning and Usage. *Human Relations*, 45(7), 659–686. doi:10.1177/001872679204500702

Bagozzi, R. P., & Yi, Y. (1988). On the evaluation of structure equation models. *Journal of the Academy of Marketing Science*, 16, 74–94. doi:10.1007/BF02723327

Bahli, B., & Benslimane, Y. (2004). An exploration of wireless computing risks: development of a risk-taxonomy. *Information Management & Computer Security*, 12(3), 245–254. doi:10.1108/09685220410542606

Belanger, F., & Carter, L. (2008). Trust and risk in e-government adoption. *The Journal of Strategic Information Systems*, 17(2), 165–176. doi:10.1016/j.jsis.2007.12.002

Biasiotti, M. A., & Nannucci, R. (2004). Teaching egovernment in Italy. In R. Traunmóller (Ed.), *Proceedings of the Third International Conference* (pp. 460–463). Zaragoza, Spain: EGOV.

Browne, C. (2001). Saudie –Commerce Conference Lauded by Major Saudi Industry Experts, ITP.

Carter, L., & Bélanger, F. (2005). The Utilization of E-Government Services: Citizen Trust, Innovation and Acceptance Factors. *Information Systems Journal*, 15(1), 5–25. doi:10.1111/j.1365-2575.2005.00183.x

Colesca, S. E. (2009). Increasing e-trust: a solution to minimize risk in the e-government adoption. *Journal of Applied Quantitative Methods*, *4*(1), 31–44.

Colesca, S. E., & Dobrica, L. (2008). Adoption and use of e-government services: The case of Romania. *Journal of Applied Research and Technology*, *6*(3), 204–217.

Commission of European communities (2003). *The Role of eGovernment for Europe's Future* SEC(2003) 1038 Retrieved June 8 2010, from http://ec.europa.eu/ information_society/ eeurope /2005/doc/all_about/ egov_communication_en.pdf

Dashti, A. Benbasat, I., & Burton-Jones, A. (2009). *Developing trust reciprocity in electronic government: The role of felt trust*. European and Mediterranean Conference on Information Systems 2009 (July 13-14 2009, Crowne Plaza Hotel, Izmir. Retrieved March, 25 2010, from http://www.iseing.org/ emcis/EMCIS2009/ Proceedings/Presenting%20Papers /C16/C16.pdf

Davis, F. (1980). Perceived Usefulness, Perceived Ease of Use, and User Acceptance of Information Technology. *Management Information Systems Quarterly*, *13*, 318–341.

DeLone, W., & McLean, E. (1992). Information Systems Success: The Quest for the Dependent Variable. *Information Systems Research*, *3*(1), 60–95. doi:10.1287/isre.3.1.60

DeLone, W., & McLean, E. (2003). The DeLone and McLean Model of Information Systems Success: A Ten-Year Update. *Journal of Management Information Systems*, *19*(4), 9–30.

Devaraj, S., Fan, M., & Kohli, R. (2002). Antecedents of B2C channel satisfaction and preference: Validating e-commerce metrics. *Information Systems Research*, *13*(3), 316–333. doi:10.1287/ isre.13.3.316.77

Featherman, M. S., & Pavlou, P. A. (2002). Predicting E-services adoption: a perceived risk facets perspective. *Proceeding in the Eight Americas Conference on Information Systems*, 1034-1045.

Fishbein, M., & Ajzen, I. (1975). *Belief, attitude, intention, and behavior: An introduction to theory and research*. Reading, MA: Addison-Wesley.

Fornell, C., & Larcker, D. F. (1981). Evaluating structural equation models with unbearable and measurement error. *JMR, Journal of Marketing Research*, *18*, 39–50. doi:10.2307/3151312

Gefen, D. (2002). Customer Loyalty in e-Commerce. *Journal of the Association for Information Systems*, *3*, 27–51.

Gefen, D., Karahanna, E., & Straub, D. (2003a). Trust and TAM in online shopping: an integrated model. *Management Information Systems Quarterly*, *27*(1), 51–90.

Gefen, D., Karahanna, E., & Straub, D. (2003b). Inexperience and experience with online stores: the importance of TAM and Trust. *IEEE Transactions on Engineering Management*, *50*(3), 307–321. doi:10.1109/TEM.2003.817277

Giamouridis, A. (2006). Policy, Politics, and Social Inequality in the Educational System of Greece. *Journal of Modern Greek Studies*, *24*(1), 1–21. doi:10.1353/mgs.2006.0004

Gil-Garcia, J.-R., & Pardo, T. (2006). Multi-Method approaches to understanding the complexity of e-government. *International Journal of Computers, Systems and Signals, 7(2)*. Retrieved May 9 2010, from http://citeseerx.ist.psu.edu/ viewdoc/download? doi=10.1.1.102.3801&rep=rep1&type=pdf

Gold, A. H., Malhotra, A., & Segars, A. H. (2001). Knowledge management: an organization capabilities perspective. *Journal of Management Information Systems*, *18*(1), 185–214.

Goodhue, D. L. (1995). Understanding user evaluations of information systems. *Management Science, 41*(12), 1827–1844. doi:10.1287/mnsc.41.12.1827

Goodhue, D. L., & Thompson, R. L. (1995). Task-technology fit and individual performance. *Management Information Systems Quarterly, 19*(2), 213–236. doi:10.2307/249689

Gupta, M. P. (2004). *Promise of E-Governance: Operational Challenges.* New Delhi: Tata Mc-Graw-Hill Publishing Company Limited.

Hair, F. Jr, Anderson, R. E., Tatham, R. L., & Black, W. C. (1998). *Multivariate data analysis* (5th ed.). Upper Saddle River, NJ: Prentice Hall.

Han, L., & Jin, Y. (2009). *A Review of Technology Acceptance Model in the E-commerce Environment,* 2009 International Conference on Management of e-Commerce and e-Government.

Horst, M., Kuttschreuter, M., & Gutteling, J. (2007). Perceived usefulness, personal experiences, risk perception and trust as determinants of adoption of e-government services in The Netherlands. *Computers in Human Behavior, 23,* 1838–1852. doi:10.1016/j.chb.2005.11.003

Huang, S.-Y., Chang, C.-M., & Yu, T.-Y. (2006). Determinants of user acceptance of the e-Government services: The case of online tax filing and payment system. *Government Information Quarterly, 23*(1), 97–122. doi:10.1016/j.giq.2005.11.005

Jaeger, P. T., & Matteson, M. (2009). e-Government and Technology Acceptance: the Case of the Implementation of Section 508 Guidelines for Websites. *Electronic. Journal of E-Government, 7*(1), 87–98.

Jain, A., & Patnayakuni, R. (2003). Public Expectations and Public Scrutiny: An agenda for research in the context of e-government. *Ninth Americas Conference on Information Systems.*

Jain Palvia, S., & Sharma, S. (2007). E-Government and E-Governance: Definitions/Domain Framework and Status around the World. *5th International conference on e-governance,* 28-30 December, Hyderabad, India

Johnson-George, C., & Swap, W. (1982). Measurement of Specific Interpersonal Trust: Construction and Validation of a Scale to Access Trust in a Specific Other. *Journal of Personality and Social Psychology, 43,* 1306–1317. doi:10.1037/0022-3514.43.6.1306

Joia, L. A. (2006). A Framework for Developing Regional E-Government Capacity- Building Networks. *The Massachusetts Institute of Technology Information Technologies and International Development, 2*(4), 61–73. doi:10.1162/154475205775249328

Karamanlis, K. (2009). The developmental vision in an upcoming word. *SEPE news, 30,* 6-9.

Koufaris, M. (2002). Applying the Technology Acceptance Model and flow theory to online consumer behavior. *Information Systems Research, 13*(2), 205–223. doi:10.1287/isre.13.2.205.83

Koutouzis, E., Bithara, P., Kyranakis, S., Mavraki, M., & Verevi, A. (2008). Decentralizing Education in Greece: In search for a new role for the school leaders. *CCEAM 2008 Conference* April 20, 2009 from http://www.emasa.co.za/ files/full/H2.pdf

Lau, E. (2004). Principaux enjeux de l'administration ılectronique dans les pays membres de l'OCDE. In *Revue Franηaise d'Administration Publique, 110* (pp. 225–244). Paris: Icole Nationale d'Administration.

Lee, S., Kim, I., Rhee, S., & Trimi, S. (2006). The role of exogenous factors in technology acceptance: The case of object-oriented technology. *Information & Management, 43*(4), 469–480. doi:10.1016/j.im.2005.11.004

Lehmann, K. (2004). *Innovation Diffusion Theory* Rogers & Bass Model DiscussionHumboldt-Universität Berlin, Wirtschaftswissenschaftliche Fakultät Institut für Entrepreneurship/ Innovationsmanagement Retrieved April 3, 2010, from http://www.grin.com/ e-book/80117/ innovation-diffusion-theory

Lim, N. (2003). Consumers' perceived risk: sources versus consequences. *Electronic Commerce Research and Applications*, *2*, 216–228. doi:10.1016/S1567-4223(03)00025-5

Malhotra, Y., & Galletta, D. (1999). Extending the Technology Acceptance Model to Account to Account for Social Influence: Theoretical Bases and Empirical Validation. In *Proceedings of the 32nd Hawaii International Conference on System Sci*ences.

Massialas, V. (1981). The Educational System of Greece. *Superintendent of Documents*, Washington, DC 20402: U.S, Government Printing Office.

Mistree, D. (2007). Exploring e-governance. Salience, Trends and Challenges. *Mapping Sustainability*, 261-275

Mofleh, S., & Wanous, M. (1999). Understanding Factors Influencing Citizens Adoption of e-Government Services in the Developing World: Jordan as a Case Study. *Journal of Computer Science*, *7*(2), 1–11.

Moon, J.-W., & Kim, Y.-G. (2001). Extending the TAM for a World-Wide-Web context. *Information & Management*, *38*(4), 217–230. doi:10.1016/S0378-7206(00)00061-6

Moore, G. C., & Benbasat, I. (1991). Developing of an instrument to measure the perceptions of adopting an information technology innovation. *Information Systems Research*, *2*(3), 192–222. doi:10.1287/isre.2.3.192

Observatory for the Greek Information Society. (2009). *Measurment of eEurope/i2010. Indicators for Greece 2008* Findings. Retrieved October 10 2009, from htt://www.observatory.gr

Panagis, Y., Sakkopoulos, E., Tsakalidis, A., Tzimas, G., Sirmakessis, S., & Lytras, M. D. (2008). Techniques for mining the design of e-government services to enhance end-user experience. *Int. J. Electronic Democracy*, *1*(1), 32–50. doi:10.1504/IJED.2008.021277

Papandreou, G. (2009).e-governance for the citizen. *SEPE news*, 30,12-15.

Patel, H., & Jacobson, D. (2008). Factors Influencing Citizen Adoption of E-Government: A Review and Critical Assessment In Golden W, Acton T, Conboy K, van der Heijden H, Tuunainen VK (eds.), *16th European Conference on Information Systems* (pp.1058-1069), Galway, Ireland.

Pavlou, P. A. (2003). Consumer Acceptance of Electronic Commerce: Integrating Trust and Risk with the Technology Acceptance Model. *International Journal of Electronic Commerce*, *7*(3), 69–103.

Petty, R. E., & Cacioppo, J. T. (1981). *Attitudes and Persuasion: Classic and Contemporary Approaches*. Dubuque, Iowa: Wm. C. Brown Company Publishers.

Robinson, L. (2009). A summary of Diffusion of Innovations. Retrieved May 5 2010, from http://www.enablingchange. com.au /Summary_Diffusion_Theory.pdf

Rogers, E. M. (1995). *Diffusion of innovations* (4th ed.). New York: Free Press.

Rotchanakitumnuai, S. (2008). Measuring e-government service value with the E-GOVSQUAL-RISK model. *Business Process Management Journal*, *14*(5), 724–737. doi:10.1108/14637150810903075

Saade, R., & Bahli, B. (2005). The impact of cognitive absorption on perceived usefulness and perceived ease of use in on-line learning: an extension of the technology acceptance model. *Information & Management, 42*(2), 317–327. doi:10.1016/j.im.2003.12.013

Sang, S., Lee, J.-D., & Lee, J. (2009). E-government adoption in ASEAN: the case of Cambodia. *Internet Research, 19*(5), 517–534. doi:10.1108/10662240910998869

Schaupp, L. C., & Carter, L. (2008). The impact of trust, risk and optimism bias on E-file adoption. *Information Systems Frontiers*. doi:.doi:10.1007/s10796-008-9138-8

Shih, H. P. (2004). Extended technology acceptance model of Internet utilization behavior. *Information & Management, 41*(6), 719–729. doi:10.1016/j.im.2003.08.009

Singh, M., Sarkar, P., Dissanayake, D., & Pittachayawan, S. (2008). Diffusions of e-government services in Australia: Citizens' perspectives In *16th European Conference on Information Systems* Golden W, Acton T, Conboy K, van der Heijden H, Tuunainen VK (eds.) (pp. 1227-1238), Galway, Ireland.

Singh, V. (2007). Full Circle of Governance: How to Leverage Age Old Organic Structure of Governance. Paper presented at *5th International Conference on e-governance. 28-30 December 2007* Hyderabad,India Retrieved November 28, 2009, from http://www.iceg.net/2007/books/3/2_281_3.pdf

Tassabehji, R., & Elliman, T. (2006).Generating citizen trust in e-government using a trust verification agent: a research note. *European and Mediterranean Conference on Information Systems* (EMCIS) 2006, July 6-7 2006, Costa Blanca, Alicante, Spain. Retrieved November 12, 2009, from http://www.iseing.org/ emcis/EMCIS2006/Proceedings/Contributions/ EGISE/eGISE4.pdf

Taylor, S., & Todd, P. (1995a). Assessing IT usage: The role of prior experience. *Management Information Systems Quarterly, 19*(4), 561–570. doi:10.2307/249633

Taylor, S., & Todd, P. (1995b). Understanding Information Technology usage: A test of competing models. *Information Systems Research, 6*(2), 144–176. doi:10.1287/isre.6.2.144

Teo, T., Srivastava, S., & Jiang, L. (2008). Trust and Electronic Government Success: An Empirical Study. *Journal of Management Information Systems, 25*(3), 99–131. doi:10.2753/MIS0742-1222250303

Thompson, R. L., Higgins, C. A., & Howell, J. M. (1991). Personal computing: Toward a conceptual model of utilization. *Management Information Systems Quarterly, 15*(1), 125–143. doi:10.2307/249443

United Nations. (2008). UN e-government survey 2008 From E-Government to connected governance, Retrieved April 23, 2009 from http://unpan1.un.org/intradoc /groups/ public/ documents/ UN/ UNPAN028607.pdf

United Nations. (2010). United Nations e-government survey 2010. Retrieved June 10, 2010 http://www2.unpan.org/ egovkb/global_reports /10report.htm

Venkatesh, V., & Davis, F. (2000). A theoretical extension of the technology acceptance model: Four longitudinal field studies. *Management Science, 46*(2), 186–204. doi:10.1287/mnsc.46.2.186.11926

Venkatesh, V., Morris, M., Davis, G., & Davis, F. (2003). User Acceptance of Information Technology: Toward a Unified View. *Management Information Systems Quarterly, 27*, 425–479.

Vijayasarath, L. (2004). Predicting consumer intentions to use on-line shopping: the case for an augmented technology acceptance model. *Information & Management, 41*(6), 747–762. doi:10.1016/j.im.2003.08.011

Vrana, V., Zafiropoulos, K., & Karavasilis, I. (2007). Quality Evaluation of local government website. A case of a primary education administration. Paper presented at *10th Toulon-Verona conference*, 3-4 September 2007, Thessaloniki.

Wangpipatwong, S., Chutimaskul, W., & Papasratorn, B. (2008). Understanding Citizen's Continuance Intention to Use e-Government Website: a Composite View of Technology Acceptance Model and Computer Self-Efficacy. *The Electronic.Journal of E-Government, 6*(1), 55–64.

Warkentin, M., Gefen, D., Pavlou, P. A., & Rose, G. (2002). Encouraging Citizen Adoption of eGovernment by Building Trust. *Electronic Markets, 12*(3), 157–162. doi:10.1080/101967802320245929

Wu, I.-L., & Chen, J.-L. (2005). An extension of Trust and TAM model with TPB in the initial adoption of on-line tax: An empirical study. *International Journal of Human-Computer Studies, 62*, 784–808. doi:10.1016/j.ijhcs.2005.03.003

Yi, M., Jackson, J., Park, J., & Probst, J. (2005). Understanding information technology acceptance by individual professionals: Toward an integrative view. *Information & Management, 43*(3), 350–363. doi:10.1016/j.im.2005.08.006

Zafiropoulos, K., Karavasilis, I., & Vrana, V. (2010). (to appear). Exploring E-governance by Primary and Secondary Education Teachers in Greece. *International Journal of Electronic Democracy.*

Zain, M., Che Rose, R., Abdullah, I., & Masrom, M. (2005). The relationship between information technology acceptance and organizational agility in Malaysia. *Information & Management, 42*(6), 829–839. doi:10.1016/j.im.2004.09.001

Chapter 8
E-Government Maturity Levels in Brazil:
Lessons Drawn from Several Brazilian States

Ciro Campos Christo Fernandes
Getulio Vargas Foundation, Brazil

Luiz Antonio Joia
Getulio Vargas Foundation, Brazil

ABSTRACT

This chapter examines the experiences of e-government programs in state public administrations, identifying differences in trajectory and levels of maturity achieved, by focusing on the Brazilian states of Alagoas, Minas Gerais, Paraná, Pernambuco and São Paulo. The study devised and implemented a framework for analyzing the development of e-government, incorporating components and factors related to strategy and organizational structure. The evidence collected corroborates the hypothesis that strategic vision, planning and organizational coordination structures are associated with experiences that have progressed through to the deployment of e-government projects of greater complexity. It was further detected that the alignment between strategy and program is a critical factor for achieving higher stages of maturity, although a linear and sequential linkage is not always verifiable between the stages of vision, planning, organization and implementation of electronic government.

DOI: 10.4018/978-1-61350-192-4.ch008

INTRODUCTION

In general, experiments in e-government are more easily recognized by the presence of Internet services, which is a high visibility aspect that seems to represent a means for obtaining tangible results swiftly and inexpensively. However, escalation by simply placing a growing number of Internet services should not be dissociated from concerns about their quality, comprehensiveness and adequacy to the needs of citizens (OECD, 1998; 2003; UKP-POST, 1999; Commission, 2003). Electronic government has the potential to transform the manner of rendering services to citizens and, from a broader perspective, the political relationship between the two parties (Fountain, 2001; Burn & Robins, 2003). However, e-government is faced with the characteristics of functional insularity that are typical of public administration. The integrating potential of new technologies can be undermined by the institutional bureaucracy of public administration (Marche & Mcniven, 2003).

In Brazil, e-government has been included on the agenda of federal government policies since 2000, incorporating a comprehensive vision of the strategic application of Information Technology (IT) in building the information society (Fernandes & Pinto, 2003). The prior trajectory of the organization of IT left a technological and institutional legacy that hinders progress, particularly in terms of functional verticalization and specialization that was exacerbated by the obsolete technology of centralized data processing (Saur, 1997).

In the Brazilian states, e-government is an item that is currently being assimilated in the government agenda, with several experiences in progress. A survey in 2003 found that IT management in state government is characterized by dismantling and decentralization, as strategic positioning plans are adopted separately in each organ (PNAGE, 2004). This situation reveals a degree of fragmentation and a lack of a coordinated and comprehensive policy. Another survey in 2006 detected advances in policy implementation, organizational struc-

tures and projects identified with the concept of e-government, particularly the dissemination of portals of unified services (Fernandes, 2006).

Thus, this chapter analyzes the trajectory of electronic government programs in Brazil focusing on the progress achieved in its states. It adopts the premise that there are identifiable levels of maturity associated with the degree and intensity with which projects and initiatives are transforming agents of the structures and processes. The hypotheses of the research consider that the maturity of e-government depends on the ability to give ongoing support to a process of transformation, requiring the alignment between strategies and structures of public administration and the e-government program.

BACKGROUND

The experiences of e-government are advanced applications of IT in the highly complex context of public organizations (Snellen, 2000). The need to provide prescriptive indications generated models for comparative analysis of experiences, based on parameters of maturation or development (Deloitte Research, 2000; Heeks, 2001; Accenture, 2002; PWC, 2002; UN/DPEPA-ASPA, 2002). The enhancement of these models depends on the incorporation of organizational factors and dimensions, and especially the strategic perspective, considering that it involves longitudinal experiences of prolonged maturation (Davison et al., 2005).

The application of information technologies can work towards a change in processes and the transformation of the organization, provided that it is geared to meeting the perceived needs for the achievement of institutional goals and objectives (Davenport, 1994; Hammer and Champy, 1993). A similar approach is found in the literature on the public sector, as the integration of IT systems and infrastructure on the management process is essential for effective results and reflects the

Figure 1. The Model of Davison et al. Source: Davison et al. (2005), adapted from Henderson & Venkatraman (1993).

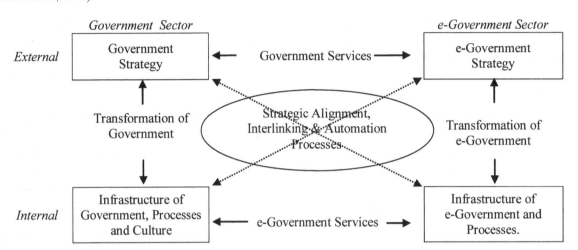

strategic vision of the organization (Kraemer e King, 1986; 2005; Kraemer & Dedrick, 1997; Margetts, 2003). But, the identification of the needs of the organization is far from occurring in an uncomplicated manner, as the politics within the organization and the interests and intentions of the participants affect the diffusion of innovations in IT (Markus & Robey, 1988).

The theoretical reference base of this research applies a model of strategic alignment adapted to the organizational context and the characteristics of electronic government, deploying and optimizing their development with the incorporation of constructs for a detailed analysis of the experiences in progress in the public administration of Brazilian states.

An Integrated Model of e-Government Maturity

An integrated model for assessing the maturity of e-government established by Davison, Wagner & Ma (2005) combines elements of traditional models of maturity with the approach of strategic alignment in IT of Henderson & Venkatraman (1993). The latter represents an application in the IT field of the theory of adjustment between the or-

ganization's strategy and its internal structure, the classic reference of which is the work of Chandler (1962). Thus, besides the adjustment between the organization's strategy and its internal structure, the adjustment between the IT strategy with the IT organizational structure and management is also required. The imperative of this double adjustment presupposes the organization's ability to coordinate and build support internally for sustaining a coherent orientation by aligning the IT area with the overall strategy. Figure 1 presents the model of Davison et al. (2005), developed from the original approach of strategic IT alignment, according to Henderson & Venkatraman (1993), and applied to the public sector.

The model assumes four critical areas for the alignment and sustainment of strategic coherence: (i) government strategy; (ii) infrastructure, processes and organizational culture of government; (iii) e-government strategy; and (iv) infrastructure and e-government processes. The strategic fit is the core variable that indicates the alignment between the (overall and e-government) strategies and the organizational components (infrastructure, processes and organizational culture).

Applying this approach to alternative trajectories of e-government development is the advance

Figure 2. Possible Sequences of Trajectories of e-Gov Deployment. Source: Davison et al. (2005)

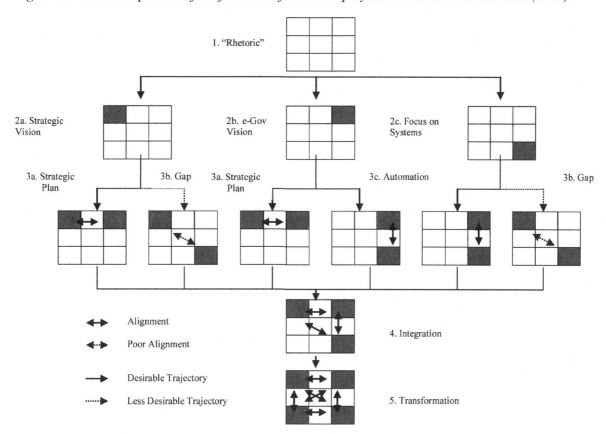

afforded by the integrated model. This model analytically incorporates various combinations between the development of electronic government services - the subject of several maturity models - and the construction and implementation of a strategy within the complex government context. The model stipulates five stages of electronic government maturity, with different configurations and alternative trajectories. Figure 2 shows the possible sequences of trajectories between the aforesaid stages and, for each of them, it presents in the boxes the matrix of alignment between general strategy, e-government strategy, government infrastructure and e-government infrastructure. Each domain is represented by the darkened box within the matrix.

In general terms, the model seeks to reflect the complexity and disparities that may occur between structure and strategy, considering that the organization responsible for conducting e-government can be organized and conducted with a degree of autonomy in relation to the government as a whole. The stages of maturity are linked together under different possible sequences, leading to specific configurations of alignment between strategy and structure. Stage 1 represents the manifestation of the outline of the intent of an e-government policy without a strategy or plan being configured in this sense. It is defined as the "rhetoric stage," witnessed by the mere presence of the website on the Internet.

Stage 2 is structured around the alternatives of initial engagement in e-government either by formulating a strategic vision of government (2a), building a strategic vision of electronic government (2b) or by the immediate development of electronic government systems or projects (2c). While the first two alternatives reflect a more conventional path structured around a formal-rational sequence, the latter reflects the choice for implementation without a previously outlined strategy.

Stage 3 permits very different configurations determined by the preceding trajectory, on a case-by-case basis. The trajectories that were initiated by the construction of the strategic vision of government (2a) can advance sequentially towards the achievement of a strategic plan of government, with its simultaneous deployment in the area of electronic government (3a), or follow a less desirable - though more plausible - path of immediate implementation of e-government services (3b). In this case, the achievement of progress will be negatively affected by the emergence of a gap between the strategy of government and the attempt to develop e-government systems and applications that are not adequately compatible with this strategy.

The trajectories initiated with the design of a specific strategic vision of electronic government (2b) may, in turn, be moving either toward the inclusion of this vision in a strategic vision of government as a whole (3a), yet to be defined, or toward the implementation of e-government services (3c). Both directions may be considered desirable, because they allow for adjustments, in the first case between strategies, and in the second between strategy and structure.

The trajectories that dispense with a strategic vision, whereby electronic government is launched via initiatives of introduction of IT systems and innovations (2c), can progress to the construction of an e-government strategy (3c), albeit led by the technological area. This is a desirable trajectory, as opposed to the unfavorable alternative of misalignment with the planning of the government as a whole (3b). The gap generated in this trajectory may originate either from a strategic vision that does not incorporate the treatment of e-government, and therefore a specific vision

and planning for IT, consistent with its requirements and potential (trajectory 2a-3b), or from the deployment of systems and services without the support of an e-government strategy (trajectory 2c-3b).

Stage 4 represents a confluence in which full alignment between government and e-government strategies and the structures and systems of electronic government is achieved (4). It enables the integration between services and a strong collaboration between agencies, although without resulting in changes in structures and processes in the back office. Stage 5 marks the end of the transition to e-government, with the transformation of structures and integrating organizational redesign, with full use made of the potential of IT (5).

Operationalization of the Model in the Research

As a core purpose of this research, an attempt was made to refine and operationalize the integrated model for detailed analysis of e-government programs and their institutional inclusion, incorporating evidence from recent surveys of Brazilian state experiences (Fernandes, 2006). With this in mind, the stages of development of electronic government defined by Davison et al. (2005) were itemized as typical sets of evidence, systematically defined on the basis of the model (Table 1). The construction of a descriptive framework of the trajectories (Table 2) sought to go beyond the elaboration of the formulators of the model, characterizing them in more detail with a vision to their inclusion in the research.

The first evolutionary stage of maturation is the configuration of electronic government as mere "rhetoric" (1) and not as effective public policy. The second stage may adopt one of three configurations: strategic vision of government (2a); vision of electronic government (2b) or focus on systems (2c). The third stage may also adopt one of three configurations: strategic plan-

Table 1. Typical evidence of configurations of the stages of electronic government

Stage/Configurations Typical Evidence
1. "Rhetoric"
Initiatives such as the creation of service and information sites on the Internet occur in an isolated manner conducted by organs and entities or as mere institutional disclosure of government. The organization and manner of operation of the IT area is traditional, inserted as a specialized tool or technical service.
2a. Strategic vision of government
The government has a clearly formulated and widely known strategic vision that identifies, gives unity and directs the administration toward transformation of the infrastructure, processes and culture. However, taking advantage of the potential of electronic government is not incorporated in this vision.
2b. Vision of electronic government
There is a strategic vision of e-government, but it is not based on a vision of government as a whole. The implementation of electronic government is hampered by the lack of strategic alignment of government.
2c. Focus on systems
Typical projects and initiatives of e-government are implemented in a sectorialized manner: service and information sites on the Internet, intranets, electronic mail (e-mail) and sectorial systems and databases. There is not a strategic vision of its alignment with overall public administration and government policy. These projects are limited in their scope and effectiveness due to the lack of coordination and integration.
3a. Strategic government planning
The planning of government objectives and goals includes electronic government. This planning expresses a strategic vision and is effective in its implementation, resulting in an e-government program aligned with the priorities of the government as a whole.
3b. Maladjustment between government strategy and electronic government
The lack of a strategic vision and planning of IT policy leads to the implementation of projects without the integrating and transforming potential of electronic government. There is a misalignment between government vision and planning and IT projects and initiatives. This situation can be attributed either to the strategic vision of government as a whole, or to the sectorialized deployment of IT projects.
3c. Automating electronic government
There is an e-government policy structured around strategic vision and planning of IT. Within the scope of this policy, there is a partial implementation of comprehensive projects in its development, with potential impacts on the entire structure of public administration: a unified portal of information and services; integration of systems and databases; government intranet (information highway) and electronic communication (e-mail and others). The implementation of this policy is limited by its isolation in the IT field.
4. Integrating electronic government
E-government policy is structured around a strategic vision and planning of IT, aligned with the vision and planning of the government as a whole. There is an advanced implementation of e-Government projects mentioned in stage 3c, spurred on by coordination and collaboration among agencies and entities. These projects create impacts on the entire structure of public administration, notably via standards for electronic services; integrated electronic systems and services involving systems and sectors; and information highway, government intranet and electronic communication throughout public administration.
5. Transforming electronic government
E-government policy and government policy as a whole aligned their strategic vision and planning, thereby enabling projects with an impact on government performance. These projects require prior restructuring of organs and entities geared to the integration between processes. A set of projects in advanced implementation includes: integration between unified attendance desk services; virtual organizational networks in strategic areas; electronic services for problem-solving with back office automation; electronic transactions; government intranet with telephone link-up and dissemination of virtual communication tools.

ning of government (3a); maladjustment between government strategy and e-government (3b), or automating e-government (3c). The next stage is integrating e-government (4) and the final stage is transforming e-government (5). The typical characteristics of these configurations of maturity stages of e-government are presented in Table 1.

The temporal sequencing between the configurations of stages results in alternative trajectories of

Table 2. Typical evidence of alternatives of maturation trajectories

Advance of Stage Trajectory Alternatives	Typical Evidence
From "rhetoric" to the insertion of electronic government in the government agenda Sequence of trajectory 1 - 2	
From "rhetoric" to a strategic vision of government Trajectory 1-2a	The government decides to formulate a transforming strategic vision, but there is no intention to adopt electronic government. The activities and projects in the IT area continue following the traditional model. Initiatives to provide services and information on the Internet continue to occur in an isolated and sporadic manner.
From "rhetoric" to a strategic vision of electronic government Trajectory 1- 2b	The intention to adopt electronic government is demonstrated in strategic management agencies or organs of the administration, leading to the decision to formulate a strategic vision of e-government. That vision remains limited to the areas involved with IT management.
From "rhetoric" to a "focus on systems" Trajectory 1-2c	Sporadic and isolated initiatives advance toward the implementation of projects and actions of electronic government, upon the initiative of the IT areas or organs and entities with entrepreneurial skills and resources.
From inclusion in the government agenda to planning and implementation of e-government projects Sequence of trajectory 2-3	
From a strategic vision of government to e-government inserted in strategic planning Trajectory 2a-3a	The transforming strategic vision requires the incorporation of IT as an enabling component of the integration and transformation of structures and processes. Consequently, the strategic planning of objectives and goals includes a series of e-government projects, aligned with government priorities.
From a strategic vision of government to strategic planning disconnected from e-government projects and initiatives Trajectory 2a-3b	The transforming strategic vision does not assimilate the potential of IT. Strategic planning does not include e-government projects as a central and priority issue. IT projects and initiatives are formulated in alignment with government planning, albeit without a long-term vision, thus falling short of its transforming potential.
From a strategic vision for e-government to electronic government inserted in strategic planning Trajectory 2b-3a	The strategic vision of electronic government spurs on and influences the construction of comprehensive and transforming strategic planning of government. Consequently, the strategic planning of government objectives and goals is aligned with the vision of electronic government.
From a strategic vision for e-government to automating electronic government Trajectory 2b-3c	The strategic vision of electronic government guides the formulation and implementation of e-government projects. These projects are conducted by different bodies and mechanisms of coordination and networking among agencies and entities that are restricted to the IT field.
From a "focus on systems" to automating e-government Trajectory 2c-3c	The performance of IT areas or of departments or organs responsible for computerization projects with horizontal impacts promotes progress toward electronic government as emerging policy and planning, albeit without support in government planning as a whole. These areas and/or agencies strengthen their integration into government with the formulation of strategic planning for IT that incorporates the concepts of electronic government. The projects are increasingly formulated and implemented in alignment with comprehensive e-government planning, but this policy remains limited.
From a "focus on systems" to the implementation of e-government projects and initiatives Trajectory 2c-3b	The performance of IT areas or agencies responsible for computerization projects enables the advance of projects to incorporate the concepts of electronic government, but government planning and its priorities are obstacles to projects with such characteristics. Consequently, its performance tends to be entrepreneurial in style, with the occupation of spaces and mobilization of support and resources to make projects viable with horizontal impacts on the whole public administration area. Unlike the 2a-3b trajectory, the projects incorporate an advanced vision of IT that finds no support in the planning of government as a whole.

continued on following page

Table 2. Continued

Advance of Stage Trajectory Alternatives	Typical Evidence
From planning and implementation of e-government projects to integrating electronic government	
Trajectory 3-4	The implementation with the results of a structured set of e-government projects is made possible by the strategic planning of government and its development into an e-government program (trajectory from 3a onwards) or the advancement of e-government programs when they are able to influence planning and organization of the government as a whole (trajectory from 3c onwards). These projects depend on collaboration and coordination among government organs, entities and areas, which requires the creation of sectors of strategic guidance from the government as a whole and from electronic government. In the first situation described, there is successful performance by pre-existing sectors of strategic coordination of government. In the second case, the coordination of e-government manages to break out of isolation and exploit the ramifications of IT projects and initiatives to achieve impacts at a strategic level. This results in structuring of government planning as a whole and its coordination agencies. The same trajectory may occur starting from the adjustment between government planning and the projects in the IT area (trajectory from 3b onwards).
From integrating electronic government to transforming e-government	
Trajectory 4-5	The transformation in structures and processes is made possible in a crucial manner by the implementation of electronic government projects. Levels of strategic coordination of government and electronic government tend toward convergence, and IT areas are increasingly intertwined with management. The agendas of modernization and innovation of management and electronic government also converge. The integrating potential of IT is used as an important facilitator for change in management.

maturation of e-government, as per the description presented in Table 2. Eleven alternative trajectories that are distributed throughout the four sequences of advancement from one stage to another more advanced stage were systematically devised.

Then, from mere "rhetoric," e-government can be included in the government agenda as part of a strategic vision of government (trajectory 1-2a); as a strategic vision of electronic government (trajectory 1-2b); or as projects and actions with components of e-government implemented in isolation (trajectory 1-2c).

The advance from the inclusion in the agenda to the structuring of e-government plans and projects can occur via different trajectories: the inclusion of e-government as a government planning program supported by a strategic vision of government (trajectory 2a-3a) or a strategic vision of electronic government (trajectory 2b-3a); the implementation of projects and initiatives of e-government planning disconnected from government planning as a whole, due to the lack of a vision of electronic government (trajectory 2a-3b) or the absence of vision and planning of the government as a whole (trajectory 2c-3b); and

lastly, the implementation of e-government as a structured program based on a strategic vision of the theme (trajectory 2b-3c), or an advance in e-government projects and initiatives for their horizontal dissemination, although without the backing of global government planning (trajectory 2c-3c).

The trajectories between the configurations of stage 3 and 4 and between stages 4 and 5 do not allow for alternatives. In the first situation, it is a question of evolving from projects or a program in e-government being implemented to the generation of impacts on the integration between government organs, entities and areas, spurred on by IT (trajectory 3-4). Advanced integration, with the transformation of structures and processes that provide new organizational models, marks the transition to a stage of greater e-government maturity (trajectory 4-5).

METHODOLOGY

This research is a multiple case study focused on the application of a model for analysis of the trajectory development of electronic government in five Brazilian states. The choice of a case study research strategy is based on the complexity and profusion of factors and circumstances that affect government policies with a transversal impact and range, such as electronic government (Yin, 2001; Vergara, 2005). The multiple case study enables the comparison and identification of critical factors for development of these experiences, particularly the association between these factors and the stages of electronic government.

The research drew on documentary sources and people linked to the organs responsible for e-government programs. Semi-structured interviews were conducted between October and December 2006, based on a list of open questions, directed at eight leaders of these organs in each state. A written record was generated after each interview and ratified by the source. In addition to this, documentation collected directly or by indication of the respondents was examined. The evidence obtained from the interviews was compared with the documentation. The survey sought to provide evidence for so-called literal replication of the approach under scrutiny (Yin, 2001: 123-127). The treatment of the data was guided by iterative analysis in light of the systematic dimensions, factors and evidence in the theoretical sphere (Eisenhardt, 1989).

DESCRIPTION OF THE CASES

The description of the cases that follows focuses on the experiences of the creation and implementation of electronic government through to the end of 2006 in the five states surveyed, namely Alagoas, Minas Gerais, Paraná, Pernambuco and Sao Paulo. The evidence was systematized in the form of narratives that seek to reconstruct the sequence of events and their relevant relationships for an analysis based on the evidence and the typical systematized trajectories unveiled in the previous section.

Alagoas: The state IT organization was the precursor in creating the government information and service website in 1996, which was an isolated initiative that already incorporated an embryonic vision of electronic government. From 2001 onwards, it began to deploy an information highway to serve the organs and entities of state government. The expansion of the information highway was linked to the provision of network services, especially e-mail, triggering the widespread use of micro-computers (PCs) and Internet access among state departments. The formulation of the vision of electronic government in the state emerged as an initiative of managers and technicians of that organ who during the course of 2003 successfully advocated its inclusion in the multi-annual planning for the 2004-2007 period.

Electronic government was included as an activity comprising one of the basic pillars of government planning, geared to the introduction of innovations in management. An intersectorial coordination structure established in 2004 set up the departments with transversal intercommunication, attributing the key role in formulating and implementing technical and operational projects to the IT sector. The IT support areas in all organs were also linked to a coordination structure reporting to the strategic command of electronic government.

The expansion of the information highway gained momentum with its institutional configuration as the government's information highway, use of which is mandatory and which integrates all the organs bodies. Major sectorial advances have occurred in projects structured around the provision of an Internet connection: distance learning; administration of management information about schools; automation and interconnection of procedures in police stations and the deployment of the health information system, using the interconnection between municipalities. In the area of government procurement, an Internet portal was launched in 2005 concomitantly with organizational restructuring of the sector through the creation of an entity providing administrative support services. The establishment of standards, supported by assessment evaluation and technical support mechanisms for government sites on the Internet, began to be introduced from 2006 onwards, though a single integrating portal of information and services on the Internet has yet to be implemented.

Minas Gerais: Electronic government arose pursuant to a request from the managers responsible for formulating the vision and strategic planning of the government that came into office in 2003. A survey conducted by technical consultants produced recommendations and the definition of actions incorporated in the government's plan, preparation of which was completed at the end of the same year. The electronic government proposed consists of a selected set of programs submitted to an intensive system of management, controlled by government command.

The program is conducted from a unit created in 2003 in the department responsible for the planning, budgeting and administration areas, supported by an intersectorial coordination structure that brings together all departments heads. In addition to this, an informal structure elicits broader participation of all IT area managers in a forum for exchanging information and discussing projects. The implementation of e-government projects during the 2003-2006 period was endorsed by the political weight and transversal insertion of that department, in a context in which alignment of the organs to a policy of fiscal adjustment supported by innovations in management was sought. The department in question was also responsible for coordinating this policy.

Electronic government reported advances in the generation of managerial information afforded by the corporate systems, enhancing the control of expenses, notably via tax collection and the payroll. The creation of a shopping portal on the Internet in 2004, and the dissemination of electronic bidding procedures and coordinated tenders between various organs enabled the unification

of relationship channels with suppliers and improved procedures, covering a significant portion of government purchases. With greater visibility, advances have also occurred in the provision of services and information via the Internet, namely a single integrating portal established in 2005, and the setting of standards, guidelines and goals for the sites linked to the portal. The integration between call centers and the single portal was another step forward that had a transforming impact on traditional work processes, as the call centers were unified and the attendance restructured to use information from the portal.

Paraná: The e-government policy was the result of a specific request from the state governor in 2000, involving managers and technicians of the Office of the Governor's Chief-of-Staff, the ombudsman, the department responsible for science and technology and the state IT company, for the development of the vision and planning of the program. In 2001, the program was formally institutionalized by a decree which defined its guidelines and coordination structure. Simultaneously, it launched the unified information and services portal of the government on the Internet.

E-government emerged in a context of weak state planning, marked by fragmentation and the lack of a unifying vision or priorities with a mobilizing impact on the entire administration. This assessment, taken from interviews, is corroborated by the absence of documentation containing the strategic vision and/or definitions of government except for multi-annual plans for budget programming that are mandatory in Brazilian public administration. This situation remained unchanged during the two subsequent government mandates after 1999.

The program is conducted at the strategic level by an intersectorial committee, from inside the Office of the Chief-of-Staff, based on working groups and on a systemic structure of coordination of all state departments, through their chief executives. The bulk of the technical and operational works is carried out by the state IT company, which plays an influential role in the articulation and formulation of projects. With a track record of solid performance in government through the provision of services on the Internet since 1995, this company has accumulated expertise in the area, coming to occupy a prominent position in the arrangements to sustain the program. Since the start of the new government mandate in 2003, the company acquired more autonomy in formulating and implementing projects, due to the exodus of personnel from the strategic coordination areas.

There has been a marked expansion and development in services offered on the Internet supported by cooperative efforts of the state IT company – responsible for updating the unified portal – along with other organs. The ongoing dissemination of data and information on the budget and public accounts has been conducted through a transparency website maintained by the government. The management of services remains fully decentralized and standards and mechanisms for monitoring and evaluation are not adopted.

The advances made in integration among systems are sectorial initiatives, a highlight in the recent period being the integration between systems in the area of collection and inspection for the control of the taxpayer's tax situation, involving registration in the income tax and highway department areas. Despite having a unified network infrastructure, provided by the state IT company, hiring and utilization of services remains the responsibility of each organ. The hiring of equipment and services and management of IT resources also remains fully decentralized

Pernambuco: Interest in electronic government came in the form of precursory initiatives in the supply of connectivity, network services, communication via email and website development by the state IT company from 1995 onwards. The company incorporated Internet coordination within its structure, by organizing training and disseminating events, thereby fostering the interest of state departments in the new tools and technologies. In the period prior to 1998, it

developed these services and enhanced the exploitation of their potential, with the provision of public Internet access in the state library and the computerization of the official gazette. These were innovations that resulted from projects developed for clients of the company within the sphere of public administration.

The period of government between 1999 and 2002 saw the creation of a vision, in tandem with government planning, marked by an emphasis on state reform, though without specific treatment of IT in the strategic formulation of the time. Nevertheless, leaders of the IT company concentrated on designing models and gaining acceptance of a comprehensive e-government program by the upper echelons of government. Transition planning for the subsequent government mandate – one of continuity, since the governor was re-elected – was marked by the explicit incorporation in early 2003 of electronic government as a program with its related structures for coordination and implementation. This e-government program was included as a support tool for the modernization of management and institutional reform in the state.

The organizational structure adopted houses the e-government program in the sector responsible for state reform. There are also sectors of intersectorial strategic coordination and operationalization of projects and activities, the latter involving the IT areas of the departments. One notable characteristic is that this structure was created in the wake of widespread organizational restructuring of the state as part of a new design seeking to establish mechanisms for horizontal coordination between the departments and agencies. Moreover, the restructuring included the state IT company, which was transformed into an agency to reflect a new format for organization and action, focused on project development and outsourced procurement of services.

The creation of an inclusive information highway to integrate the organs and entities of state administration was a priority project that was completed in 2005. Since then, it has been managed by hiring unified access and network services, with the introduction of this previously untried outsourcing model. A similar project is underway to engage services of data storage, applications and equipment maintenance. The period from 2003 to 2006 saw sectorial advances in the development of electronic systems and services with the intensive use of Internet and network communication. These include the computerization of the highway area (State Traffic Department) and the Department of Finance, the implementation of online appointment scheduling over the Internet for the National Health System, as well as school enrollment controlled by a single computerized system for the public elementary school grid.

Corporate systems for automation of administrative activities common to the organs and entities are in the process of being technologically upgraded in the areas of payroll, personnel and purchasing control, including the creation of services and access to information on the Internet. In the case of government procurement, the creation of a portal on the Internet gave rise to more profound change, transforming traditional procedures, with the spread of electronic bidding procedures and services to government suppliers. In general, the provision of Internet services through government websites continues to be decentralized with the consequent dispersion of initiatives. There is no progress toward creating a unified portal for information and services. Similarly, the initiatives of integration between systems are still sporadic, though with important innovations such as the deployment of an integrated management system for managerial information.

São Paulo: Since 1995, there emerged a government strategy directly geared toward tax adjustment, promoting projects and initiatives in the area of management that require coordination and transversality covering the entire state public administration. The implementation of this strategy has generated a demand for information and control systems with advanced IT applications. However, there was a lack of strategic vision of electronic government at that time. The planning and building of organizational structures consistent with strategic IT inclusion were postponed for a prolonged period. Thus, in Sao Paulo the implementation of electronic government relied on informal arrangements and its structuring as a program only occurred in 2003.

In the period from 1995 to 1998, projects with a critical impact on the performance of tax adjustment were implemented, as they enhanced the integration and control over the entire state administration structure. A strategic information system supported the coordination of projects and priority actions under the direct control of the governor. Other systems were developed for the control of expenses with personnel and outsourcing, and the registration of real estate and governmental actions by municipalities. These initiatives were accomplished without the use of Internet resources, using a technological infrastructure that fell far short of its needs.

In the area of finance, a major sectorial breakthrough was achieved during this period with the computerization of tax collection and financial administration. On the other hand, innovation in the delivery of services to citizens was introduced using what had been a highly successful precedent, though removed from the use of new IT resources, namely the unification of services in a single physical space (a project called "Poupatempo" i.e. Timesaver) was not associated with the computerization of procedures and use of the Internet.

The construction of an information highway infrastructure with network services and the subsequent unification of procurement and management of services occurred in the period from 1999 through 2002. Also during this period, the creation of online Internet auctions, combined with other support tools of government procurement, sparked off changes in government tendering procedures in all organs. The creation of government sites was relatively insignificant as a first step in e-government, though the supply of services and information over the Internet spread

Table 3. Configurations and trajectories of electronic government

Case	Configuration				
Alagoas	Rhetoric (1)	Focus on systems (2c)	Automating electronic government (3c)	Integrating electronic government (4)	
Minas Gerais		Strategic vision of government (2a)	Strategic government planning (3a)	Integrating electronic government (4)	
Paraná	Rhetoric (1)	Vision of electronic government (2b)	Automating electronic government (3c)		
Pernambuco	Rhetoric (1)	Focus on systems (2c)	Maladjustment between strategy and electronic government (3b)	Integrating electronic government (4)	
São Paulo		Strategic vision of government (2a)	Maladjustment between strategy and electronic government (3b)	Integrating electronic government (4)	
Level of Maturity	1	2	3	4	5

widely, albeit without systematic monitoring and evaluation structures. The creation of a unified portal with advanced resources of information and navigation organization in 2005 replaced the previous portal, which had been operated using a simple redirect function

Between 1995 and 2002, the e-government initiatives were conducted by a team of multi-institutional origin, constituted within the Office of the Governor's Chief-of-Staff subsequently converted into the government and management department. This team benefited from the ease of interaction with the whole government, as well as privileged access to the governor and the technical support of the state IT company. The concern with the creation of a formal structure emerged with the distancing and subsequent death of the governor during the period from 1999 to 2001. The governor had been directly involved with e-government projects and had exercised personal leadership over them

However, the program and its organizational structure were only implemented in 2003 with the creation of an intersectorial coordination body that resulted from the transformation of the structure originally focused on management quality strategic actions. Thus, the strategic control

unified e-government with the innovation agenda in management. The technical team that had worked informally was incorporated in the new arrangement, including pre-existing IT coordination units structured in a traditional manner. An important step was the creation of strategic-level positions in the structures of all organs and entities to conduct projects in IT, giving capillarity to the operationalization of projects and activities of e-government.

Despite the inclusion and scope of this structure, the managers interviewed revealed an emerging dispute over control of the program involving the state IT company's attempt to broaden its sphere of action and influence. This evidence indicates a possible weakening of the ties between e-government and government strategy as a whole, which might eventually result in more autonomous operation of the company and the consequent isolation of the program in the IT area.

ANALYSIS OF THE RESULTS

The configurations and trajectories followed by electronic government are quite varied, as shown in Table 3, which also indicates the level of maturity attained in each state. An attempt was made to compare the evidence of the cases with the typical systematized evidence in Tables 1 and 2. The following paragraphs list the analysis on a state-by-state basis.

Alagoas: There are reports of sporadic website creation initiatives on the Internet since 1996, revealing an early stage ("rhetoric") of e-government. The deployment of the information highway and network services from 2001 onwards represents an innovative mode of intervention by the state IT agency, which is geared to transversal projects and focused on the customer. This marks the transition to evolution to the "focus on systems" stage (2c). The formulation by the IT organ of a strategic vision of electronic government and commitment to its assimilation by government planning as a whole indicates progress to the next stage, namely "automating electronic government" (3c) in the course of 2003. The incorporation of e-government to statewide planning and concomitant creation of its strategic coordination structures marks the transition to "integrating electronic government" (4). Projects that depend on intersectorial coordination, such as the creation of a unified shopping portal, standardization of government websites and consolidation of the information highway, are associated with this stage in Alagoas.

Minas Gerais: No evidence was collected of a precursory stage (1) in Minas Gerais. Electronic government emerges in the course of 2003, due to the need perceived during the discussion of the strategic vision of the government to focus on IT and its potential. This short stage can be construed as that of the "strategic vision of government" (2a), the dynamic of which is moving towards the incorporation of e-government projects to the planning of priority actions of the government as a condition for making that vision viable. However, there is temporal simultaneity between the construction of the strategic vision of government, carrying out a diagnosis of the IT area, strategic government planning and the decision on priority

projects. Thus, the stage of "strategic government planning" (3a) does not fit in sequentially and is hardly distinguishable from the previous stage (2a). Similarly, the integrating electronic government (4) has already been mapped out since 2003, with the creation of coordination structures and the e-government program. Evidence of implementation of projects based on the integration between organs and entities are identified after 2004, with the unified information and service portal and the government procurement portal.

Paraná: Since 1995 there were precursory initiatives by the state IT company, especially the creation of a website on the Internet. In 2000, the creation of an e-government policy was requested by the governor, but it was disconnected from the vision and planning of government. This situation can be classified as the "vision of electronic government" stage (2b), which in the case of Paraná was unable to elicit the construction of more comprehensive planning. The implementation of a unified government portal, already in construction by the state IT company, occurred simultaneously with the creation of the e-government program and its coordination structure in 2001. The "automating electronic government" stage (3c) was outlined since then, with the weakening of the strategic coordination throughout the subsequent period. The weakness of government planning has led to a more autonomous role of the state IT company, accentuating the isolation of electronic government. The implementation of integrating projects such as the unified portal and the information highway are operating below their potential, possibly due to a lack of coordination capacity over government as a whole.

Pernambuco: Precursory initiatives had occurred since 1995, with intense activity of the state IT company that evolved from isolated and experimental projects, associated with the first stage of electronic government ("rhetoric") to the effective dissemination of models, tools and services typical of electronic government. The advance to the "focus on systems" stage (2c) can be associated with the introduction of advanced projects of electronic services, witnessed by the computerization of transactions and the publication of the official gazette. However, it is not possible to define precisely the beginning of that stage.

The performance of the state IT company remains isolated, though during the period of government between 1999 and 2002, the leaders advocated the need for an e-government program in a context in which the government was building its strategic vision and planning geared toward the reform of the state. Thus, this period is associated with the configuration of a "maladjustment between government strategy and systems of e-government" (3b), the main characteristic of which seems to be the dispute and possible resistance to assimilation of electronic government at the strategic decision level. From 2003 onwards, the creation of the program and the structures for its coordination and the subsequent restructuring of the IT area throughout the state administration are a clear indication of the emergence of "integrating electronic government" (4). However, the profile of the progress achieved since then indicates a certain prevalence for actions for the construction of infrastructure in relation to developments in electronic government services. Taking advantage of the installed infrastructure in the development of electronic government services is recommended for the maturation of this experience and progressing to the next stage.

São Paulo: There is no precursory stage seen in the trajectory of São Paulo, because the assimilation of new information and communication technologies and the Internet in particular occurs out of step in relation to the needs arising from a strong strategic vision and planning of government. In the period from 1995 to 1998, this strategic vision emerges at the same time that IT projects critical to the performance of government are implemented, though without vision and planning of electronic government. Throughout this period, projects for information and control and network communications systems are implemented through an informal

arrangement and without a strategic horizon in IT. Nevertheless, the projects are successful, but the state does not advance in a planned manner in the construction of infrastructure, systems and electronic government services, despite many sectorial achievements. Thus, the stage of "maladjustment between government strategy and electronic government systems" (3b) was present since 1995 and is indistinguishable from the previous stage ("strategic vision of government" – 2a), because the implementation of priority projects and actions occurred since the beginning of the government that same year. The creation of the e-government program and its convergence with the management modernization program occurred in 2003 during the third continuity mandate. It is then configured at the "integrating electronic government" stage (4). The prolonged period of misalignment indicates the effectiveness of the informal arrangement adopted, but meant that poor strategic advantage was taken of the synergies between innovative actions in management and electronic government, witnessed by the creation and dissemination of "Poupatempo" disconnected from the Internet. In addition to this, it weakened the strategic performance of government, which saw the advance of e-government projects though without institutional support for their long-term continuity, generating disputes over their control since 2005.

CONCLUSION

This chapter applied a comprehensive framework for analyzing the development of electronic government, incorporating components and factors related to the organizational strategy and structure. The evidence gathered supports the hypothesis that the construction of a strategic vision, planning and organizational coordination structures accompany the experiences of electronic government that advance through to the deployment of more complex projects. These projects depend on collaboration and coordination between the organs and at the same time deepen the integration between them and their customers. The contrast between the case of Paraná and the others is clear proof of this: it is the only state that has not advanced to the "integrating electronic government" stage due to the weakness of its government strategy.

The alignment between strategy and electronic government as a critical factor for advancement to higher stages of maturity is found in the trajectories of Pernambuco and São Paulo. The circumstances in both cases are different, indicating that disparities can occur as much from lack of support at the strategic level for advancement or making e-government projects viable (Pernambuco), as from accepting informal arrangements for the conduct of electronic government (São Paulo).

The model outlined in the theoretical references has proved effective in the systematization of chains of events assumed for the formulation of vision and planning, the creation of organizational structures and project implementation. The cases support the premise that the sequences are not necessarily linear and, indeed, a trajectory based on a formalist and rational sequencing seems unusual. This trajectory, which assumes the vision-planning-implementation-organization sequence, was only found in Minas Gerais, though with the stages being almost simultaneous or even chronologically merged.

In all the cases investigated, a certain amount of difficulty was encountered in defining the transition between stages of the second level ("strategic vision of government", "vision of electronic government" and "focus on systems") and the third level ("strategic government planning," "automating electronic government" or "maladjustment between government strategy and electronic government"). The rapid progression to stage 4 indicates that decision styles with characteristics of flexibility, informality and focus on results seem surprisingly more frequent in Brazilian public administration.

It should be pointed out that the framework itself loses credibility in its ability to categorize and identify factors affecting the trajectory of electronic government, because the probable differences in performance and perhaps the most important obstacles to the maturation of these experiences are concentrated in stage 4. A possible improvement of this framework should therefore examine the analytical denouement of "integrating electronic government," seeking factors that enable the comparison of experiences located at this same stage.

As inferences on the cases and their respective trajectories that can inspire further research, it is clear that the different configurations assumed at each stage affect the subsequent stages in different ways. It is in this sense that electronic government reveals a greater tendency towards projects geared to infrastructure – especially the construction of information highways – in cases starting out at the "focus on systems" stage, namely Alagoas, and even more characteristically, Pernambuco. In both cases, the state agency responsible for IT in public administration played a key role in the emergence of e-government policy.

The cases that originated from the strategic needs of government resulted in the rapid implementation of projects, the results of which were deemed to be critical to the overall performance of governments. This is seen clearly in Sao Paulo, though it also occurred in Minas Gerais with projects that generated a reduction in costs and an improvement in controls and management. One question suggested by the analysis of these experiences is to what extent "skipping steps" in Minas Gerais or implementation expedited by informal arrangements in São Paulo, eventually weaken the long-term consolidation of electronic government.

The case that originated from the construction of a vision of electronic government that does not "contaminate" government strategy as a whole – exemplified by Paraná – did not evolve very favorably as an isolated program that failed to reach the stage of "integrating electronic government" (4). The impact of the strategic weakness of the government on that trajectory has already been mentioned. Its probable evolution will be towards a resumption of control by the state IT company, which already appears to be happening. The emergence of the program from the IT area is therefore a circumstance to which the tendency to isolation and greater difficulty in providing strategic breadth to the program may be attributed.

REFERENCES

Accenture (2002). *E-Government Leadership – Realizing the Vision.* The Government Executive Series.

Burn, J., & Robins, G. (2003). Moving towards eGovernment: a case study of organizational change processes. *Logistics Information Management, 16*(1), 25–35. doi:10.1108/09576050310453714

Commission (2003). *The Role of eGovernment for Europe`s Future*, Communication from the Commission of the European Communities, Brussels Chandler, A.D. (1962). *Strategy and Structure.* New York: Doubleday

Davenport, T. H. (1994). *Reengenharia de processos.* São Paulo: Campus.

Davison, R. M., Wagner, C., & Ma, C. K. (2005). From government to e-government: a transition model. *Information Technology & People, 18*(3), 280–299. doi:10.1108/09593840510615888

Deloitte Research. (2000). *At the Dawn of E-Government.* New York: Deloitte Consulting.

Eisenhardt, K. M. (1989). Building theories from case study research. *Academy of Management Review, 14*(4), 532–550.

Fernandes, C. C. C. (2006). Governo Eletrônico. In: FUNDAP/CONSAD. *Avanços e Perspectivas da Gestão Pública nos Estados.* Foundation for Administrative Development / National Council of Federal State Management Secretaries, 135-167

Fernandes, C. C. C. & Pinto, S. L. (2003). Sociedad de la Información en Brasil: balance y perspectivas. *Nueva Sociedad* (187),153-168

Fountain, J. E. (2001). *Building the Virtual State: Information Technology and Institutional Change.* Washington, D.C.: Brookings.

Hammer, M., & Champy, J. (1993). *Reengenharia. S. Paulo.* Campus.

Heeks, R. (2001). *Understanding e-Governance for Development.* i-Government Working Paper Series, 11

Henderson, J. C., & Venkatraman, N. (1993). Strategic alignment: leveraging information technology for transforming organizations. *IBM Systems Journal, 32*(1), 4–16. doi:10.1147/sj.382.0472

Kraemer, K., & Dedrick, J. (1997). Computing and public organizations. *Journal of Public Administration: Research and Theory, 7*(1).

Kraemer, K. L., & King, J. L. (1986). Computing and Public Organizations. *Public Administration Review*, (46): 488–496. doi:10.2307/975570

Kraemer, K. L., & King, J. L. (2005). Information technology and administrative reform: will e-government be different? *International Journal of Electronic Government Research, 2*(1).

Marche, S., & Mcniven, J. D. (2003). E-government and e-governance: the future isn't what it used to be. *Canadian Journal of Administrative Sciences, 20*(1), 74–86. doi:10.1111/j.1936-4490.2003.tb00306.x

Margetts, H. (2003). Electronic Government: a revolution in public administration? In Peters, B. G., & Pierre, J. (Eds.), *Handbook of Public Administration.* London: Sage.

Markus, M. L., & Robey, D. (1988). Informational technology and organizational change: Causal structure in theory and research. *Management Science, 34*(5), 583–594. doi:10.1287/mnsc.34.5.583

OECD. (1998). *Information Technology as an Instrument of Public Management Reform: a Study of Five OECD Countries*. Paris: Organization for Economic Co-operation and Development

OECD. (2003). *The E-Government Imperative*. E-Government Studies. Paris: Organization for Economic Co-operation and Development

PNAGE (2004). *Diagnóstico Geral das Administrações Públicas Estaduais*. Ministry of Planning, Budget and Management, 2004

PWC. (2002). *Estudo de Benchmarking Global em e-Government*. Price Waterhouse & Coopers.

Saur, R. (1997). *A tecnologia da informação na reforma do estado. Ciência da Informação, 26(1)*. Jan/Apr.

Snellen, I. (2000) Public Service in an Information Society. In: Peters, B. G. and Savoie, D. *Governance in the Twenty-first Century*: Revitalizing the Public Service. Montreal & Kingston: McGill-Queen's University Press

UKP-POST. (1999). *Electronic Government - Information Technologies and the Citizen*. London: United Kingdom Parliament - Parliamentary Office of Science and Technology.

UN/DPEPA-ASPA. (2002). *Benchmarking E-government: A Global Perspective*. York: United Nations / Division for Public Economics and Public Administration - American Society for Public Administration. N.

Vergara, S.(2005). *Métodos de pesquisa em administração*. S. Paulo: Atlas

Yin, R. K. (2001). *Estudo de caso – planejamento e métodos*. Porto Alegre: Bookman.

Chapter 9
Digital Transition in Alaska

Ping Lan
University of Alaska Fairbanks, USA

ABSTRACT

This chapter conducts a preliminary assessment on the early digital transition in Alaska by systematically examining the usage of the Internet in Alaska from five aspects: local information and communication technology providers, top 100 private firms, small private firms crossing different programs, the Government, and varied Alaskan communities. Over 1,000 websites were analyzed. It finds that Alaska is very committed to turning digital opportunities into a development force. The digital transition in Alaska is at various stages throughout the State. This digital transition benefits consumers instead of suppliers. It is driven by government instead of private sectors. It is strong at basic components or lower levels instead of demonstrating a balanced structure.

INTRODUCTION

Great expectations of E-business existed for Alaska in the late 1990s, leading to the progresses of its digitizing process. However, contrary to many studies of the impact of information and communication technology (ICT)—particularly the internet on firms, there has been a few systematic study of how a region such as Alaska is turning digital opportunities into a development force. In theory, major advances in ICT have transformed businesses and markets, revolutionized learning and knowledge-sharing, generated global information flows, empowered citizens and communities in new ways that redefine governance. At a regional level, this "digital revolution" could offer enormous opportunities to support sustainable local wealth creation, and thus help to achieve the broader development goals (DOT Force 2001). In reality, however, turning digital opportunities into a development force is not an automatic process. Even to measure it is difficult, due to different criteria and agendas of varied stakeholders. Therefore, it is understand-

DOI: 10.4018/978-1-61350-192-4.ch009

able that different picture of a digitizing process can be observed in different context. For example, Dunt and Harper (2002) painted a positive picture about Australian experience, while Evans (2002) argues that e-commerce has not changed relative status of Greater Manchester and Merseyside.

As one of two states which do not adjoin the mainland of USA, Alaska is seen as broadly well placed to benefit from the Internet and e-commerce. Traditionally isolated from the US main economic centers and reliant on commodities in its trade, the advent of the Internet is ideal for a region to overcome the geographical limitations. However, statistics does not support the claim. Most economic indicators show a downward tendency in Alaska since 1995, although the Federal Government expenditure has been increasing (ASTF 2002). This raises several questions. Are there "sunk" benefits of digital revolution in such context which can not be measured by the traditional methods? Is it only hype that digital opportunities can become a development force for changing relative status of a comparatively backward region? Or is it too early to judge the changes which will be released from a new infrastructure?

Given this background, a research with an Alaska focus is of interest in several aspects. First, Alaska's economy is different from those of other states, making it worth of studying its digitizing process. Second, Alaska is a good test bed for checking digital divide in such a context of a developed country due to its unique geographical, social and economic structure. Third, the isolation of Alaska offers an opportunity to examine the linkage of different components in a comparatively closed environment.

This chapter is based on a large scale survey with over 1,000 websites analysis undertaken by the author and his students over several years. It is structured as follows. In the next section, the framework for the examination is discussed. It is the combination of two components. The second section highlights the characteristics of the Alaska economy. In the third section, it summarized the findings of the survey on the usage of the internet among private firms, government agencies and communities in Alaska. The final section concludes the preliminary assessment on Alaska's digitizing process.

ACTION CONE IN A DIGITAL SPACE

Generally speaking, the changes brought about by the ICT to Alaska are results of the interface of the following two components as shown in Figure 1. One is a digital space on which various activities are taking place. The other is the efforts made by Alaskan to catch digital opportunities. This section first describes briefly the structure of the digital space; then it discusses contents of the action cone which are relevant to Alaska. The combination of the two components constitutes the working framework for this investigation.

A Digital Space

The major advances in ICT enable us to operate in a digital space consisting of three dimensions: ICT technologies, ICT applications or digital activities, and management of ICT projects or digital activities. ICT technologies are consequences of invention and innovation happened in computing, software engineering and telecommunication areas. Within this dimension, three sets of technology play important roles: digitizing technologies, networking technologies and authoring technologies. Digitalizing technologies are originated from development of computer, and extended to software engineering and digital information handling. The development of digitalizing technologies, on the one hand, dramatically increases computing power. On the other hand, it offers possibilities for shifting business operation from a material-based paradigm to an information-based paradigm (Lan 2006). Networking technologies result from the convergence of telecommunication technol-

Figure 1. An action cone in a digital space (Developed by the author based on Lan, 2002 and DOT Force, 2001, 2002)

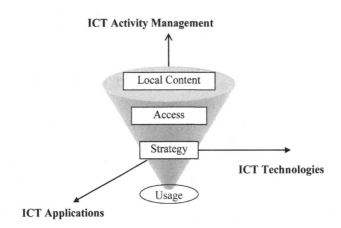

ogy and electronic technology (Panko 2001, Lan 2006). The development of networking technologies enables information exchange to enjoy an unimaginable freedom, judged by bandwidth, connectivity, accessibility, and diversity. This freedom of information exchange provides possibility for reorganising business and whole society (Gilder 2000, Keen and Mackintosh 2001). Authoring technologies are a collection of various tools for enabling dynamic and multimedia Websites. They are generated from convergence of digitalizing technologies and networking technologies, and are specialized in creating virtual existence. The development of authoring technologies provides solutions for not only changing ways of interface between an organization with its stakeholders by adding a virtual dimension, but also enlarging boundaries of mass creation (Loudon 2001, Von Hippel 2001).

The second dimension is ICT applications, which displays the usage spectrum of enabled technologies in digital operations. The following three applications are key components in this usage spectrum: eMessaging, eTransaction and eIntegration. eMessaging is reflected in various flows of information through the Internet such as online marketing, online education and online publication. eTransaction is characterized by electronic payments and related information flows, such as EDI, credit card and electronic cash payment. eIntegration displays restructuring or convergence of activities, functions and organizations occurred at different levels from units, departments, enterprises, industries to the whole society (Fingar et al. 2000, Rayport and Jaworski 2001).

The third dimension is digital activity management which deals with common managing challenges brought about by ICT technologies and ICT applications. As pointed out by Christensen (1997), a disruptive technology usually generates a chaos in a traditional management paradigm. To deal with co-evolution of technology and market requires panorama thinking, and three key issues have to be considered: define/redefine a value chain, formulate/reformulate a strategy, and design/redesign implementation. Defining/ redefining a value chain aims to locate a target from a chaotic environment, and have an idea of the operation scope (Mckenzie 2001). Formulating/reformulating a strategy means to find a path for channelling into a value pool (Lan 2000b) and set a hierarchy of priority. Designing/redesigning implementation requires continuous innovations for leveraging inside and outside resources into a designed operation (Rayport and Jaworski 2001, Yoffie and Cusumano 1999).

An Action Cone

The above three dimensions constitute the digital space. The interaction among the three dimensions displays the novelty, diversity and dynamic of the space. In this new environment, players position or reshape themselves with certain freedom. However, for a region, especially for a comparatively backward region, turning Digital Opportunities into a development force is not an automatic process. DOT Force (2001, 2002) offers guidelines for catching digital opportunities. Borrowing the concept from Physics that events happen in a four-dimension time-space form a light cone (Hawking 1998), an "action cone" was used here to organize various measures recommended by DOT Force and to illustrate the interaction between the digital platform and various efforts. The action cone has a three-level structure. It consists of, from bottom up, strategy formation, access improvement, and local content generation and knowledge sharing.

In terms of strategy formation, the ideal model of the DOT Force shows the following features: it should be the result of a consultative process involving all relevant interested parties in the region, including the private sector and non-profit organizations (NPOs); eStrategy should be regularly reviewed and updated, and benchmarked internationally; It should be reinforced by regional and sub-regional coordination efforts, notably in the context of economic integration; eStrategy should commit to the establishment of an enabling, pro-competitive regulatory and policy framework; and eStrategies should distinguish and recognize the importance of eGovernment for internal efficiency and effectiveness within government, as well as of eGovernance for institutional capacity

building, transparency, accountability and its ability to enhance democratic governance;

In terms of access improvement, the following items are in the action agenda of the DOT Force (2002): multiple technologies should be allowed to compete for communications networks and services and access terminals; the establishment of public and community ICT access points should be supported as a key means to facilitate timely, broad, affordable and sustainable access to ICT; approaches to promote universal access for rural and remote areas should be pursued; and R&D efforts for the development and adaptation of cost-effective technologies suitable for local conditions should be encouraged.

In terms of supporting local content and applications creation, the DOT Force offers several tips for integrated efforts. They include: encourage the software community, including the open source and commercial software communities, to develop applications relevant to local context and localize software applications; encourage the growth of eGovernment as a means of achieving a critical mass of on-line content and encourage governments to provide widely-available free-of-charge access to state-owned information and local content, except where it is private or classified; encourage local content development, translation and/or adaptation in local context to fulfil the needs of learners, scholars, professionals, and citizens for education, learning, training and application development; support national and international programs for digitizing and putting public content online, focusing on multilingual applications and local heritage; encourage networking of bodies which acquire, adapt and distribute content on a non-commercial basis; encourage commercial publishers to explore possible business models to enhance greater accessibility for poor people to relevant content; support university-based "networked centers of excellence" focusing on research and learning at the intersection between ICT and development; foster Enterprise and Entrepreneurship for Sustainable Economic

Development including incubation activities; and encourage private-public partnerships involving companies, local entrepreneurs, governments, non-profit organizations and labour organizations.

COMBINING THE ACTION CONE AND THE DIGITAL SPACE IN THE CONTEXT OF ALASKA

The prospects for digitizing Alaska should be seen against the backdrop of the economy, which in relative terms is simple and small. Petroleum has boosted Alaska's economy since the 1970's, peaked in 1988, and has been on decline since. Other basic industries (seafood, tourism, logging, mining, air cargo, agriculture) contribute less to gross state product (GSP) than petroleum, but create more jobs. Infrastructure and support industries (utilities, communications, trade, and service industry) have grown rapidly as Alaska's population grew and economy matured. Government remains a big contributor to GSP. Private industry has grown associated to government. State and local governments have grown associated to federal government. This structure determines that Alaska's economy is driven by the price of oil and federal spending, since primarily producing commodities are with little value added. During the last decade, Alaska's growth in gross state product has been anemic to declines in the petroleum, fishing, and forest products industries. Alaska's economy relies heavily on oil and therefore swings in oil prices impacts Alaska's GSP significantly

Another feature of Alaska's economy is that it does not follow the suits of national economy. For example, during the time period 1996-2001, Alaska had only one new company, Alaska Communications Systems Group, used initial public offering (IPO) to raise $140 million. Only one company, livepostcard.com of Anchorage received $3.5 million venture capital (VC) investment in 2000. While the national economy suffers from the crash of technology stocks, Alaska's economy

keeps steady growth (ASTF 2002). While many places were hurt by housing crisis, Alaska real estate market only shows limited fluctuations.

These above features make Alaska a very unique state for checking its digitizing process. First, its economy is small and is highly dependent on the oil production. Secondly, governments play a very important role both for employment and for adopting new technology. Thirdly, geographical and social conditions offer either challenges or opportunities for facilitating digital transition.

Given the uniqueness of the Alaska, the internet usage was selected as the survey focus for this research. On the one hand, it is comparatively easier to start and to organize for a region with very limited literature and documentation. On the other hand, it does provide a good opportunity to melt the two components together. Through analyzing of current usage of the Internet, Alaskan efforts in turning digital opportunities into a development force can be scrutinized. At the same time, the features of the current digital platform emerged in Alaska can be examined along with various activities.

Based on this design, a survey involving analyzing over 1,000 websites in Alaska was conducted. The students from University of Alaska Fairbanks worked on five topics: (1) the usage of the Internet by ICT technology providers, which aims to examining the supply side or technology dimension of the digital platform. (2) Large Alaska firms' usage of the Internet, which intend to explore the depth of digital transition in Alaska's private sector. (3) Small private firms' adoption of the electronic media, which aims to reveal the current market gap in different industries. (4) Government usage of the Websites, which aims at revealing how eGovernance capacity is built up in Alaska, and (5) Alaskan communities' website usage, which aims to check either how rural/remote areas were involved in catching digital opportunities, or how the Government has promoted the digital transition. The five topics are interwoven. The combination of the surveys on the topics does

Table 1. Online Activeness of Alaskan ICT Technology Providers

Sector	Total Firms	No. of Firms with a Website	% of Firms with a Website
Cable & other pay television services	12	3	25
Computer & Data processing	42	6	14
Computer Data Services	5	5	100
Miscellaneous communication services	11	3	27
Research & testing services	11	2	18
Telegraph & other message communications	11	0	0
Telephone communications	31	6	19
Utilities Services	3	3	100
Total	**121**	**28**	**23**

Source: Herman et al. (2002)

provide a picture about the digital transition rooted in Alaska, although the inconsistence in handling different topics exists.

SURVEY FINDINGS AND DISCUSSION

Online Operations of Technology Providers

As mentioned in the last section that Alaska's growth in gross state product has been declined during the last decade. Among a few of bright spots, growth of technology industry is one. However, it is worth noting that this technology platform is very small. Examining the structure of the technology industry, it also shows an imbalance, i.e. most expertise in Alaska is confined to networking area. There is only 9% of jobs are directly related to digitizing technology. This imbalance not only required Alaska to outsource digitizing services from other states, but also limited local content development.

Started from the fact that Alaska ICT technology dimension is short and imbalanced, a survey was conducted to check the online activeness of

ICT technology providers, since they are one necessary component of digital platform. In order to understand who provides information technology, what information technology they provide, and how they provide the information technology to people in Alaska, eight sectors listed in *Alaska Science & Technology Innovation Index* were selected which include wireless phones, text messaging, online transactions, and so forth. By using specific SIC codes to search the Alaskan corporation database, 121 companies based in Alaska among the eight sectors were identified. After the company names were found, a systematic online survey was conducted through search engines and sites analysis. Table 1 shows the sector distribution of these companies, as well as the website usage among these firms.

It is apparent that Computer & Data processing and Telephone communications have the majority of firms. However, most of them even did not have a Website. Adding up together, less than a quarter of ICT providers in Alaska had a website. Among the 28 companies with website 23 or 82.5% of them are located in Anchorage, the largest city in Alaska. The rest five are distributed in five small cities.

Digital Transition in Alaska

Online Operations of Private Firms

Two measurements were carried out in the survey to understand the current state of businesses using the electronic medium. The first is to examine the depth of the Internet usage among the top 100 private firms in Alaska. The second is to examine width of the Internet usage among various firms, particularly small firms. In terms of the examination on top 100 private firms, the survey includes collecting information on the number of web pages for each Website that businesses used to convey information, the number of links that other companies had to these websites, and the ranking of their Websites usage on messaging, transaction and integration as shown in Table 2. In addition to personal ranking, Google and other search engines are tools for carrying out the investigation.

It is worth noting that although the companies operate in Alaska, they may not be based in Alaska. Of the 100 companies studied, 54 were based in Alaska as the others were based elsewhere throughout the country. Those that were based outside of Alaska did indeed have a regional, national, or international presence in the marketplace. It is apparent that the average size of Alaska based companies' website is much smaller than that of firms based elsewhere. In fact, the average web pages per site are 258 for Alaska based firms, while for firms based outside Alaska the number is 2,640. If the size of a website reflects its richness in the content, the web links of a website to other websites are a good indicator for the broadness of a website's networking in the World Wide Web. The survey finds that average outside links per site for Alaska based firm are 92, and average outside links per site for non-Alaska based firm are 555, another big difference. Among the Alaska firms, the widest linked site is the Anchorage Daily News. The sites with 2000 or more out links were Williams Express, McDonalds, United Postal Service, AT&T Alascom, Blockbuster Video, Bristol Bay Area Health Corp.,

and Hilton. However, the majority of websites had less than 1000 other sites with links to their website.

To judge how a website marketed its product to customer, three different categories are employed. High level online marketing means that the website actively tries to sell their product/service. In so doing they provide and display much information in a format that was very easy to understand and very convenient to navigate. Medium level online marketing means that there is some information available, which would help a customer to understand about the company and their product/service. But there is no means to sell product or service online, or make it easy to purchase. Low level online marketing means that there is no much information pertinent to what a consumer might want to know about the company or its product/service.

In categorizing the interaction offered by a website to its customers, three types of integration were used in the analysis. "Point and Click" is designated for websites that just have links to sort their information. "Search and query" is labeled for websites that allowed users to search for the information that they want to know about. This allows users to quickly find information when the information provided is abundant. "Product/service customization" describes companies like Dell where you can take their product and change it to fit your needs right on the website. The degree of interactivity with users on a firm's website can be an indication of how sophisticated a website is.

Further analyzing the Website usage between Alaska firms and companies based outside of Alaska, it reveals Alaska's firms are not so active in using electronic media. For example, of all the websites that were evident of high online marketing, 15 were located in Alaska and 19 outside of Alaska. Of all the websites that were evident of low online marketing, 12 were from companies outside of Alaska and 26 from companies in Alaska. Of the 15 companies which utilized some form of product customization on their website,

Table 2. Usage of Website among the Top 100 Private Companies in Alaska

Industry	No of firms	Online Marketing			Online Interaction				Online Sale	Community formation	Intranet & Extranet Usage			
		High	Medium	Low	Customize	Search	Point	Other	Yes	Yes	Intra	Extra	None	Both
Health Care/ Social Service	17	3%	5%	9%	0%	3%	13%	1%	1%	12%	2%	2%	12%	1%
Air Carrier/Bus/ Shipping Service	13	7%	2%	4%	5%	1%	5%	2%	8%	6%	2%	5%	6%	0%
Hotel/Eating Service	13	6%	4%	3%	5%	5%	3%	0%	10%	6%	1%	1%	8%	3%
Oil/Gas Extraction	13	2%	6%	5%	0%	3%	10%	0%	0%	5%	2%	4%	7%	0%
Seafood Processing	9	0%	2%	7%	0%	2%	7%	0%	0%	5%	1%	2%	6%	0%
Grocery/General Merchandise	8	5%	1%	2%	3%	0%	3%	2%	5%	4%	0%	2%	6%	0%
Hospital/Medical Center	6	1%	3%	2%	1%	0%	5%	0%	0%	4%	0%	0%	5%	1%
Communication/ Public Utility	5	3%	2%	0%	1%	1%	1%	2%	5%	3%	0%	0%	4%	1%
Building/Facility Construction	4	1%	1%	2%	0%	1%	2%	1%	1%	2%	0%	0%	4%	0%
Pine/Mining	4	0%	3%	1%	0%	0%	4%	0%	0%	2%	1%	0%	3%	0%
Banking/ Credit Union	3	3%	0%	0%	0%	2%	0%	1%	3%	2%	0%	2%	1%	0%
Department Store	2	2%	0%	0%	0%	2%	0%	0%	2%	0%	0%	0%	2%	0%
Others	3	1%	0%	2%	1%	0%	2%	0%	1%	1%	0%	1%	2%	0%
Total	**100**	**34%**	**29%**	**37%**	**16%**	**20%**	**55%**	**9%**	**36%**	**52%**	**9%**	**19%**	**66%**	**6%**

Source: O'Neil et al. (2002)

143

Table 3. Usage of the Internet in Alaska's Small Firms

Program	No. of Firms	E-mail Usage	Website Usage
MIA	709	77.6%	31.5%
ASTF	31	46.4%	44.0%

Source: Atkisson et al. (2002).

only 5 were from Alaska where as 10 were from elsewhere (O'Neil et al. 2002).

In order to overcome the bias in analysis of the 100 top private firms, a much large examination on the usage of the internet was undertaken, which targets two programs. One is "Made in Alaska" (MIA). The other is technology sectors of certain importance to Alaska listed by Alaska Science & Technology Foundation (ASTF). Briefly, MIA was designed to promote and increase Alaskan made products in 1986 by then Governor Bill Sheffield. Over the years, MIA has gone through many changes by the way of the legislation and regulations. Currently, the MIA program has about 1,200 certified businesses. ASTF was established in 1988 to help develop science and technology to benefit Alaskans, as well as help to promote innovation within Alaska.

As shown in Table 3, 709 firms were selected from MIA grogram, which consist of 17 industries according to MIA's statistics. Besides that, 31 firms were randomly selected from ASTF technology sector listing except sectors which were regarded as ICT providers and have been covered previously.

The data shows that there is quite big market gap in the usage of Internet for small Alaska firms, no matter they are in export oriented MIA program, or in technology intensive ASTF listing. For example, in the Arts & Crafts Industry of MIA, which accounts for about 40% of the all samples of the survey, 89% has e-mail access, 28% have websites, and 22% have e-mail and a website. Out of the 28% of the websites, 35% have some sort of on-line marketing, and 28% have on-line transactions. The Clothing & Apparel Industry

(which has 192 small firms and accounts for 25% of the total samples) is not much better, 25% have e-mail access, 24% have a website, 70% of the 24% have on-line marketing, and only 7% have on-line transactions. The Alaskan Novelty Wood Products Industry (which ranks number three and accounts for 9.1% of the total MIA samples), 48% have e-mail's, 27% have websites, and 1% have both, out of the 27% that have websites 93% of them have on-line marketing, and 28% have on-line transactions.

Online Operations of Governments

Alaska government's website lists about 150 State Government web links. After the exploration of all the websites 81 were selected in this research. The reason for this minimization was due to the un-necessary detail (for this study) in which some departments sub-divided themselves into.

To formulate a consistent guideline for checking the contents of the Government websites, a simple 5-criterium method was adopted in the survey. The five criteria were: (1) valuable information, which measures if the information in the website gives viewers a clear picture of what that department's main function was, and the availability of resources that department had; (2) the amount of "filler" information. "Filler" information in here was defined as information located on the site was invaluable to the citizens in terms of the function of that department; (3) existence of mission statement on the homepage, which shows viewers what they feel is valuable and what services they provide. (4) Department's contact information on the homepage; and (5) the

Table 4. User-Friendly Ranking of Alaska Government's Websites

Total Websites	Ranking: 1 lowest and 5 highest				
	Level 1	Level 2	Level 3	Level 4	Level 5
81	3	15	27	19	17

Source: Chukwu et al. 2002

information orientation, which aims to find out if a site is more community oriented or more along the lines of a form of intranet for the department. If all of the criteria points were met the site received a score of 5, which is the highest amount of points possible. Yet if any of the key factors was missing, then a point was taken away. Table 4 display the results of the ranking based on these criteria.

On this grading scale 18 sites scored below average 3. Yet shockingly enough 3 of those sites received a score of 1. The Department of Revenue/Tax Division site www.tax.state.ak.us/#top had major problems. Even though most people know what this department does they may not understand its function clearly. Many people have questions about their taxes on a daily bases, yet the website is not user friendly at all. The source of information is rather obscure and not very relevant to the department's main function, which is not stated on the homepage. Another department webpage that received a 1 was the Department of Revenue/Administrative Services Division. In order to contact the department you would have to go to another page. The mission statement is so small and obscure it would appear it was placed on the page as an after thought. It is worth noting that poorly sites scored website are the sites that deal with money, not theirs but the communities.

There were a few sites that may not have received a perfect score, but did have valuable information for the public. For instance the DMV offers vehicle registration on-line and also you can purchase fishing licenses as well. On the Department of Law website you can e-mail them legal questions or concerns and you will receive a response. This function of the site is valuable

for the citizens because you can receive legal advice for free.

Out of those 81 records only 8 had online transaction function. They are Department of fish and game, sub-department of Wildlife and conservation, sub-department of Commercial Fisheries, sub-department of Sport Fish, Department of Administration, Department of Alaska Railroad Corporation, Department of Administration for Motor Vehicles, and Department of Natural Resources of Public Information Centre. Users are able to purchase all types of things like: fishing licenses, hunting licenses, personalized driving plates, land leases (NRPC), mining rentals (NRPC), vessel licenses, and Alaska railroad gift items etc. Most of the Departments websites allowed users to retrieve copies of applications or forms off their websites. But when it came to transactions the user had to mail in the form with a money order or check.

Online Operations of Communities

Alaska is the most unique state in the United States of America. It is the biggest state by area, yet it almost has the smallest population. Many rural villages even do not have road access. In order to obtain a complete picture about the usage of the Internet in Alaska, a survey on varied communities was conducted. In Alaska, only 6% of communities have a population of over 5,000 people, leaving the other 94% of Alaskan communities to be categorized as small. Of this 94%, 68 percent have a population that is less than 500 people. Considering the amount of communities in Alaska, 90 communities were selected, which

Table 5. Online Popularity and Community Size

Community size	<100	100-499	500-999	1000-4999	>=5000
No. of Communities	12	27	18	24	11
Online name search results	2,555	2,301	13,615	23,768	29,504

Source: Uzzell et al. (2002).

include all the larger cities and randomly selected the smaller communities. The samples covered all locations (which were reflected in Alaska Native corporation geographic area that the community was located in) and 95% of the population in Alaska.

In addition to checking the usage of community websites in marketing, transaction and community formation as did for private firms and government, special attention was paid for checking online popularity of different communities. It was conducted through check online search engines such as Google for full community name search. The number of hits was used to indicate its online exposure. Table 5 is a summary of the relationships between the community size, main business activities and its website usage.

It is apparent that the large communities in the state have the best Internet access and online usage. Some remote communities had no ISP's and no known Internet usage. In order to have Internet access, some have to dial long distance and pay as much as $6.00 an hour. Other communities are able to obtain Internet access through satellite dishes. A community's main business did influence their online activities. In cities that have government as their major business, they are all good or excellent in the ranking of online performance. The communities that listed subsistence as what is spurring their economy typically were rated as poor. Communities with a service based economy were shown to have better Internet usage than communities with a fishing-based economy. Aside from fishing communities everything fit into very nice patterns of Internet use, some poor and some good.

Features of Action Cone in Alaska

The above usage of the Internet reflects the collective efforts committed by all stakeholders in Alaska, which also made action cone in Alaska show the following features: steady and active strategy, high level access and limited local content/application development.

Contrast to DOT Force's suggestions, Alaska government's performance in formulating eStrategy and put the strategy into practice are far beyond the benchmarking framework. As early as 1996, Alaska government made its *Telecommunications and Information Technology Plan* with a state wide consultation. In the plan, the following goals and implementation time line were set up: (1) improve public access to government information; (2) maximize service to the public through voice, video and data systems; (3) optimize government efficiencies; (4) explore innovative and cost-effective services that meet Alaska's challenges; and (5) stimulate the development of private and public services

In addition to making plan, Alaska has paid much more attention to build an eGovernment for internal efficiency and effectiveness, as well as for institutional capacity building, transparency, accountability and its ability to enhance democratic governance. The previous online usage of government has proved that the efforts are productive. These efforts are also recognized national wide. Table 6 shows the performance of Alaska in government digitizing. Alaska ranked third overall in the 2000 survey, up from ninth in 1998. In the 2001 survey, Alaska regained its number one position in digital democracy, but

Table 6. Alaska's Rank among the 50 States in Digital State Government

Category	1998 survey	2000 survey	2001 survey
Digital Democracy	1	7	1
Higher education	26	3	na
K-12 education	29	17	na
E-commerce & business regulation	1	2	8
Taxation & revenue	10	2	na
Social services	1	5	24
Law enforcement & the courts	15	12	21
Management & administration	na	4	25
GIS/transportation	Na	Na	14
Overall	9	3	18

Sources: The Center for Digital Government, 2001 and 2000 Digital State Surveys and the Progress and Freedom Foundation, Digital State 2000, September 2000.

lost ground in other areas to states catching up. One of Alaska's significant accomplishments was the passage of a digital signature law that updates state statutes and codes to make digital signatures legally binding. In March 2002, the Progressive Policy Institute ranked Alaska 6th in the nation in their study "The Best States for E-Commerce" which examined how state governments make it easy or difficult for their citizens to fully take advantage of the Internet to buy things, engage in legally binding transactions, and interact with government. Based on the achievements during the last several years, a more technical implementation oriented plan was formulated in 2002. This plan paid more attention to improve the overall infrastructure for catching digital opportunity, particularly for government.

As part of Alaska's *Telecommunications and Information Technology Plan,* online access has been dealt with seriously. Also the efforts were paid off. Online access as a whole and online access for school students in Alaska are both better of than the national average. The number of people online is probably the most basic indication of a state's progress toward the digital economy. In 2000 Alaska ranked 2nd in the nation in terms of percent of households with internet access

following only New Hampshire, and 2nd in the nation in terms of percent of households with computers following only Utah. Alaska's schools have fewer students per computer and fewer students per internet connected computer than the national average. However, Alaska's great distances and small rural school populations cause it to fall behind the national average in the percentage of schools with internet accesses and high speed service.

Contrast to eStrategy formulation and access provision, Alaska's achievements in developing local contents and applications are limited, which can be seen from low online existence of small private firms, no matter they are in supplying products or services for accelerating digitizing process, or in export oriented products or service providers. The situation is not limited to small firms. They can be observed from large firms and government branches. The average small size of websites founded in various situations can be another indicator.

Several reasons may be attributed to the case. One is the weak of Alaska in generating new knowledge as shown by patent generation. Generally speaking, the number of patents generated is a good indication of how active the idea creation process is. These new ideas are the basis for future products and companies. Utility patents are inventions. Other patents include design patents, plant patents, reissues, defensive publications, and statutory inventions registrations. From 1997 -2001 total 257 Utility patents were issued to Alaskan, the oil industry led Alaska with 33, followed by the medical profession (8), Static structure (e.g. building 6), fishing and packaging (both 5). Alaska's recent utility patents 2000-2001 per 100,000 population was 7, the lowest in the nation. The second is the lack of expertise in software development, which is a key component to generate or modify local applications. Among the portfolio of Alaska's invention, software development related portion is very marginal. Thirdly, the generation of local application, the share of knowledge and facilitation of innovation did not appear or did not get enough attention on the agendas of stakeholders.

CONCLUSION

This study was based on the combination of two frameworks. One is a digital space which consists of three dimensions: ICT technology, ICT application and management of ICT activity. The three dimensions in a given region could determine the feature of its digital space. The other is an action cone, which consists of collective efforts made by different stakeholders at different layers in a given region. The interaction between the action cone and the digital space offers a handy tool to examine the digitizing process in a region. In the context of Alaska, ICT technology providers, ICT applications in private firms, governments and communities, as well as collective efforts in making strategy, creating online access opportunities and generating local contents were selected as check points. Over 1,000 Alaskan websites and all available literature were surfed or reviewed during the research.

The survey finds that Alaska is very committed to turn digital opportunities into a development force. However, the digital transition in Alaska is in various stages throughout the state. It is an ongoing process. This digital transition shows three features. Firstly, it benefits consumers/citizen instead of suppliers. Secondly, it is driven by government instead of private sectors. Thirdly, it is strong at basic components or lower levels instead of having a balanced structure.

The first conclusion can be drawn from the following contrast of weak points and strong points. The weak points include: the short ICT technology dimension, imbalanced ICT technology structure, limited growth of ICT technology jobs, and the lowest online existence of ICT technology providers among private sectors (only 23%). The strong points include easy access, active online consumers, and convenience to residents brought about by eGovernance.

The second conclusion can be observed from the performances of both Government and private sectors. While government has been active in making strategy, formulating policy framework and generating eGovernance capacity, private sectors have been slow in moving even into the preliminary level. The survey finds that market gap—measured by number of firms not having a website to total firms --in Alaska small firms is 68%.

The third conclusion is drawn from fact that Alaska enjoys a high level of online access, but shows a low level of local content generation. This is further exemplified by: (1) The existence of a website for each community, but most of them are no more than "brochureware". (2) The usage of website in most private firms lacks of useful active components.

Data presented in the chapter does answer the questions raised in the introduction at certain degree. Firstly, there are indeed some "sunk" benefits of digital revolution which do not show in the traditional indicators. In the Alaska context, households and individual consumers do benefit a lot from online messaging and online transactions. Through focus group survey, it found that Alaskan people were less hesitation in giving their credit card number for online shopping due to limited local choice. Therefore, a high internet access rate in Alaska means not only a high readiness for e-commerce as suggested by OECD (2000), but also a reality for increasing purchasing power, customer satisfaction and improving life quality. These benefits, generally speaking, were not reflected in traditional indicators.

Secondly, it is possible that digital opportunities can become a development force for changing relative status of a region. However, it needs a coherent and persistent effort from all stakeholders. Alaska's experience shows that it has changed its status in governance by promoting digitizing government. It also shows that this change can be short-lived without continuity, interaction with, and progressing of other key stakeholders. Therefore, turning digital opportunities into a development force is not a fashion. It is a down to earth transition. This transition could shorten the development gap. However, realizing such a transition needs a long term commitment and effective execution.

Thirdly, the changes brought about by the Internet, although may not be accurately measured statistically, have been felt positively in the context of Alaska, not only economically, but also socially. However, due to the comparative small size of digital platform in the regional economy, Alaska's gains in this area do not counter with the declines in its traditional industry sectors.

REFERENCES

G8 Kyushu-Okinawa Summit. (2000). *Okinawa Charter on Global Information Society.* Retrieved from http://www.dotforce.org./ reports/ it1.html

ASTF. (2002). *Alaska Science & Technology Innovation Index.* Report of the Foundation Alaska Science & Technology Foundation (ASTF). Retrieved from http://www.astf.org

Atkisson, J., O'Hara, B., Harvy, E., & Roland, J. (2002). Market *Gap in Alaska's E-Commerce, an unpublished report.* University of Alaska Fairbanks.

Burr, T., Gandara, M., & Robinson, K. (2002). E-commerce: Auditing the Rage. *Internal Auditor, 59*(5), 49–55.

Chukwu, O., Ward, L., Chan, C., & Epperson, R. (2002). *Alaska Government's Internet Usage, an unpublished report.* University of Alaska Fairbanks.

Dunt, E., & Harper, I. (2002). E-Commerce and the Australian Economy. *The Economic Record, 78*(242), 327–342. doi:10.1111/1475-4932.00061

Evans, R. (2002). E-commerce, Competitiveness and Local and Regional Governance in Greater Manchester and Merseyside: A Preliminary Assessment. *Urban Studies (Edinburgh, Scotland), 39*(5-6), 947–975. doi:10.1080/00420980220128390

Fingar, P., Kumar, H., & Sharma, T. (2000). *Enterprise E-Commerce.* Tampa, FL: Meghan-Kiffer Press.

Force, D. O. T. (2001). *Digital Opportunities for All: Meeting the Challenge.* Report of the Digital Opportunity Task Force (DOT Force). Retrieved from http://www.dotforce.org./ reports/ DOT_ Force_ Report_ V_ 5.0h.html#ac

Founrain, J. E. (2001). *Building the Virtual State: information technology and institutional change.* Washington, D.C: Brookings Institution Press.

Hawking, S. (1998). *A Brief History of Time: updated and expanded tenth anniversary edition.* New York: Bantam Books.

Herman, T., Laner, J., Keough, D., & Towne, S. & Mayes, L. (2002). *Alaska Technology Providers, an unpublished report*. University of Alaska Fairbanks.

Huizingh, E. K. R. E. (2002). Towards Successful E-business Strategies: A hierarchy of three management models. *Journal of Marketing Management, 18*(4), 721–747. doi:10.1362/0267257022780615

Keen, P., & Mackintosh, R. (2001). *The Freedom Economy: gaining the mCommerce edge in the era of the wireless Internet*. New York: McGraw-Hill.

Lan, P. (2000a). Changing Production Paradigm and the Transformation of Knowledge Existing Form. *International Journal of Technology Management, 20*(1/2), 44–57. doi:10.1504/IJTM.2000.002857

Lan, P. (2000b). The Technology-component matrix: a tool for analyzing and managing knowledge. *International Journal of Technology Management, 20*(5/6/7/8), 670-683.

Lan, P. (2002). *E-Business Space for E-innovation*. Proceedings of the 3rd World Congress on Management of E-commerce (CD-Rom format).

Lan, P. (2006). A New Vision of Innovation Management: Towards an Integrated Paradigm. *I. J. of Technology Marketing., 1*(4), 355–374. doi:10.1504/IJTMKT.2006.010732

Loudon, A. (2001). *Webs of Innovation: the networked economy demands new ways to innovate*. London: Pearson Education Ltd.

McKenzie, R. (2001). *The Relationship-Based Enterprise: powering business success through customer relationship management*. Toronto: McGraw-Hill Ryerson.

O'Neil, J., Byrne, A., Liddle, M., Talley, E., & Hoyos, C. (2002). *Profiles of Users, an unpublished report*. University of Alaska Fairbanks.

OECD. (2000). *Measuring the ICT Sector, Organisation for Economic Cooperation and Development*. Paris: OECD.

OECD. (2001). *The New Economy: Beyond the Hype-Final Report on the OECD Growth Project, Executive Summary*. Meeting of the OECD Council at Ministerial Level 2001. Organisation for Economic Cooperation and Development (OECD). Retrieved from http://www.oecd.org/pdf/ D00018000/ M00018624.pdf

Panko, R. R. (2001). *Business Data Communications and Networking* (3rd ed.). Upper Saddle River, NJ: Prentice Hall PTR.

Rayport, J., & Jaworski, B. (2001). *E-Commerce*. Boston: McGraw-Hill/Irwin.

Uzzell, B., Wornath, J., & Graves, J. & Ferris, D. (2002). A*n Analysis of Alaska's Community Websites, an unpublished report*. University of Alaska Fairbanks.

Von Hippel, E. (2001). Innovation by User Communities: Learning from Open-Source Software. *MIT Sloan Management Review, 42*(2), 82–86.

Yoffie, D. B., & Cusumano, M. A. (1999). Judo Strategy: the competitive dynamics of internet time. *Harvard Business Review, 77*(1), 71–81.

Chapter 10
Pressures or Weapons?
Applying Information Technologies to Innovate Organizational Structures in the Information Age

Liang-Hung Lin
National Kaohsiung University of Applied Sciences, Taiwan

ABSTRACT

Innovating organizational structures by using information technologies (IT), this study introduced new IT-enabled structures, and presented how managers scan firms capabilities and design suitable structures in the information age. Another purpose of this chapter is to verify the role of IT-enabled structures in the multilevel study of innovation management. Findings based on hierarchical regression analyses revealed that IT-enabled structures are critical in the management of innovation. Furthermore, IT-enabled structures can explain the difference of both organizational innovation and individual creativity in organizations. It also can moderate the relationship between organizational innovation and individual creativity.

INTRODUCTION

Organizational structure describes the "blueprint for activities which includes, first of all, the table of organization: a listing of office, departments, positions, and programs" (Meyer and Rowan, 1977, pp.341-42). To emphasizing the importance of organizational structure design, Mintzberg (1979, p.2) stated the problem: "Every organized human activity … gives rise to two fundamental and opposing requirements: the division labor into various tasks to be performed and the coordination of these tasks to accomplish the activity. The structure of an organization can be defined simply as the sum total of the ways in

DOI: 10.4018/978-1-61350-192-4.ch010

which it divided its labor into distinct tasks and then achieves coordination among them". Since large complex organizations in last century have become increasing heterodox nowadays, the new post-Bureaucratic forms of organizations, which are adaptive to the rapidly changing environment, should be introduced and discussed in the digital age (Arndt and Bigelow, 2000; Gordon and Gordon, 1996; Ku and Fan, 2009). Meanwhile, new and more flexible organizational structure is a core issue in the management of organizational change. Innovating organizational structures by using information technologies (IT), this study introduced new IT-enabled structures, and presented how managers scan firms capabilities and design suitable structures in the information age. Facing keen competition, organizations advance their structure to reduce outside pressures. Besides suggesting innovative structures, the second part of this research wish to verify the roles IT-enabled structures played in organizational innovation and individual creativity, or, in the innovation management of different levels.

IT-DESIGN VARIABLES AND IT-ENABLED ORGANIZATIONAL STRUCTURES

Structure, as the blueprint for activities, includes the table of organization covering departments, positions, and programs. Three affective contextual variables exist, including environment, technology, and size that allow organizations to generate different types of structures (Woodward, 1970; Chandler, 1962; Child, 1972). From this perspective, information technologies are not merely changes of organizational environment, but also are an important technology for a firm, particularly for information and e-business related industries. Managers can use information technologies to develop IT-enabled design variables that can help in designing suitable structures to manage strategy/environment fit. Lucas and Ba-

roudi (1994) and Boudreau et al. (1998) reported useful IT-enabled design variables for designing new structures to facilitate corporate coordination and inter-organizational communication among organizations. These variables include:

1. virtual components, which can create virtual departments via electronic data exchange and inter-organizational delivery system (For example, if some firms wish their parts suppliers to replace the inventory, they may ask the suppliers to offer parts on demand OR at the last minute by using electronic mail and express delivery);
2. electronic linking, by using electronic mail and telecommunication technologies;
3. technological leveling, which can refine the organizational hierarchy by using electronic communication tools;
4. mass customization technology;
5. internet, intranet, and extranet; and
6. technological matrixing, which forms matrix structures by electronic mail, fax, and telecommunication technologies.

Organizations must modify their structure continuously when the environment changes more rapidly than before. Facing keen competition, firms should maintain and improve competitive advantage by developing collaborative strategies such as joint venture, strategic alliance, and vertical integration (Hamel, 1991; Porter, 1987). Accordingly, some organizational activities must be separated and become the business of the collaborative partners, indicating changing of operational processes for both parties. From this perspective, organizations should adopt the appropriate competitive strategy and at least one modified structure to respond to these considerations. According to information technologies, organizations have addressed and implemented numerous innovative structures. Virtual organization recently has been identified as the most representative and innovative of these new structures in the information related industries. Virtual organization can be considered the general application of IT-enabled design variables and traditional design variables.

The virtual organization is considered a rapidly respondent organization of marketing orientation and satisfying customer need designed to orient itself to the market and satisfy customer needs (Black and Edwards, 2000; Davidow and Malone, 1993; DeSanctis and Monge, 1999). Estallo (2000) addressed that within this structure members are organized in distinct geographical spaces and in different times, from managerial to operating levels, to accomplish organizational tasks. The characteristics of this structure are flexible, indicating the capability to adapt to the environment, fluid communication, the capability to discover potential consumer needs, and virtuality, which controls the breaking of formal structure. Virtual structure is limited in two respects: the lack of physical flow and equipment, and incomplete knowledge transportation (Chau et al., 2003; Howard et al., 2003; Koch, 2000). Meanwhile, virtual organization has three advantages: dependence on federation; spatial and temporal independence; and flexibility.

Besides virtual organization, this study also introduces four other representative and innovative structures in the digital age.

Process-Oriented Structure

In the literature on business processes restructuring, Davenport and Short (1990) proposed a process-oriented structure using information and communication technologies to redesign boundary-crossing and customer-driven process. Manufacturing firms adopt process-oriented structures in response to the need of mass and automatic production. Most electronic OEM companies in East Asia are typical examples of this structure. To redesign a process-oriented structure, five major steps were proposed (Davenport and Short, 1990):

1. develop the business vision and process objectives;
2. identify the processes to be redesigned;
3. understand and measure the existing process;
4. identify IT levers; and
5. design and build a prototype of the new process.

Modular Design

In the practice of new product design, a component represents a specific function of a product; thus, the integration of all components has to be considered in the early stage of innovating products. Product architecture, as a complete group of interfaces standards, will defines the relationships among components. Daft and Lewin (1993) addressed modular organizational structure in response to the decomposability of product development process and radical organizational changes. The modular organizational structure comes from the concepts of standardized component design and cooperative interfaces relationship (Sanchez and Mahoney, 1996; Thomas et al., 1999). The essential knowledge of a successful modular structure is based on two respects: the information of all separated components, and the information exists in the relationships of associated components; that is, the knowledge of product architecture.

Virtual Department

Large firms could build departments that are not actually located in the organization in order to reduce inventory and security costs (Arndt et al., 1999; Lucas and Baroudi, 1994). Component suppliers play the roles of virtual departments of large firms by using electronic data interchange (EDI) and express delivery system. Large firms could order their outside suppliers to provide components or raw materials in the suitable time at cheap price without causing any transaction cost because the suppliers are considered to be the virtual departments of the large form. For example,

General Motors (GM) asked its suppliers to be virtual departments of GM by owning the right to modify outside suppliers' master production schedule (MPS). Virtual departments could only occur if there are significant power imbalances between organizations.

Virtual Integration

Firms can combine the use of virtual departments and vertical integration strategy by adopting virtual integrated structures. "Focusing on the inter-organizational control and collaboration, this structure has properties of flexibility and production cost reduction that diminishes the risk and uncertainty of environmental and technological change (Lin and Lu, 2005; p.187)." The existence and advantage of a virtual integration depends on the contracts and agreements it has with its co-operative enterprises, and the goods and services provided to its customers by other organizations. Lucas and Baroudi (1994) introduced a typical virtual integration - Calyx and Carolla flower company to represent the essential practice of such a new organization, which is based on two integrated agreements. First, Calyx and Carolla contracted with Federal Express to deliver flowers within one night to any place in United States. Second, Calyx and Carolla also contracted with flower farmers deliver flowers to Federal Express, instead of selling to flower wholesalers. Thus, the central part of this company is clerks who take orders via phone, tax, or e-mail. In fact, most Internet direct selling companies operates similarly to virtual integration in some respects including the following major activities:

1. **Negotiation:** Business coordinates its intra-organizational activities and functions with extra-organizations, especially the sharing and interchange of information.
2. **Commercial affairs:** Internet and ICT provide standardized and globalized tools of low cost to contact with potential consumers worldwide.
3. **Community:** The temporal and spatial diversities no longer exist by advanced information technologies.
4. **Content:** Information, goods, and services provided by integrated organizations.
5. **Communication:** Including phone call, fax, e-mail, video telephone, mobile phone and other possible media.

IT-ENABLED STRUCTURES IN THE MANAGEMENT OF INNOVATION

The second part of this research draws the roles IT-enabled structures played in organizational innovation and individual creativity, or, in the innovativeness of different levels. General systems theory (GST) has been the most dominant perspective of the 20th century which originate in that the whole is greater than the sum of its parts, and organizations are proposed to have similar structures and process (Kozlowski and Klein, 2000). However, in the studies of multi-levels perspectives, GST is not usually useful because its lack of testable principles. In this study, organizations are divided into five forms of structure and statistic evidences will show the strategic differences among different structures.

Multi-level models are proposed to bridge micro and macro viewpoints and specify relationships between higher and lower levels. Thus, a multi-level model must present how phenomena are linked in different levels: by top-down or bottom-up process (James and Williams, 2000). Top-down process describes the effects of higher-level factors on lower levels of organizations. Bottom-up process presents how lower-level attributes emerge to form higher-level phenomena. Emergence process can be separated into composition and compilation types: composition process describes phenomena that are the same as they emerge upwards; and compilation process presents properties that comprise a similar domain but are quite different as they emerge upwards (Kozlowski and Klein, 2000).

Considering effects of individual creativity on organizational innovation, it's clear to be a compilation form of bottom-up emergency. Since individual creativity is only an important component of organizational innovation, successful innovation adoption and diffusion still needs the coordination of different functions, the integration of organizational resources, the support of top management, etc. Thus, the models applied in this study consider individual creativity as an important determinant of organizational innovation, and, models should also include other major determinants on levels of individual, organization and environment. Moreover, top-down effects are to admit of no doubt in the model because organizations of different structures must have impacts on individual creativity. Base on the top-down theory, this study take types of structure as a moderator of the relationship between organizational innovation and individual creativity.

Based on the above discussion, the objectives of this empirical study can be summarized with two research questions.

Research question 1. Do individual creativity and structure types affect the performance of organizational innovation?

Research question 2. Does structure type positively moderate the relationship between organizational innovation and individual creativity?

METHODS

Sample and Data Collection

The stated Research questions were tested on a sample of information and computer firms in Taiwan's largest science park, Hsinchu Science-based Industrial Park (HSIP). HSIP provides advanced information and manufacturing infrastructure for information and computer firms. All important firms of this industry in Taiwan, about 320 firms are in HSIP. Sampling data were obtained from questionnaires sent to all 320 firms in HSIP. Questionnaires were divided into two parts: one questionnaire was sent to the firm's top manager to ask organizational product innovation, process innovation, and other control variables of firm size, firm age, etc; another 30 creativity questionnaires were randomly sent to 30 employees to measure the individual creativity of this firm. In this survey, 320 questionnaires were delivered to the firms (320×30 creativity questionnaires were sent to employees), 135 of which were returned after three times followed up by phone calls. Withdrawing invalid respondents and outliers by computer checking, yielded a sample of 145 companies.

Measurement

To address the research question described previously, this study adopt quantifiable measurements that are clear and easy for respondents. In the organizational innovation measurement, this study used two questionnaires, product innovation and process innovation measure which were developed by Damanpour and his colleagues (1984, 1991, 2001). Product innovation includes 20 items (such as new products, new services, patents, etc.) and process innovations includes 6 items (such as new production process, feasible process for customers, low cost production process, etc.). The alpha values were 0.86 and 0.81 separately. In the measure of individual creativity, this study adopted Creative Personality Scale (CPS) developed by Gough (1979) that contains 30 items (18 of them are positive questions such as perspicuous, self-confident, individualism, etc.; 12 of them are negative such as conservative, traditional, etc.). Each positive item scored +1 and each negative item scored -1. The sum of 30 items scores presents the individual creativity for each employee. The alpha value was 0.83. Type of organizational structure was the major variable discussed in

Table 1. Correlation Matrix

Variable	1	2	3	4	5	6	7
1.Product innovation							
2.Process innovation.	.01						
3. Creativity	.56***	.55***					
4. Structure type	.43**	.37**	.18				
5. Professionalism	.26*	.20	.17	.24			
6. Training	.25*	.32	.29	.24	.16		
7. Organizational size	.28*	.12	.05	.12	.22	.26	
8. Competition	-.03	-.12	.11	.08	.09	.04	-.21

Notes: $n = 145$, * $p < 0.05$,.** $p < 0.01$, *** $p < 0.001$

this study which was separated into five types: process-orient structure, modular organization, virtual department, virtual integration and virtual organization. Types of higher virtualization have higher scores: virtual organization scored 5, virtual integration scored 4, virtual department scored 3, modular organization scored 2 and process-orient structure scored 1. The higher scores presents firms' organizational structures were highly virtualized, IT-enabled and more feasible; lower score presents more traditional structures were adopted by firms.

Considering control variables, this study adopted top manager's professionalism and employee's training as individual control variables. These two variables were operationalized by top manage's formal education years and employee's average annual on-the job training (Daft, 1978; Damanpour, 1991). Organizational control variables consisted of firm size which was measured based on the number of full time workers. Environmental control variable include the number of major competitors of this firm.

RESULTS

This study adopted hierarchical regressions to test the research questions. Before discussing the regression results, all variables were standardized

(Table 1) to proceed refined diagnostic analyses for confirming the adequacy of all models. The resulting average variance inflation factor (average VIF) for each regression coefficient in models 2, 3, 5 and 6, introduced in tables 4 and 5, were 1.105, 1.130, 1.120 and 1.210. All of the VIFs of all associated variables fell in the range 1.11 to 1.35, implying minor multicollinearity. The Dubin-Watson statistics for models 2, 3, 5 and 6 were 2.14, 2.13, 1.99, and 2.02, also suggesting the fitness of random assumption for regression models. Four outlying sample points were removed according to the test of DFFITS, DFBETAS and Cook's distance (Johnson and Wichern, 1992; Neter et al., 1999).

Research Question 1. Do Individual Creativity and Structure Types Affect the Performance of Organizational Innovation?

Tables 2 and 3 showed a series of hierarchical regressions concerning organizational product and process innovations. Model 1, containing only four control variables, revealed low multiple squared correlation coefficient ($R^2=0.19$) which only suggested the influences of training and organizational size variables ($b = 0.23$ and 0.26, $p < 0.05$). Adding two major variables, individual creativity and structure type, increased R^2 by 33

Table 2. Results of Product Innovation

	Product innovation					
	Model 1		Model 2		Model 3	
Independent variables	b	t	b	t	b	t
Controls						
Professionalism	0.19	1.81	0.17	1.54	0.15	1.43
Training	0.23	2.01*	0.20	1.92	0.23	1.8
Firm Size	0.26	2.03*	0.22	1.85	0.18	1.64
Competition	-0.04	-0.45	-0.14	-1.48	-0.09	-0.75
Direct effects						
Individual creativity			0.55	3.67***	0.51	3.42***
Structure type			0.46	2.92**	0.40	2.49**
Moderating effect						
Individual creativity × Structure type					0.35	2.38**
R^2	0.19		0.52		0.62	
ΔR^2			0.33***		0.10**	
F	4.99*		12.06***		8.22***	
Partial F			10.67***		3.80**	

*Note: n = 145, * $p < 0.05$,.** $p < 0.01$, *** $p < 0.001$*

percent over model 1 ($\Delta R^2 = 0.33$, $p < 0.001$). After introducing the interaction term of individual creativity ×structure type in model 3, R^2 increased to 0.62($\Delta R^2 = 0.10$, $p < 0.01$). Higher regression coefficients of individual creativity (b = 0.55, $p < 0.001$) and structure type (b = 0.46, $p < 0.01$) implied the direct effects of individual creativity and structure type were strong and stable. These also suggested individual creativity and structure type to be important determinants of organizational product innovation.

Model 4, also containing the same control variables, revealed fair multiple squared correlation coefficient ($R^2 = 0.22$) which suggested the importance of employee training (b = 0.32, $p < 0.01$) in the adoption and development of process innovation. Skilled employees seemed helpful to organizational process innovation due to their practiced experience. Adding two major variables in model 5, individual creativity and structure type, increased R^2 by 24 percent over model 4 ($\Delta R^2 = 0.24$, $p < 0.01$). After introducing the interaction term of individual creativity ×structure

type in model 6, R^2 increased to 0.54($\Delta R^2 = 0.08$, $p < 0.01$). Higher regression coefficients of individual creativity (b = 0.36, $p < 0.01$) and structure type (b = 0.33, $p < 0.01$) implied the direct effects of individual creativity and structure type were strong and stable. These also suggested individual creativity and structure type to be important determinants of organizational process innovation. Moreover, by using ANOVA test, the findings also supported that structure type can discriminate the between-group difference of individual creativity (F = 8.31, $p < 0.01$). Employees of highly virtualized organizations had higher creativity performance.

Research Question 2. Does Structure Type Positively Moderate the Relationship between Organizational Innovation and Individual Creativity?

In Table 2, after adding the interaction term, individual creativity ×structure type, to model 3 increased R^2 by 10 percent ($\Delta R^2 = 0.10$, $p <$

Table 3. Results of Process Innovation

	Process innovation					
	Model 4		Model 5		Model 6	
Independent variables	b	t	b	t	b	t
Controls						
Professionalism	0.10	1.02	0.09	0.08	0.05	0.07
Training	0.32	2.34**	0.30	2.23**	0.31	2.51**
Firm size	0.11	0.41	0.03	0.06	0.04	0.08
Competition	-.014	-.035	-.010	-1.28	0.12	0.97
Direct effects						
Individual creativity			0.36	2.61**	0.34	2.54**
Structure type			0.33	2.58**	0.31	2.40**
Moderating effect						
Individual creativity × Structure type					0.30	2.12*
R^2	0.22		0.46		0.54	
ΔR^2			0.24**		0.08**	
F	5.07**		15.01***		7.06***	
Partial F			6.04**		5.23**	

Note: $n = 145$, * $p < 0.05$, ** $p < 0.01$, *** $p < 0.001$

0.01), from that for model 2, revealing significant moderating effect in organizational product innovation. Positive regression coefficient ($b = 0.35$, $p < 0.01$) also indicated that firms of higher virtualized structures presents stronger relationship between organizational product innovation and individual creativity. In Table 3, similar findings also supported that firms of higher virtualized structures presents stronger relationship between organizational process innovation and individual creativity.

DISCUSSION

This article focuses on the decisions that firms make when facing IT-enabled structures and associated strategic choices, especially on the impacts to innovation management. Since Innovation involves factors and processes that exist at different levels and most researchers tend to focus at single level of analysis, this study also wish to operate at different levels to know about how variables at one level of analysis influence innovation at another level. Klein et al. (1999) stated the relevant barriers to multilevel research included the difficulty of determining the appropriate scope, the difficulty of subtle properties and the difficulty of gathering multilevel data. This study thus chose innovativeness of organizational and individual levels to be major considerations and gathered data of environmental, organizational and individual levels as controlling variables in order to clarify relationship between organizational innovation and individual creativity. Finally, IT-enabled structure type was introduced as another determinant and major moderator in this investigation. Data gathering undoubtedly played an important role in this study. Considering appropriate sample size, each sample firm finished one organizational innovation questionnaire accompanying with other

30 individual creativity questionnaires. Large sampling data provided a reliable base of analysis.

First finding of this research suggested that individual creativity had direct effect on organizational innovation although some other control variables, such as training, also had fair influence on it. This implies organizational innovation to be a complex function of specific and dyadic-networked contributions. From a bottom-up perspective, organizational innovation really shows its characteristic of compilation process. Since individual creativity is only an important component of organizational innovation, successful management of organizational innovation still needs the coordination of different functions.

Second set of findings revealed information technologies and IT-enabled structures to be more influential than individual creativity and all control variables because it is a major determinant as well as a moderator in this investigation. On the one hand structure type can discriminate the between-group difference of both organizational innovation and individual creativity; on the other hand it can moderate the relationship between organizational innovation and individual creativity. Firms of highly virtualized structure not only possess higher degree of organizational innovation and employee creativity but also strengthen the relationship between innovations in two levels. Innovativeness in organizational and individual levels co-develop in the same direction if the firms are highly virtualized. The reason may be due to the adoption of IT strategy. High density IT strategy may help the development of R&D activities in all levels as well as help the communication among different levels (Ahuja and Carley, 1999; Kraut et al., 1999).

Whether managers view information technologies as environmental pressures or strategic advantages, information technologies are essential in redesign organizational structures and selecting successful corporate strategies. Coping with the challenge of change and competition, organizations should undertake structural innovation enabled by building appropriate IT capabilities during the initial stage of strategic changes. Managers should keep themselves informed regarding the latest developments in information technologies. Top management commitment to deriving strategic IT capabilities is extremely important and may require the support of information departments to help top manager recognize the potential and benefits of information technologies.

Generally, organizational structures change or innovate in response to different strategic choices, and appropriate adoption of information technologies assists the redesign of restructuring and the implementation of corporate strategy. However, extended learning and adaptation is required for all organizational members to understand and master new technologies. Managers thus should punctiliously assess the need for various IT capabilities, and should select the most suitable technologies to help in undertaking structural innovation. Furthermore, the adoption of fitting structure is just one feature of cooperation among organizations. The key to success is the focus on inter-organizational management system, coordinating mechanism, and process control that incorporates flexibility and efficiency into the practice of organizational changes. In addition to structure and technology, an organization contains people and tasks. Without considering the challenge created by its people and tasks, it maybe hard to change an organization if the managers only try to change the structure

This investigation is informative in two respects. First, externally oriented aggression clearly provides a continuous advantage compared to a passive strategy. Structural innovation accompanied with advanced information technologies is essential to successful strategic change. Second, different organizations might generate and develop various innovative structures if restructuring was considered an administrative innovation. Applying IT capabilities to structural innovation is effective when treating information technologies as strategic weapons, not environmental pressures. Thus, unlike traditional organizations, fit among

IT capabilities, innovative structure, and corporate strategies enables organizations to meet potential consumer demand in the information age.

REFERENCES

Ahuja, M. K., & Carley, K. M. (1999). Network structure in virtual organizations. *Organization Science, 10*(6), 741–757. doi:10.1287/orsc.10.6.741

Arndt, M., & Bigelow, B. (1995). The adoption of corporate restructuring by hospitals. *Journal of Healthcare Management, 40*(3), 332–347.

Arndt, M., & Bigelow, B. (2000). Presenting structural innovation in an institutional environment: hospitals' use of impression management. *Administrative Science Quarterly, 45*(3), 494–552. doi:10.2307/2667107

Arndt, M., Bigelow, B., & Dorman, H. G. (1999). In their own words: how hospitals present corporate restructuring in their annual reports. *Journal of Healthcare Management, 44*(2), 117–131.

Black, J. A., & Edwards, S. (2000). Emergence of virtual or network organizations: fad or feature. *Journal of Organizational Change Management, 13*(6), 567–576. doi:10.1108/09534810010378588

Boudreau, M., Loch, K. D., Robey, D., & Straud, D. (1998). Going global: using information technology to advance the competitiveness of the virtual transnational organization. *The Academy of Management Executive, 12*(4), 120–128. doi:10.5465/AME.1998.1334008

Chandler, A. D. (1962). *Strategy and structure: Charters in the history of the American industry enterprise*. Cambridge, MA: MIT press.

Chau, P. Y. K., & Lai, V. S. K. (2003). An empirical investigation of the determinants of user acceptance of internet banking. *Journal of Organizational Computing and Electronic Commerce, 13*(2), 123–145. doi:10.1207/S15327744JOCE1302_3

Child, J. (1972). Organizational structure, environment and performance: the role of strategic choice. *Sociology, 6*(1), 1–22. doi:10.1177/003803857200600101

Daft, R. L. (1978). A dual-core model of organization innovation. *Academy of Management Journal, 21*(2), 193–210. doi:10.2307/255754

Daft, R. L., & Lewin, A. Y. (1993). Where are the theories for the new organizational form? an editorial essay. *Organization Science, 4*(4), i–iv.

Damanpour, F. (1991). Organizational innovation: A meta-analysis of effects of determinants and moderators. *Academy of Management Journal, 34*(3), 555–590. doi:10.2307/256406

Damanpour, F., & Evan, W. (1984). Organizational innovation and performance: The problem of organizational lag. *Administrative Science Quarterly, 29*(3), 392–409. doi:10.2307/2393031

Damanpour, F., & Gopalakrishnan, S. (2001). The dynamics of the adoption of product and process innovations in organizations. *Journal of Management Studies, 38*(1), 45–65. doi:10.1111/1467-6486.00227

Davenport, T. H., & Short, J. E. (1990). The new industrial engineering information technology and business process redesign. *Sloan Management Review, 31*(4), 11–17.

Davidow, W. H., & Malone, M. S. (1992). *The Virtual Corporation: Structuring and Revitalizing the Corporation for the 21st Century*. New York, NY: Harper Business.

DeSanctis, G., & Monge, P. (1999). Introduction to the special issue: communication processes for virtual organizations. *Organization Science, 10*(6), 693–703. doi:10.1287/orsc.10.6.693

Estallo, J. (2000). The new organizational structure and its virtual functioning. *International Advances in Economic Research, 6*(2), 241–255. doi:10.1007/BF02296105

Gordon, S. R., & Gordon, J. R. (1996). *Information Systems: A Management Approach*. New York: Harcourt Brace & Company.

Gough, H. G. (1979). A creative personality scale for the adjective check list. *Journal of Personality and Social Psychology, 37*(8), 1398–1405. doi:10.1037/0022-3514.37.8.1398

Hamel, G. (1991). Competition from competence and interpartner learning within international strategic alliances. *Strategic Management Journal, 12*(Special Issue), 83–103. doi:10.1002/smj.4250120908

Howard, M., Vidgen, R., & Powell, P. (2003). Overcoming stakeholder barriers in the automotive industry: building to order with extra-organizational systems. *Journal of Information Technology, 18*(1), 27–43. doi:10.1080/0268396031000077431

James, L. R., & Williams, L. J. (2000). The cross-level operator in regression, ANOVA, and contextual analysis. In K. J. Klein, S. W. J. Kozlowski, (eds). *Multilevel Theory, Research, and Methods in Organizations: Foundations, Extensions, and New Directions*, 382-424. San Francisco: Jossey Bass.

Johnson, R. A., & Wichern, D. W. (1992). *Applied Multivariate Statistical Analysis*. Upper Saddle River, NJ: Prentice Hall.

Klein, K. J., Tosi, H., & Cannella, A. A. (1999). Multilevel theory building: Benefits, barriers, and new developments. *Academy of Management Review, 24*(2), 243–248. doi:10.5465/AMR.1999.1893934

Koch, C. (2000). Building coalitions in an era of technological change: virtual manufacturing and the role of unions, employees and management. *Journal of Organizational Change Management, 13*(3), 275–288. doi:10.1108/09534810010330922

Kozlowski, S. W. J., & Klein, K. J. (2000). A multilevel approach to theory and research in organizations: Contextual, temporal and emergent processes. In K. J. Klein, S. W. J. Kozlowski, (eds). *Multilevel Theory, Research, and Methods in Organizations: Foundations, Extensions, and New Directions*, 3-90. San Francisco: Jossey Bass.

Kraut, R., Steinfield, C., Chan, A., Butler, B., & Hoag, A. (1999). Coordination and virtualization: The role of electronic networks and personal relationships. *Organization Science, 10*(6), 722–740. doi:10.1287/orsc.10.6.722

Ku, E. C. S., & Fan, Y. W. (2009). Knowledge sharing and customer relationship management in the travel service alliances. *Total Quality Management & Business Excellence, 20*(12), 1407–1421. doi:10.1080/14783360903248880

Lin, L. H., & Lu, I. Y. (2005). Adoption of virtual organization by Taiwanese electronics firms: An empirical study of organization structure innovation. *Journal of Organizational Change Management, 18*(2), 184–200. doi:10.1108/09534810510589598

Lucas, H. C., & Baroudi, J. (1994). The role of information technology in organization design. *Journal of Management Information Systems, 10*(4), 9–24.

Meyer, J. W., & Rowan, B. (1977). Institutionalized organizations: Formal structure as myth and ceremony. *American Journal of Sociology, 83*(2), 340–363. doi:10.1086/226550

Mintzberg, H. (1979). *The Structuring of Organizations*. Englewood Cliffs, NJ: Prentice-Hall.

Neter, J., Kutner, M. H., Nachtsheim, C. J., & Wasserman, W. (1999). *Applied Linear Regression Models*. New York: McGraw-Hill.

Porter, M. E. (1987). From competitive advantage to corporate strategy. *Harvard Business Review, 65*(3), 43–59.

Sanchez, R. & Mahoney, J. T. (1996). Modularity, flexibility, and knowledge management in product and organization design. *Strategic Management Journal, 17*(Winter Special Issue), 63-76.

Thomas, H., Pollock, T., & Gorman, P. (1999). Global strategic analyses: frameworks and approaches. *The Academy of Management Executive, 13*(1), 70–82. doi:10.5465/AME.1999.1567340

Woodward, J. (1970). *Industrial Organization: Behaviour and Control*. London: Oxford University Press.

Chapter 11
Improving Cognitive Load on Students with Disabilities Through Software Aids

Rubén González Crespo
Universidad Pontificia de Salamanca, Spain

Oscar Sanjuán Martíne
Universidad de Oviedo, Spain

Juan Manuel Cueva Lovelle
Universidad de Oviedo, Spain

B. Cristina Pelayo García-Bustelo
Universidad de Oviedo, Spain

Vicente García Díaz
Universidad de Oviedo, Spain

Patricia Ordoñez de Pablos
Universidad de Oviedo, Spain

ABSTRACT

This chapter proposes a new way to improve the cognitive load and construction of e-learning environments making them more usable and accessible using emerging design. This causes a significant improvement in cognitive load. Accessibility within the area of Web applications, is actually present in different laws of many countries, trying that information could be used for everyone. This objective is limited when you are dealing with severe disabilities. An example of this is people with hearing disabilities who have never hear or speak. To solve these problems the authors propose a platform that brings a complete solution to accessibility.

INTRODUCTION

This paper propounds a way in which emerging design and programming techniques can be used to convert and build accessible web sites. Accessibility, in the scope of the web applications, is a reality present in multiple countries' different laws that must be confronted so anyone, regardless his condition or nationality, can communicate and use technology without any kind of impediment.

This maxim is limited when we deal with people with severe disabilities, where the problems existing currently, can make almost impossible the use of web sites as a door to the society's information, in which we found ourselves immerse. An example are people with auditory prelocutive disability, people who were never able to hear or speak. The complexity it implies for them learn

DOI: 10.4018/978-1-61350-192-4.ch011

the language, the writing and the people with disabilities expressions, implies a serious entry barrier. If we bear in mind as well, Spain has more than a million people with auditory problems and since October 2007, the Spanish sign language is a language recognized by law, wouldn't it be more obvious to find a communication mechanism, familiar to them, which removed their accessibility problems? This solution adapts the Signwriting, mechanism of graphic representation of the sign language, to the environments of the already mentioned information society.

Besides this problem, there is another one even bigger. From January 2006 on the Public Administration sites must be accessible with AA level, according to the WAI (Web Accessibility Initiative) accessibility guidelines. And from January 2009 on, the big companies that render general purpose services and all of those entities and companies that receive public financing, including educational centers, and universitaries, and the private centers financed by the Administration. Then, would it be possible to mitigate the costs of this transformation? or on the contrary, is it necessary to go through a whole redesign process of the web sites, with the high costs it implies? We must not forget the Spanish SMBs will adopt these measures as well, and they are a high percentage of the Spanish business sector (BOE, 2005).

In order to solve these problems we raise a platform which has a complete solution for accessibility. An approximation to this global platform would consist of two architectures, each one oriented to solve things separately, but as a whole when required, depending on the kind of user, the expounded problems on the previous paragraphs, being able to obtain accessible web applications with AA level for people with severe auditory disability by means of Signwriting.

The first one solves the accessibility problem expounded on the third paragraph. In order to do so, we build an Accessibility Adaptor that, using templates allows us to build the interfaces that currently are "drawn" with JavaScript in the client, in the server. With this we get to reduce drastically the costs of rebuilding web applications with AA level, according to the WAI accessibility guidelines and the LSSICE and the LISI (BOE, 2005) (LSSI, 2009).

The second one contributes with a solution to make every web site accessible for anyone with an auditory disability. The problem has been expounded in the second paragraph. In order to solve it the SWMLSVG language has been developed, which allow us to specify, through XML, the sign language in writing mode, already known as SignWriting. This way, using vectorial graphics a new language could be used so every web site can be defined from spoken language to signed language.

This proposal not only solve the problems mentioned at the beginning of this introduction, but to improve existing solutions for e-learning market, as discussed below as the sociology of disability means that the learning mechanism that are placed at their service are tailored to their specific needs, something that is evident in the people who need to communicate properly signwriting.

CULTURE IN THE DISABILITIES FIELD. DEAF PEOPLE SOCIOLOGY

"…An autobiography, in case such thing does exist, is like asking a rabbit what does it look like when it jumps through a meadow. How is it going to know it? But, on the other hand, in case we want to know something related to the meadow, there is no one in a better situation than the rabbit to tell us, always having in mind we don't pretend to know those things the rabbit didn't notice due to its position on a given moment." (Golden, 2005)

In order to understand the concepts of the Deaf Culture and the Deaf Community, we must accept the point of view of the persons that make it up (Marchesi, 1999), deaf people, as we accept the rabbit's opinion to get to know the meadow from all the possible points of view, including his and our owns.

The definition Padden suggests related to the Deaf Community is the following (Padden, 19989): "A Deaf community is a group of people who live in a particular location, share the common goals of its members, and in various ways, work toward achieving these goals. A Deaf community may include persons who are not themselves deaf, but who actively support the goals of the community and the work with Deaf people to achieve them."

Padden defines Deaf Culture as (Padden, 19989): "A set of learned behaviors of a group of people who have their own language, values, rules of behavior, and traditions. Members of the Deaf Culture behave as Deaf people do, use the language of Deaf people, and share the beliefs of Deaf people towards themselves and other people who are not Deaf."

The basic attribute of every culture is the language they use, without it, from every point of view, culture among humankind would be impossible. Every language, spoken or written, is a system based on symbols with meaning that have been learned and are used to describe, classify and catalogue experiences, concepts and objects.

Sign language, as most of other languages, can be signed in different ways, depending on the geographic location of the group signing them or their society. This way, every language adapts to each culture's needs, so those who use them can communicate their thoughts, feelings, etc... But, at the same time, the language's own structure subtly shapes the way in which a group notices the reality of the world.

In the Deaf Culture, all these feelings, problems, emotions, etc, are transmitted basically through vision, which is the reason why it is a culture based on vision and space. This influence process between culture and language is mutual and gives a personal and particular vision of the world, as language has an influence in the perception (audible in the case of the listener, visual for the one with auditory disability), perception has an influence in concepts, concepts in thoughts, thoughts in ideas, and the ideas revert in the world again.

This interaction basically leads to adapt their lifestyle to their specific situation, and the fact that for generations people with auditory disability have been living in a particular way, makes what was firstly an adaptation to a specific situation, turn into a tradition or custom, that belonging to a particular community follows a series of fixed rules.

For a long time, many years, Sign Language has been present in society as a way to communicate for all people. Because of its characteristics, the lack of need to learn it and the ruled set by society, the Sign Language is used, basically, by people who are deaf or have some kind of relation with the Deaf Community (Maher, 1996).

Therefore is required that the Signwriting Language were designed to improve the on-line solutions that exist to promote learning. As discussed in the following paragraph signwriting is the ideal mechanism to bring this language to the web, since by their morphological features is easily represented and could be introduced in high demand and free solutions such as Moodle (Moodle, 2009) and Blackboard (Blackboard, 2009) with low cost and efficiently.

FROM THE SIGN LANGUAGE TO SIGNWRITTING: A MULTIMEDIA APPROACH

The sign language is used to communicate through gestures but, what happens when we communicate through writing? The usual thing is to do it in Spanish, using characters which represent sounds but, what happens with those who have never heard a sound, a word? SignWriting, through the development of alphabetization materials tries to teach the deaf to write their own sign language. Where's the point in writing a sign language?

Figure 1. SignWriting configurations

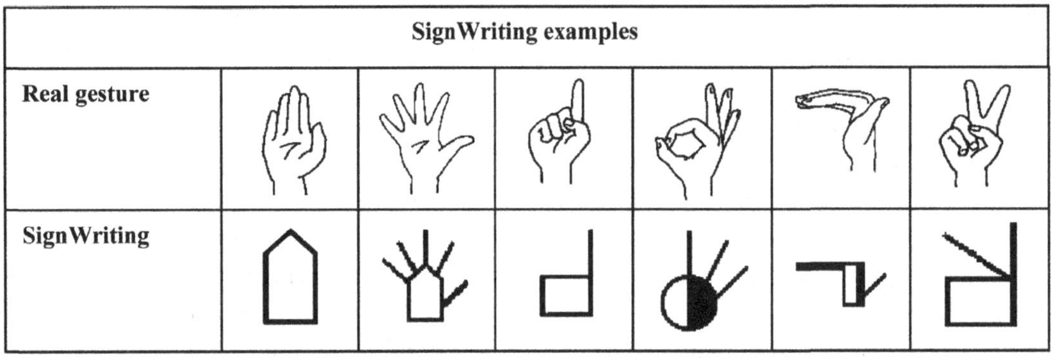

SignWriting examples						
Real gesture						
SignWriting						

Can't deaf read Spanish? Some of them can, but for many others it is a really difficult task. Written words are made of letters that represent sounds. For someone who never heard those sounds learning to read consists basically in memorizing. It is like memorizing a telephone number for each word. This writing method is meant for deaf people who know sign language but don't understand Spanish well enough to read long or complicate texts.

As can be read in various scientific publications (Mimbela, 2009) the use of multimedia improves learning efficiency. Since the theoretical basis of learning should be redesigned for use in e-learning systems in the deaf community is the same. Thanks to this system it is possible that by its nature based on multimedia and cognitive theory (Sweller, 1999) of multimedia learning provide, in this case makes no sense to contemplate inhibition, learning for prelingually deaf (Paas, 2004) (Moreno, 2007).

Approximately 35% of deaf people in Spain (INE, 2006) prelingually hearing impaired, they would make to improve their skills.

This writing system is called SignWriting (invented by Valerie Sutton for the American Sign Language) (Parkhurst, 2000). SignWriting is basically a simple graphic representation of the real sign. We write hand configurations, movements and facial expressions, using symbols which are easy to write. The written signs are very similar to simplified drawings of the symbols deaf people

really use. As a result, a deaf who knows the system should quickly be able to read and easily write his own language, his Sign Language.

The following examples show the simplicity of the system (Figure 1):

So, some words written in SignWriting could be (Figure 2):

Trying to explain the functionality of SignWriting in a few pages is really impossible. Firstly we must get things straight; this is a system used to write and read *Sign Languages*. With this witting system we can write any kind of sign regardless its origin (Spanish Sign Language, American Sign Language, etc...). Therefore the SignWriting elements could be compared to the alphabet, in the sense that every word developed with an Arabic writing are made with the same characters; without forgetting the existing exceptions (in Spanish, the use of the letter "ñ"). So, using the same elements, we can develop a phrase in English "Signing for the Deaf" or in Spanish "La Comunidad Sorda". The comprehension of these will obviously depend on knowledge the writer has on English Language or Spanish Language.

The same happens in SignWriting. It puts at our disposal a set of "drawings" that, technically are known as **"queiremas"** and **"queirotropemas"** (Torres, 2008). With them we will develop signs with an appropriate union.

We want to represent the sign **HELLO.** In order to make this sign we need the following elements:

Figure 2. SignWriting examples

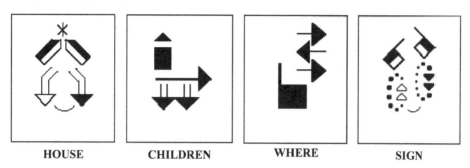

| HOUSE | CHILDREN | WHERE | SIGN |

a head, a hand with the fingers stretched out and something that will represent movement from left to right (in this case we will use the arrows). Joining these three elements correctly we get the desired sign (Figure 3).

As we can see in this example, it is very easy to build an element in SignWriting. What makes this system more complicated is the great variety of possible combinations we can find. If this knowledge is acquired, we just have to take a look at the Sign Language's sign, choose the needed symbols and the correct configurations, and we will have the new sign.

This sign is the union of the three parts described in the two previous paragraphs, as we can see on the following explanation (Figure 4).

As we can see in the previous examples, all the elements that compose SignWriting are vectorial graphics and therefore can be easy treated with the variety of web applications we have nowadays. With the mark language SWMLSVG, Signwriting Markup Language SVG (Standard Vectorial Graphics), we will be able to bring SignWriting closer to web developments for people with auditory disability.

Figure 3. "Hello" sign

A SOLUTION: ON-LINE CONTENT ADAPTATION ARQUITECTURE

Accessibility is a worldwide reality that must be supported currently or shortly by every company, specifically the Spanish ones, with presence in the web, regardless their work field. Many laws or recommendations in force or not in force (Aenor, 2008) (ONU, 2006) (W3C, 2005) (WCAG, 1999) (WCAG2, 2008), show the administrations desire to offer web contents that everyone, regardless their physical limitations, can have access to.

For example we can see that according to the LSSI (LSSIC, 2009), "Ley de Servicios de la Sociedad de la Información y del Comercio Electrónico", from January 2006 on, the Public Administration sites must be accessible with AA level, and from January 2009 on, the big companies that render general purpose services and all of those entities and companies that receive public financing, including educational centers,

Figure 4.

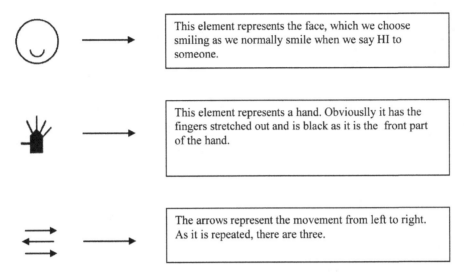

Figure 5. Accessibility Global Platform components

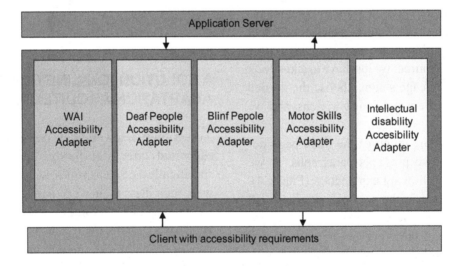

and universitaries, and the private centers financed by the Administration.

The theoretical solution for the platform would consist of an architecture based on components that allow us to obtain the objectives we have just described (Figure 5).

Proceeding to describe each one of the components of the shown architecture we have:

- **Application Server:** In the application server we will have the web application. Its accessibility level is irrelevant as it will be the platform the one in charge of, in case it is necessary, adapting the contents to obtain the accessibility level requested by the user.

- **Client with Adaptation needs:** Any kind of client with adaptation needs, such as, web browsers, text processors, image processors, spreadsheets, etc.

- **WAI Accessibility Adapter:** Component in charge of the conversion of any kind of web application located in the application server, regardless its accessibility level, to the expected accessibility level.

- **Auditory Disability Accessibility Adapter:** Component in charge of the adaptation of the application's content for people with severe auditory disability, through accessibility techniques not defined in WAI.

- **Visual Disability Accessibility Adapter:** Component in charge of the adaptation of the application's content for people with severe visual disability, through accessibility techniques not defined in WAI.

- **Motor Disability Accessibility Adapter:** Component in charge of the adaptation of the application's content for people with severe motor disability, through accessibility techniques not defined in WAI.

- **Intelligence Disability Accessibility Adapter:** Component in charge of the adaptation of the application's content for people with severe intelligence disability, through accessibility techniques not defined in WAI.

A simple approximation to this accessibility global platform that allows us to solve the two problems expounded at the beginning of this paper would be (Figure 6).

These two components would be in charge of the following operations:

- **Accessibility Adapter:** The accessibility adapter expresses the adopted solution to adapt the accessibility problems caused, mainly, by the use of JavaScript, in the development of web applications in order to be accessible with AA level.

Figure 6. Accessibility Global Platform approximation

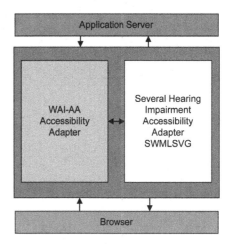

- **SWMLSVG Accessibility Adapter for Severe Auditory Disability:** In order to face the problem of people with severe auditory disability, a component that allows the translation of standard web applications to web applications based on SignWriting is suggested. The developed middleware is based on the framed language SWMLSVG (Signwriting Markup Language for Scalable Vector Graphics), which has been defined to easily visualize, through XML and SVG, sign language signs in any web browser that supports the visualization of this kind of graphics.

A REALITY: WAI-AA ONLINE CONTENT ADAPTER

This adapter will be in charge of allowing the web applications which currently are not in AA level, essentially due to the use of JavaScript, to acquire this accessibility level and therefore obey the current law.

The WAI-AA adapter's main functionality would be (Figure 7):

Figure 7. Schema of the communication between the adapter elements

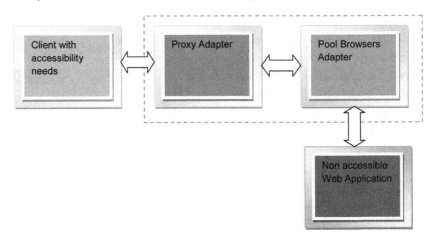

1. The client with accessibility needs makes a request to the adapter instead of the application server (this request contains the original application's address).
2. The adapter requests the web page to the web application and renderizes its content.
3. The adapter applies the appropriate transformations.
4. The adapter answers the client with the accessible contents.

The adapter consists of two elements, each one of them with different characteristics and needs:

- The **component proxy** is an application developed in J2EE that takes on the following responsibilities:
  - Receive the requests of the accessible clients.
  - Request the Pool the execution of the petitions in the browser associated to that client.
  - Obtain the HTML code generated from that request.
  - Apply the transformations to the obtained HTML code.
- The **component pool** is an application developed in.net which is executed in a web browser capable of executing asp.net, Cassini and that assumes the following responsibilities:
  - Instanciate the browsers (Internet Explorer processes) needed to *renderize* the pages on the Server.
  - Manage the assignment of the Internet Explorer instances to specific clients (Each IE, will be associated to a specific accessible client and will maintain its state during the whole life of the session).
  - Control the Internet Explorer instances' release.
  - Receive the proxy requests and request its execution on the associated Internet Explorer (through session) to the client who made the petition.

ANOTHER REALITY: SWMLSVG

SWML is the acronym for Signwriting Markup Language. It is based on XML and is used to store and process documents made in the sign language writing system (Rocha, 2004). Due to its characteristics and that its objective public is small, there aren't many developments to make

Figure 8. SWMLSVG Schema

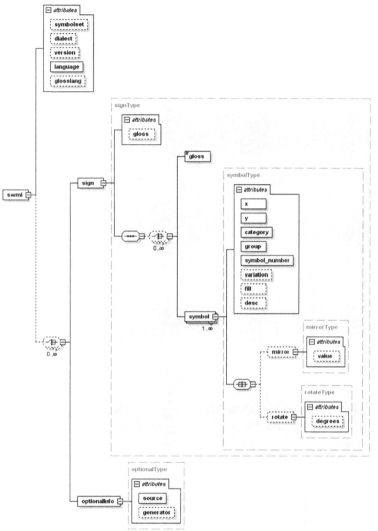

tasks with it with a computing equipment. If we add that each one of these programs stores information generated in its own format, the standardization, evolution and improvement of the kind of tools will be seriously affected.

That is the reason why in 2000 SWML's first version was born. Based on XML and with the intention of standardize the existing signwriting formats and open the doors to the Internet.

SWMLSVG is the evolution of SWML language. Until in 2004 the first SSS (Sign-Symbol-Sequence) data storage for vectorial graphics SVG

was generated, all the SignWriting storing sources were based on graphics PNG or GIF, with their respective limitations.

SSS is the acronym for Sign - Symbol – Sequence (Signwriting, 2008). SSS constitutes the official sequence in which signwriting symbols are organized. This way, the symbols can be accessible in a lexicographic way. We could say it is this system's alphabetical order and is basic in order to build dictionaries and do translations. SSS-2004-svg (Figure 8) is the file used to store images in SVG format that will make up the alphabet.

Figure 9. Architecture adapted to SWMLSVG for the generation of Signwriting

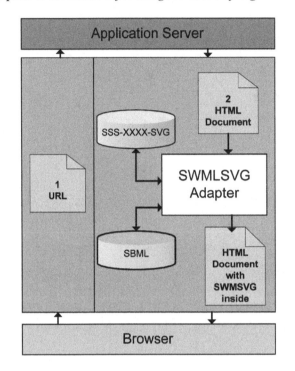

The SWMLSVG schema shown in the previous graph allows us to design Signwriting elements through SVG easily but, why should we bother to defend SVG as vectorial graphic medium?

If we understand vectorial graphics as those graphics in which its representation is made through the description of "traces" (lines, circles, curves,...) instead of a dot surface such as bitmaps or raster, the sign language elements creation would adjust perfectly to this definition. It is clear that, we can use them as bmp, png, gif, etc, format. But if we pretend or developments to be accessible for people with other kind of disability, it is necessary for the drawing to be able to enlarge its size as much as the user way want to, without losing quality, being this one of this kind of graphics' main characteristics. As for its main characteristics we can stand out four:

- They need less disk space than a raster (bitmap). Vectorial drawings usually take less space for simple representations, how-

ever, if we use complex images the difference decreases and the advantage reverts to bitmaps.
- They can be easily re-edited.
- Animations are much easier to do. For example, we can draw a leg and then move it or rotate it easily to represent movement.
- Besides, due to the fact the graphic is defined by vectors, we can modify its size without losing quality.

With the language implemented and justified we can set the architecture in charge of making the adaptations to written sign language (Figure 9):

- **Web Browser:** The web browser would be the client from which we will request a web application located in the application server, and will be in charge of showing the new web page with imbued SVG symbols.

Figure 10. Obtained results with the web designed for the application

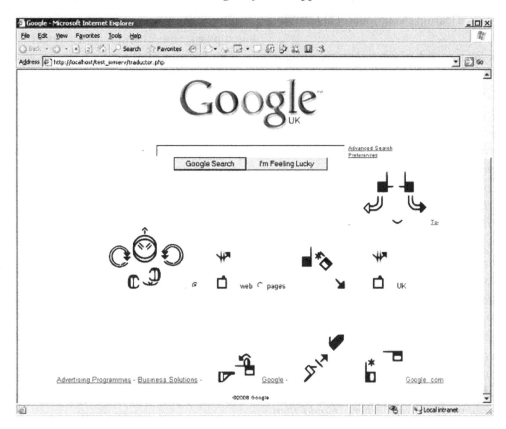

- **Application Server:** The web application will be located in the application server.
- **HTML Document with SWMLSVG:** Element that fulfills the specifications indicated in SWMLSVG.XSD, and is useful to storage the contents generated with the middleware.
- **SSS-200X-SVG:** Standard data storage that contains the different configurations a SVG Sign Language sign may have.
- **SWMLSVG:** Application executed in an intermediate server, allowing the full conversion of the HTML document to HTML with imbued SWMLSVG format.
- **SBML:** Data base with symbols previously configured and stored for a quick use.

With this architecture we obtain a simple way to communicate the Deaf Community with the rest of the members of the society, allowing through a web server, the publication of documents based on SWMLSVG, easily executable from any computer (Figure 10).

The developed middleware, SWMLSVG, is based on the framed SWMLSVG (Signwriting Markup Language for Scalable Vector Graphics) language, which has been defined to visualize easily, through XML and SVG, sign language signs in any web browser that supports the visualization of this kind of graphics.

WRAP UP

As future work is intended to provide further improvements to facilitate increasing integration of persons with disabilities in the social field in which there are today and more specifically as related to online learning techniques. This aims to:

- *Develop a sociological study of the various applications within the IT field is signwriting and break new ground and generate new ideas. This would favor the creation of an integration program for people with hearing impairment in formal education through the signwriting.*
- *Accessibility Platform approach to the problem of global accessibility worked in this thesis covers only two aspects. It would therefore be good to open as many lines of research as there are accessibility issues so that solutions were found are added to the platform.*
- *Introduce a new research line for the adaptation of any client in need of adaptation through the platform. Common applications market, such as word processors, databases, multimedia environments (Gonzalez, 2008) and others. Could then be used as a method of writing as signwriting and storage mechanism in swmlsvg signs.*
- *Open a research line about how swmlsvg can be the basis for two-dimensional animations through Signwriting symbols. This would be possible thanks to the capabilities of SVG for animation with vector graphics with the capabilities of SMIL, proposed as a language to facilitate accessibility in WCAG 2.0.*
- *Start a research line to expand and improve swmlsvg to allow a source of data storage for generating three-dimensional virtual signers.*
- *Improve our research line about achieving accessibility using the adapter (gateway) and get an accessibility level AAA instead of AA, under the current rules.*

Lastly, and regardless formats, schemas and other technical and computing elements, we must emphasize these two are at the service of the society with the aim of allowing people with disability and auditory disability, specifically, with serious communication problems to improve their quality of life through different means and existing mechanisms. The investment in this field and the involvement of the rest of the society to promote developments as the ones described previously will make feasible the reduction of the existing differences to equality.

REFERENCES

W3C - World Wide Web Consortium, (2005). Web Accesibility Initiative. Retrieved from http://www.w3c.es/ traducciones/ es/ wai/ intro/ accessibility, [01/08/2009]

Aenor. (2008). *Asociación española de normalización y certificiación.* Retrieved from http://www.aenor.es, [01/08/2009]

Blackboard. (2009). *Aplicación del Aprendizaje en Línea.* Retrieved from http://www.blackboard.com, [16/07/2009]

BOE - Boletín Oficial Del Estado. (43 de 19/02/2005). Retrieved from http://www.boe.es, [25/07/2009]

Golden, A. (2005). *Memorias de una Geisha.* Punto de Lectura.

Gonzalez, R. (2008). *Arquitecturas Intermedias de Adaptación de Contenidos Online para Lograr la Accesibilidad en Entornos Cambiantes Mediante Técnicas Emergentes.* Pontifical University of Salamanca.

INE - Instituto Naciaonal De Estadística. (2006). Retrieved from http://www.ine.es, [01/07/2006]

LSSIC - Ley Servicios de la Sociedad de la Información y de Comercio Electrónico. (2009). Retrieved from http://www.congreso.es/ public_ oficiales/ L7/ CONG/ BOCG/ A/ A_068-13.PDF.

Maher, J. (1996). *Seeing Language in Sign: The Work of William C. Stokoe*. Washington, DC: Gallaudet University Press.

Marchesi, A. (1999). *Psicología de la Comunidad Sorda*. Madrid, Spain: Fundación CNSE.

Mimbela, J. (2009). *e-learning, bases teóricas*. Santa Cruz, Cajarmarca: Universidad Nacional Pedro Ruiz Gallo Lambayeque.

Moodle. (2009). *Open-source community-based tools for learning*. Retrieved from http://www. moodle.org, [16/06/09]

Moreno, R. (2007). Optimizing learning from animations by minimizing cognitive load: Cognitive and affective consequences of signaling and segmentation methods. *Applied Cognitive Psychology, 21*, 1–17..doi:10.1002/acp.1348

ONU. (2006). Convención De Derechos De Las Personas Con Discapacidad. Ed. ONU.

Paas, F., Renkl, A., & Sweller, J. (2004). Cognitive Load Theory: Instructional Implications of the Interaction between Information Structures and Cognitive Architecture. Instructional Science, 2 (1-2). New York: Springer.

Padden, C., & Humhries, T. (1988). *Deaf in America: Voices from a culture*. Cambridge, MA: Hardvard University Press.

Parkhurst, S., & Parkhurst, D. (2000). *Un sistema completo para escribir y leer las Lenguas de Signos*. Madrid: PROEL.

Rocha, A., Pereira, G., & Baldez, J. (2004). A sign matching technique to support searches in sign language texts. Workshop on the Representation and Processing of Sign Languages, (LREC), Lisboa, Portugal.

SIGNWRITING. (2009). Read, Write, Type Sign Languages. Retrieved from http://www.signwriting.org, [10/05/2009]

Sweller, J. (2009). *Cognitive Load Theory*. Retrieved from http://tip.psychology.org/ sweller. html, [13/09/2009]

Torres, S. (2008). *Curso de Bimodal. Sistemas Aumentativos de Comunicación*. Universidad de Málaga. Retrieved from http://campusvirtual.uma. es/ sac/ _contenidos/, [11/04/2009]

WCAG1 - Web Content Accessibility Guidelines 1.0, (1999). Pautas de Accesibilidad al Contenido en la Web 1.0. Recomendación W3C de 5 de mayo de 1999. Retrieved from http://www.w3.org/ TR/ WCAG10/, [01/08/2009]

WCAG2 - Web Content Accessibility Guidelines 2.0, (2009). W3C Candidate Recommendation 30 April 2009. Retrieved from http://www.w3.org/ TR/ WCAG20/, [01/08/2009]

Chapter 12
Reviewing the European Innovation Activities and Industrial Competitiveness

George M. Korres
University of Newcastle, UK & University of the Aegean, Greece

Aikaterini Kokkinou
University of Glasgow, UK

ABSTRACT

The purpose of this chapter is to analyse and examine the evaluation and the development of Community's policy and how it can be implemented to European member states. This chapter also attempts to examine the effects of innovation activities and the impact of innovation policy on growth and productivity and integration process. More specifically, this chapter relates Research and Development with industrial infrastructure, productivity effects and regional development. Moreover, it analyses "national system of innovations" indicating the national technological capabilities, and also the structure and the planning on research and development. The main conclusion focuses on European technological policy and its important role for the economies of European member states with technological policy aiming to reinforce the competitiveness and enhance the convergence between member states.

INTRODUCTION

Since the early days of European economic integration, one of the central goals for the European Union has been greater equality of income and productivity among member states and regions. However, more recently, the process of European economic convergence has slowed down considerably and according to a widening group of economists, has ceased at the regional level after 1980. As a consequence, the costs and benefits of economic and monetary integration may not be equally distributed across European regions; it is possible that less developed regions will receive fewer benefits from the integration process. Therefore, it is of crucial importance to design

DOI: 10.4018/978-1-61350-192-4.ch012

European policies directed to reduce such dispari-ties, and to promote equality of opportunities in the territory. Indeed, if this is not achieved, the process of economic and monetary integration itself can be at risk.

Different studies dealing with the territorial cohesion in Europe highlight that income in-equalities inside the E.U. are very pronounced, especially across regions. Moreover, European income disparities, in terms of per capita Gross Domestic Product (GDP), are more accentuated at a regional level than at a country level. If per capital income across countries seems to have converged (especially across poor countries), the same pattern is not observed across European regions, either if the E.U. is taken as a whole or inside each of the country members of the Union. It seems that poor European regions do not tend to completely converge with rich regions. One of the possible solutions could be the enhancement of capital investment, as well as the innovation and R&D promotion, with one main channel be-ing the FDI activities. E.U. – 27 has a major FDI policy orientation regarding the FDI activities, as far as both inward and outward investments are concerned:

This paper attempts to examine the ef-fects of innovation activities and the impact of innovation policy on growth and productivity, and integration process.

THE EUROPEAN INNOVATION POLICY

As it has been broadly described above, innova-tion is a key factor to determine productivity growth. Innovation helps in understanding the sources and patterns of innovative activity in the economy, as a fundamental prerequisite to de-velop better policies. As such, innovation assists member states in identifying their own strengths and weaknesses and in designing corresponding policies and programmes. Notably to overcome

weaknesses and valorise strengths by identifying policy priorities, providing examples to articu-late policy strategies and to measure the impact of those strategies. Figure 1 illustrates that the innovation performance of the US and Japan is well above that of the EU27. The EU27-US gap has dropped significantlyup until 2007, but in the last 3 years the relative progress of the EU27 has slowed down. The EU27-Japan gap has remained stable between 2005 and 2009 although the gap has decreased up until 2008 but has increased again in 2009.

The 2009 European Innovation Scoreboard (EIS) provides a comparative assessment of the innovation performance of EU27 Member States, under the EU Lisbon Strategy, reporting overall innovation performance as calculated on the basis of 29 indicators covering five dimensions of innovation:

1. **Innovation drivers** measure the structural conditions required for innovation potential;
2. **Knowledge creation** measures the invest-ments in R&D activities;
3. **Innovation & entrepreneurship** mea-sures the efforts towards innovation at the firm level;
4. **Applications** measures the performance expressed in terms of labour and business activities and their value added in innovative sectors; and
5. **Intellectual property** measures the achieved results in terms of successful know-how.

The 2009 EIS report shows that most Member States until 2008 were steadily improving their innovation performance. The economic crisis may, however, be hampering this progress. Early indications show that the worst hit are Member States with lower levels of innovation perfor-mance, potentially reversing the convergence process witnessed over recent years. Meanwhile, the latest statistics show that the E.U. is having difficulty in catching up with the US in innovation

Figure 1. E.U. Innovation Gap

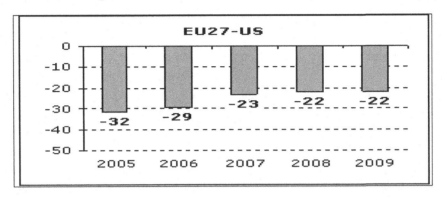

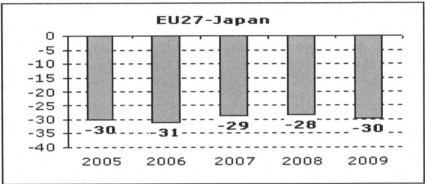

Note: Performance for each reference year is measured using, on average, data with a two-year lag (e.g. performance for 2009 is measured using data for 2007).
Source: European Union (2009), http://www.proinno-europe.eu/repository/51-us-and-japan

performance, although it maintains a clear lead over the emerging economies of Brazil, Russia, India and China, despite rapid improvements in China. More specifically, the members states of the E.U. - 27 fall into the following four country groups:

1. Denmark, Finland, Germany, Sweden and the UK are the **Innovation leaders,** with innovation performance well above that the EU27 average and all other countries. Of these countries, Germany and Finland are improving their performance fastest while Denmark and the UK are stagnating.

2. Austria, Belgium, Cyprus, Estonia, France, Ireland, Luxembourg, the Netherlands and Slovenia are the **Innovation followers,** with innovation performance below those of the

Innovation leaders but close to or above that of the EU27 average. Cyprus, Estonia and Slovenia have shown a strong improvement compared to 2008, providing an explanation why these countries have moved from the Moderate innovators in the EIS 2008 to the Innovation followers,

3. Czech Republic, Greece, Hungary, Italy, Lithuania, Malta, Poland, Portugal, Slovakia and Spain are the **Moderate innovators,** with innovation performance below the EU27 average. The EIS 2009 Moderate innovators are a mix of 5 Member States which were Moderate innovators in the EIS 2008 and 5 Member States which were Catching-up countries in the EIS 2008.

4. Bulgaria, Croatia, Latvia, Romania, Serbia and Turkey are the **Catching-up countries.**

Although their innovation performance is well below the EU27 average, this performance is increasing towards the EU27 average over time. All the countries are rapidly closing their gap to the average performance level of the EU27, and Bulgaria and Romania have been improving their performance the fastest of all Member States. This year's assessment shows that there continues to be convergence amongst the groups, with Moderate innovators and the Catching-up countries growing at a faster rate than the Innovation leaders and Innovation followers.

As far as each country is concerned, Germany, Cyprus, Malta and Romania are the EU27 countries displaying the largest improvement within their peer groups. Within each of the country groups there is variation in growth performance, with Finland and Germany showing the best growth performance of the Innovation leaders. Cyprus, Estonia and also Slovenia are the fastest growing Innovation followers. Czech Republic, Greece, Malta and Portugal are the fast growing Moderate innovators and Bulgaria and Romania are not only the fastest growers among the Catching-up countries but also overall.

On the other hand, an impressive average annual growth rate over the last five years has led Estonia and Cyprus to catch up with the EU27 average innovation performance in 2009. Both Cyprus and Estonia have improved their performance from below the EU27 average in the EIS 2008 to an above average performance in the EIS 2009. For Cyprus strong growth in Finance and support, Linkages & entrepreneurship and Throughputs have been the main drivers of its improvement in innovation performance. For Estonia strong growth in Firm investments and Throughputs have been the main drivers of its improvement in innovation performance.

Although the EU27 has been, overall, improving its innovation performance, the economic crisis may threaten this good progress, particularly in moderate innovators and catching-up countries. The EU27 is making overall progress, with particularly strong increases in the numbers of graduates in science, engineering, social sciences and humanities, venture capital, private credit, broadband access, community trademarks, community designs, technology balance of payments flows and sales of new-to-market products. The strong increases in venture capital and private credit most likely do not yet capture the impact of the economic downturn in 2008. However, the economic crisis may lead to a reversal of the convergence between EU27 countries in innovation performance. The 2008 European Innovation Scoreboard showed a clear process of convergence between EU27 Member States. The 2009 Scoreboard does not capture any possible impacts of the crisis, as most data come from 2007 and 2008. However, data from the 2009 Innobarometer survey suggests that the rapid advances in innovation performance made in many lower performing countries may not be maintained, at least in the short term, due to the severity of the economic crisis.

As the regional level is important for economic development and for the design and implementation of innovation policies, it is important to have indicators to compare and benchmark innovation performance at regional level. Such evidence is vital to inform policy priorities and to monitor trends. As a result, the 2009 RIS is able to replicate the methodology used at national level in the European Innovation Scoreboard (EIS), using 16 of the 29 indicators used in the EIS for 201 Regions across the EU27 and Norway. Changes over time are considered using principally data from 2004 and from 2006.

The 2009 Regional Innovation Scoreboard (2009 RIS) adopts the European Innovation Scoreboard approach at regional level and provides richer analysis compared to previous reports due to the availability of more comprehensive regional Community Innovation Survey data. The analysis shows that all major EU27 countries have diverse levels of performance and relative strengths within their regions, and that Spain, Italy and the Czech Republic are the most heterogeneous. The 2009 RIS marks a significant step forward in measuring regional innovation performance although it also shows that more progress is needed on the availability and quality of innovation data at regional level.

Despite this progress, the data available at regional level remains considerably less than at national level. Due to these limitations, the 2009 RIS does not provide an absolute ranking of individual regions, but ranks groups of regions at broadly similar levels of performance

The main findings of the 2009 Regional Innovation Scoreboard are:

1. **There is considerable diversity in regional innovation performances.** The results show that all countries have regions at different levels of performance. This emphasizes the need for policies to reflect regional contexts and for better data to assess regional innovation performances. The most heterogeneous countries are Spain, Italy and Czech Republic where innovation performance varies from low to medium-high.

2. **The most innovative regions are typically in the most innovative countries.** Nearly all the "high innovators" regions are in the group of "Innovation leaders" identified in the European Innovation Scoreboard (EIS). Similarly all of the "low innovators" regions are located in countries that have below average performance in the EIS. However, the results also show regions that outperform their country level:
   ◦ Noord-Brabant in the Netherlands is a high innovating region located in an Innovation follower country.
   ◦ Aha in the Czech Republic, Pais Vasco, Comunidad Foral de Navarra, Comunidad de Madrid and Cataluρa in Spain, Lombardia and Emilia-Romagna in Italy, Oslo og Akershus,

Sur-Ustlandet, Agder og Rogaland, Vestlandet and Trundelag in Norway are all medium-high innovating regions from Moderate innovators.
   ◦ The capital region in Romania, Bucuresti—Ilfov, is a medium low innovating region in a Catching-up country.

3. **Regions have different strengths and weaknesses.** A more detailed analysis was conducted for those regions with good data availability. This shows that regions are performing at different levels across three dimensions of innovation performance included in the EIS: Innovation enablers, Firm activities and Innovation outputs. Although there are no straight forward relationships between level of performance and relative strengths, it can be noted that many of the "low innovators" have relative weaknesses in the dimension of Innovation enablers which includes Human resources.

While a substantial minority of innovative firms in the EU27 are involved in product and process modification (about 30%), more than half of these firms involve users in support of their innovative activities. A sectoral analysis for the European countries shows that there are only limited differences between manufacturing and services sectors. Whereas for services sectors innovative sales are supported by growing demand and technology adoption, for manufacturing sectors it is firm size which drives innovative sales.

The financial crisis which started in 2007 has triggered a global economic downturn. This has resulted in at first falling economic growth rates followed by a real economic decline in many countries. Indicators of innovation performance, including those used in EIS, have a time lag of one or more years and therefore do not yet reveal the full impact of the crisis that reached its height in the second half of 2008. A thematic paper has been produced16 based on an analysis of the

Innobarometer 2009 survey (EC, 2009b) of innovating firms in the EU27 which was conducted in April 2009. The survey data indicates that 23% of innovative firms had decreased their innovation expenditures as a direct result of the economic downturn, and that 29% of firms expected their 2009 innovation expenditures to be lower than in 2008. This showed a marked transition from the period 2006-08 where only 9% of firms had decreased innovation expenditures.

The type of growth experienced by the countries of European Union seems to have been a spurt rather than progressive catch-up, and the 2007-2009 global financial crisis in particular has demonstrated the fragility of this growth. At the same time, there are several growth accounting exercises that suggest that growth in this region during the late 1990s and early 2000s was based mainly on total factor productivity (TFP), which from a conventional economic perspective suggests that this growth should be sustainable since it is based on technical change. We argue here that productivity growth in the region is based mainly on production, not innovation capability. Whether this production capability can be converted into greater productivity as well as S&T outputs depends largely on the efficiency of the national systems of innovation (NSI). So, in institutional terms, the long-term growth of EE countries will depend on whether their 'broad' and 'narrow' NSI can become efficient and effective carriers of innovation based growth.

The literature on the determinants of productivity suggests several related reasons for productivity growth: increased capital intensity; human capital; technological change; and competition (OECD, 2001). The key problem in trying to explore the determinants of productivity growth is whether it is appropriate to consider each individual component as a separate factor, since their contributions are closely interrelated (OECD, 2001). One of the most important drivers of technological change is R&D. Hence, as is the case with other factors, the issue is whether it is appropriate to isolate R&D as

a driver of productivity growth, from other factors. Aggregate studies often find that R&D provides a positive contribution to productivity growth.

The countries that are technologically backward have a potentiality to generate more rapid growth even greater than that of the advanced countries, if they are able to exploit the new technologies which have already employed by the technological leaders. The pace of the catching up depends on the diffusion of knowledge, the rate of structural change, the accumulation of capital and the expansion of demand. The member states that are lagging behind in growth rates can succeed in catching up, if they are able to reduce the technological gap. An important aspect of this is that they cannot rely only on the combination of technology imports and investment, but they should increase their innovation activities and improve locally produced technologies (such as in the case of new industrialized countries Korea and Singapore).

THE EUROPEAN INNOVATION POLICY AND COMPETITIVENESS

The analysis of system of innovations helps to understand and to explain, why the development of technology is necessary in a certain direction and at a certain rate. We should be very careful in the definition of the "regional systems" according to which sub-systems should be included and which process should be studied in the different countries.

Figure 2 illustrates, that even if EU–27 has real GDP growth rate similar to Japan and USA, in certain periods even higher, however, since 2007 there is a huge declining trend in the rate. Keeping in mind that EU–27 experiences a severe economic crisis, it is also worth mentioning that the members states do not all have the same GDP per capital levels, on the contrary there are significant differences, as seen in figure 3:

Figure 2. Real GDP growth

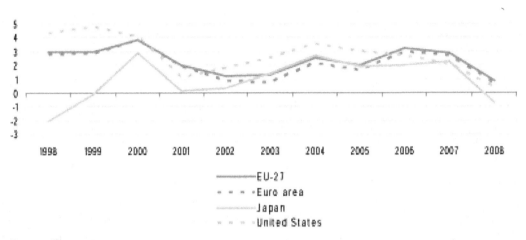

Source: Eurostat

We are using the term of "innovation" rather broadly, in order to encompass the processes by which firms master and get into practice product designs and manufacture processes that are new to them, if not to the nation. We are adopting in the term of "innovation" the actors that do research and development. The term "system" indicates something that is designed and built, but this concept is far from the orientation here. The term here indicates a set of institutions whose interactions determine the innovative performance. The term of "system" concept is a set of institutional actors that play the major role, influencing the innovative performance. We are using the term "regional system of innovations", in order to indicate the policies that are related with research and technological activities planning, (both from a macro and micro economic view) in a region.

The first approach and definition of "system of innovations" is that, it's a social system that is constructed by a number of elements, while there is a close-relationship between these elements. These elements are "interacting" in the production, diffusion, and economic cycles. We can define "the system of innovations" from a "narrow" view. According to "the narrow definition" it includes

organizations and institutions that of involved in searching and exploring the new technologies (such as technological institutes, and research departments). From the other side, the "broad" definition follows the theoretical perspective and includes the different parts of economic structure (such as the production system, and the marketing system). On international scene, when the large countries change the orientation of research activities, this is affects the small countries. Any improvement and technological sophistication in the traditional sectors for the large countries have usually pushed the small country' firms for the same sectors to follow the new technologies.

The development and diffusion of new technologies for a small country usually depend on the actions that have been undertaken by private enterprises and public sector organizations and institutions. However, this is a complex and interactive process that is taking place in the national system of production and affecting the competitiveness of the market and economy. In the contexts of bibliography, usually there are two different approaches analyzing the international competitiveness for the small countries. The first approach is mainly based on the trade theory and on

Figure 3. GDP per capita at current market prices, 2008

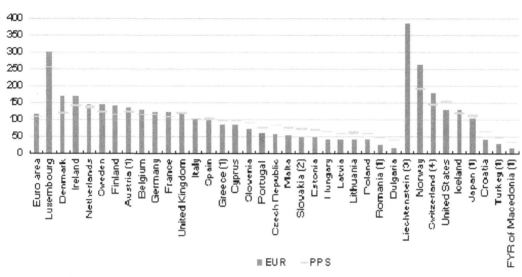

Source: Eurostat

the "relevant advantages" for the small countries. The second approach is based on the long-term accumulation of innovative and technological capabilities and in the technological specialization for the small countries.

There are a lot of reasons suggesting that a "free-enterprise market system" without government intervention (particularly for small size countries) is likely to support insufficient scientific effort and sometimes this does not allocate to an efficient pattern. We can summarize some of these reasons: First, companies (especially small medium enterprises) are usually unable to allocate the appropriate and adequate share of total gains in such efforts. Second, risk and uncertainties associated with such efforts that cannot be undertaken fully by private agents. Third, social problems that imply the transmission of scientific and technological activities. Fourth, imperfections in capital markets that is in the provision of funds for scientific efforts and technological changes. Fifth, avoidance of wasteful duplication of scientific services. Sixth,

consideration of national security. Seventh, the development of large scale-economies and the importance of the markets. These reasons advocate that the government technological intervention is an important point for the development of research and scientific activities.

Usually, it is also true that the small and weak technological countries have fewer resources than the larger countries. Small countries can be allocated to less resources for research and technological activities than the larger countries. Due to these reasons, the small size countries are usually forced either to allocate their resources more thinly in different areas and related activities, or to select some "certain areas" for research and technological priorities.

On the other side, the advanced technological countries are usually investing in the development of new technologies in "associated strategic industries" that aim to increase the competitiveness, the economic growth and the living standards. However, in practice different countries choose different priorities for technological and economic subjects and put emphasis, in these areas in which they believe they will have more potential in future. The advanced technological countries make their plans with more long-term scientific intensive criteria and usually the priorities that choosed are based in the most expensive and high technology areas, while sometimes they carry out research in collaboration with other countries. On the other side, the small countries are forced to choose these sectors, that they easily to develop, and to compete and furthermore try to strengthen the technological basis in international competitive scene. The existence of specialized research and technological institutions, the amounts allocated for research and technological activities and the availability of resources in the large countries, give an additional advantage and imply that the large countries are usually leading in the trends and in the fashions for the different research and technological topics. Therefore, the small countries tend to follow the "direction" set by the leading-large countries, and sometimes they are forced to follow even if the relevant research and technological topics are not the most appropriate and necessary to cover their specific needs. It is necessary, for the small countries to pay more attention to identify the specific priorities that can exploit the particular advantages (such as natural and human resources, and to increase their research expenditures). An important thing for the weak technological countries is to establish and to improve the technological infrastructure.

POLICY IMPLICATIONS AND CONCLUSIONS

The Commission calls upon Member States to make the structural reforms necessary to deliver the results required. In the context of the Lisbon strategy, the Commission has adapted its regulatory framework on State aids to enable Member States to develop new measures in favour of the support of innovation, taking into account the identified market failures of Europe in this domain. This should also encourage Member States and regions to redirect State support, for instance from structural funds, towards activities that are most directly correlated with the Lisbon agenda.

Small countries are likely to need a more comprehensive and oriented policy of co-operative innovative effort, in order to develop their future capabilities and to make the necessary choice for technological priorities. Looking first at scientific and technological output, the EU is still ahead of the US and Japan in its share of scientific publications, but lags behind in most of the other performance indicators, especially patents. There is, nonetheless, a substantial variation within the EU and certain EU Member States often score better than the US and Japan (most notably Sweden and Finland), yet the overall situation in the EU-27 is far from satisfactory. Although there are some noticeable encouraging tendencies in several acceding countries, one can expect that with the enlargement of the Union, the «European Paradox» will be, at least temporarily, further accentuated. In other words, in relation to its enlarged population, the EU-25's strong performance in science will contrast increasingly with its weaker development and commercialization of technology. The slowing down of EU-27 investment in the knowledge-based economy is likely to be reflected sooner or later in a significant decline in its performance. This trend underlines the urgency of implementing the Lisbon Strategy. In particular, the EU needs to increase its efforts, so as to give renewed impetus to the catching up of some countries with the rest of the EU-27 and to close the gap as soon as possible with the US and provide the economic opportunities and quality jobs needed in less favored regions.

Today, the innovation-gap is nearly twice as great as the cohesion gap. Many of the causes of disparities among regions can be traced to disparities in productivity and competitiveness. Education, research, technological development and innovation are vital components of regional competitiveness. Long-term foreign private capital flows have a complementary and catalytic role to play in building domestic supply capacity as they lead to tangible and intangible benefits, including export growth, technology and skills transfer, employment generation and poverty eradication. Policies to attract FDI are essential components of national development strategies.

The inter-regional innovation-gap is not only of a quantitative nature but also of a qualitative one. There are a number of characteristics of regional innovation systems in less advance regions which make them less efficient:

- Firms may not be capable of identifying their innovation needs or maybe unaware of the existence of a technical solution.
- There may be poorly developed financial systems in the area with few funds available for risk or seed capital, which are specifically adapted to the terms and risks of the process of innovation in firms.
- There may be a lack of technological intermediaries capable of identifying and 'federating' local business demand for innovation (and RTD&I) and channeling it towards sources of innovation (and RTD&I) which may be able to respond to these demands.
- Co-operation between the public and private sectors may be weak, and the area may lack an entrepreneurial culture which is open to inter-firm co-operation, leading to an absence of economies of scale and business critical mass which may make certain local innovation efforts profitable.
- Traditional industries and small family firms may dominate which have little inclination towards innovation. There may be a low level of participation in international RTD&I networks and a low incidence of large, multinational firms.

Given all the above, we believe that regional policy should increasingly concentrate its efforts on the promotion of innovation to prepare regions for the new economy and close the 'technology gap' if it is to be successful in creating the conditions for a sustained (and sustainable) economic development process in less favoured regions. Now, before we turn to what has been our policy response over the last decade and what our ideas about the future are, let me briefly pick up the second question. Regional policy should evolve from supporting physical innovation infrastructure and equipment towards encouraging co-operation and a collective learning process among local actors in the field of innovation. A policy which facilitates the creation of rich, dynamic regional innovation systems and which assists in the exchange of skills and expertise which small and medium sized firms may not have available in-house.

In this context, a stable economic, legal and institutional framework is crucial in order to attract foreign investment and to promote sustainable development through investment. In this regard a conducive international financial environment is also crucial. Promoting a conducive macroeconomic environment, good governance and democracy, as well as strengthening structural aspects of the economy and improved institutional and human capacities, are important also in the context of attracting FDI and other private external flows.

REFERENCES

David, P. A. (1975). *Technical choice, innovation and economic growth.* New York: Cambridge University Press.

European Commission. (2009). *European Innovation Scoreboard.* EIS.

European Commission. (2009). *Regional Innovation Scoreboard.* RIS.

Greene, W. (2003). *Distinguishing Between Heterogeneity and Inefficiency: Stochastic Frontier Analysis of the World Health Organization's Panel Data on National Health Care Systems.* Working Paper 03-10, Department of Economics, Stern School of Business, New York University, New York.

Koetter, M. (2006). Measurement Matters – Alternative Input Price Proxies for Bank Efficiency Analyses. *Journal of Financial Services Research, 30*, 199–227.. doi:10.1007/s10693-006-0018-4

Korres, G. (1996). *Technical change and Productivity Growth: an empirical evidence from European countries.* London: Avebury-Ashgate.

Kravtsova, V., & Radosevic, S. (2009). Are Systems of Innovation In Eastern Europe Efficient? *Economics Working Paper No.101,* Centre for Comparative Economics, UCL School of Slavonic and East European Studies UCL SSEES, Centre for Comparative Economics.

Malecki, E. J. (1991). *Technology and economic development: the dynamics of local regional and national change.* Essex, UK: Longman Scientific and Technical.

Mansfield, E. (1968). *Economics of technological change.* New York.

Meeusen, W., & van Den Broeck, J. (1977). Efficiency estimation from Cobb – Douglas Production Functions with Composed Error. *International Economic Review, 18*(2), 435–444.. doi:10.2307/2525757

Movshuk, O. (2004). Restructuring, productivity and technical efficiency in China's iron and steel industry, 1988–2000, purch. *Journal of Asian Economics, 15*(1), 135–151. doi:10.1016/j.asieco.2003.12.005

Nelson, R. (1993). *National innovation systems: a comparative analysis.* Oxford University Press.

OECD. (2001a). *Basic research: statistical issues. OECD/NESTI Document DSTI/EAS/STP/NESTI(2001)38.* Paris: OECD.

OECD. (2001b). *The new economy: beyond the hype.* Final report on the OECD growth project. Meeting of the OECD Council at ministerial level, 2001. OECD, Paris.

OECD. (2002a). *Frascati Manual. Proposed standards practice for surveys on research and experimental development.* Paris: OECD.

OECD. (2002b). *Public funding of R&D - trends and changes. OECD Document DSTI/STP(2002)3/REV1 prepared by the ad hoc working group on «Steering and Funding of Research Institutions».* Paris: OECD.

Stoneman, P. (1987). *The economic analysis of technology policy.* Oxford, UK: Oxford University Press.

Stoneman, P. (1995). *Handbook of the Economics of Innovations and technological change.* Oxford, UK: Blackwell.

Timmer, M. O'Mahony, M. & van Ark, B. (2008). *The EU KLEMS Growth and Productivity Accounts: An Overview.* University of Groningen & University of Birmingham.

Chapter 13
City Structure in Transition:
A Conceptual Discourse on the Impact of Information and Communication Technology (ICT)

Kh. Md. Nahiduzzaman
King Fahd University of Petroleum and Minerals, Saudi Arabia

Adel S. Aldosary
King Fahd University of Petroleum and Minerals, Saudi Arabia

ABSTRACT

With the technological advancement of ICT, the cities of the world are becoming so dependent that ICT is challenging the conventional ideas and classic theories of city structure. The cities of the world are undergoing a transition that is caused by the shift of principle from 'physical movement' to 'virtual movement'. The state-of-the-art ICT featured by internet and e-commerce (Business-to-Commerce - B2C) is facilitating such shift which influences in changing the conventional ideas and structure of CBD, core business areas, city center, etc. Though the magnitude of influence on the transition process is yet to be known, there is an obvious transition that almost all cities of the world are experiencing. This book chapter conceptually discusses and portrays the potential changes in the conventional city structure by analyzing three classic city models (i.e., multi-nuclei, concentric and sector models), exploring the technological advancement in ICT and increasing dependencies on it and by drawing evidence from a pilot case study. This chapter argues that ICT induced change in the city structure, which we may call 'future city' or 'transitional city', would bring positive impacts on the physical and social environment, competitive land and transportation system in the city.

DOI: 10.4018/978-1-61350-192-4.ch013

INTRODUCTION

Information and communication technology (ICT) has increasingly become so important that everyday life cannot be thought of without it. The benefits of ICT have been spreading at a rate higher than ever and its effects are rooted to almost every aspects of everyday life such as from home, business, office and to every other domain (Aoyama, 2001; Abbate, 1999; Castells, 1989). There is a conventional wisdom that ICT and city planning are two different domains of knowledge that rarely have any mutual interdependence and inter-disciplinary effects (Aoyama, 2001; Audretsch, 1998). In many occasions, they are considered as two complete different disciplines without properly exploring and advancing the fact on the nature of their relationships and influences. It is evident, therefore, that there is a knowledge gap on the facts of their level of influences and its magnitude. Given this knowledge gap, this paper attempts to conceptually explore and analyze how the increasing dominance of ICT has been influencing to shape or re-shape the city structure. Though this paper draws a conceptual discourse, a pragmatic evidence of the current influence of ICT on a few aspects of the city structure is brought and analyzed to be able to open up a few windows of thoughts and scopes for further research on spatial planning. Among different areas of ICT, this paper explores the following two broad segments: e-commerce (B2C: Business-to-consumer) and online based multi-media, to explore and analyze their current and imminent effects on the city fabric.

CITY STRUCTURE AND ICT: A THEORETICAL CONSTRUCT

This section discusses and reviews literature on the typical city structure (e.g., location of CBD, development of sub-urban areas, location of industries, major commercial activities, and other service facilities, etc.) and the advancement of ICT, particularly focusing on e-commerce (i.e., B2C). This will conceptually help to re-visit the conventional city structure and its hierarchy. Therefore, classic theories on city structure are discussed in this paper based on two approaches namely, ecological and economic approaches. Burgees', Hoyt's and Thunen's models are brought in to be able to understand the possible impact of ICT on the existing and popular wisdom of city structure and its hierarchy. This impact eventually demonstrates the power towards positive environmental changes, such as reduced number of trips, traffic congestion, low carbon emission, decreasing competition for acquiring high priced land in the CBD, etc.

Analysis of City Spatial Structure

The application of ecological approach for spatial structure of a city is a straightforward projection of ecological orientation directed to look for regular patterns of spatial distribution. This concept was first given by Burgess' in 1920s that was associated with a graphical description of ecological map of Chicago city, as a series of five concentric zones (Alshuwaikhat, 1988). Central Business District (CBD) which is known as inner most zone with all the dominant commercial activities, such as shopping areas, theatre districts, hotels, office buildings, banking districts and other businesses where land value is very high compared to other parts of the city. The next order zone often termed as 'zone of transition' which is easily identified by variety of changing feature of uses, such as residential areas, island-like cluster of first-citizen, homes persisting behind brick walls and iron fences, clinging tenaciously to the respectability that once marked in the entire area. Old structures may be still standing, but some signs of new usages and large apartment houses. The Third order zone is largely known as workingmen's homes of factory workers, laborers, low-income residents, etc. The Fourth zone is containing the large residential areas where the white collar workers and middle-class families are mostly prevalent. The Fifth or outer most zone which is also known as commuters' zone where suburban communities are found along the arteries of transport corridor. According to the model, this is where the middle and high-income classes reside (see Figure 2). Burgess' model clearly portrays the structuration of a city according to different landuses which are directly or indirectly determined by land prices. This model conventionally depicts the strong relationship between landuse and land price where transportation, in terms of accessibility, plays a major role. The CBD facilitates the citizens by bringing the entire commercial and other daily facilities together where there is a regular need of physical access to the CBD. This model clearly demonstrates that the regular needs of each citizen have to be physically transported and, therefore, the city has been stratified on account of accessibility and land price.

As Burgess' developed his model on the basis of empirical observations of some cities in the U.S., it was criticized by many critics at the later stage. One of the significant criticisms was that it would not be applicable for relatively small size non-industrial cities. However, in the late 1930s, Homer Hoyt, an economist, developed the 'sectoral model' which is treated as the modification to Burgess' model as it retains many of the concentric model's features. The sector model provides some new insights into the landuse pattern and rents paid for several clusters where different income-classes of a city tend to be found in distinct areas describable in terms of sectors of a circle centered on the CBD. The high rent or high price residential areas can be identified in particular sectors and there is a gradation of rentals downward from these high rental areas in all directions. Intermediate rental areas adjoining the high rental areas on one or more sides and tend to be located in the same sectors as high rental areas, whereas low rent areas occupy other entire sectors

of the city from the center to the periphery (see Figure 2).

The Hoyt's model is also criticized because of its definitional oversimplification of sectors and narrow perspective of identification of forces behind the distribution and movement of different rental areas. In 1945s, Harris and Ullman argued that the land use pattern of the city grows around several district nuclei rather than single center or multi-sector. They developed a multi nuclei model which was first introduced by McKenzie (Alshuwaikhat, 1988). It was a deliberate attempt to develop a generalization form about the city structure and growth. The model demonstrates that there are a series of nuclei in urban landuse pattern rather than single center core where the number and function of each nucleus varies from one metropolitan area to another. The CBD serves as one nucleus while others may appear in the form of industrial or wholesaling centers. Suburban center and other more distant satellite communities for commuters are also mentioned as nuclei (see Figure 2). Despite the criticisms of the above mentioned models, there are some basic lessons learnt from the models i.e., land price is one of the determinants that influence the location of landuses, such as CBD, residential areas, recreation areas, location of industries, etc. and land price is a function of transport accessibility which facilitates citizens to meet their daily needs. This explicitly implies that in order to meet the daily needs, the citizens have to be physically transported to different places where different land uses are located. Location of such landuse is strongly determined by the land price.

The economic approach analyzes the spatial structures of the cities introduced by the earlier works of land economists based on the neoclassical economic theory. The central theme of the economic theories was to establish and recognize the relationships between distance and accessibility in the distribution of landuses where land is supposed to be allocated for its most profitable use. Among the theories, Alonso's theory of urban

Figure 1. Conceptual diagram of the pattern of physical transportation to different landuses determined by and price (Source: Own construct)

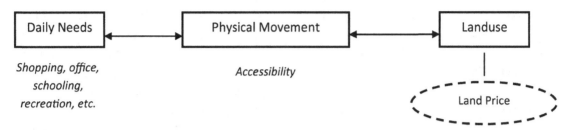

Figure 2. Models of spatial structure of city (Source: Chapin, 1979)

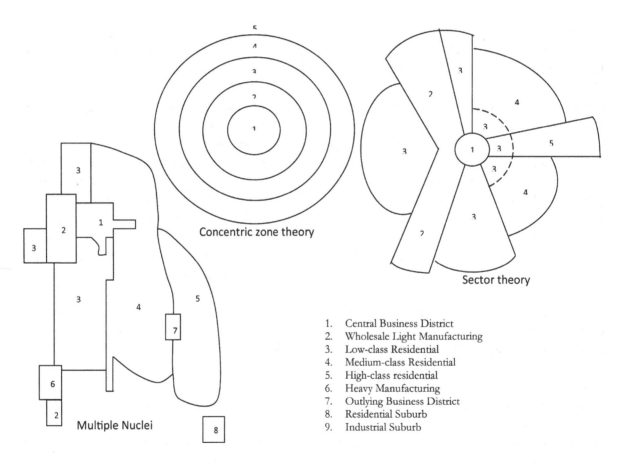

1. Central Business District
2. Wholesale Light Manufacturing
3. Low-class Residential
4. Medium-class Residential
5. High-class residential
6. Heavy Manufacturing
7. Outlying Business District
8. Residential Suburb
9. Industrial Suburb

landuse showed marked continuity and conformity with earlier writers of the industrial city based on observations (Alshuwaikhat, 1988). The theory developed by Alonso is the urban and mathematical version of Von Thunen's agricultural model. It is applicable to both firms and individual household as consumers of space. The central theme of Alonso's theory is the historical explanation of urban structure and contrasting them with a structural explanation as that household locates in urban space so as to maximize their utility. It is shown that the high-income class prefers low densities which take a longer journey to workplace (Alshuwaikhat, 1988).

In regard to the diagram presented in Figure 1, this paper analyzes the possible impacts of ICT on the need of physical transportation to different places of the city where different uses are located. The above models describing different conventional city structures have been developed based on the conceptual diagram shown in Figure 1. But with the increasing advancement of ICT, the need for physical transportation might be immaterial and hence pressure in acquiring locations for different landuses might be decreased to a substantial extent as the daily needs of the citizens might be served by other mode of transportation or by other means which is different than the conventional transportation, such as private cars. In the end based on the trend of technological advancement of ICT, this paper conceptually sketches the imminent changes in the spatial pattern of the conventional city structure.

E-Commerce: Business-to-Consumer (B2C)

Within the technological advancement of ICT, Business-to-consumer (B2C), a type of e-commerce, are briefly discussed here to explore the possible ways that might impact on the transformation of people's behavior towards 'physical transportation' and hence influence the physical structure and hierarchy of the city. B2C e-commerce, between companies and consumers, is the earliest and one of the largest forms of e-commerce. It involves consumer gathering information, purchasing physical (consumer products tangible in nature) or information (intangible in nature, such as software, e-books, etc.) of goods that are purchased over an electronic network, via credit card or some other means (Andam, 2003; Aoyama, 2001). Among others, Andam (2003) mentions several areas of its application including

purchasing of products and information, managing personal finance using online banking tool, data base development and management, management information system etc. Many B2C e-commerce researches show that there is a substantial increase in revenue in the recent years due to the benefits in different aspects both from consumer and producers point of views.

First of all B2C e-commerce reduces transactions costs, particularly search cost for products and services, by increasing access to products, services and information to find the most competitive price for that product or service. Secondly, it reduces market entry barriers as the cost of putting up and maintaining a web site is much cheaper than buying or renting a land parcel in the competitive commercial zone to install a 'brick and mortar' structure for a store. It also saves stores or firms from factoring the additional cost of physical distribution of networks (Andam, 2003). Now the question is how B2C possibly influences in shaping or re-shaping the city structure in a manner that could be unconventional in nature. Next section develops a conceptual discourse on the current and possible transition of city structure based on the ongoing technological advancement in ICT. On the part of a pilot case, the influence of internet, home based multimedia and satellite channels on the city structure is explored and analyzed by drawing pragmatic evidence from a small city, called Rajshahi, of Bangladesh.

ICT AND DAILY LIFE IN TRANSITION

ICT has brought dramatic changes in our daily lives (Arndt, 2001). Knowingly or unknowingly people have become very dependent on ICT, resulting in changes in our social life. Until the early 90s shopping mall was one of the most popular places where people roam around, observe, examine, and purchase different products from different stores of their choices and it may still be the case. With the advent of B2C e-commerce, a significant outcome of ICT, a new dimension and an increasing trend of shopping has been noticed lately. Beside conventional shopping, people also examine and purchase products without making any physical trip to the shopping mall, rather they order for those products while being at home or any place where they have access to the internet. Through internet based websites people are able to experience a virtual shopping world where detailed features of different products are presented in a realistic manner (Anddam, 2003; Arndt, 2001; Leinbach, 2001). In that virtual platform, online purchase is being performed by B2C e-commerce at their discretion. Until to date, country wise there is no specific data/information on the fact of shift of purchase from traditional shopping to B2C e-commerce, but understandably with the increasing dependencies on the internet based B2C e-commerce, a substantial amount of shopping is performed in virtual world where physical observation and existence of the buyers and sellers, as seen in traditional shopping, is becoming immaterial. For example, in traditional shopping for ornaments, books, clothing, or other daily necessities, the prospective buyer needs to make one or several trips via car or other mode of transport to the stores to be able to purchase them with the aid of cash or credit card. Contrarily, through B2C e-commerce buyers does not necessarily need to make any trip to the stores, but they can perform the selection and purchasing jobs though e-commerce being seated in front of the computer irrespective of their locations in the city – whether at home, out in the fringe areas, city center or somewhere else. Once the order is processed through e-commerce, the products are sent to the buyer's place of choice within a promised duration of time.

Likewise, with the technological advancement of ICT and with the advent of online library and purchasing system, there is no absolute necessity for the readers to go to the library, may be located perhaps somewhere in the down town or in the neighborhood center, to get the required books to purchase. Rather this service is more conveniently offered through different online based libraries by various companies where the buyers can select from a wide variety of books of their interests and purchase them (i.e., both conventional hard paper binding book and e-book) using the credit card or other online banking system. In such practice, the acquisition of land space for traditional large establishment for libraries is an immaterial thinking that has normal opening hours and that demands physical visit for any tiny purchase or reading.

It is an undeniable fact that the trend of using credit card (e.g., master cared, visa, American express, etc.) has been increasing over the years and daily life has become very dependent on it both in the west and eastern world. This increasing trend is also an indication that a large volume of transaction has been taking place in the virtual world through internet, which has significantly reduced people's conventional and physical movement that is associated with trips, traffic congestion, carbon emission and the like.

Amazon is one of the most popular and giant companies and is known to be one of the best examples of online based library, which offers a wide variety of book choices to the readers to purchase from. Not only books, it is also engaged in e-commercing a wide variety of other daily products, such as electronic equipments, movies, music, games, computers, clothing, shoes, jewelry items, etc. Understandably, such online based purchasing method has substantially impacted people's movement and the need for space for physical establishments for that wide variety of products. Among others, eBay is another online shopping giant offering a similar and wide range of services and products. Other multi-national giants, such as Adidas, Nike, GAP, L'Oreal, etc. are also increasingly shifting toward online based purchase operation beside their conventional feet on the traditional method for trade.

Same line of trend is noticeable in performing office tasks. With the internet based e-mailing system and video conferencing options, physical presence of the office personnel at the office desks has become less relevant. People do not need to make any office trips as they can perform most of their tasks, if not all, by being at home or at any places where they have access to internet. They do not even need to physically attend the regular (e.g., weekly, bi-monthly, monthly, etc.) office meeting, but through video conferencing they would be able to contribute in the same way as they would have done by their physical presence. Contrarily, in traditional office movement practice, people need to make daily trips to and from offices, which significantly contributes to the traffic congestion in the road, which is popularly known as congestion in the peak hours (e.g., during the opening and closing office hours). Not only this, offices are also physically located in the prime locations (i.e., office business district in the CBD) of the city where land price is not only high, but also land acquisition process is lengthy and very competitive.

In the academic practice, conferences, workshops, symposiums, etc. are considered to be the most popular and effective scientific platforms for sharing and disseminating experiential and contextual knowledge of different fields. But traditionally those scientific gatherings demand physical participation of the research scholars/practitioners by flying, for instance, thousands of mileages to attend there. In the era of global climate challenge, this is an increasing and long-standing concern. The air traffic movement of this sort and for other purposes (e.g., vacation trips, official trips, etc.) has been substantially increased and thus adversely affecting the global environment (Zook, 2000; Kolko, 1999). Contrarily, for the scientific congregation, this has been a wide and popular practice to rent an exquisite hotel, resort or convention center that is, perhaps, located in strategic places of the city where understandably land value is pretty expensive and there is an acute competition for land acquisition. In contrast to this, since the last decade an increasing practice has also been noticed that international, national or regional conferences, workshops, symposiums are taking place in the virtual world where there is absolutely no necessity for the participants to fly to a luxurious and expensive locations in other parts of the world to meet other scholars. Rather they meet each other in the virtual world and discuss theories, discourses, principles, etc. through the video conferencing option. In that circumstance, it is absolutely irrelevant for the participants where they are located in the world or if they need to fly thousands of miles at the cost of the environment. Though some might consider time differences in different time zones as a barrier for the participants to meet in the virtual world in one time, this could be overcome by a mental satisfaction by looking at the big picture of not producing any carbon that would have adversely affected the environment by their air traffic movements.

Arguably, from the above discussion it is understood that ICT has brought many changes that has been affecting people's movement, especially in the areas of trip generations, distributions, and occupancy of land space in the prime locations (Figure 1), which has a strong influence in reshaping the city structure. With this notion a pilot study was carried out in a metropolitan city of Bangladesh, called Rajshahi, where the physical and social effects of internet based multimedia, home theatre (DVD, VCD player) and satellite channels were observed to measure their effects on the operation and physical existence of cinema theatres.

Before the advent of internet based multimedia, home theatre and satellite channels, watching movies in the cinema theatres was one of the most popular recreational and social events for the city populations. Therefore, those cinema theatres were located in the prime locations (i.e., in the core business areas) of the city where land value was comparatively higher than other places. With the advancement of ICT, when those home based theaters, internet based multimedia and satellite channels came into operations and rapidly expanded to the entire city, the city people inclined

Figure 3. Transformation of landuse from a cinema theatre (under construction) to a shopping mall in Rajshahi city (Photo courtesy: Mr. Akhtaruzzaman)

to stay at home for watching movies rather going out to the theaters. Monthly subscription cost of the satellite channels, internet and cost of DVD, VCD, etc. were cheaper than the ticket costs for movies shown in the cinema theatres. Moreover, movies at home gave viewers a greater flexibility to watch at per their comfort and conveniences. Due to the agglomeration effects of these ICT based industries, a diminishing trend of people going to the cinema theatres was noticed and eventually the theatres were found almost abandoned. Degraded quality of the local movies was a factor that contributed partly not to attract many customers, but this is also associated with the fact that they have better and wider list of movie choices at home at an affordable cost. As multiplier and perpetuating effects, the small scale industries being developed around the cinema theaters were excruciatingly impacted. Therefore, the owners of the cinema theaters were compelled to convert the use of the theatre buildings to, for example,

shopping malls, residential buildings, hospitals and other commercial establishments that have higher market demand and brings financial profits (see Figure 3) Such transformation has been significantly influencing the entire city structure too. As a primary effect, land value around those cinema theaters was drastically decreased and the infrastructure (e.g., wide roads, etc.) developed around them started to be used in the least extent (both in time and number of users) than what capacity they were designed for. Number of traffic flow was gradually reduced towards those cinema theatres, but the flow started to increase to other parts of the city where the DVD, VCD, satellite channel and internet provider stores are located (see Figure 4).

There was also a significant shift of inner city traffic flow caused by the landuse changes i.e., transformation of cinema theatres to other uses, increasing trend of in-house home theatre, shift of supporting and small scale commercial activi-

Figure 4. Different ICT based stores have started to develop that primarily meet the demand for online and satellite based home theatre (Photo courtesy: Mr. Akhtaruzzaman)

ties that started to develop around those ICT based industries. There was a noticeable change in the recreation part of the city life. Earlier the nature of people was relatively outgoing due to the fact that watching movies in cinema theatres was one of the most popular, social and recreational weekly events. With the increasing invasion by home based theatres, the need for going out for movie-based recreation was decreased which, in turn, reduced the number of trips in the inner city (see Figure 5). This is because of the fact that the demand for open space, parks, play ground, river side areas, etc. in the social and recreational areas has increased as the city population gradually got used to in-house recreational activities through satellite channels, home based theatres, etc.

It was notice worthy that land value also started to increase in the newly developed ICT based industrial areas. This, eventually, affects the city landscape and structure to a considerable extent which is presented in Figure 5. The associated and supporting small scale industries around the cinema theatres lost their business and thereby commercial value of those lands became

significantly low. This is why a large portion of the areas surrounding cinema theatres remained vacant. A number of residential compounds were under development which understandably is the result of shift of landuses caused by the indirect pitcher effects of ICT based industries. It is shown in the map (Figure 5) that the traffic movement in the inner city has reduced and increased towards the open spaces, parks, gardens and especially to the riverbank side areas.

This pilot study proves the assertion that the increasing dependencies on ICT have been influencing the city's conventional physical structure. It is obvious that the ICT will, and still is, undergo a massive technological advancement which will directly and indirectly influence the life style of the citizens reflecting in their 'physical movement' and this will eventually impact in the transition of city structure. But the question remains on the quest that how fast or slow the state-of-the-art ICT will accelerate the transformation process. Next section, therefore, develops a discourse on the possible impacts of above mentioned technologi-

Figure 5. Transformation effects of ICT based industries in Rajshahi city (Source: modified by the authors from Google map, 2010)

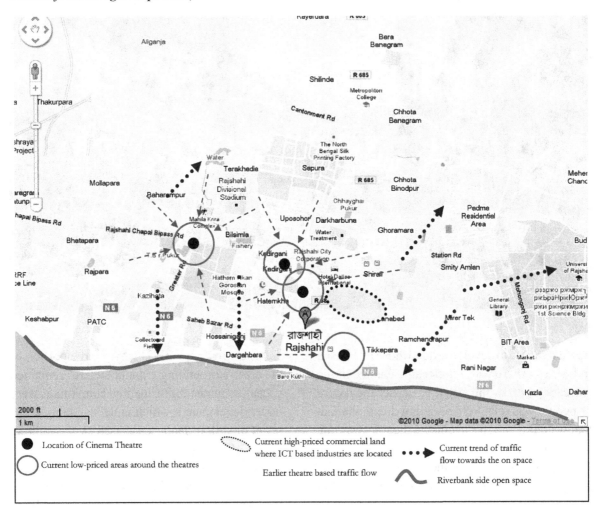

CHANGING CITY STRUCTURE

This section starts by putting a simple question: what sort of spatial and social changes the ICT are going to bring in the conventional city structure? The aforementioned discussion and pilot study's evidence on the transition of city's daily life focuses on the crux issue that 'physical movement' of the citizens is becoming less relevant for daily activities, such as for office work, any kind of shopping, reading, academic gathering, etc. The effects on the 'physical movement' are, however, not confined to the above discussed areas only. But based on the insights drawn from those examples and on the evidence of the pilot study, a conceptual and holistic picture is drawn on how increasingly less dependency on the 'physical movement' would influence the entire city structure to be re-shaped. Changing city structure is also associated with the positive environmental

cal advancement of ICT and B2C e-commerce on city's physical structure.

factors that help the city to be more resilient and sustainable.

Let's just concentrate on different types shopping that are carried out by making at least 2 trips (going there and coming back) by one person. If the shopping job is being performed without making any trip, we can imagine that how many trips will be saved in shopping for a family alone. If we aggregate all the families in the city and take shopping alone as a purpose for trip, we can estimate how many trips are getting reduced which in turn affecting in emitting less carbon in the city air and in contributing less traffic to the already congested roads. This same function is applicable for any trip ('physical movement') that is generated by different purposes that we discussed earlier. It is understandable that with the application and use of state-of-the-art ICT in daily life how such purpose oriented trips for each individual would be reduced. Not only from environmental (i.e., less carbon affecting the city and global environment) and less congested transportation system point of views, but also increasing dependencies on ICT has a wide range of influence on the land price too. In the traditional shopping culture, one of the most attractive parts of trading is presentability of the products. For this, most of the shopping malls and stores are well decorated, designed and they are located in the prime locations in the city where land price is fairly high, but easily accessible to the customers. The principal aim of the entire sellers is to attract customers and, therefore, they are competing for the strategic locations in the city that are convenient and attractive to the customers. Due to high competition among the sellers, land price and rent automatically experiences a hike that is also accelerated by the limited supply of land in those strategically attractive locations. If the increasing trend of shopping in the virtual world continues (which is very likely to be the case), there will be no necessity to locate those shopping malls in the prime locations of the city through an acute competition for lands, land acquisition process and with a payment of high

price. The virtual shopping world will take over the expensive presentation of the traditional malls where the buyers experience the same, even more attractive, shopping environment and do not need to drive ('physical movement') to those prime locations. In that case, the city might experience the prime places where there would be rarely any shopping malls located. Only the storehouse of different stores will be located far in the fringe areas of the city or villages where land price is low. Those storehouses will supply different products at the customer's choice to different parts of the city. The direction of traffic flow will solely be observed form the product suppliers, not from the buyers. Then it is likely that land price in the prime locations, such as in the CBD, etc. will be lower with virtually no competition for business and the empty spaces of shopping malls will be occupied by rather other uses that the citizens create demand for. This transition is similarly applicable to all other commercial establishments that are located in different parts of the city. Only concern would be the locations of storehouses for different commercial products that would take place anywhere in or outside the city boundary and where there would a good transportation facility connecting the city.

The next questions would be: what kind of uses would replace the empty spaces that are currently occupied by different business establishments in the core business areas? What kind of changes this transformation would bring to the social life of the city? It is assumed that with the advancement of ICT, people would be able to perform most of his daily tasks without making any 'physical move' and it would be irrelevant where they are living or located. This implies that most of the daily activities would be taking place in 'in-house' environment with the aid of, for example, an internet connection, online banking system or credit cards. People would be spending more time in the virtual world which will tremendously excel the demand for 'outside the house' activities and environment i.e., fresh, green and 'easy to meet people' environment outside that is generally found in the park, playground, garden, jogging trail, etc. This utmost and increased demand for-outing of the citizens will gradually invade and replace the empty spaces in the city center or in other prime locations of the city for social gathering and recreation. There parks, gardens, playgrounds, etc. will be located with a few small scale commercial activities, such as restaurant, etc. around. Then city centers or CBDs would be safest and attractive places for daily social gathering and recreation as there would be a significantly less number of traffic in the downtown areas. This transformation, in fact, would entirely change the conventional city structure theorized in aforementioned multiple nuclei, concentric and sector models. Because there would be no city centers *per se*, but different pockets of refreshment and social gathering zones where walking will be the priority and general practice of the citizens.

It is very clear that all the classical and conventional models of city structuration are assumed on the principle of 'physical movement'. Contrarily in the transitional city structure, caused by the increasing dependency on ICT, 'virtual movement' is the key determinant. Some might argue that the dire need for outing might increase the traffic volume in the city and thus contribute more to the traffic congestion. Yes, it has an obvious contribution to the traffic volume, but 'recreation' is *one* of many daily needs/activities which would be satisfied by the 'physical movement' where vehicular transport is a guaranteed medium along with walk. The rest tasks would be performed based on the 'virtual movement' paradigm where vehicular transport of the citizens would become less relevant.

Still a question remains to be explored on the acceleration rate of the transitional process in the city i.e., how slow or fast of the above transition will take place in the city influenced by the increasing dependency of ICT. It is understandable that the magnitude and rate of influence of ICT on the city structure is a locally contextual answer.

Different cities of the world are undergoing and experiencing different magnitudes of technological developments in ICT that would primarily determine the influence rate on the changes of conventional city structure. Therefore, there is an urgent need for further research to explore and understand the transitional rate and process that almost every city of the world are currently undergoing and thus experiencing a new transition in the city structure that we may call our 'future city' or 'transitional city'.

REFERENCES

Abbate, J. (1999). *Inventing the Internet*. Cambridge, MA: MIT Press.

Alshuwaikhat, H. (1988). *The Role of Sociocultural Values and Planning Policies in Urban Spatial Structure*. Evanston, IL: Northwestern University.

Anddam, R. Zorayda (2003). *E-commerce and e-business*. E-ASEAN Task Force, UNDP-APDIP. UN Press: Manila

Aoyama, Y. (2001). The Information Society, Japanese Style: Corner Stores as Hubs for Ecommerce Access. In Leinbach, T. R., & Brunn, S. D. (Eds.), *Worlds of e-commerce: economic, geographical and social dimensions*. Chichester, UK: J. Wiley.

Arndt, S. W., & Kierzkowski, H. (2001). *Fragmentation: new production patterns in the world economy*. Oxford, UK: Oxford University Press.

Audretsch, D. B. (1998). *Agglomeration and the location of innovative activity*. Oxford, UK: Oxford Review of Economic Policy.

Castells, M. (1989). *The informational city: information technology, economic restructuring, and the urban-regional process*. Oxford, UK: Blackwell.

Chapin, S. (1979). *Urban Land use Planning*, pp. 14-20. Chicago: University of Illinois press.

Kolko, J. (1999). *The Death of Cities? The Death of Distance? Evidence from the Geography of Commercial Internet Usage.* Paper read at Cities in the Global Information Society: An International Perspective, November, at Newcastle upon Tyne, UK.

Leinbach, T. (2001). Emergence of the Digital Economy and E-Commerce. In Leinbach, T. R., & Brunn, S. D. (Eds.), *Worlds of ecommerce: economic, geographical and social dimensions.* Chichester, UK: J. Wiley.

Zook, M. (2000). *The web of production: the economic geography of commercial Internet content production in the United States.* Environment & Planning A, March, 411(16)

Chapter 14

European Learning Resource Exchange:
A Platform for Collaboration of Researchers, Policy Makers, Practitioners, and Publishers to Share Digital Learning Resources and New E-Learning Practices

Eugenijus Kurilovas
Vilnius University, Lithuania; Ministry of Education and Science, Lithuania & Vilnius Gediminas Technical University, Lithuania

ABSTRACT

The chapter presents European Learning Resource Exchange (LRE) system and scientific research results used for its development. LRE is a platform for collaboration of researchers, policy- and decision-makers, content providers (publishers), and practitioners (teachers) to share digital learning resources/ objects – LOs and new e-learning practices. The chapter presents research on LRE architecture, interoperability, reusability and quality of LOs, and new e-Learning practices using LOs. Importance of pan-European collaboration of scientists, policy makers, publishers and practitioners is shown using examples of several LRE best practice networks. Scientific models and methods to evaluate quality and reusability of LOs are presented in more detail. The chapter also presents the results of several large scale R&D projects co-funded by EU programmes that were and are implemented currently to support LRE. The author believes that research results and best practices presented in the chapter will be useful for all aforementioned educational stakeholders groups.

DOI: 10.4018/978-1-61350-192-4.ch014

INTRODUCTION

European Learning Resource Exchange (LRE) system is a federation of learning objects (LOs) repositories that currently offers over 130,000 LOs and assets from over 25 providers. LRE is run by European Schoolnet (EUN, 2011), a unique public-sector consortium funded by 31 European Ministries of Education (MoE) and supported by the European Commission. EUN was created more than 10 years ago to bring about innovation in teaching and learning to its key stakeholders: MoE, schools, teachers and researchers. With some 40 staff in Brussels, EUN serves the needs of education policy-makers and researchers, schools and suppliers. It exists to help develop learning opportunities for young people across Europe through communication and information exchange at all levels. Its activities are determined by the needs of the MoE, the European Commission and industrial partners, including companies from the publishing and ICT industries.

European Schoolnet's activities are divided among three areas of work:

- Policy, research and innovation
- Schools services
- Learning resource exchange and interoperability

EUN and its supporting MoE have started to create LRE while implementing EU 5FP CELE-BRATE project in 2002, and since that time several large scale EU-funded R&D projects have been implemented to develop LRE. The most important of them were: CALIBRATE (2005-2008), MELT (2007-2010), ASPECT (2008-2011), INSPIRE (2008-2009), and also ongoing eQNet (2009-2012) and iTEC (2010-2014) projects.

The author was/is a leader of Lithuanian research and development teams in FP6 CALI-BRATE and eContent*plus* ASPECT projects mainly aimed at LRE architecture and interoperability issues, and also in LLP INSPIRE, eQNet,

and FP7 iTEC projects aimed at LOs application in teaching and learning. The author also was/is a leader of research work packages in INSPIRE and eQNet projects, and also an expert member of several international interoperability organisations such as LTSO and IMS.

The chapter presents research on LRE architecture, interoperability, reusability and quality of LOs, and new e-learning practices on using LOs and its impact on learning. Importance of pan-European collaboration of scientists, policy makers, publishers and practitioners is shown using examples of several best practice networks such as ASPECT and eQNet. Scientific models and methods to evaluate quality and reusability of LOs are presented in more detail. The chapter also presents the main results of several large scale R&D projects co-funded by European Commission that were and are implemented to support LRE, and also the main results of the author's own research on the analysed topics obtained while implementing the aforementioned projects in Lithuania.

The rest of the chapter is organised as follows. The 2nd section presents the main stages and projects on LRE creation; the 3rd section presents the main research results on federating repositories, interoperability and standards, the 4th section presents main results on reusability of LOs and evaluation of their quality, the 5th section presents the main research results of use of LOs in real pedagogical practice in schools and its impact on learning. Those sections are also enriched by the author's own research results on the analysed topics. The 6th section offers further research trends, and conclusions are provided in the 7th section.

CREATION OF LRE

CALIBRATE

The CALIBRATE project built on the work of three previous R&D projects (CELEBRATE,

ITCOLE and ValNet). Its key aims were: to facilitate greater collaboration between MoE (in both old and new member states) related to the exchange and reuse of learning content (LOs) in schools; and the development of strategies and tools to support collaborative learning based on this content. CALIBRATE involved research activities related to brokerage system architectures, collaborative learning environments and semantic interoperability of content. It was also a service-oriented project designed to add value to the services provided by national content portals and to help EUN to implement a new Learning Resource Exchange (LRE) service for schools.

At the end of the CELEBRATE project in November 2004, MoE supporting EUN asked the EUN Office to move forward with the development of a European LRE for schools based on a federation or network of MoE repositories. CELEBRATE was a large-scale, €7m IST demonstration project that had developed and successfully demonstrated a federated Learning Object Brokerage System architecture and made available over 1350 LOs to schools produced by both public and private sector content developers.

In October 2005, EUN was able to take forward its earlier work in a new project called CALIBRATE (Calibrating eLearning in Schools) which, as well as building on the achievements in CELEBRATE, also built on work started in the successful ITCOLE and ValNet projects. The ITCOLE School of Tomorrow project (2001-2003) had developed the Fle3 open source server software for computer supported collaborative working and ValNet (2000-2004) had developed an advanced validation methodology suitable for large-scale validations of ICT systems and services in schools.

CALIBRATE sought to advance the state-of-the art by building on the results of these projects in order to:

- Better integrate European research in the areas covered by these initiatives (broker-

age architectures, semantic interoperability of content, collaborative learning environments and advanced ICT validation methodologies)

- Enable greater collaboration between MoE related to content exchange and the development of strategies to support collaborative learning based on this content
- Encourage new forms of collaborative learning between pupils.

CALIBRATE was a 30-month (2005 – 2008) project coordinated by EUN. CALIBRATE brought together eight Ministries of Education, leading research institutions, validation experts, technology providers and SMEs to carry out a multi-level project designed to support the collaborative use and exchange of LOs in schools.

The objectives of the project were to:

- Carry out multi-level research activities (related to 'brokerage system' architectures, collaborative learning environments and semantic interoperability of curricula descriptions of LOs) that will strengthen the ICT research effort in an enlarged Europe
- Develop and implement a European LRE, based on this research and involving a federation of LO repositories supported by six Ministries of Education (incl. Lithuania)
- Evaluate the use of the LRE, (including a CALIBRATE 'learning toolbox' and new approaches to semantic interoperability) with up to 100 schools in seven countries, and to report on the extent to which project results are capable of supporting advanced pedagogical models including more collaborative forms of learning
- Disseminate the results of the project, including via open source modalities, and to offer ongoing LRE services to all interested MoE participating in the EUN initiative

and to large numbers of teachers and learners across Europe.

The main project activities and achievements, the challenges and lessons learned and the prospects for future work and further developments are as follows:

European Added Value: Extensive information exchange and knowledge building took place between project partners as well as important new research activities. The project evaluation concludes that the CALIBRATE LRE and LeMill were especially important for Eastern European countries, successfully catalysed modernisation processes in these countries and stimulated high quality use of digital resources in education.

Exploitation of Results: CALIBRATE results are already being taken forward in other EUN projects such as MELT, INSPIRE, ASPECT, and eQNet. The project exploitation strategy also involved: ongoing support from MoE; building synergies with other projects and initiatives; providing services to LRE Associate Partners. Future work will particularly address challenges related to the IPR and quality assessment of LRE resources.

Conclusions: CALIBRATE has been a pivotal project in enabling EUN and its supporting Ministries to develop the strategic vision for a European LRE that was first outlined in the CELEBRATE demonstration project. By working particularly with Ministries in both old and new member states, it has been possible to strengthen the integration of the ICT research effort in an enlarged Europe via increased information exchange, collaborative knowledge building and new research. At the same time, CALIBRATE has enabled EUN to begin to put into place some of the key components that will enable it to launch a publicly available LRE service for schools at the end of 2008.

In addition, the LeMill learning toolbox developed in CALIBRATE has: (1) produced distributable open source software and an attractive user-friendly learning platform; (2) established a stable user base in both Estonia and Georgia;

and (3) built up an active global community of LeMill users.

Important new research in the project has also advanced the state-of-the-art related to semantic interoperability of curricula descriptions of LOs and new personalised search approaches based on agent technology.

The setting up of a new LRE Working Group by EUN Ministries of Education in April 2008 confirms that work carried out in CALIBRATE remains of strategic importance to MoE and will be taken forward and led by Ministries themselves. This new body will be key to: (1) defining criteria and mechanisms to improve the quality of LRE content; (2) developing an operational plan for running a sustainable, publicly available LRE service; and (3) determining how the LRE can relate to and work with providers of commercial content.

ASPECT

ASPECT is a large-scale, 30-month Best Practice Network, supported by the eContent*plus* Programme that involves 22 partners from 15 countries, including 9 MoE (incl. Lithuania), four commercial content developers and leading technology providers. This project has examined how the practical implementation of standards and specifications will enhance the pan-European interoperability of educational resources in the publicly available LRE and the systems that are used to develop, discover, transfer, and use that content. An important issue was the implementation of Creative Commons licenses in order to address some of the problems related to the adoption of open licenses that were highlighted in CALIBRATE.

For the first time, experts from all international standardisation bodies and consortia active in e-learning (CEN/ISSS, IEEE, ISO, IMS, ADL) worked together in order to improve the adoption of learning technology standards and specifications.

In the course of thirty-two months (2008-2011), the ASPECT consortium implemented and tested two categories of specifications: specifications for content use (e.g., content packaging formats, access control, and licensing); and specifications for content discovery (e.g., metadata, vocabularies, protocols, and registries). Through this work, the project identified best practices for learning content discovery and use and produced recommendations for the education community in Europe.

INSPIRE

INSPIRE (Innovative Science Pedagogy in Research and Education) was a two-year (2008-2009) project coordinated by EUN under the EC Lifelong Learning Programme (LLP). The aim is to set up a limited validation observatory where 60 schools in Europe (incl. 10 in Lithuania) have tested and analysed the use of Maths, Science and Technology (MST) LOs in the LRE.

INSPIRE project has been proposed on the following reasons: (1) Europe's future competitiveness in the global economy will depend to a great extent on its supply of scientific specialists and on ensuring that they are put to good use; (2) MST, including computer science, environmental science and engineering are vital for the development of the knowledge-based and increasingly digital economy.

Although quite a small project, INSPIRE is of strategic importance for the future development of the LRE as there is now considerable political momentum behind the need to implement new approaches to MST teaching and learning. Being able to provide greater access to MST resources at a European level should mean that INSPIRE has the potential to be a very important driver for the initial success of the LRE as a publicly available service to schools.

eQNet

eQNet is a three-year (September 2009-2012) Comenius Multilateral Network funded under the EC LLP. The project is coordinated by EUN and involves 9 Ministries of Education or agencies (incl. Lithuania) nominated to act of their behalf. The primary aim is to improve the quality of LOs in EUN's LRE. As a pan-European service, the LRE particularly seeks to identify LOs that "travel well" (i.e., reusable) across national borders and can be used in a cultural and linguistic context different from the one in which they were created.

eQNet is doing this by establishing a network consisting of researchers, policy makers and practitioners (teachers) that develops and applies "travel well" quality criteria to both existing LRE content as well as that to be selected in future from national repositories. The vision driving the LRE is that a significant percentage of high quality LOs developed in different countries, in different languages and to meet the needs of different curricula can be re-used at European level.

eQNet provides a forum for joint reflection and co-operation related to the exchange and re-use of educational content and allows network members to:

- Better share information and expertise particularly related to "travel well" quality criteria (i.e., pedagogical, technical and intellectual property rights (IPR) factors)
- Develop new frameworks to improve the quality of LOs and metadata in both national repositories and the LRE, including the growing volume of user-generated content and metadata, as well as to improve the multilinguality of LRE content as a result of the translation of metadata, making use, where appropriate, of automatic metadata translation approaches and technologies
- Enable schools to participate in a community of practice related to the use LOs at European level.

Major results will include:

- The development of "travel well" quality criteria to more easily identify LOs with the potential for cross-border use (this work package is coordinated by the Lithuanian partner, in particular by the author of a chapter)
- The practical application by teachers of these criteria to >3,500 LOs in the LRE
- 'Showcases' of the best of these LOs in a "travel well" section of the LRE portal
- Where necessary, the enrichment of selected LOs with new or better metadata
- A community of practice for teachers around these LOs.

iTEC

iTEC (Innovative Technologies for an Engaging Classroom) is a four-year, pan-European project focused on the design of the future classroom. iTEC is the largest and most strategic project yet undertaken by EUN and its supporting Ministries.

Starting in September 2010, iTEC will bring together policy makers, researchers, technology suppliers, other technology-enhanced learning experts and innovative teachers in order to design and build scalable learning and teaching scenarios for the future classroom with recognition of the realities of pace of the educational reform process. Rigorous testing of these future classroom scenarios in large-scale pilots will then be carried out in order to significantly increase the possibility that innovation can be mainstreamed and taken to scale when the project ends.

With 27 project partners, including 14 Ministries of Education (incl. Lithuania), and funding from the European Commission of 9.45 million Euros, iTEC will provide a model describing how the deployment of technology in support of innovative teaching and learning activities can move beyond small scale pilots and become embedded in all Europe's schools. The strategic nature of the project is underlined by the fact that the iTEC piloting in >1,000 classrooms in 12 countries is by some margin the largest pan-European validation of ICT in schools yet undertaken.

The key aim is to develop engaging scenarios for learning in the future classroom that can be validated in a large-scale pilot and be subsequently taken to scale. This will be achieved through an increased understanding of the ways in which new and emerging technologies can support more effective forms of learner engagement.

While iTEC will develop ambitious scenarios for the future classroom, it will also recognise the realities and pace of the educational reform process. By the end of the project, schools will most certainly still exist but the organisation of learning will be changing as social interaction and personalisation becomes much more prevalent.

iTEC, therefore, will explore a vision of the future where schools will remain the key location for learning and assessment as part of a wider network of physical and virtual learning locations. In doing so, the project recognises that the learning process will increasingly engage with other stakeholders including parents and cultural and business sector members and draw in adult and informal learning. iTEC also begins with a clear understanding that the starting point for change is current teaching practice and that educational policy making in the real world must be understood as the context for this change. The project will not only examine how innovative technologies can be deployed but also the underlying change processes that are required in order for innovative teaching and learning practices to be mainstreamed and taken to scale.

An underpinning principle of the project's approach is an appreciation that the power of technology to significantly enhance learning and teaching is not always transparent to practitioners. The iTEC learning centred approach is based upon the understanding that technology in itself cannot bring about schools that are competent in the use of ICT without other factors such as vision and competency, and technology that is designed with usability in mind.

The increasing use of Web 2.0 content and social tools to extend learning beyond the physical learning space is the focus for iTEC's pedagogical and technical analysis. The strategy is particularly to look beyond how schools are currently using learning platforms (VLEs, etc.) which arguably support a more formal approach to teaching and learning, and which have shown disappointing levels of adoption. Moving forward, iTEC will aim to build upon the popularity of community driven learning using personal learning spaces created by individuals through interaction with multiple personal online learning services.

Current trends suggest that tools and services supporting learning are increasingly likely to be fairly small, autonomous applications. Ways must be found to ensure that teachers and learners can reliably discover, assemble and fully exploit these tools. It is also recognised that interactive whiteboards have played a valuable role in demonstrating; how technology can engage both teachers and learners, drive transformational change in the classroom, and act as a 'gateway' to more enhanced adoption of technology. With a range of interactive, multi-touch technologies being deployed at large scale in classrooms across Europe, it is now time to examine how these technologies can be successfully integrated with other emerging tools and services to ensure ease of adoption and maximise potential benefits.

A central objective for European MoE in order to help engage and motivate learners of the future should be to ensure that the richness of ICT used in schools does not pale in comparison to how pupils are using ICT for personal recreational use. To achieve its aims, the iTEC project may particularly need to challenge the tendency for schools to limit the learner's use of personal technologies and instead encourage and support learners in exploiting the potential of Web 2.0 approaches to content creation and social networking.

iTEC objectives are:

- To develop and refine a range of teaching and learning scenarios for the future classroom
- To develop decision support criteria (technological, pedagogical and policy-related) that facilitates the selection of scenarios that can be mainstreamed and taken to scale
- To develop specific teaching and learning activities, based on the scenarios, and test these in a pre-pilot phase, and to carry out large-scale pilots in up to 1,000 classrooms in at least 12 European countries exploring both the integration of technologies and how these impact on teaching and learning practices and the engagement of a wider group of stakeholders outside the school
- To evaluate the extent to which the iTEC scenarios have been successful in supporting collaboration, individualisation, creativity and expressiveness and identify those with maximum potential to have a transformative effect on the design of the future classroom
- To select technologies resources (i.e., technologies: tools, learning platforms, services, and plug-ins; content; and people, necessary to carry out the selected learning and teaching scenarios) and then to group these resources into meaningful categories (i.e., depending on the way they contribute to the different scenarios) and provide a conceptual framework for describing each of these categories
- To describe these selected resources according to the corresponding frameworks and to register them in one or more registries and then to apply a set of specifications and standards to the selected resources in order to make them interoperable and easy to combine (mash-up)
- To develop shells that will support the combination of resources in order to provide classrooms with the technical set-

ting necessary to support the teaching and learning activities corresponding to the selected scenarios

- To explore conceptual modelling paradigms (e.g., learning design, semantic-web ontologies) to formally describe learning and teaching scenarios
- To build a prototype assistant for advising users how to find, select and combine resources that support the project scenarios.

RESEARCH ON FEDERATING REPOSITORIES, INTEROPERABILITY, AND STANDARDS

Federating Repositories in CALIBRATE

CALIBRATE operated at the leading edge of global initiatives related to developing brokerage system architectures and federated searching. At the end of the project, organisations could connect to the LRE federation in a matter of days rather than months and LRE users could exploit new personalised and curriculum search features.

The 'brokerage system' architecture demonstrated in the earlier CELEBRATE project was significantly extended and new tools were developed to enable developers to more easily connect to the federation of repositories. At the end of the CELEBRATE project, approximately 2-3 months of effort was required to connect to the federation. However, as a result of work in CALIBRATE, it is now possible for a skilled software engineer to establish a connection to the federation in a matter of 2-3 days.

More specifically, in achieving this major step forward:

- CALIBRATE has led to the design and implementation of LIMBS, an open source brokerage system that relies on open standards and open content to promote exchanges of learning resources within a federation of e-learning systems. Contrary to the CELEBRATE brokerage system, from which it derives, LIMBS's role is limited to carrying and routing messages exchanged by the federation members rather than to enforcing semantic interoperability. With LIMBS, semantic interoperability becomes the responsibility of the federation members that rely on "clients" to communicate with the brokerage system and to support the negotiation of common query languages and metadata formats. LIMBS itself adopts a service-oriented architecture so that each service (e.g., resource discovery, digital rights management) can be used separately and combined with any (group) of the others. Current services include: connection management, federated searching, and metadata harvesting

- CALIBRATE has produced tools to help developers to connect systems (e.g., repositories, search interfaces) to the federation. Tools include: a test instance of the federation, a test repository, a test search interface, a "query watcher", a tool for monitoring connections, and a connection toolkit

- CALIBRATE developed an Agent-Based Search System to help rank search results according to the profiles of users. This was implemented in the CALIBRATE portal/federation as follows: (1) the ABSS collects LRE metadata using the LRE harvesting service, (2) the CALIBRATE portal provides the ABSS with user profiles and Contextual Attention Metadata (CAM) using a SQI (Sequential Inquiry Interface) service, and (3) the ABSS is queried using the SQI service (by means of an ad hoc query language).

In conclusion, as a result of the development of new services and tools in CALIBRATE, it is now much easier for repositories to join the LRE federation. At the end of the project, CALIBRATE was still operating at the leading edge of global initiatives related to brokerage system architectures and federated search and work in the project has fed directly into international standardisation bodies.

Federated Searching vs Federated Metadata

The evolution of the LRE confirms that such a federation cannot be limited to federated searching or harvesting but must combine both approaches in order to accommodate the requirements of the different metadata providers.

When choosing whether to support 'live' searching, harvesting or both, repository owners should bear in mind that these are not equivalent and each has its pros and cons. During a federated search, the repository is queried in real time, whereas, with harvesting, exposed metadata is gathered into a central cache and it is this cache that is queried.

On the one hand, the former means that, during a search operation, a repository can take advantage of unexposed information to process queries more efficiently (unexposed information is information about resources that a repository stores but does not make directly available either because it is not part of the selected metadata standard or because its access is restricted for some reason).

On the other hand, it means that, during a federated search, each repository needs to be powerful enough to support the load of processing queries, which, in a federation can be a significant overhead, particularly if the default option for a federated search service is to search all repositories. Real time searching of repositories will always produce up-to-date results. This is an advantage when collections are volatile with frequent updates. The drawback of live searching is that repositories that are temporarily unavailable at query time, for whatever reason, are

ignored. In contrast, when searching cached (i.e. harvested) metadata, complete results are always returned (even if some repositories are unavailable at the time of the query). But the results might be outdated.

Within Europe, there is no other initiative that is aiming to implement a federation of national learning content repositories for schools. The expertise developed in the project is well recognised at an international level and work begun in CALIBRATE is now being taken forward in other EUN-led projects such as MELT and ASPECT.

Specific further developments planned include:

- A New Context Set based on a LRE federated schema
- Improving performance by implementing a caching mechanism at the brokerage system level
- Development of new tools and reference implementations
- Further exploring models to support a federation of federations
- Building and supporting communities (brokerage system, repositories, educational portals)

Research on Semantic Interoperability in CALIBRATE

CALIBRATE carried out innovative research related to the semantic interoperability of curricula descriptions. This included a comparative analysis of the curricula semantics of two subject domains in four European countries and the development of a Topic Mapper application to support curriculum mapping experts in mapping their curricula. At the end of the project, this work is being fed into key standards bodies such as CEN/ISSS and IMS.

The earlier CELEBRATE project developed a LOM-based application profile (AP) that was well received by MoE, adopted by national school networks and was referred to by many LOM AP initiatives. CELEBRATE also confirmed that, when searching for resources, the most common criteria used by teachers and learners are the language of the resource, intended age group, and subject. Also for the evaluation of resources, these are the top three evaluation criteria. However, while vocabularies about language and intended age group are sufficiently uniform, this is not the case for 'subject of the learning resource'. CALIBRATE suggested that there is scope for improvement concerning the use of subject keywords, even if one uses the multilingual thesaurus that had been developed in earlier EUN projects. The reason is that (1) using the same thesaurus across national borders requires a considerable adoption effort, and (2) the vast majority of teachers would prefer to see the subject expressed in terms of their national curriculum. At the start of CALIBRATE, the only option available, following the LOM standard, was for content providers to provide different sets of metadata each according to a national curriculum. However, this option was far too expensive.

The objective in CALIBRATE, therefore, was to explore new approaches concerning how we relate the subject of a LO to the national curriculum. Two approaches were addressed in the project: (1) A user driven approach; teachers were given tools where they could indicate for which part of their own national curriculum they were able to successfully use a learning resource; (2) Associating or mapping national curricula through knowledge representation techniques. Mapping and association are two techniques for 'harmonising' vocabularies including thesauri and simple ontologies. In a mapping, the underlying vocabularies remain unchanged and only mapping relationships are added. In an association, the vocabularies are merged more tightly. Both approaches require that interoperable formats for expressing national curricula are used. Following that, the project investigated how the chosen knowledge representation(s) can be used for relating the different national curricula to each

other in order to preserve the highest degree of semantic interoperability as possible.

The driving motive was to understand the underlying semantics of topics, goals/competencies and learning activity directions for teachers and learners. Research was carried out into the appropriate semantics for three curriculum topics: Mathematics, Natural Science/Environmental Studies and (partly) for English as a Foreign Language. As part of this work, there was also an investigation of how national curricula are related to practices at different education system levels in order to inform the construction of curricula ontologies that can assist teachers when searching for learning resources. These system level analyses provide an important foundation for how use cases and mapping/association approaches should be designed and have helped direct technological tools' development.

Ontology/taxonomy developments: CALIBRATE searched for and tested different ontologies/taxonomies (represented as vocabularies) that could assist the processes of curricula mapping/association. Partners also did some curriculum dry run analyses based on competencies represented as action-verb tuples for evaluation purposes in teaching practices. This system was compared with another classification model (Topic, Goal and Activity – model) based on a bottom-up analysis of curricula in the CALIBRATE project.

Use cases for system and tools development: A set of use case scenarios were developed that described basic structures for the mapping/association tools for MoE and portal services for teachers. These use case scenarios cover topics such as vocabulary management, curricula mapping and searching and browsing.

Experiment with RDF/OWL mapping technologies such as Annotea, Protegé and IAnnotate: CALIBRATE experimented with existing and mature open source mapping technologies. The idea was to inform partners' work regarding: user interfaces for mapping and vocabularies; how to store relations in-between vocabulary items;

how to store relations between vocabulary items and sections in curriculum documents, relations between sections in curriculum documents and learning resources; and how these relations can be expressed in a LOM AP as well as in the CALIBRATE portal. The experimentation, with these existing technologies provided partners with a clear idea of what the user interface of a linking tool (contained within the portal) should look like. In addition, the experimentation provided a clear indication of how to maintain relations between different items in the system.

Based on this work, CALIBRATE developed and tested a curriculum mapping tool and integrated this in the CALIBRATE portal so that teachers could discover LOs as a result of searches that used terms from their own national curriculum documents.

Key achievements in the project are as follows:

- The project made a thorough, bottom-up comparative analysis of curricula semantics of two subject domains in four European countries with the intention to create a harmonised ontology representing the semantics of European national curricula and their relation to LOs. At the higher governmental levels semantic meaning is expressed through the national curricula as topics and learning goals (competencies). At the lower level, close to teachers looking for LOs, semantic meaning is expressed as meaningful learning activities for the pupils. Based on these findings, the project concluded that it is best from an educational point of view that ontologies used for the discovery of LOs should reflect topics, learning goals (competencies) and learning activities – known as the TGA approach (Hauge *et. al.*, 2007). Drafts of these three ontologies have been produced and worked well in curriculum mapping tests

- However, the project found that the bottom-up approach was quite time consuming. Thus, for practical reasons, a top-down analysis was made in order to try to relate the existing Bloom's extended taxonomy to the various curricula. With this approach, partners developed ontologies for topics and competencies (Van Assche, 2007). This approach was fast and provided CALIBRATE with readymade terms that worked well during the final curriculum mapping

- CALIBRATE developed a Topic Mapper (2008) application to support curriculum mapping experts in mapping their curricula. It allows users to identify concepts in a text and to associate them with concepts contained in several vocabularies. This process is called mapping of the text. But it also supports users in building and enhancing these vocabularies by adding relations between existing terms or adding missing terms that have been identified in a text. Topic Mapper has been designed to make the mapping process as comfortable as possible so that the user can simply map the document by several mouse clicks or just by dragging and dropping vocabulary terms to text paragraphs. The application supports multilingual vocabularies and the user interface can also be easily translated

- CALIBRATE has provided an empirical demonstration that it is possible to map different countries' curricula to each other, even though they have different curricula constructs and languages. Further, it has shown that we can use this as a basis for the discovery of LOs. Until now, using curricula to discover LOs has only been done in areas where language and curricula constructs are the same

- A small-scale validation of this work has been carried out where teachers have browsed their national curriculum in order to find suitable LOs and have actively participated and linked resources to a curriculum.

Interoperability Research in ASPECT

Work in developing ASPECT best practices involved project partners and teachers using a version of the EUN LRE service that enables schools to find open educational content from many different countries and providers. In ASPECT a customised and password protected version of the LRE was developed for schools in the project that contained LOs from commercial providers and some additional search and retrieval features related to the exploration of the standards under investigation in the project.

During ASPECT, content providers from both the public and private sectors applied content standards to their LOs and made them available via the LRE. This represents a large-scale implementation of standards and specifications for content discovery and use.

As a result, the following elements, not directly linked to the quality of the specifications themselves, were identified as necessary for the successful adoption of a standard:

- Availability and quality of tools for producing compliant content and metadata
- Availability and quality of tools to test for compliance
- Availability of solutions adapted to the different needs of content providers from both the public and private sectors.

An important focus in the project was the exploration of content standards and specifications for content packaging (SCORM and Common Cartridge) by both MoE and commercial content developers. ASPECT tested existing tools for creating, validating content packages and using these specifications. Having identified areas in need of improvement, ASPECT also developed new tools to enhance content packages and to validate them more accurately.

After the end of the project, ASPECT continues to make publicly available a variety of tools and services to support the best practices that emerged from its work. These can be accessed via the LRE Service Centre (2011)

The LRE Service Centre includes:

- A Learning Technology Standards Observatory (LTSO) serving as a focal access point to updated information on projects, results, news, organisations, activities and events that are relevant to the development and adoption of e-learning technology standards and specifications
- An application profile (AP) registry providing information about the data elements and vocabularies used by different application profiles and mappings between different profiles of a given standard
- A Vocabulary Bank for Education (VBE) providing a browsable and searchable interface to locate, view and download controlled vocabularies
- LO Repository Registries providing up-to-date information about repositories of LOs and their collections.
- Validation services for testing conformance of metadata records to different metadata specifications and APs
- Metadata transformation services for converting metadata records from one AP to another
- An automatic metadata translation service integrated in the LRE enabling the discovery of LOs in various languages.

The various ASPECT activities were driven by the needs of the different stakeholders as identified at the start of the project. ASPECT conducted several studies on the different stakeholders' adoption and awareness of content discovery/repository standards (e.g., IEEE LOM, IMS LODE, etc.) and content packaging standards (SCORM & IMS Common Cartridge). This work included interviews with the ASPECT content providers (MoE and commercial content providers), ascertaining their readiness and willingness to adopt content standards. Insights from these interviews informed the development of the ASPECT recommendations.

ASPECT general recommendations are as follows:

- Use standards and specifications. There are four core reasons to use standards and specifications: (1) They avoid dependency on single vendors (vendor lock-in); (2) Their use facilitates interoperability; (3) Their use lowers costs by making it possible to build higher-level services on top of proven and standard compliant systems; and (4) They represent best-practice solutions to known problems even when interoperability is not at issue
- Check conformance
- Select appropriate standards. Given the profusion of standards available, it is critical to identify the existing standards of communities with which you want to interoperate. When a standard exists that addresses a certain requirement, using it, even if it is complex or incomplete – is often better than creating a new specification
- Don't profile without consent. It is necessary to use standards and specifications 'as-is' as much as possible. A profile must always have a clearly defined scope and purpose for the target community whose needs it should meet. If no formal consensus can be reached in this community, it is recommended to meet the needs of its common practice
- When profiling, preserve interoperability. When profiling is unavoidable, keep any customisation as limited as possible and

profile in a way that preserves interoperability with the original specifications. For example, do not make mandatory elements optional or do not remove terms from an existing controlled vocabulary. If new elements must be introduced, do it only at the extension points foreseen in the specification
- Combine standards and specifications consistently
- Use a progressive strategy. Adopting a complete solution can be expensive but interoperability can be built gradually. Build interoperability in stages by adopting specifications most pertinent to your immediate requirements and progressively add other complementary specifications.

ASPECT recommendations for content providers and repository owners are as follows:

- Only use content specifications when required
- For learning assets, stick to web-standards
- Learning assets (i.e., single file content) should not be packaged
- The distribution of complex content requires packaging
- Use content package specifications used by your intended audience
- "Creative Commons" maximises reuse of the open content
- Make sure the distribution of interoperable commercial content does not conflict with your business model
- Make metadata creation easy and, where possible, try to generate metadata automatically
- Combine as many sources of information as possible about the resource. Descriptive metadata provided by content providers is only one of the possible sources of information about a LO. It can be comple-

mented by other valuable information such as: (1) Usage data, such as the number of times a resource is retrieved; (2) Explicit feedback from users, such as ratings and annotations (Web 2.0 tools and practices); (3) Third-party metadata provided by aggregators or reviewers. This type of information provides feedback to enhance searching by users and ranking and feedback helps providers better understand issues related to the quality and usage of their content

- Expose metadata and content in as many ways as possible
- Register your repository to ensure its discoverability
- Describe each re-usable part of content.

ASPECT recommendations for tools providers are as follows:

- Build tools that support all features and options in a specification
- Support content specifications best adapted to the type of learning scenarios a platform supports.

ASPECT recommendations for federation and discovery service builders are as follows:

- Minimise the cost of joining a federation
- Offer persistent management of LOs and metadata
- Establish good communication channels between the different stakeholders of a federation
- Use already existing best practices and tools when setting up a federation. ASPECT recommendations for standards organisations are as follows:
- Support the development of free and user-friendly tools to edit, deploy, rearrange, and play educational content

- Provide community-based conformance competence forums, supporting stakeholders which apply open educational standards
- Support the development of application profiles and domain profiles of existing standards reflecting what is used in common practice
- Maintain backward compatibility
- Do not encode controlled vocabularies in bindings
- Uniquely identify each controlled vocabulary and controlled vocabulary term and only use identifiers in metadata records.

The following stakeholders can benefit directly or indirectly from the ASPECT best practices network related to the implementation of standards and specifications for content discovery and use:

- Educators will have an easy way to discover learning content that addresses the needs of their students, making their jobs easier, and maximising re-use and minimising costs by repurposing materials
- Students benefit from having access to high-quality LOs; these can make a significant impact on the quality of their learning experience and their learning outcomes
- Content providers will be able to more easily make their products interoperable and to promote/market them by making them globally discoverable
- System vendors will only need to support a limited set of specifications to make their systems compliant with learning resources from major federations
- Finally, repository and federation builders will secure and maximise their investment by developing infrastructures based on standard specifications.

RESEARCH ON REUSABILITY AND EVALUATION OF QUALITY OF LEARNING OBJECTS

Methodology of the Research in eQNet

One of the main features achieving the high LOs effectiveness and efficiency level is LOs reusability. The need for reusability of LOs has at least three elements (McCormick et. al., 2004; Kurilovas, 2009ab):

1. Interoperability: LO is interoperable and can be used in different platforms
2. Flexibility in terms of pedagogic situations: LO can fit into a variety of pedagogic situations
3. Modifiability to suit a particular teacher's or student's needs: LO can be made more appropriate to a pedagogic situation by modifying it to suit a particular teacher's or student's needs.

Reusability of LOs (or their ability to "travel well" between different contexts and education systems) is considered by the author as a part of the overall quality of LOs. This means that any high quality LO has some reusability level (or potential to "travel well"), but this does not mean that any reusable LO is quality one.

The main problem analysed in section is how to establish:

- A 'proper' set of LOs "travel well" quality evaluation criteria that should reflect the objective scientific principles of construction a model (criteria tree) for LOs "travel well" quality evaluation, and
- 'Proper' methods for evaluation of LOs "travel well" quality.

According to (Oliver, 2000), evaluation can be characterised as "the process by which people make judgements about value and worth". In the context of learning technology this judgement process is complex and often controversial. Although the notion of evaluation is rooted in a relatively simple concept, the process of judging the value of learning technology is complex and challenging. Quality evaluation is defined as "the systematic examination of the extent to which an entity (part, product, *service* or organisation) is capable of meeting specified requirements" (ISO/IEC 1999). Expert evaluation is referred here as the multiple criteria evaluation of LOs aimed at selection of the best alternatives (i.e., LOs) based on score-ranking results (Kurilovas & Dagiene, 2009ab).

According to (Zavadskas & Turskis, 2010), there is a wide range of multiple criteria decision making (MCDM) problem solution techniques, varying in complexity and possible solutions. Each method has its own strength, weaknesses and possibilities to be applied. But, according to (Zavadskas & Turskis, 2010), there are still no rules determining the application of multi-criteria evaluation methods and interpretation of the results obtained. If the set of decision alternatives (LOs) is assumed to be predefined, fixed and finite, then the decision problem is to choose the optimal alternative or, maybe, to rank them. But usually the experts have to deal with the problem of optimal decision in the multiple criteria situation where the objectives are often conflicting. In this case, an optimal decision is the one that maximises the expert's utility. These principles of identification of quality evaluation criteria have been analysed in multiple criteria decision making/analysis (MCDM/MCDA) theory related research works, e.g., Belton & Stewart (2002).

Evaluation of LOs quality is a typical case where the criteria are conflicting, i.e., LOs could be very qualitative against several criteria, and not qualitative against the other ones, and vice versa. Therefore, the author proposes to use MCDA approach for creation of LOs quality evaluation model.

LOs multiple criteria evaluation method used by the author in eQNet is referred here as the experts' additive utility function represented by formula (1) below including LOs evaluation criteria, their ratings (values) and weights (Kurilovas & Serikoviene, 2010a,b).

This method is well-known in the theory of optimisation and is named "scalarisation method". A possible decision here could be to transform multi-criteria task into one-criterion task obtained by adding all criteria together with their weights. It is valid from the point of view of the optimisation theory, and a special theorem exists for this case (Kurilovas & Serikoviene, 2010b).

Therefore, here we have the experts' additive utility function:

$$f(X) = \sum_{i=1}^{m} a_i f_i(X) \tag{1}$$

where $f_i(X_j)$ is the rating (i.e., non-fuzzy value) of the criterion i for the each of the examined LOs alternatives X_j. The weights here should be 'normalised' according to the 'normalisation' requirement

$$\sum_{i=1}^{m} a_i = 1, a_1 > 0. \tag{2}$$

According to (Zavadskas & Turskis, 2010), the normalisation aims at obtaining comparable scales of criteria values. The major is the meaning of the utility function (1) the better LOs meet the quality requirements in comparison with the ideal (i.e., 100%) quality.

The following sub-sections are aimed to apply the aforementioned scientific approaches in order:

- To propose a suitable scientific model for evaluation of quality of LOs
- To propose suitable scientific methods for evaluation of quality of LOs

- To present the experimental evaluation results using the proposed evaluation model and methods.

Learning Objects Quality Evaluation Model

According to Belton & Stewart (2002), the following principles of identification of quality evaluation criteria are relevant to all MCDA approaches:

Value relevance: Are the decision makers able to link the concept to their goals, thereby enabling them to specify preferences which relate directly to the concept?

Understandability: It is important that decision makers have a shared understanding of concepts to be used in an analysis

Measurability: All MCDA implies some degree of measurement of the performance of alternatives against specified criteria, thus it must be possible to specify this in a consistent manner. It is usual to decompose criteria to a level of detail which allows this

Non-redundancy: Is there more than one criterion measuring the same factor? When eliciting ideas often the same concept may arise under different headings. One can easily check for criteria which appear to be measuring the same thing by calculating a correlation coefficient if appropriate data is available, or carrying out a process of matching as associated with analysis of repertory grids

Judgmental independence: Criteria are not judgementally independent if preferences with respect to a single criterion, or trade-offs between two criteria, depend on the level of another

Balancing completeness and conciseness: a number of authors note that desirable characteristics of a value tree are that it is complete, i.e., that all important aspects of the problem are captured, and also that it is concise, keeping the level of detail to the minimum required

Operationality: The model is usable with reasonable effort – that the information required

Table 1. LOs quality evaluation model (criteria tree)

Criteria group	Nr.	Quality criteria
		Technological quality criteria
"Internal" quality criteria	1	Technological interoperability and reusability
	2	Layered architecture
	3	Technical stability and robustness
"Quality in use" criterion	4	Design and usability: aesthetics, navigation, user-friendly interface and information structure, personalisation
		Pedagogical quality criteria
	5	Trans-national or multidisciplinary / cross-curricular topic
	6	Interactivity, strong visual element
	7	Language independence
	8	Ease of use, intuitiveness
	9	Methodological support for teachers is not needed
		IPR criterion
	10	Clear license: open, free to use, cost-effective

does not place excessive demands on the decision makers. The context in which the model is being used is clearly important in judging the usability of a model

Simplicity vs complexity: The value tree, or criteria set is itself a simple representation, capturing the essence of a problem, which has been extracted from a complex problem description. The modeller should strive for the simplest tree which adequately captures the problem for the decision maker.

LOs quality evaluation model based on these MCDA criteria identification principles is presented in the Table 1. This model consists of 10 quality criteria, four of them dealing with technological quality, three – with pedagogical quality of LOs, and one – with IPR issues. This model includes three groups of criteria, namely, technological, pedagogical and IPR criteria.

The author's analysis has shown that the model presented in Table 1 fits all MCDA criteria identification principles. Taking into account Non-redundancy, Judgmental independence, Balancing completeness and conciseness, Operationality, and Simplicity versus complexity MCDA

criteria identification principles, the author considers that the following 10 LOs evaluation criteria should construct the comprehensive LOs quality criteria tree (see Table 1):

Technological Quality Criteria:

'Internal Quality' Criteria:

1. Technological reusability (according to Kurilovas & Dagiene (2009b):
   a. Interoperability: Metadata accuracy; Compliance with the main import/export standards (e.g., IMS CP, IMS CC, SCORM 2004)
   b. Decontextualisation: Is LO indivisible (atomic)? – LO aggregation (granularity) level; Is LO modular (i.e., are the parts of a content item fully functional on their own?)
   c. Cultural and learning diversity (Adaptability): LO flexibility (LO can be modified, for instance from a configuration file, from a plain text file or because it is provided along

with its source code or an authoring tool); LO internationalisation level; LO suitability for localisation

d. Accessibility (design of controls and presentation formats to accommodate disabled and mobile learners): Is LO designed for all? Compliance with accessibility standards (W3C)

2. Architecture: Is LO architecture layered in order to separate data, presentation and application logics? (Kurilovas & Dagiene, 2009b)

3. Robustness, technical stability (according to Becta (2007):

a. Having help functions that identify common user problems and their solutions

b. Having navigational actions that can be undone

c. Giving quick, visible and audible responses to user actions

d. Allowing the user to exit at any point

e. Not being adversely affected by user experimentation and error. If users do experience an error they should be able to recover quickly and, where appropriate, be informed about the nature of the error.

'Quality in use' criterion (according to Kurilovas & Dagiene (2009b):

4. Design and usability (design of visual and auditory information for enhanced learning and efficient mental processing): Aesthetics; Navigation; User-friendly interface; Information structuring; Personalisation.

According to the standards-based technological quality criteria classification principle, we can divide technological quality criteria into 'internal quality' and 'quality in use' criteria of the educational software (e.g., LOs). 'Internal quality' is a descriptive characteristic that describes the quality of software independently from any particular context of its use, while 'quality in use' is evaluative characteristic of software obtained by making a judgment based on criteria that determine the worthiness of software for a particular project (Kurilovas & Dagiene, 2009a).

Any LOs quality evaluation model (set of criteria) should provide the experts (decision makers) the clear instrumentality who (i.e., what kind of experts) should analyse what kind of LOs quality criteria in order to select the best LOs suitable for their needs. According to aforementioned technological quality criteria classification principle, 'internal quality' criteria should be mainly the area of interest of the software engineers, and 'quality in use' criteria should be mostly analysed by the programmers and users taking into account the users' feedback on the usability of software (Kurilovas & Serikoviene, 2010b).

The author has applied the aforementioned principle in his previous papers (Kurilovas & Dagiene, 2010a, 2009ab; Kurilovas & Serikoviene 2010b) on technological evaluation of the learning software, and thus have identified a number of LOs technological quality evaluation criteria presented in the technological part of the LOs quality evaluation model (see Table. 1).

Presented LOs technological quality criteria are included into a majority of already existing LOs evaluation models. 'Interoperability' and 'Accessibility' criteria being independent criteria in, e.g., Leacock & Nesbit (2007) or Becta (2007) are included as sub-criteria into 'Technical reusability' criterion in the presented model. There are several reasons for this, e.g., both 'Interoperability' and 'Accessibility' criteria deal with international interoperability standards and specifications, both influence LO technical reusability level in different repositories and platforms, etc. MCDA Non-redundancy principle is applied here.

On the other hand, the author has analysed a number of existing models (sets of quality evaluation criteria) for evaluation of pedagogical quality of LOs, e.g., Becta (2007), Leacock &

Nesbit (2007), MELT (2010), Vargo *et. al.* (2003), etc., and also the results of communication with eQNet partners during project partners meeting in Florence in April 2011.

Suitable pedagogical reusability criteria based on MCDA principles (Belton & Stewart 2002) are as follows:

5. Trans-national or multidisciplinary / cross-curricular topic: the LO addresses curriculum topics that could be considered trans-national. For example, teaching 'geometric shapes' or 'the parts of the cell' are usually covered in every national curriculum, but teaching the folklore of a very specific region is not. It can also be a LO well suited for use in multi-disciplinary or cross-curricular contexts (eQNet, 2011)

6. Interactivity, strong visual element or structure, e.g., LOs include animations, images, short videos and simulations that are self-explanatory or have just a few text labels or icons/buttons for start, stop, etc.; strong visual structure (MELT, 2010)

7. Language independence: LO is not text-heavy; LOs may have little or no text; or low language dependence (easily translatable); or LOs are multilingual, i.e., LOs have been designed to be language customisable and are already offered in more than one language (MELT, 2010)

8. Ease of use, intuitiveness:

    a. Users can find their way through the resource almost intuitively; they can broadly understand what is the intended learning objective or topic (MELT 2010)

    b. LOs provide appropriate guidance, where necessary, for learners and/or practitioners

    c. LOs make appropriate assumptions about the ICT skills of users, both learners and practitioners, or provide straightforward guidance on this

    d. LOs not present a barrier or impede the learning experience (Becta 2007).

9. Methodological support for teachers is not needed: subject teachers can easily recognise how this LO meets their curriculum requirements or how this LO could be used in a teaching scenario without further instructions.

The aforementioned LOs pedagogical quality criteria are included into the analysed LOs evaluation models (Leacock & Nesbit, 2007; Becta, 2007; MELT, 2010; Vargo *et. al.,* 2003).

There are also several criteria included into the aforementioned models. They are: 'Content quality' (Leacock & Nesbit, 2007), 'Match to the curriculum', 'Assessment', 'Learner engagement', and 'Innovative approaches' (Becta, 2007).

In the author's opinion, 'Content quality' criterion should not be included into the proposed LOs quality evaluation model. The main reason for this is "a need for a common (more narrow) definition of what is, and what is not a LO" (Paulsson & Naeve, 2006). Therefore, since a LO is "any digital resource that can be reused to support learning" (Wiley, 2000), we can conclude that scientific content of any LO should be relevant, accurate and trustworthy, in other case the digital resource could not be used and reused "to support learning".

'Match to the curriculum' criterion could be suitable for nationally recognised quality criteria of learning resources, but taking into account the "more narrow definition" (Paulsson & Naeve, 2006) of LOs, we should consider only the resources "that can be reused" to support learning (Wiley, 2000). Since there are different curricula in different countries, reusable resources should be curriculum independent. Reusable LOs could be often used in other pedagogic situations and learning scenarios that have been planned by LOs authors. Such approach has been, e.g., applied by the author's leaded team in CALIBRATE project when Lithuanian teachers have been created and

Table 2. Linguistic variables conversion into triangular fuzzy numbers

Linguistic variables	Triangular fuzzy numbers
Excellent	(0.700, 0.850, 1.000)
Good	(0.525, 0.675, 0.825)
Fair	(0.350, 0.500, 0.650)
Poor	(0.175, 0.325, 0.475)
Bad	(0.000, 0.150, 0.300)

implemented their own lesson plans using foreign LOs from LRE.

Criteria such as 'Assessment to support learning' and 'Robust summative assessment' (Becta, 2007) often do not fit the LO reusability principle—they are mostly suitable for entire learning courses with high semantic density and aggregation level.

Criteria such as 'Learner engagement' and 'Innovative approaches' are interconnected on the one hand, and are closely related to 'Interactivity' and 'Intuitiveness' criteria included into the proposed model, on the other.

Intellectual property rights (IPR) criterion (10) should also be considered here. It is about Open license, free to use, open code: Licensing (clear rules, e.g., compliance with Creative Commons); Economic efficiency – Cost vs Quality taking into account probable LO reusability level.

Learning Objects Quality Evaluation Methods

The widely used measurement criteria of the decision attributes' quality are mainly qualitative and subjective. Decisions in this context are often expressed in natural language, and evaluators are unable to assign exact numerical values to the different criteria. Assessment can be often performed by linguistic variables: 'bad', 'poor', 'fair', 'good' and 'excellent'. These values are imprecise and uncertain: they are commonly called 'fuzzy values'. Integrating these different judg-

ments to obtain a final evaluation is not evident (Kurilovas & Serikoviene, 2010b).

Therefore, the author has proposed to use fuzzy group decision making theory (Ounaies *et. al.*, 2009) to obtain final assessment measures. The fuzzy numbers are: (1) triangular fuzzy numbers, (2) trapezoidal fuzzy numbers, and (3) bell-shaped fuzzy numbers. In the presented sub-section, the author uses triangular and trapezoidal fuzzy numbers for evaluating quality and reusability of LOs.

Use of Triangular Fuzzy Numbers

According to Zhang Li Li & Cheng De Yong (1992), triangular fuzzy numbers are a class of the fuzzy set representation. A triangular fuzzy number is expressed by three real numbers $M = (l, m, u)$; the parameters l, m and u, respectively, indicate the lower, the mean and the upper possible values. Triangular fuzzy numbers membership functions are as follows:

$$\mu_M(x) = \begin{cases} \dfrac{x-l}{m-l}, & if \quad x \in [l,m], \\ \dfrac{x-u}{m-u}, & if \quad x \in [m,u], \\ 0, & if \quad x \notin [l,u]. \end{cases} \quad (3)$$

Conversion of these qualitative values into fuzzy numbers is shown in Table 2.

Therefore, in the case of using average triangular fuzzy numbers, linguistic variables conver-

Table 3. Linguistic variables conversion into trapezoidal fuzzy numbers

Linguistic variables	Trapezoidal fuzzy numbers
Excellent	(0.800, 1.000, 1.000, 1.000)
Good	(0.600, 0.800, 0.800, 1.000)
Fair	(0.300, 0.500, 0.500, 0.700)
Poor	(0.000, 0.200, 0.200, 0.400)
Bad	(0.000, 0.000, 0.000, 0.200)

Box 1.

$$a_g = \begin{pmatrix} 0,100 & 0,100 & 0,100 & 0,100 & 0,100 & 0,100 & 0,100 & 0,100 & 0,100 & 0,100 \end{pmatrix} \qquad (5)$$

Box 2.

$$a_{tw} = \begin{pmatrix} 0,130 & 0,080 & 0,080 & 0,080 & 0,130 & 0,080 & 0,130 & 0,080 & 0,130 & 0,080 \end{pmatrix} \qquad (6)$$

sion into non-fuzzy values of the evaluation criteria should be as follows: 'excellent'=0.850; 'good'=0.675; 'fair'=0.500; 'poor'=0.325; 'bad'=0.150 (Kurilovas *et. al.*, 2011; Kurilovas & Serikoviene, 2010b).

Use of Trapezoidal Fuzzy Numbers

A trapezoidal fuzzy number is a fuzzy number represented by four points as follows: $M = (a, b, c, d)$.

In this case, a membership function can be attached to the level fuzzy function (4):

$$\mu_M(x) = \begin{cases} 0, & if \quad x < a, \\ \dfrac{x-a}{b-a} & if \quad a \leq x \leq b, \\ 1, & if \quad b \leq x \leq c, \\ \dfrac{d-x}{d-c} & if \quad c \leq x \leq d, \\ 0, & if \quad x > d. \end{cases} \qquad (4)$$

Conversion of these qualitative values into fuzzy numbers is shown in Table 3.

Therefore, in the case of using secondary trapezoidal fuzzy numbers, linguistic variables conversion into non-fuzzy values of the evaluation criteria should be as follows: 'excellent'=1.000; 'good'=0.800; 'fair'=0.500; 'poor'=0.200; 'bad'=0.000.

Weights of Quality Criteria

The weight of the evaluation criterion reflects the experts' opinion on the criterion's importance level in comparison with the other criteria for the particular needs. For example, for the most simple (i.e., general) case, when all LOs evaluation criteria are of equal importance (i.e., we pay no especial attention to LOs reusability criteria), the experts (decision-makers) could consider the equal weights $a_i = 0,100$ according to the normalisation requirement (2) and get general weights matrix a_g as follows: (see Box 1)

But if we pay a special attention to LOs reusability criteria, we can, e.g., consider the increased weights for the 1st, 5th, 7th and 9th quality evaluation criteria (see Table 1), because those criteria deal with LOs reusability mostly. In this case, according to the normalisation requirement (2), we'll get special "travel well" weights matrix a_{tw} as follows: (see Box 2)

Example of Practical Evaluation of LOs from LRE

The presented evaluation model and fuzzy numbers methods have been applied in eQNet project by the author and Lithuanian Mathematics expert teacher Silvija Serikoviene.

A number of probably qualitative reusable LOs have been identified in LRE and evaluated against the aforementioned model and method (see experts' additive utility function (1) and normalisation requirement (2)).

There were three examples of those LOs examined in the practical evaluation exercise:

- LO$_1$: "Mixed Numbers" (available in LRE at: http://celebrate.ls.no/english/animations/mathematics/tilblanda/index.html);
- LO$_2$: "Practice with Tangents and Circles" (available in LRE at: http://regentsprep.org/Regents/math/geometry/GP14/PracCircleTangents.htm);
- LO$_3$: "Tangent to a Circle" – geometry construction using a compass and straightedge (available in LRE at: http://www.mathopenref.com/consttangent.html).

The criteria ratings (values) obtained while evaluating the aforementioned LOs using triangular fuzzy numbers method are presented by matrix (7):

$$f_i(X) = \begin{pmatrix} 0,675 & 0,850 & 0,850 \\ 0,850 & 0,675 & 0,500 \\ 0,500 & 0,675 & 0,675 \\ 0,675 & 0,325 & 0,675 \\ 0,675 & 0,850 & 0,675 \\ 0,850 & 0,675 & 0,850 \\ 0,675 & 0,500 & 0,675 \\ 0,500 & 0,675 & 0,500 \\ 0,850 & 0,675 & 0,850 \\ 0,850 & 0,850 & 0,850 \end{pmatrix} \qquad (7)$$

The results of experimental evaluation of those Mathematics LOs general quality (g) using triangular fuzzy numbers method are presented by matrix (8):

$$a_g \cdot f(X_j) = \begin{pmatrix} 0,7100 & 0,6750 & 0,7100 \end{pmatrix} \qquad (8)$$

The results of experimental evaluation of those Mathematics LOs "travel well" quality (tw) using triangular fuzzy numbers method are presented by matrix (9):

$$a_{tw} \cdot f(X_j) = \begin{pmatrix} 0,7118 & 0,6838 & 0,7205 \end{pmatrix} \qquad (9)$$

The obtained evaluation results mean that LO$_1$ meets 71.00% general quality (g) in comparison with the ideal, LO$_2$ – 67.50%, and LO$_3$ – 71.00%.

They also mean that LO$_1$ meets 71.18% "travel well" quality (tw) in comparison with the ideal, LO$_2$ – 68.38%, and LO$_3$ – 72.05%.

Therefore, using triangular fuzzy numbers method, one could see that both LO$_1$ and LO$_3$ are the best alternatives (among the evaluated) from general quality point of view, but LO$_3$ is the best from "travel well" quality point of view.

The criteria ratings (values) obtained while evaluating the aforementioned LOs using trapezoidal fuzzy numbers method are presented by matrix (10):

$$f_i(X) = \begin{pmatrix} 0,800 & 1,000 & 1,000 \\ 1,000 & 0,800 & 0,500 \\ 0,500 & 0,800 & 0,800 \\ 0,800 & 0,200 & 0,800 \\ 0,800 & 1,000 & 0,800 \\ 1,000 & 0,800 & 1,000 \\ 0,800 & 0,500 & 0,800 \\ 0,500 & 0,800 & 0,500 \\ 1,000 & 0,800 & 1,000 \\ 1,000 & 1,000 & 1,000 \end{pmatrix} \qquad (10)$$

The results of experimental evaluation of those Mathematics LOs general quality (g) using trapezoidal fuzzy numbers method are presented by matrix (11):

$$a_g \cdot f(X_j) = \begin{pmatrix} 0,8200 & 0,7700 & 0,8200 \end{pmatrix} \quad (11)$$

The results of experimental evaluation of those Mathematics LOs "travel well" quality (tw) using trapezoidal fuzzy numbers method are presented by matrix (12):

$$a_{tw} \cdot f(X_j) = \begin{pmatrix} 0,8260 & 0,7810 & 0,8360 \end{pmatrix} \quad (12)$$

The obtained evaluation results mean that LO_1 meets 82.00% general quality (q) in comparison with the ideal, $LO_2 - 77.00\%$, and $LO_3 - 82.00\%$.

They also mean that LO_1 meets 82.60% "travel well" quality (tw) in comparison with the ideal, $LO_2 - 78.10\%$, and $LO_3 - 83.60\%$.

Therefore, using trapezoidal fuzzy numbers method, one could see the same results in comparison with the application of triangular numbers: both LO_1 and LO_3 are the best alternatives (among the evaluated) from general quality point of view, but LO_3 is the best from "travel well" quality point of view.

In real life situations a teacher is the only suitable expert to decide on quality of LOs, and, therefore, on purposefulness to use these LOs in his / her teaching process in particular school. In the analysed case, it is clear that Math teacher should choose LO_1 or LO_3 as the best alternatives from general quality point of view, and LO_3 – from "travel well" quality point of view.

Recommendations on Evaluation of LOs Quality

The research results presented in LOs quality evaluation sub-section show that the complex application of the principles of multiple criteria decision analysis for identification of quality evaluation criteria, technological quality criteria classification principle, fuzzy group decision making theory to obtain final evaluation measures, and normalisation requirement for the weights of evaluation criteria, as well as triangular and trapezoidal fuzzy numbers methods for LOs quality optimisation are (1) applicable in real life situations when schools have to decide on purchase of LOs for their education needs, and (2) could significantly improve the quality of expert evaluation of LOs by noticeably reduce of the expert evaluation subjectivity level.

The experimental evaluation results show that the proposed scientific approaches are quite objective, exact and simply to use for selecting the qualitative LOs alternatives in the market.

On the other hand, the proposed LOs "travel well" quality evaluation approach is applicable for the aims of eQNet project in order to select "travel well" LOs from LRE or elsewhere to use them in the other education contexts and countries.

Therefore, those approaches have been recommended by the author to be widely used by European policy makers, publishers, practitioners, and experts-evaluators both inside and outside eQNet project to evaluate quality and reusability level of LOs.

RESEARCH ON USE OF LEARNING OBJECTS IN REAL PEDAGOGICAL PRACTICE AND ITS IMPACT ON LEARNING

LeMill Learning Toolbox

CALIBRATE demonstrated innovative approaches to the creation of LOs through the development of templates and tools that are specifically designed to help create content that can be used for collaborative learning. At the end of the project, the LeMill offers an open source service platform for teachers and schools and provides an active web community for finding, authoring and sharing learning resources.

At the start of the project, the high expectations set for Virtual Learning Environments (VLEs) were not yet being met, even by the latest second generation learning platforms. A key problem was that many VLEs were either designed to support collaborative learning or had been developed primarily to allow teachers and pupils to follow what are seen as more directed forms of 'instruction' based upon the use of SCORM compliant LOs.

The objective in CALIBRATE was to try to advance the state-of-the art concerning learning platform development by integrating what are usually two quite distinct development methodologies – the first coming from a background in social constructivist pedagogies and collaborative knowledge building and the second coming from a background in SCORM and Leaning Content Management Systems. By drawing on both these approaches, partners in CALIBRATE sought to develop, in close collaboration with teachers, a new open source, 'learning toolbox' (building on Fle3 and Plone/Zope) that would offer a much richer feature set. As part of this work, CALIBRATE also carried out an empirical study of IMS Learning Design (IMS LD) in order to determine to what extent it is possible to successfully model "multi-learner" activities in a way that teachers can understand and find useful.

In CALIBRATE, the work involved both: research and technological development designed to gain new knowledge leading to the development of an original open source product for schools; and support for the demonstration and validation of this 'learning toolbox' in order to test its viability in several countries.

What was particularly important in this work was the innovative way that it took the views of teachers in several countries (incl. Lithuania) to be the main driver of service development and then combined this input and feedback with the latest pedagogical and psychological research on learning. As a result, LeMill developers also produced a hypothesis that "there is a growing demand in schools for intuitive, easy to use tools that will allow teachers and pupils to: (1) develop community-driven learning content repositories, and (2) carry out collaborative learning activities using both content developed by the schools themselves and content from commercially available resources."

In LeMill, CALIBRATE has provided a functional service platform for teachers and schools that want to take the first steps towards open content, the knowledge economy, social networking, and pedagogical reform for the 21st century.

More specifically, in working towards this goal, CALIBRATE has:

- Produced distributable, open source server software than can be used for building up a platform for the collaborative development and delivery of LOs. LeMill supports and utilizes open standards such as IEEE LOM, SCORM, RSS, XHTML, etc.
- Explored the extent to which IMS LD is able to model collaborative learning processes and scenarios
- Demonstrated innovative approaches to the creation of LOs through the development of templates and tools that are specifically designed to help create content that can be used for collaborative learning. "Stories",

or descriptions of how teachers use LeMill content, methods and tools, have also been provided

- Established an active, global community of LeMill users. Its major difference to traditional learning management systems is that all content is open, searchable via the web, and modifiable by anyone.

A Creative Commons Attribution-ShareAlike license5 was applied to all resources in LeMill (content, methods, tools, stories, group fora). This enables teachers to use the content found in LeMill freely and also protects their rights as authors. The license allows anyone to modify and improve the content in LeMill, but also guarantees that original authors are always listed as the authors of the content they have made and any improvements are also published using the same license. This allows users to also benefit from improvements made by others.

While the open approach of LeMill has received varied responses in different countries, however, the overall design of LeMill has been successful and the hypothesis behind its development appears to have been broadly accurate. LeMill has proved challenging to some teachers and is unnecessary for others but current indications are that significant numbers of teachers find it a potentially useful tool.

While project developers believe that LeMill is pedagogy-neutral, it is obvious from its collaborative and open nature that some forms of pedagogy are a poor fit. This is particularly the case with teacher-centric traditional practices with closed content. Exams and assessment may also not benefit much from the collaborative and open resources in LeMill. In general LeMill developers suggest that it is useful and can be more easily exploited in democratic educational settings where students are able to influence the practices and tasks that constitute their education.

The project has carried out an empirical study into whether IMS LD is able to model collabora-

tive processes and scenarios and whether it can help the project to develop prototype LOs that are IMS LD compatible. The conclusion of this work was that the disadvantages outweighed the advantages of using IMS LD structures for creating pedagogical templates in the project.

Evaluation and School Pilots in CALIBRATE

CALIBRATE adapted the methodology developed in the ValNet project to train, support and work with approximately 100 primary and secondary schools incl. 10 in Lithuania. Teachers in these countries tested CALIBRATE results in workshops, summer schools and directly via authentic trials in classrooms.

The main objectives of CALIBRATE school pilots were:

- To evaluate how existing national content repositories were being used by teachers
- To integrate the results from other work packages in a CALIBRATE LRE portal and provide support/training materials for teachers in up to 100 schools in Europe
- To evaluate the use of the CALIBRATE LRE portal and LeMill by schools in seven countries, and to report on their potential to facilitate collaborative uses of LOs and support more advanced pedagogical models.

A starting point was the validation framework first developed in ValNet project. This was designed to capture changes in education systems, schools and teaching and learning and the impact of project outputs on them. The original five dimensions were extended to cover education system and institutional elements, summed up as SIPTEC (System, Institutional, Pedagogical, Technological, Economic and Cultural). CALIBRATE National Validation Moderators – NVMs (incl. the author) began their work by examining whether it was possible to adapt the framework to specific local conditions while retaining the overall structure.

Validation and evaluation work was divided into four tasks:

1. Create the conditions for a successful validation exercise: identifying, training and supporting the network of schools; developing a shared vision for collaborative learning; helping to integrate and make project research work packages results visible via a CALIBRATE portal
2. Pre-validation' with a small number of schools and development and implementation of a teacher training course
3. Develop the validation framework and teacher training before the validation starts
4. Carry out full validation, collect and analyse results.

Four hypotheses were examined during the evaluation process:

1. European teachers with an average level of ICT skills and competences are able to make good use of the LRE
2. Computer supported collaborative learning in knowledge building communities and trialogical learning – co-operation around shared LOs – is successfully supported by LeMill
3. Long-term use of the LRE and LeMill will promote the advancement of the integration of ICT in education on technical, economic and cultural/linguistic levels
4. Regular use of the LRE and LeMill will promote the advancement of the integration of ICT in education on an institutional (school level) and on a pedagogical (teacher/ student) level as well.

Three evaluation methods were used:

1. Authentic trial (school based search, retrieval and processing of content for immediate teaching). Reporting back experiences was also carried out in an authentic way, through Lesson Plans, in a format close to those normally prepared and stored for later use by practicing teachers
2. National focus group discussions (CALIBRATE philosophy of free of charge, international exchange of valuable open educational resources in a community of contributing user-developers) were contrasted with current educational practice in different countries
3. International co-evolutionary process of the repository and toolbox that involved:
   ◦ Pre-pilots: the usability of the CALIBRATE LO repository and LeMill was first tested in two pre-pilots with expert ICT using teachers from 5 countries (incl. Lithuania). The activity facilitated the design of tools as it provided first hand information for developers on user requirements and problems arising in user practice
   ◦ Presentations by developers (not only about CALIBRATE but also about its cultural context: social tagging, Web 2.0 technologies, communities of practice, interactive teaching strategies etc.)
   ◦ Evaluation exercises in international groups in a workshop setting.

Evaluation was not only targeted towards CALIBRATE tools, it also identified user needs: definition of necessary competences, motivation and attitudes towards ICT, personal characteristics relevant for its educational use, and type of preparation needed for the minimal, average and optimal use of the LRE portal and LeMill.

CALIBRATE carried out a two-stage evaluation, using a hypothesis-based approach, of how teachers worked with the CALIBRATE LRE portal and LeMill. The general conclusion from the available evidence was that; teachers' were willing and, given support, had the ability to use the LRE; and could collaborate successfully in LeMill.

Did the evaluation support the four hypotheses? The evaluation has shown that:

1. European teachers with an average level of ICT skills and competences are able to make good use of the LRE, the first federated European learning content repository.

The evaluation presumed that: a satisfactory for educational innovation ICT competence level for teachers can be defined, based on substantial international studies; and teachers who possess an average ICT competence will make optimal use of the LRE. Optimal use is characterised by the following activities:

*   Search for international digital learning assets and resources with the help of metadata in mother tongue and English
*   Retrieve assets and resources (in mother tongue and in foreign languages alike)
*   Adapt and use them in authentic educational activities (e. g., self improvement, preparation for teaching, development of teaching aids, classroom work, assignment of home work, etc.)
*   Evaluate assets and resources before/after use according to criteria defined by LRE developers,
*   Produce an account about educational use of LRE assets and resources in the form of Lesson Plans.

This assumption was proven because both experienced users and novices to ICT were able to search for, download, adapt, test and evaluate international LOs. Their motivation and skill to do so varied according to:

*   Previous training in the educational use of digital learning content
*   Availability of resources through national repositories
*   The range of LOs offered in the repository in the disciplines taught by the teachers
*   The quality of LOs: preferably little text but high quality visualisation and/or interactive teaching-learning options.

2. Computer supported collaborative learning in knowledge building communities and trialogical learning – cooperation around shared educational objects – is successfully supported by LeMill.

The evaluation proved the hypothesis that LeMill as a collaborative VLE would act as a catalyst for shared knowledge creation and dissemination. Shared knowledge is a trialogical learning concept that refers to knowledge that is uniform across all members of a team and is represented in each member's individual competence rather than unequally distributed in the team. The evaluation also proved the hypothesis that LeMill would be an excellent form for mentored innovation as it offers a variety of tools for scaffolding – a process by which a more experienced person supplies supporting structures or simplifies a situation or a task in a way that allows one less experienced to solve complex problems that would otherwise be beyond the latter's capability. Scaffolding may also be created by computer tools that structure enquirers' activities in a way that facilitates complex problem solving.

The Forum function of LeMill had the potential to create social presence, a strong feeling of community. The main idea behind LeMill was appreciated and, although technical problems were identified, satisfaction rose significantly towards the end of the project.

3. Long term use of the LRE and LeMill will promote the advancement of the integration

of ICT in education on technical, economic and cultural/linguistic levels.

CALIBRATE tools resulted in more intensive educational use of ICT in piloting schools and, as dissemination commences, also on local, regional and ultimately national scale.

NVMs witnessed a large increase in the integration of ICTs in countries with no digital educational content repositories and this shows the real potential of the tools and resources: initiating large numbers of newcomers in different countries simultaneously in high level ICT use in education. Discipline based collaboration was found to be most efficient in piloting countries.

4. Regular use of the LRE and LeMill will promote the advancement of the integration of ICT in education on institutional – school level and on pedagogical – teacher/student level as well.

The concept of symmetric knowledge advancement was introduced to describe the nature of change incurred by CALIBRATE tools. Symmetric knowledge advancement occurs when ICT makes a network's discourses and practices public to a larger community, fostering knowledge creation across a large professional network. In CALIBRATE, piloting teachers and NVMs who gained access to the discourses of software developers and their fellow teachers and evaluation experts learned to model expert practice more effectively and distribute it with more ambition and success. Similarly, teachers who had access to the discourses and practices of students may improve their own practices and develop deeper understanding of students' needs and goals, etc. Symmetric knowledge advancement is realised when communities of learners cross-discursive and practice-related boundaries of the classroom and organisation and promote one another's advancements.

The hypothesis proved while the evaluation team analysed (1) Policy documents of participating countries about the role of ICT in education and related educational policies; (2) Accounts of the NVMs about Evaluation Days; and (3) Final reports by NVMs on the results of CALIBRATE evaluation procedure in their countries and prospects of further use.

In this case, piloting teachers and NVMs who had gained access to the discourses of software developers and their fellow teachers and evaluation experts did indeed learn to model expert practice more effectively and distribute it with more ambition and success. Symmetric knowledge advancement was also realised when communities of learners cross-discursive and practice-related boundaries of the classroom and organisation and promote one another's advancements. During the CALIBRATE project, such processes were witnessed during the mentored innovation process that accompanied testing of international LOs at school, at the Summer School in Portoroz, Slovenia, where international teams collaborated and during national Evaluation Days.

Motivation for use of European LOs seems to be vital for sustainability in order to avoid the regrettably frequent fate of ICT-related innovations that are often overpaid and underused. Innovation results in CALIBRATE were successfully communicated through carefully selected channels over time among the members of a social system in a 5-step process, involving innovators first (in this case, these are the piloting teachers), early adopters, (in the project, those interested teachers who, at educational exhibitions, were involved in national Evaluation Days), and early majority (who were reached through dissemination conferences for CALIBRATE). Therefore, it is hoped that the LRE and LeMill will be successfully used in the future by an increasing number of teachers in participating countries.

"Travel Well" Resources:

CALIBRATE teachers appeared motivated to use resources from other countries and in other languages. An important finding was that 93% of respondents surveyed in the project said that would be interested in having access to digital LOs from other countries even if they are not in their own language.

One of the most important issues of the pilot was to identify LOs that teachers could use in all or most of the piloting countries – that is, resources that had the potential to 'travel well'. Teachers and NVMs identified two major sets of selection criteria: (1) Suitability to the national curriculum/ guidelines of the users; and (2) Overall quality of the learning material.

This work was continued in the next EUN's INSPIRE and eQNet projects.

In conclusion, the CALIBRATE evaluation made the following ten key recommendations:

1. Communicate the results of CALIBRATE, including the LRE and LeMill, to new EU member states, not only through conference presentations, but also through introductory workshops and demonstrations of the LRE and LeMill best practice. The CALIBRATE 'Evaluation Days' model shows how both systems can be successfully introduced to novices

2. Ensure that both pre-service and practicing teachers fully exploit the opportunities for collaboration provided by the LRE and LeMill through local peer support or longer-term mentoring. This will particularly be important in those countries where ICT supported methods are not yet fully embedded in teachers' daily practice

3. Continue international teacher workshops and training events for teachers in order to help promote pan-European knowledge building communities for the LRE and LeMill

4. Continue to use the Topic Mapper approach but consider providing more exemplification and applying more rigour in vocabulary

5. Share only the best resources at an international level, in order to make the LRE attractive, particularly for teachers in countries that have rich, national LO repositories

6. MoE, repository owners and other content partners should pre-select sufficient high quality resources and assets with appropriate metadata from national collections, to guarantee high quality content in the LRE federation

7. Undertake further work in the other projects (such as MELT, INSPIRE and eQNet) to reach a wider agreement on quality criteria for resources/assets that "travel well" and, if necessary, develop new mechanisms to ensure that these criteria are applied to national content collections. It also needs to be recognised that the "best" resources at a national level may not always be those that "travel well".

8. Continue to involve teachers as co-developers of both the LRE and LeMill. In terms of future development of the LRE and LeMill, it is also important to recognise that didactic teaching still prevails and ICT resources are still demanded by teachers for use in this classic instructional model

9. Carry out a second evaluation of LRE and LeMill use a year after the completion of the CALIBRATE project in order to show whether those countries that do not make LRE and LeMill use a national priority develop large numbers of active users and teacher communities.

10. Accompany major educational innovations by an evaluation process using the Design Based Research paradigm that is most suited to the interdependent educational and technological processes identified in CALIBRATE.

Validation of CALIBRATE Services in Lithuania

Two CALIBRATE project tools validation days were organised in Lithuania by the author of the chapter: (1) October 24, 2007, in Druskininkai – 30 participants; (2) November 30, 2007, in Vilnius – 11 participants. Totally 41 teachers participated from 21 schools from all over Lithuania.

The following subjects' teachers have participated mostly: Mathematics – 14 teachers, Information Technologies – 11, and Physics – 6.

One of the validated tools was CALIBRATE portal. Portal's usability and different LOs search strategies implementation level were evaluated mostly.

The main results of CALIBRATE portal validation in Lithuania were as follows:

- 85% teachers can (re-)use LOs, and 80% can create LOs by themselves with no or little help
- 97% teachers prefer (i.e., find it useful and very useful) full query conformity, 82% would take into account other teachers ranks, 81% prefer LOs sorting adequate to search method, 42% would take into account LOs popularity, 68% prefer LOs sorted accordingly with their profile, and 52% would take into account similar users opinion (tagging)
- Most of the teachers would use the found LO as illustration or include it in presentation (i.e., as Learning Asset, in project work, as background information, or include LO in test / task sheet
- It is obvious that the majority of teachers prefer to reuse "small" assets, and they intend to reuse the majority of assets in another way and in another learning context than it was primarily designed by assets authors
- The majority of teachers prefer to have the mechanism of advance search of ul-

timately reusable resources. Therefore it is extremely important to identify LOs metadata standard's elements suitable to describe LOs reusability level, and to develop software for such kind of advanced search in the repositories. It is clear that these elements are extremely important to fill in while creating LOs metadata
- 77% teachers were satisfied or very satisfied with LOs they found in LRE portal
- All 100% teachers would find the LOs again in LRE portal
- 95% teachers would use LRE very soon or perhaps, only 5% did not know.

LRE validation in Lithuania has shown that the teachers prefer LOs from national repositories which have the potential to "travel well" and can be used in different national contexts. These reusable LOs preferred by the teachers are mainly "small" decontextualised assets. Therefore in order to maximise LOs reusability in Europe LRE should consist mainly of decontextualised learning assets. There are two main conditions for LOs reusability elsewhere:

- LOs have to fit different countries' national curricula
- Different countries' LOM APs have to be oriented towards quick and convenient search of reusable resources.

The main tools for this are curricula mapping and right guidelines for LOM AP. Approaches concerning application profiles and curricula mapping (incl. controlled vocabularies) are the main while creating any metadata guidelines or strategies (Reigeluth & Nelson, 1997). Indeed, LRE at the moment contains about 130.000 LOs, and the main problem is to provide more quick and convenient suitable LOs search possibilities in the repositories for the users.

LRE validation in Lithuania has shown that the majority of teachers prefer to have the mechanism of advance search of ultimately reusable resources. Therefore, it is extremely important to identify LOs metadata standard's elements suitable to describe LOs reusability level, and to develop software for such kind of advances search in the repositories. It is clear that these elements are extremely important to fill in while creating LOs metadata.

Content Packaging Application Research in ASPECT

An important aim in ASPECT was to help redress a perceived 'disconnect' between standards' organisations and the educational community by working directly with teachers to help them explore and implement standards. From the perspective of MoE, it is important that teachers' views as well as those of technical experts are fed into the pre-standardisation process. In line with this objective, 46 teachers from Belgium, Lithuania, Portugal and Romania took part in a series of ASPECT workshops to elicit their opinions and observe their use of content packaging, search features and mechanisms developed in the ASPECT project. The tests were carried out between October 2009 and May 2010, and involved three independent workshops:

1. National workshops on content discovery
2. Online workshops on content reuse
3. An international workshop for all participants on content packaging and access control.

Lithuanian validation report provides the data collected from experiments conducted with 9 Lithuanian teachers of Science subjects who took part in three separate ASPECT school pilot workshops. The report includes: background information on the teachers selected for the experiments; data we gathered on teachers' search behaviours and satisfaction with the ASPECT LRE portal vs. Google; teachers' attitudes toward

LOs reuse and sharing of; and teachers' feedback on packaged content in SCORM and IMS CC formats. Workshop 1 with Lithuanian teachers took place Vilnius (Lithuania), Sat 24 Oct 2009 eliciting teachers' feedback on search tools and collecting data on teachers' search behaviours. The second workshop was carried out online in March 2010 covering content discovery as well as the functionalities of the ASPECT LRE portal vs. Google. The third workshop was a joint summer school for 45 teachers from all four countries in May 2010.

Main Results

Discovery of Resources

Workshops 1 and 2 used questionnaires to elicit data on search and user satisfaction among teachers searching for LOs and compared their behaviours using the ASPECT LRE portal vs. Google. 60% of Lithuanian teachers reported successful searches of the ASPECT LRE portal for images to fit their lesson plans. Simulations were also found by 50% of the teachers. 60% of teachers used keywords in their successful searches for images.

In most of the cases, LOs were found when teachers searched via keywords or subjects. This is mainly the traditional way of finding resources, and seems to be teachers want. It is important to note that they didn't find any resources when recommended or tagged by others. Given that the Lithuanian teachers had no previous knowledge of the ASPECT LRE portal, they were asked to assess its features and point out which features they liked best. Teachers liked the availability of information about different kinds of LOs (100% liked the descriptions they found of applets) and they also appreciated the ability to search for LOs in different languages (90% of teachers).

Google vs. ASPECT LRE

To understand search behaviours and user satisfaction, researchers have administered a test to compare the time it took teachers to find the "same" resource using the ASPECT LRE or Google. This usability test also illustrated teachers' search behaviours.

On average, when these teachers searched by subject or via target group, they took less time to find resources in Google than with the ASPECT LRE portal. However, when they searched via keywords, they took less time with the ASPECT LRE portal than with Google.

Lithuanian teachers are fully aware of tagging and rating systems. In 100% of the cases:

- Teachers can see themselves tagging LOs or adding them to favourites in the future
- Teachers found tagging very useful because they can find LOs they liked quickly
- They could give ratings to LOs they have reviewed
- They trust more ratings done recently
- They trust the rating if given by someone they know
- They consider ratings when they are choosing
- They find both ratings and tagging useful.

Building Lesson Plans with Packaged Content: SCORM and IMS CC Formats

Teachers' reactions and use behaviour patterns with IMS CC and SCORM were elicited during a workshop organised in May 2010 in Lisbon that brought together all the teachers in the project. User testing focused on the integration of LOs into VLE and content packaging, in particular exploring how different types of "content packaging" can add value to the learning experience. The VLE used was Moodle. Teachers who had not experience with Moodle were provided with a basic training session in its use.

All teachers underwent a training session on the use of Moodle and the integration of packaged resources in the VLE. Once they were familiar with this platform, the teachers were asked to create the same lesson plan four times: (1) normal lesson plan using the Moodle VLE in a "traditional" way, i.e., by combining different LOs; (2) using a LO on the same topic that had been 'packaged' by ASPECT content developers using the SCORM standard; (3) using a LO on the same topic that had been 'packaged' by ASPECT content developers using the IMS CC standard; and, finally, (4) just embedding parts of the IMS CC.

27% Lithuanian teachers found it really easy to create a lesson plan using a normal web page, and only 9% found it really easy to use an IMS CC package or taking parts of it. Using an IMS CC package and web pages was reasonable for another 45% of teachers. A large proportion (64%) of teachers encountered "some problems" taking parts of an IMS CC package. When it came to creating a forum using normal web pages, a SCORM package, an IMS CC package or by taking parts of an IMS CC package, less then forty percent of teachers encountered "some problems".

Less than 10% considered creating questionnaires really easy with any of the formats. Slightly more teachers reported that web pages were "reasonable" to work with for this task in comparison to the other formats.

Lithuanian teachers found that the best option for them would be to take a piece of the LO from one of the IMS CC packages and use it with other teaching materials. 55% of teachers thought that, although they would initially loose time working with IMS CC formats, it was worth the investment. For SCORM, 45% thought it was worth the time investment to master the features.

Teachers' preferences regarding interfaces were mixed. No single format garnered a majority of teachers as a preferred interface in different kinds of teaching activities. 45% of Lithuanian teachers thought that IMS CC packages in Moodle would be useful for teaching an entire online course, and 36% of them also thought it would be useful for giving students online homework assignments and extra credit.

73% of teachers preferred to use bits of materials they found online and mix them with other materials.

For 55% percent of teachers, the quality of the content was of vital importance.

Access Control Mechanisms

Most of the teachers (90%) indicated that their schools buy LOs online. When asked if they were interested in a credit-based system, 80% indicated that they were interested but it was important for them that they receive credits without having to pay for these.

All Lithuanian teachers created their own learning resources and in 90% of the cases said they will continue doing so. 70% said they would not mind sharing their own resources if they received other resources in exchange. 40% of teachers were interested in being paid for sharing their resources.

In order for teachers to gain credits, two proposals were made. First, teachers could gain credits by rating other people's LOs or providing feedback on them. Second, teachers could gain credits by uploading LOs they had created. 80% of Lithuanian teachers are interested in earning credits by providing ratings and feedback on other people's LOs. 90% would agree to a credit system that would allow them to upload their own LOs in exchange for other LOs.

In Lithuania, 9 teachers participated in the AS-PECT project. Most had many years of teaching experience as well as high rates of computer literacy and regular use patterns of web materials and Moodle. Lithuanian teachers were more successful and satisfied with their searches using Google vs. the ASPECT LRE. Lithuanian teachers preferred to create lesson plans, forums or questionnaires using a normal web page rather than IMS CC or SCORM. They were interested in using any format that could allow them to modify and edit content rather than using a structured packaged.

INSPIRE Learning Objects Validation Observatory and School Pilots

INSPIRE has set up a limited validation observatory where 60 schools in Europe used, tested, and analysed new LOs from LRE in the field of MST. On the INSPIRE website the pilot schools were able to choose from 60 LOs to be applied in their science lessons. During the project, schools regularly provide reports of students' and teachers' feedback on the new teaching methods.

The project has relied on previous R&D activities and implemented the following activities:

- Implement three school pilots involving a total of 60 schools in Germany, Austria, Italy, Spain and Lithuania
- Define the protocol of experimentation and organise the training of the pilot schools via training of trainers' session
- Launch and monitor the experimentation activity for a period of 10 months with the pilot schools
- Analyse the impact and feedback of this experimentation
- Draw the lessons and propose recommendations, action plan and concrete support (i.e., a handbook for teachers) for generalising such an approach
- Ensure the exploitation of this project via the organisation of an international summer school and the development of an online community of practice for educators regarding the use of LOs in MST.

INSPIRE consolidated report on school pilots has provided several conclusions on the use of LOs. They are as follows:

General Conclusions:

- The INSPIRE project has been successful as far as participation is concerned – 62 schools, over 200 teachers and nearly 5000 pupils participated in the project

- The INSPIRE project has also been very successful as it clearly proves that the use of LOs enhances the quality of learning and teaching of MST. Furthermore the use of LOs greatly contributes to enhancing the acquisition of various lifelong learning competences and skills

- Most of the schools involved are very much interested in ICT, have strategies for implementing ICT in as many disciplines as possible and were already participating in ICT projects. Many are also active in European, interregional or bilateral projects. One can thus conclude that most of the schools involved are schools that are open to innovation in education in general and not only in MST. These schools can truly be said to be innovative

- The schools took the preparation of the INSPIRE project very seriously as virtually all of them discussed the project and its objectives with the head and management and with the teachers involved. Three quarters also kept the teachers involved updated. Only parents were less informed (40%) and even less updated about the project activities. Three quarters of the schools also trained the pupils and or the teachers involved. The serious preparation is also proven by the fact that motivated and experienced school coordinators were appointed in each school

- The countries involved also took the preparation of the project very seriously by nominating experienced and committed national coordinators and by organising meetings with all the schools and teachers concerned involving information and training sessions

- The organisation of the project work was successful thanks to the participation of several ministries, the schools, the national coordinators, the school coordinators and the support of the EUN team. The satisfaction rate with the monitoring of the national coordinators and school coordinators was very high. It can therefore be said that the organisation of the project team, with the training of the national coordinators has been very efficient. The idea of the Protocol of Experimentation is also to be welcomed although there are elements of it that could be improved

- Most of the participating schools were secondary schools. This can be explained by the fact that most of the LOs proposed by the project team were to be used at secondary school level. Also as far as the respondent pupils were concerned the large majority of them were in the age group between 11 and 18. Some of the younger pupils would probably lack the skills to fill out the questionnaires

- About two thirds of the teachers who participated in the project already had experience with ICT experiments and about one quarter had experience with science experiments

- All 60 proposed LOs were used in the project. Lithuania chose to use each of the LO ten times. Some of the LOs were only used 10 times, others over thirty times. The main selection criterion to use the LO was the fact that the topic of the LO was part of the national curriculum. Also the fact that the LO combined MST with ICT and that the LO took into account the ICT experience of teachers and pupils were important criteria. When the LO did not deal with a topic of the curriculum it had to develop a creative learning environment in order to be chosen

- The LOs were subdivided in five clear categories: Biology, Chemistry, Mathematics, Physics and ICT. The LOs for the subcategories ICT and Mathematics were used most. The LOs were used for a wide range of subjects going from ICT to languages and image education. The subjects for which the LOs were used most were ICT and Physics. The LOs were not only used during lessons but also during extracurricular activities, ranging from Comenius projects, over Science clubs to project work

- The pedagogical approach was usually an approach consisting of several elements of the Inquiry-Based Science Education approach

- The majority of the pupils (40%) worked on their own but others worked in pairs or even in large groups which had an impact on skills such as teamwork

- The schools that were fully involved had the necessary and appropriate IT equipment. Schools with no equipment or limited equipment had difficulties getting involved or dropped out. Although only 90% of the schools who participated in the project stated that they used special equipment to carry out the experiments, it turned out that a number of the schools (especially in Germany and Austria) considered computers to be standard equipment. In fact all the schools that participated in the project had computers available. They usually had one computer per child, very often with Internet access. One third of the teachers used multimedia or a beamer and two thirds say there was Internet access to carry out the experiments. Only one school could not participate in the project because of lack of equipment

- The LOs do not only have an impact on the pupils but also on the teachers. Indeed, three quarters state that their interest in and motivation for teaching MST has increased. Moreover, two thirds say that the LO have increased their motivation for teaching MST using LOs and that the latter have facilitated teaching MST to differentiated groups

- As far as the impact on the pupils is concerned the views of the teachers and the pupils differ. According to 80% of the teachers the ability to study autonomously has increased most, followed by the ability of the pupils to understand and use ICT in general. As far as the attitudes and skills of the pupils are concerned the skill that has improved most according to 70% of the teachers is the learning to learn skill. Also around two thirds of the teachers state that the pupils have acquired scientific vocabulary, are more motivated to study MST and can better work in team

- When assessing the appreciation of MST before the use of the LOs it is clear that the attitude of boys is in general much more positive towards MST than that of girls. However, in the three pilots considerable differences were found. Because the majority of pupils responding to the survey (around 80%) were German and Austrian the overall figures have strongly been influenced by the German and Austrian results. In Lithuania and in the pilot for Spain and Italy girls seemed to have a more positive attitude towards MST

- According to the pupils the LOs had a very positive impact on making a better link between MST and everyday life. Also a positive impact is experienced on making it easier to study MST and to evaluate scientific data and experiences more critically

- When assessing the impact on MST taking into account gender differences it is clear that the LO have a bigger impact on boys than on girls except for linking MST with everyday life and for studying MST autonomously where the impact is the same. However, also here, the overall figures have been strongly influenced by the results from the Austrian-German pilot. In fact it seems that whenever pupils (girls or boys) have a positive attitude towards MST the impact of the LOs seems to be greater. When taking into account the age differences it is clear that the impact on the pupils is higher with younger than with older pupils. This is the case as well with boys as with girls. The number of LOs used seems to have no impact on the appreciation of MST

- There might also be a higher impact of the LOs if the expectations of the teachers are higher. However, the higher impact might also be linked to the fact that some pupils were already used to working with LOs whereas for others they were relatively new. Especially for those pupils who have already been working with LOs, the choice or selection of LOs is very important. In order to have an important impact on all pupils they should be creative, innovative and interactive

- The project did not only have an impact on the direct beneficiaries (pupils and teachers) but also on the schools involved and even on the educational system of the countries involved. This was clearly illustrated by the fact that schools stated that one of the outcomes would be that more MST teachers are trained to use ICT-based tools and that the lessons learned from the project would be mainstreamed in the education system

- Lastly, the main success factors of the project are the motivation of the pupils and teachers involved, the help and support of the national and school coordinator but also the small financial help that was given to the schools. The fact that the support and monitoring by the national and school coordinator were much appreciated proves that the organisational structure set up by EUN in cooperation with the partners to the project worked very well.

Relevance: The activities of the project focusing on the testing of LOs can be said to be very relevant to the countries involved. The project definitely contributes to innovative policies in the promotion of MST which are implemented in all the countries concerned and which are also at the core of the Lisbon agenda 2010: the promotion of quality education in general, the promotion of creative learning environments, the promotion of interest for science and technology and the promotion of ICT. The activities of the project are also particularly relevant as to Inquiry-Based Science Education which proves more and more to be one of the key methods to improve the quality of the learning and teaching of MST as highlighted in the Rocard report "Science education now: a renewed pedagogy for the future of Europe".

Efficiency: The activities of the project as to the work done with the LOs have been very efficient. A clear support and organisational structure was set up to organise, support, monitor and evaluate the work with the LOs in the different countries involved. The well defined and complementary roles of the national and the school coordinators have proven to be crucial for the implementation of the INSPIRE activities. The support of the MoE also proved to be very important both at the level of the implementation and at the level of the dissemination and valorisation of what has been achieved. The coordinating role played by EUN has also proven to be stimulating and synergetic in many respects. All the competencies and skills of the different partners and parties involved have been put at use in a very efficient and cost effective way. When taking into account the money that has been used to support the coordinators and the schools it has to be clearly stated that the investment was minimal in comparison to what has been achieved. The money spent has been efficiently and very well spent leading to very positive outcomes.

Effectiveness: All the objectives of the project as described in the Comenius application have definitely been reached and one can easily state that they have been reached beyond expectations. The data collected through the protocol of experimentation prove that the objectives have been reached. The findings will also prove to be useful not only for the schools involved but for many schools and educational systems across Europe that can make use of the outcomes and the findings of the INSPIRE project. The project team has been working in a very flexible way in close in cooperation with the representatives of the ministries, the national coordinators and the school coordinators to the benefit of the quality of the outcomes.

Impact: The data collected clearly show that there is a clear impact of the use of LOs on the learning and teaching of MST. The impact is clear shown on all the actors involved: on the teachers, the national coordinators, the school coordinators, the ministries and the education systems as such. The schools stress that there is an impact on the school strategy to use LOs not only in MST but in all subjects which will be reflected in training teachers to work with those LOs. The findings also prove to have an impact on the one hand the MoE in their decision-making process and on the other hand on those in charge of curriculum-development or those in charge of developing LOs and or manuals for MST. The impact is definitely also enhanced by the fact that the lessons learnt through the INSPIRE project have been mainstreamed in several of the countries involved.

Sustainability: The feedback and the evaluation made by the schools and teachers involved clearly show that schools subsequent to their

involvement in the project will promote more use of LOs not only in MST but in as many subjects as possible. Measures will be taken within the schools to promote the use of LOs such as in-service training of teachers. Also the ministries are convinced that LOs should be more used in many disciplines. The stimulus of the ministry will no doubt have an influence on the curriculum development people and on those in charge of developing LOs and manuals or textbooks. The fact that the outcomes and the findings of the project have been largely disseminated and mainstreamed across the education systems will definitely contribute to the sustainability.

INSPIRE Experimentation Results in Lithuania

According to Kurilovas & Serikoviene (2010c), through INSPIRE project experimentation, special attention has been given and reported on as regards:

- The impact of the new LOs and teaching methods at the level of pupils and their motivation
- The analysis of the pre-requisites to be defined for enabling the teachers to integrate these new techniques in their pedagogy
- The critical success factors to be mastered at the level of the teacher and the school for the generalisation of such practices.

The author while being INSPIRE coordinator in Lithuania has performed the questionnaires-based survey of the MST teachers in 10 Lithuanian comprehensive schools. 10 IT teachers from 10 schools have participated in the survey. 12 LOs on IT subject from LRE have been proposed to the teachers to evaluate during the experiment in real pedagogical contexts in their schools.

Some results of this survey are presented further. Tables 4, 5, and 6 present the results of the survey aimed to analyse the IT subject's learn-

Table 4. General information

Names	Values	Ratings
Learner profile information	High knowledge / skills level	0
	Average knowledge / skills level	9
	Low knowledge/skills level	0
	Gifted	0
	Motivated	5
	Needs personalisation	0
Learning aims / General competences	Communication in mother tongue	6
	Communication in foreign language	4
	Competence in MST	2
	Digital competence	6
	Learning to learn	3
	Social competencies	1
	Enterprising and Creativity	3
	Personal and Cultural understanding	4
Subject competences	Fit the curriculum	10
	Do not fit the curriculum	0
Digital environment used in the experiment	Moodle	3
	LeMill	1
	Other	5
	Not used	0
Conclusion on LOs usability	To localise and use	3
	To use without localisation	7
	Not to use	0

ers' pre-requisites, enhanced competences (both general and subject), learning and assessment methods and VLEs used by IT teachers during the experiment, as well as the teachers' conclusion of LOs usability in future.

Learning methods taxonomy in Table 2 has been developed according to Kurilovas & Dagiene (2010b).

Tables 4, 5, and 6 show that all general competences were addresses by the proposed LOs, and different pedagogically sound proactive learning and assessment methods have been used during the experiment.

In IT teachers' opinion, VLE Moodle is the most suitable digital environment to implement these learning and assessment methods while working with personalised and decontextualised LOs.

They also think that the majority of LOs are suitable to use without localisation, and the others require localisation before implementation in school practice.

Table 5. Learning methods used during the experiment

Learning methods	Description	Ratings
By information source	Word-based methods	3
	Visual-based methods	7
By theory and practice ratio	Theoretical methods	0
	Practice-based methods	10
By teacher and students activity relationship	Active learning methods	0
	Passive learning methods	7
By authoritarianism and humanity relationships	Programme-oriented methods	4
	Student-oriented methods	9
	Authoritarian methods	1
	Humane methods	1
By the students activity creativity level	Reproductive methods	5
	Creative methods	3
By the students reasoning operations relationships with the logical forms and shapes	Analysis	5
	Synthesis	6
	Abstraction and generalisation	3
	Deduction and induction	1
	Analogy	2
	Hypothesis	2
	Experiment	5

Table 6. Assessment methods used during the experiment

Description	Ratings
Test	3
Credit	0
Practical assignment	8
Creative assignment	3
Self-assessment	2
E-Portfolio	0
Project work	1

FUTURE RESEARCH TRENDS

Future Research on LOs Quality and Reusability

In the chapter, the author has analysed several tools and methods for multiple criteria evaluation of LOs.

Future research should concentrate on investigating a comprehensive scientific model and several methods suitable for the expert evaluation of quality of learning scenarios paying especial attention to their suitability to particular learner groups (i.e., profiles) in iTEC. Additional research is needed to avoid the overlap of the learning content and activity quality evaluation criteria. Other methods of vector optimisation could be also used in the future research, and their efficiency should be compared.

Several optimisation methods should be explored to optimise learning scenarios in conformity with particular learner profiles. Several practical examples of iTEC learning scenarios should be evaluated against the proposed model and methods. The further research results should analyse suitability of both Analytic Hierarchy Process

(AHP) method to establish the weights of quality criteria, and several fuzzy optimisation methods to solve learning scenarios' multiple criteria evaluation and optimisation tasks for particular learner profiles. Method of consecutive triple application of AHP for establishing the weights of evaluation criteria currently developed by the author should be absolutely novel, and those new elements should make the given work distinct from all the other earlier works in the area.

Furthermore, all the new models are to be validated. Along this line, validation of the proposed LOs quality evaluation model and methods is scheduled for the rest of eQNet project till September 2012, and validation of learning scenarios quality evaluation model and methods are scheduled in 5 stages of iTEC project, with the first stage starting in September 2011.

An additional very complicated problem is minimisation of the experts' (decision makers') subjectivity in quality evaluation process. There are some scientific approaches concerning this issue, but this is out of the scope of the chapter, and they should be analysed separately in future works.

The issues of personalisation and adaptation of learning content and activity also deserve further investigation, and a more detailed analysis in the scientific literature is needed.

Future Research on Learning Content and Activity Impact on Education

Solution of complex learning scenarios (incl. both learning content and activity modules) quality evaluation and optimisation problems could help educational institutions to select suitable learning scenarios for the particular learner profiles.

iTEC partners plan to develop specific teaching and learning activities, based on the scenarios, to test these in a pre-pilot phase, and to carry out large-scale pilots in up to 1,000 classrooms in at least 12 European countries exploring both the integration of technologies and how these impact on teaching and learning practices and the engagement of a wider group of stakeholders outside the school.

CONCLUSION

The main conclusions of the chapter are as follows.

Concerning LOs Quality and Reusability

LOs quality evaluation research results show that the complex application of the principles of multiple criteria decision analysis for identification of quality evaluation criteria, technological quality criteria classification principle, fuzzy group decision making theory to obtain final evaluation measures, and normalisation requirement for the weights of evaluation criteria, as well as triangular and trapezoidal fuzzy numbers methods for LOs quality optimisation are (1) applicable in real life situations when schools have to decide on purchase of LOs for their education needs, and (2) could significantly improve the quality of expert evaluation of LOs by noticeably reduce of the expert evaluation subjectivity level.

The aforementioned scientific approaches are quite objective, exact and simply to use for selecting the qualitative LOs alternatives from LRE or elsewhere. LOs "travel well" quality evaluation approach is applicable to select "travel well" LOs from LRE or elsewhere to use them in the other education contexts and countries. Those approaches have been recommended by the author to be widely used by European policy makers, publishers, practitioners, and experts-evaluators both inside and outside eQNet project to evaluate quality and reusability level of LOs.

Concerning LOs Impact on Education

The data collected in the chapter clearly show that there is a clear impact of the use of LOs on the learning and teaching. The impact is clear shown on all the actors involved: on the teachers, the schools, the ministries and the education systems as such.

The schools stress that there is an impact on the school strategy to use LOs in all subjects which will be reflected in training teachers to work with those LOs. The findings also prove to have an impact on the one hand the ministries of education in their decision-making process and on the other hand on those in charge of curriculum-development or those in charge of developing LOs and or manuals. The impact is definitely also enhanced by the fact that the lessons learnt through, e.g., the INSPIRE project have been mainstreamed in several of the countries involved.

The main results of LRE development are as follows:

Concerning LRE Services

European Learning Resource Exchange (LRE) system is a functioning service that currently offers almost 130,000 LOs and assets from over 25 providers.

Main outcomes of the development of LRE (LRE Service Centre) are as follows:

- A Learning Technology Standards Observatory
- An application profile registry
- A Vocabulary Bank for Education
- Learning Object Repository Registries
- Validation services for testing conformance of metadata records
- Metadata transformation services
- An automatic metadata translation service

Concerning Interoperability Issues and Curricula Mapping:

A number of recommendations have been formulated in ASPECT to help all groups of LRE stakeholders to develop interoperable systems and services. Those include the general recommendations, recommendations for content providers and repository owners concerning interoperable open and commercial content, describing and exposing content, recommendations for tolls providers, for federation and discovery service builders, for standards organisations, and for target users and their needs.

A top-down analysis was made in CALIBRATE in order to try to relate the existing Bloom's extended taxonomy to the various curricula. With this approach, partners developed ontologies for topics and competencies.

REFERENCES

W3C (2011). *World Wide Web Consortium Web content accessibility guidelines*. Retrieved on June 28, 2011, from http://www.w3.org/ TR/ WAI- WEBCONTENT/

ASPECT. (2011). *EU eContentplus programme's ASPECT (Adopting Standards and Specifications for Educational Content)*. Best Practice Network (2008 – 2011) web site. Retrieved on June 28, 2011, from http://aspect-project.org/

Becta, (2007) *Quality principles for digital learning resources.*

Belton, V., & Stewart, T. J. (2002). *Multiple criteria decision analysis: an integrated approach*. Amsterdam: Kluwer Academic Publishers.

CALIBRATE. (2008). *EU FP6 IST CALIBRATE (Calibrating eLearning in Schools) project (2005 – 2008) web site*. Retrieved on June 28, 2011, from http://calibrate.eun.org

CELEBRATE. (2004). *EU FP5 IST CELEBRATE (Context eLearning with Broadband Technologies) project (2002 – 2004) web site*. Retrieved on June 28, 2011, from http://celebrate.eun.org

Creative Commons. (2011). *Creative Commons website*. Retrieved on June 28, 2011, from http:// creativecommons.org/

eQNet (2011). *EU LLP eQNet (Quality Network for a European Learning Resource Exchange) project (2009 – 2012) web site*. Retrieved on June 28, 2011, from http://eqnet.eun.org/ web/ guest

EUN. (2011). *European Schoolnet (EUN) web site*. Retrieved on June 28, 2011, from http:// www.eun.org

Hauge, T. E., Dolonen, J. A., & Smørdal, O. (2007). *Semantic interoperability of learning resource descriptions based on national curricula*. Presented at CMC 2007, Oslo.

IMS CC. (2011). *IMS Common Cartridge specification alliance website*. Retrieved on June 28, 2011, from http://www.imsglobal.org/ common-cartridge.html

IMS CP. (2011). *IMS Content Packaging specification*. Retrieved on June 28, 2011, from http://www. imsglobal.org/ content/ packaging/ index.html

IMS LD. (2011). *IMS Learning Design specification*. Retrieved on June 28, 2011, from http:// www.imsglobal.org/ learningdesign/ index.html

INSPIRE. (2009). *EU LLP INSPIRE (Innovative Science Pedagogy in Research and Education) project (2008 – 2009) web site*. Retrieved on June 28, 2011, from http://inspire.eun.org/ index.php/ Main_Page

ISO/IEC 14598-1:1999. (1999). *Information Technology – software product evaluation – part 1: general overview*. 1st ed., 1999-04-15.

ITCOLE. (2003). *EU FP5 IST ITCOLE (Innovative Technology for Collaborative Learning and Knowledge Building) project (2001 – 2003) web site*. Retrieved on June 28, 2011, from http://www. euro-cscl.org/ site/ itcole

iTEC (2011). *EU FP7 IST iTEC (Innovative Technologies for an Engaging Classroom) project (2010 – 2014) web site*. Retrieved on June 28, 2011, from http://itec.eun.org/ web/ guest/

Kurilovas, E. (2009). Interoperability, Standards and Metadata for e-Learning. In G.A. Papadopoulos & C. Badica (Eds.). *Intelligent Distributed Computing III, Studies in Computational Intelligence, 237*, 121–130. Springer-Verlag Berlin Heidelberg.

Kurilovas, E. (2009). Learning Objects Reusability and Their Adaptation for Blended Learning. In: *Proceedings of the 5th International Conference on Networking and Services (ICNS 2009)*. April 20–25, 2009, Valencia, Spain, 542–547.

Kurilovas, E., Bireniene, V., & Serikoviene, S. (2011). Methodology for Evaluating Quality and Reusability of Learning Objects. *The Electronic Journal of e-Learning, 9(1)*, 39–51. Retrieved on June 30, 2011, from www.ejel.org

Kurilovas, E., & Dagiene, V. (2009). Learning objects and virtual learning environments technical evaluation criteria. *The Electronic Journal of e-Learning, 7(2)*, 127–136. Retrieved on June 28, 2011, from www.ejel.org

Kurilovas, E., & Dagienė, V. (2009). Multiple Criteria Comparative Evaluation of e-Learning Systems and Components. *Informatica, 20*(4), 499–518.

Kurilovas, E., & Dagiene, V. (2010). Multiple Criteria Evaluation of Quality and Optimisation of e-Learning System Components. *The Electronic Journal of e-Learning, 8(2)*, 141–150. Retrieved on June 28, 2011, from www.ejel.org.

Kurilovas, E., & Dagiene, V. (2010). eLearning in Lithuania – II. In: *e-Learning Practices. Cases on Challenges Facing e-Learning and National Development: Institutional Studies and Practices. Anadolu University, Eskisehir, Turkey*, 2010, Vol. 1, 463–484.

Kurilovas, E., & Serikoviene, S. (2010). Application of Scientific Approaches for Evaluation of Quality of Learning Objects in eQNet Project. In M.D. Lytras et al. (eds.). *WSKS 2010, Part I, CCIS 111*, 437–443. Heidelberg: Springer

Kurilovas, E., & Serikoviene, S. (2010). Learning Content and Software Evaluation and Personalisation Problems. *Informatics in Education, 9*(1), 91–114.

Kurilovas, E., & Serikoviene, S. (2010). *Personalisation of Learning Objects and Environments for Informatics Science Education in Lithuania.* Proceedings of the 4th International Conference on Informatics in Secondary Schools: Evolution and Perspectives (ISSEP 2010). Zurich, Switzerland, January 13–16, 2010, 52–72.

Leacock, T. L., & Nesbit, J. C. (2007). A Framework for Evaluating the Quality of Multimedia Learning Resources. *Journal of Educational Technology & Society, 10*(2), 44–59.

LeMill. (2011). *CALIBRATE LeMill 'learning toolbox'*. Retrieved on June 28, 2011, from http://lemill.org

LOM. (2002). *IEEE LTCS Learning Object Metadata (LOM) Standard*. Retrieved on June 28, 2011, from http://ltsc.ieee.org/ wg12/ files/ LOM_ 1484_ 12_ 1_ v1_ Final_ Draft.pdf

LRE. (2011). *European Learning Resource Exchange service for schools web site*. Retrieved on June 28, 2011, from http://lreforschools.eun.org/

LRE Service Centre. (2011). *ASPECT LRE Service Centre web site*. Retrieved on June 28, 2011, from http://aspect-project.org/ node/ 52

McCormick, R., Scrimshaw, P., Li, N., & Clifford, C. (2004). *CELEBRATE Evaluation report*. Retrieved on June 28, 2011, from http://celebrate. eun.org/ eun.org2/ eun/ Include_ to_ content/ celebrate/ file/ Deliverable7_ 2Evaluation Report02 Dec04.pdf

MCDM. (2011). *International Society on Multiple Criteria Decision Making website*. Retrieved on June 28, 2011, from http://www.mcdmsociety.org/

MELT. (2010). *EU eContentplus programme's MELT (Metadata ecology for learning and teaching) project (2007 – 2010) website*. Retrieved on June 28, 2011, from http://melt-project.eun.org

Oliver, M. (2000). An introduction to the evaluation of learning technology. *Journal of Educational Technology & Society, 3*(4), 20–30.

Ounaies, H. Z., Jamoussi, Y., & Ben Ghezala, H. H. (2009). Evaluation framework based on fuzzy measured method in adaptive learning system. *Themes in Science and Technology Education, 1*(1), 49–58.

Paulsson, F., & Naeve, A. (2006). *Establishing technical quality criteria for learning objects*. Retrieved on June 28, 2011, from http://www. frepa.org/ wp/ wp-content/ files/ Paulsson- Establ- Tech- Qual_ finalv1.pdf

Reigeluth, C. M., & Nelson, L. M. (1997). A new paradigm of ISD? In R. C. Branch & B. B. Minor (eds.). *Educational media and technology yearbook, 22,* 24–35. Englewood, Co: Libraries Unlimited.

SCORM. (2011). *Shareable Content Object Reference Model*. Retrieved on June 28, 2011, from http://xml.coverpages.org/ scorm.html

Topic Mapper. (2008). *CALIBRATE Topic Mapper application web site*. Retrieved on June 28, 2011, from http://www.tovek.cz/ produkty/ topicmapper.html

ValNet. (2004). *EU FP4 IST ValNet (European SchoolNet Validation Network) project (2000 – 2004) partners community web site*. Retrieved on June 28, 2011, from http://www.valnet.eun.org

Van Assche, F. (2007). Linking Learning Resources to Curricula by using Competencies. *CEUR Workshop Proceedings of the 1ˢᵗ International Workshop on Learning Object Discovery & Exchange (LODE'07) within the 2ⁿᵈ European Conference on Technology Enhanced Learning (EC–TEL07)*. Sissi, Crete, Greece, 17–20 September, 2007. Vol. 311, 80–91.

Vargo, J., Nesbit, J. C., Belfer, K., & Archambault, A. (2003). Learning object evaluation: Computer mediated collaboration and inter–rater reliability. *International Journal of Computers and Applications, 25*(3), 198–205.

Wiley, D. A. (2000). *Connecting learning objects to instructional design theory: A definition, a metaphor, and a taxonomy*. Utah State University. Retrieved on June 28, 2011, from http://www. reusability.org/ read/

Zavadskas, E. K., & Turskis, Z. (2010). A new additive ratio assessment (ARAS) method in multicriteria decision-making. *Technological and Economic Development of Economy, 16*(2), 159–172. doi:10.3846/tede.2010.10

Zhang Li Li & Cheng De Yong. (1992). Extent analysis and synthetic decision. In: *Support Systems for Decision and Negotiation Processes, Preprints of the /FAC/IFORS/IIASA/TIMS Workshop, Vol. 2. System Research Institute, Warsaw*, 633-640.

Compilation of References

Aaby, N. E., & Slater, S. T. (1989). Management Influences on Export Performance: A review of the Empirical Literature 1978-88. *International Marketing Review*, *6*(4), 7–23. doi:10.1108/EUM0000000001516

Abbate, J. (1999). *Inventing the Internet*. Cambridge, MA: MIT Press.

Abowd, G. D., Atkeson, C. G., Hong, J., Long, S., Kooper, R., & Pinkerton, M. (1997). Cyberguide: A mobile context-aware tour guide. *ACM Wireless Networks*, *3*(5), 421–433. doi:10.1023/A:1019194325861

Accenture (2002). *E-Government Leadership – Realizing the Vision*. The Government Executive Series.

Aenor. (2008). *Asociación española de normalización y certificiación*. Retrieved from http://www.aenor.es, [01/08/2009]

Agarwal, R., & Prasad, J. (1998). A Conceptual and Operational Definition of Personal Innovativeness in the Domain of Information Technology. *Information Systems Research*, *9*(2), 204–215. doi:10.1287/isre.9.2.204

Aghion, P., & Howitt, P. (1992). A model of growth through creative destruction. *Econometrica*, *60*(2), 323–351. doi:10.2307/2951599

Ahuja, M. K., & Carley, K. M. (1999). Network structure in virtual organizations. *Organization Science*, *10*(6), 741–757. doi:10.1287/orsc.10.6.741

Al-adawi, Z., Yousafzai, Z., & Pallister, J. (2005). *Conceptual Model of citizen adoption of e-government*. Paper presented at The Second International Conference on Innovations in Information Technology.

Álamo-Vera, F. (2005). Internationalization: firms and managerial factors. *International Journal of Entrepreneurial Behaviour & Research SMES*, *11*(4), 258–279. doi:10.1108/13552550510603298

AlAwadhi, S., & Morris, A. (2008). The Use of the UTAUT Model in the Adoption of E-government Services in Kuwait, In *Proceedings of the 41st Hawaii International Conference on System Sciences*, (pp. 1-11). Washington, DC, USA: IEEE Computer Society.

Ali, A. & Swiercz. (1991). Firm size and export behaviour: Lessons from the Midwest. *Journal of Small Business Management*, 71–78.

Almor, T., & Hashai, N. (2004). The competitive advantage and strategic configuration of knowledge-intensive, small- and medium-sized multinationals: A modified resource-based view. *Journal of International Management*, *10*(4), 479–500. doi:10.1016/j.intman.2004.08.002

Alonso, J.A. (1991/2). La Internacionalización de la Empresa Española. *Economistas, 52*, 76-86. Diciembre-Enero.

Alsaghier, H., Ford, M., Nguyen, A., & Hexel, R. (2009). Conceptualising Citizen's Trust in e-Government: Application of Q Methodology. *Electronic. Journal of E-Government*, *7*(4), 295–310.

Alshuwaikhat, H. (1988). *The Role of Socio-cultural Values and Planning Policies in Urban Spatial Structure*. Evanston, IL: Northwestern University.

Altenburg, T., Schmitz, H., & Stamm, A. (2008). Breakthrough? China's and India's Transition from Production to Innovation. *World Development*, *36*(2), 325–344. doi:10.1016/j.worlddev.2007.06.011

Alvarez, I., & Molero, J. (2005). Technology and the generation of international knowledge spillovers: An application to Spanish manufacturing firms. *Research Policy, 34*(9), 1440–1452. doi:10.1016/j.respol.2005.06.006

Amine, L., & Cavusgil, S. T. (1986). Export Marketing Strategies in the British Clothing Industries. *European Journal of Marketing, 20*(7), 21–33. doi:10.1108/EUM0000000004653

Anddam, R. Zorayda (2003). *E-commerce and e-business.* E-ASEAN Task Force, UNDP-APDIP. UN Press: Manila

Andersen, O. (1993). On Internationalization Process of Firm: A Critical Analysis. *Journal of International Business Studies, 24*(2), 209–231. doi:10.1057/palgrave.jibs.8490230

Anderson, E., & Coughlan, A. (1987). International Marker Entry and Expansion Via Independent or Integrated Channel of Distribution. *Journal of Marketing, 51*(1), 71–82. doi:10.2307/1251145

Andersson, S. (2004). Internationalization in different industrial contexts. *Journal of Business Venturing, 19*(6), 851–875. doi:10.1016/j.jbusvent.2003.10.002

Antkiewicz, A., & Whalley, J. (2007). Recent Chinese Buyout Activity and the Implications for Wider Global Investment Rules. *Canadian Public Policy - Analyse De Politiques, XXXIII*(2), 207-226.

Aoyama, Y. (2001). The Information Society, Japanese Style: Corner Stores as Hubs for Ecommerce Access. In Leinbach, T. R., & Brunn, S. D. (Eds.), *Worlds of e-commerce: economic, geographical and social dimensions.* Chichester, UK: J. Wiley.

Arcus, T. P. (1992). *Australian Business in Asia: Climbing the Mountains.* Victoria: Business Council of Australia.

Arndt, M., & Bigelow, B. (1995). The adoption of corporate restructuring by hospitals. *Journal of Healthcare Management, 40*(3), 332–347.

Arndt, M., & Bigelow, B. (2000). Presenting structural innovation in an institutional environment: hospitals' use of impression management. *Administrative Science Quarterly, 45*(3), 494–552. doi:10.2307/2667107

Arndt, M., Bigelow, B., & Dorman, H. G. (1999). In their own words: how hospitals present corporate restructuring in their annual reports. *Journal of Healthcare Management, 44*(2), 117–131.

Arndt, S. W., & Kierzkowski, H. (2001). *Fragmentation: new production patterns in the world economy.* Oxford, UK: Oxford University Press.

Arrow, K. J. (1962), Economic Welfare and the Allocation of Resources for Invention. In R. Nelson (ed.). *The Rate and Direction of Inventive Activity.* Princeton University Press, pp. 609–626. -- Collected papers of K.J. Arrow. Vol. 5, Harvard University Press.

Arvaja, M., Salovaara, H., Hakkinen, P., & Jarvela, S. (2007). Combining individual and group-level perspectives for studying collaborative knowledge construction in context. *Learning and Instruction, 17,* 448–459. doi:10.1016/j.learninstruc.2007.04.003

ASPECT. (2011). *EU eContentplus programme's ASPECT (Adopting Standards and Specifications for Educational Content).* Best Practice Network (2008 – 2011) web site. Retrieved on June 28, 2011, from http://aspect-project.org/

ASTF. (2002). *Alaska Science & Technology Innovation Index.* Report of the Foundation Alaska Science & Technology Foundation (ASTF). Retrieved from http://www.astf.org

Atkisson, J., O'Hara, B., Harvy, E., & Roland, J. (2002). Market *Gap in Alaska's E-Commerce, an unpublished report.* University of Alaska Fairbanks.

Audretsch, D. B. (1998). *Agglomeration and the location of innovative activity.* Oxford, UK: Oxford Review of Economic Policy.

Axinn, C. N. (1988). Export Performance: Do Managerial Perceptions Make a Difference? *International Marketing Review, 5*(2), 61–71. doi:10.1108/eb008353

Bagchi-sen, S. (1999). The Small and Medium Size Expoters' Problems: An Empirical Analysis of Canadian Manufacturers. *Regional Studies, 33*(3), 231–245. doi:10.1080/00343409950082427

Bagozzi, R., Davi, F., & Warshaw, P. (1992). Development and Test of a Theory of Technological Learning and Usage. *Human Relations, 45*(7), 659–686. doi:10.1177/001872679204500702

Bagozzi, R. P., & Yi, Y. (1988). On the evaluation of structure equation models. *Journal of the Academy of Marketing Science, 16,* 74–94. doi:10.1007/BF02723327

Bahli, B., & Benslimane, Y. (2004). An exploration of wireless computing risks: development of a risk-taxonomy. *Information Management & Computer Security, 12*(3), 245–254. doi:10.1108/09685220410542606

Balkundi, P., & Kilduff, M. (2005). The ties that lead: A social network approach to leadership. *The Leadership Quarterly, 16,* 941–961. doi:10.1016/j.leaqua.2005.09.004

Basch, P. F. (1993). Technology transfer to the developing world: does new technology have any relevance for developing countries? *Tubercle and Lung Disease, 74*(6), 353–358. doi:10.1016/0962-8479(93)90077-B

Beaimish, P. W. (1990). The Internationalization Process for Smaller Ontario's Firms: A Reasearch Agenda. In Rugman, A. M. (Ed.), *Research in Global Strategic Management-International Business.*

Beccatini, G. (1975). *Lo sviluppo economico della Toscana, con particolare riguardo all'industrializzazione leggera. Florencia.* IRPET.

Becta, (2007) *Quality principles for digital learning resources.*

Belanger, F., & Carter, L. (2008). Trust and risk in e-government adoption. *The Journal of Strategic Information Systems, 17*(2), 165–176. doi:10.1016/j.jsis.2007.12.002

Beldona, S., Morrison, A. M., & O'Leary, J. (2005). Online shopping motivations and pleasure travel products: a correspondence analysis. *Tourism Management, 26*(4), 561–570. doi:10.1016/j.tourman.2004.03.008

Bell, M. W. (2008). Toward a Definition of —Virtual Worldsl. *Journal of Virtual Worlds Research, 1*(1).

Belton, V., & Stewart, T. J. (2002). *Multiple criteria decision analysis: an integrated approach.* Amsterdam: Kluwer Academic Publishers.

Biasiotti, M. A., & Nannucci, R. (2004). Teaching egovernment in Italy. In R. Traunmóller (Ed.), *Proceedings of the Third International Conference* (pp. 460–463). Zaragoza, Spain: EGOV.

Biediger, J., Decicco, T., Green, T., Hoffman, G., Lei, D., & Mahadevan, K. (2005). Strategic Action at Lenovo. *Organizational Dynamics, 34*(1), 89–102. doi:10.1016/j.orgdyn.2004.11.007

Bilkey, W. J. (1978). An Attempted Integration of the Literature on the Export Behaviour of Firms. *Journal of International Business Studies, 9*(1), 33–46. doi:10.1057/palgrave.jibs.8490649

Bin, G. (2008). Technology acquisition channels and industry performance: An industry-level analysis of Chinese large- and medium-size manufacturing enterprises. *Research Policy, 37*(2), 194–209. doi:10.1016/j.respol.2007.11.004

Bjorn, J., Johannes, S., & Ingmar, K. (2005). Industry Level Technology Gaps and Complimentary Knowledge Stocks as Determinants of Intra-MNC Knowledge Flow. *Journal of Economics and Business, 8*(1&2), 137–156.

Black, J. A., & Edwards, S. (2000). Emergence of virtual or network organizations: fad or feature. *Journal of Organizational Change Management, 13*(6), 567–576. doi:10.1108/09534810010378588

Blackboard. (2009). *Aplicación del Aprendizaje en Línea.* Retrieved from http://www.blackboard.com, [16/07/2009]

Blalock, G., & Gertler, P. J. (2009). How firm capabilities affect who benefits from foreign technology. *Journal of Development Economics, 90,* 192–199. doi:10.1016/j.jdeveco.2008.11.011

Blodgett, L. L. (1992). Factors in the Instability of International Joint Ventures: An Event History Analysis. *Strategic Management Journal, 13,* 475–481. doi:10.1002/smj.4250130607

Blomstrom, M. (1991). Host country benefit of foreign investment. In McFetridge, D. (Ed.), *Foreign Investment Technology and Economic Growth.* Calgary, Canada: University of Calgary Press.

Blomström, M., & Kokko, A. (2003). *The economics of foreign direct investment incentives.* Foreign direct investment in the real and financial sector of industrial countries, pp. 37-56.

Bloodgood, J., & Sapienza, H.J. & ALMEIDA, J.G. (1996). The Internationalization of New High-Potential U.S. Ventures: Antecedents and Outcomes. *Entrepreneurship Theory and Practice, 20*(4), 61–76.

BOE - Boletín Oficial Del Estado. (43 de 19/02/2005). Retrieved from http://www.boe.es, [25/07/2009]

Bonaccorsi, A. (1992). Relantionship Between Firm Size and Export Intensity. *Journal of International Business Studies, 23*(4), 605–635. doi:10.1057/palgrave.jibs.8490280

Bopp, M. (2006). Didactic analysis of digital games and game-based learning. In M. Pivec (Ed.), *Affective and emotional aspects of human-computer interaction; Game-Based and Innovative Learning Approaches. Vol.1: The Future of Learning.* Amsterdam: IOS Press

Boudreau, M., Loch, K. D., Robey, D., & Straud, D. (1998). Going global: using information technology to advance the competitiveness of the virtual transnational organization. *The Academy of Management Executive, 12*(4), 120–128. doi:10.5465/AME.1998.1334008

Boulos, M. N., Hetherington, L., & Wheelert, S. (2007). Second life: An overview of the potential of 3-D virtual worlds in medical and health education. *Health Information and Libraries Journal, 24*(4), 233–245. doi:10.1111/j.1471-1842.2007.00733.x

Bromley, D. A. (2004). Technology policy. *Technology in Society, 26*, 455–468. doi:10.1016/j.techsoc.2004.01.005

Browne, C. (2001). Saudie –Commerce Conference Lauded by Major Saudi Industry Experts, ITP.

Bruun, P., & Mefford, R. N. (1996). A framework for selecting and introducing appropriate production technology in developing countries. *International Journal of Production Economics, 46-47*, 197–209. doi:10.1016/S0925-5273(96)00082-5

Buhalis, D. (1998). Strategic use of information technologies in the tourism industry. *Tourism Management, 19*(5), 409–421. doi:10.1016/S0261-5177(98)00038-7

Buhalis, D. (2004). eAirlines: strategic and tactical use of ICTs in the airline industry. *Information & Management, 41*(7), 805–825. doi:10.1016/j.im.2003.08.015

Burgos, D., Moreno, P., Sierra, J. L., Fernandez-Manjon, B., Specht, M., & Koper, R. (2008). *Building adaptive game-based learning resources: The marriage of IMS learning design and <e-adventure>.* Retrieved from www.eucm/publications/articles.html.

Burn, J., & Robins, G. (2003). Moving towards eGovernment: a case study of organizational change processes. *Logistics Information Management, 16*(1), 25–35. doi:10.1108/09576050310453714

Burr, T., Gandara, M., & Robinson, K. (2002). E-commerce: Auditing the Rage. *Internal Auditor, 59*(5), 49–55.

Burton, F., & Schlegelmilch, B. (1987). Profile analyses of nonexporters versus exporters grouped by export involvement. *International Marketing Review, 1*(27), 38–49.

Bush, G. W. (2006). *American Competitiveness Initiative.* Domestic Policy Council Office of Science and Technology Policy.

Byrne, M. R. (2006). Protecting National Security and Promoting Foreign Investment: Maintaining the Exon-Florio Balance. *Ohio State Law Journal, 67*, 849.

CALIBRATE. (2008). *EU FP6 IST CALIBRATE (Calibrating eLearning in Schools) project (2005 – 2008) web site.* Retrieved on June 28, 2011, from http://calibrate.eun.org

Calof, J. C. (1994). The Relationship Between Firm Size and Export Behaviour Revisated. *Journal of International Business Studies, 25*(2), 367–387. doi:10.1057/palgrave.jibs.8490205

Calvo, J. (1993). *La Internacionalización de las PME Manufactureras Españolas. Economía Industrial, 291* (pp. 66–75). Mayo Junio.

Campa, J.M. & Guillén, M.F. (1999). Internalization of exports: Firm- and location-specific factors in a middle-income country. *Management Science, 45*(11), 1463–1478. doi:10.1287/mnsc.45.11.1463

Cañas, A. J., Carff, R., Hill, G., Carvalho, M., Arguedas, M., & Eskridge, T. (2005). Concept maps: Integrating knowledge and information visualization. In Tergan, S.-O., & Keller, T. (Eds.), *Knowledge and information visualization: Searching for synergies* (pp. 205–219). Heidelberg, NY: Springer Lecture Notes in Computer Science. doi:10.1007/11510154_11

Cannice, M. V., Chen, R., & Daniels, J. D. (2003). Managing international technology transfer risk: A case analysis of U.S. high-technology firms in Asia. *The Journal of High Technology Management Research, 14*, 171–187. doi:10.1016/S1047-8310(03)00020-8

Cantwell, J. A., & Dunning, J. H. (1991). MNEs technology and competitiveness of European industry. *Aussnwirtschaft, 46*, 45–65.

Capacidades Exportadoras y Estrategia Internacional de la Empresa. (1993). *Empresas y Empresarios Españoles en la Encrucijada de los '90*. Madrid: Civitas.

Carayannopoulos, S., & Auster, E. R. (2010). External knowledge sourcing in biotechnology through acquisition versus alliance: A KBV approach. *Research Policy, 39*, 254–267. doi:10.1016/j.respol.2009.12.005

Carmeli, B., & Cohen, B. (2001). PiNet: Wireless Connectivity for Organizational Information Access Using Lightweight Handheld Devices. *IEEE Personal Communications, 8*(4), 18–23. doi:10.1109/98.943999

Carter, G. (2003). *LDAP System Administration*. New York: O'Reilly Media.

Carter, L., & Bélanger, F. (2005). The Utilization of E-Government Services: Citizen Trust, Innovation and Acceptance Factors. *Information Systems Journal, 15*(1), 5–25. doi:10.1111/j.1365-2575.2005.00183.x

Carter, B., & Click, A. (2006). *Imagine the real in the virtual: Experience your second life*. Paper presented at the 22nd Annual Conference on Distance Teaching and Learning, Wisconsin, Madison.

Castellacci, F. (2008). Innovation and the competitiveness of industries: Comparing the mainstream and the evolutionary approaches. *Technological Forecasting and Social Change, 75*, 984–1006. doi:10.1016/j.techfore.2007.09.002

Castells, M. (1989). *The informational city: information technology, economic restructuring, and the urban-regional process*. Oxford, UK: Blackwell.

Caves, R. E. (1974). Multinational firms, competition and productivity in host country market. *Economic, 41*, 176–193.

Cavusgil, S. T. (1980). On the Internationalization Process of Firm. *European Research, 8*(November), 273–281.

CELEBRATE. (2004). *EU FP5 IST CELEBRATE (Context eLearning with Broadband Technologies) project (2002–2004) web site*. Retrieved on June 28, 2011, from http://celebrate.eun.org

Ceri, S., Daniel, F., Matera, M., & Facca, F.M. (2007). Model-driven development of context-aware Web applications. *ACM Transactions on Internet Technology, 7*(1), article no. 2.

Chaintreau, A., Hui, P., Diot, C., Gass, R., & Scott, J. (2007). Impact of Human Mobility on Opportunistic Forwarding Algorithms. *IEEE Transactions on Mobile Computing, 6*(6), 606–620. doi:10.1109/TMC.2007.1060

Chan, L. (2009). *Technology Transfer to China: Case of the High-speed Rail Industry*. Paper presented at the Portland International Conference on Management of Engineering and Technology.

Chandler, A. D. (1962). *Strategy and structure: Charters in the history of the American industry enterprise*. Cambridge, MA: MIT press.

Chapin, S. (1979). *Urban Land use Planning*, pp. 14-20. Chicago: University of Illinois press.

Chaturvedi, K., & Chataway, J. (2006). Strategic integration of knowledge in Indian pharmaceutical firms: creating competencies for innovation. *International Journal of Business Innovation and Research, 1*(1/2), 27–50. doi:10.1504/IJBIR.2006.011087

Chau, P. Y. K., & Lai, V. S. K. (2003). An empirical investigation of the determinants of user acceptance of internet banking. *Journal of Organizational Computing and Electronic Commerce, 13*(2), 123–145. doi:10.1207/S15327744JOCE1302_3

Chen, N., Ko, H., Kinshuk, K., & Lin, T. (2005, May). A model for synchronous learning using the Internet. *Innovations in Education and Teaching International, 42*(2), 181–194. doi:10.1080/14703290500062599

Cheng, H. L., & Yang, L. (2004). Analysis on the Status of Beijing as International R&D Center. *Science of Science and Management of S.& T., 25*(7), 25–29.

Chetty, S. (1999).Dimensions of Internationalisation of Manufacturing Firms in the Apparel Industry. *European Journal of Marketing, 33*, (½),121-142.

Cheverst, K., Davies, N., Mitchell, K., Friday, A., & Efstratiou, F. (2000). *Developing a context-aware electronic tourist guide: some issues and experiences.* In Proceedings of the SIGCHI conference on Human factors in computing systems, p.17-24, April 01-06, The Hague, The Netherlands.

Child, J. (1997). Strategic choice in the analysis of action, structure, organizations and environment: retrospect and prospect. *Organization Studies, 18*(1), 43–76. doi:10.1177/017084069701800104

Child, J. (1972). Organizational structure, environment and performance: the role of strategic choice. *Sociology, 6*(1), 1–22. doi:10.1177/003803857200600101

Chin, C., & Chia, L. G. (2002). *Problem-based learning: Using students' questions to drive knowledge construction.* New York: Wiley Interscience.

Cho, Y. C., & Agrusa, J. (2006). Assessing use acceptance and satisfaction Toward online travel agencies. *Information Technology & Tourism, 8*(3/4), 179–195. doi:10.3727/109830506778690795

Christense, N, C.,Da Rocha, A. & Kerbel, R. (1987). An Empirical Investigation of the Factors Influencing Exporting Succes of Brazilian Firms. *Journal of International Business Studies, 18*(3), 61–77. doi:10.1057/palgrave.jibs.8490412

Chudnovsky, D., Lopez, A., & Rossi, G. (2008). Foreign direct investment spillovers and the absorptive capabilities of domestic firms in the Argentine manufacturing sector (1992-2001). *The Journal of Development Studies, 44*(5), 645–677. doi:10.1080/00220380802009159

Chukwu, O., Ward, L., Chan, C., & Epperson, R. (2002). *Alaska Government's Internet Usage, an unpublished report.* University of Alaska Fairbanks.

Clifton, R. A. (1999). The education of university students: A social capital perspective. *College Teaching, 47*(3), 114–118. doi:10.1080/87567559909595798

Clinton, W. J. (1997). *Science and Technology Shaping the Twenty-First Century.* Office of Science and Technology Policy.

Cohen, W. (2009). Enron Email Dataset. Retrieved from http://www.cs.cmu.edu/~enron/

Colesca, S. E. (2009). Increasing e-trust: a solution to minimize risk in the e-government adoption. *Journal of Applied Quantitative Methods, 4*(1), 31–44.

Colesca, S. E., & Dobrica, L. (2008). Adoption and use of e-government services: The case of Romania. *Journal of Applied Research and Technology, 6*(3), 204–217.

Coltman, T. (2007). Why build a customer relationship management capability? *The Journal of Strategic Information Systems, 16*(3), 301–320. doi:10.1016/j.jsis.2007.05.001

Commission (2003). *The Role of eGovernment for Europe's Future,* Communication from the Commission of the European Communities, Brussels Chandler, A.D. (1962). *Strategy and Structure.* New York: Doubleday

Commission of European communities (2003). *The Role of eGovernment for Europe's Future* SEC(2003) 1038 Retrieved June 8 2010, from http://ec.europa.eu/ information_society/ eeurope /2005/doc/all_about/ egov_communication_en.pdf

Cooper, R., & Kleinschmidt, E. (1985). The Impact of Export Strategy on Export Sales Performance. *Journal of International Business Studies, 16*(1), 37–56. doi:10.1057/palgrave.jibs.8490441

Corallo, A., Elia, G., Lorenzo, G., & Solazzo, G. (2005). *A semantic recommender engine enabling an etourism scenario.* ISWC2005 International Semantic Web Conference 2005, 6-10 November, Galway, Ireland.

Corr, C. F. (2003). The Wall Still Stands! Complying with Export Controls on Technology Transfers in the Post-Cold War, Post-9/11 Era. *Houston Journal of International Law, 25*(3), 441.

Cosh, A., & Hughes, A. (1996). International merger activity and the national regulation of mergers. a UK perspective. *Empirica, 23*(3), 279–302. doi:10.1007/BF00924974

Coviello, N., & McAuley, A. (1999). Internationalisation and the Smaller Firm: A Review of Contemporary Empirical Research. *Management International Review, 39*(3), 223–256.

Creative Commons. (2011). *Creative Commons website*. Retrieved on June 28, 2011, from http://creativecommons.org/

Crick, D., & Jones, M. V. (2000). Small high-technology firms and international high-technology markets. *Journal of International Marketing*, *8*(2), 63–85. doi:10.1509/jimk.8.2.63.19623

Criscuolo, P., & Narula, R. (2008). A novel approach to national technological accumulation and absorptive capacity: Aggregating Cohen and Levinthal. *European Journal of Development Research*, *20*(1), 56–73. doi:10.1080/09578810701853181

Cross, J., O'Driscoll, T., & Trondsen, E. (2007). Another life: Virtual worlds as tools for learning. *ELearn Magazine, (3).*

Cui, A. S., Griffith, D. A., Cavusgil, S. T., & Dabic, M. (2006). The influence of market and cultural environmental factors on technology transfer between foreign MNCs and local subsidiaries: a Croatian illustration. *Journal of World Business*, (41): 100–111. doi:10.1016/j.jwb.2006.01.011

Culpan, R. (1989). Export Behavior of Firms: Relevance of Firm Size. *Journal of Business Research*, *18*, 207–218. doi:10.1016/0148-2963(89)90045-3

Cunningham, M., & Spigel, R. (1971). A study in successful exporting. *European Journal of Marketing*, *5*(1), 2–12. doi:10.1108/EUM0000000005176

Czinkota, M., & Johnston, W. J. (1981). Segmenting U.S. Firm for Export Development. *Journal of Business Research*, *9*(4), 335–365. doi:10.1016/0148-2963(81)90012-6

Daft, R. L. (2009). *Organization Theory and Design* (10th ed.). Cincinnati, OH: Engage Learning.

Daft, R. L. (1978). A dual-core model of organization innovation. *Academy of Management Journal*, *21*(2), 193–210. doi:10.2307/255754

Daft, R. L., & Lewin, A. Y. (1993). Where are the theories for the new organizational form? an editorial essay. *Organization Science*, *4*(4), i–iv.

Dalkey, N., & Helmer, O. (1963). An experimental application of the Delphi method to the use of experts. *Management Science*, *9*, 458–467. doi:10.1287/mnsc.9.3.458

Damanpour, F. (1991). Organizational innovation: A meta-analysis of effects of determinants and moderators. *Academy of Management Journal*, *34*(3), 555–590. doi:10.2307/256406

Damanpour, F., & Evan, W. (1984). Organizational innovation and performance: The problem of organizational lag. *Administrative Science Quarterly*, *29*(3), 392–409. doi:10.2307/2393031

Damanpour, F., & Gopalakrishnan, S. (2001). The dynamics of the adoption of product and process innovations in organizations. *Journal of Management Studies*, *38*(1), 45–65. doi:10.1111/1467-6486.00227

Daniels, J., & Robles, F. (1982). The choice of technology and export commitment: the peruvian textile industry. *Journal of International Business Studies*, *13*(Primavera/Verano), 67–87. doi:10.1057/palgrave.jibs.8490792

Dashti, A. Benbasat, I., & Burton-Jones, A. (2009). *Developing trust reciprocity in electronic government: The role of felt trust*. European and Mediterranean Conference on Information Systems 2009 (July 13-14 2009, Crowne Plaza Hotel, Izmir. Retrieved March, 25 2010, from http://www.iseing.org/emcis/EMCIS2009/Proceedings/Presenting%20Papers /C16/C16.pdf

Davenport, T. H. (1994). *Reengenharia de processos*. São Paulo: Campus.

Davenport, T. H., & Short, J. E. (1990). The new industrial engineering information technology and business process redesign. *Sloan Management Review*, *31*(4), 11–17.

David, P. A. (1975). *Technical choice, innovation and economic growth*. New York: Cambridge University Press.

Davidow, W. H., & Malone, M. S. (1992). *The Virtual Corporation: Structuring and Revitalizing the Corporation for the 21st Century*. New York, NY: Harper Business.

Davis, F. (1980). Perceived Usefulness, Perceived Ease of Use, and User Acceptance of Information Technology. *Management Information Systems Quarterly*, *13*, 318–341.

Davison, R. M., Wagner, C., & Ma, C. K. (2005). From government to e-government: a transition model. *Information Technology & People*, *18*(3), 280–299. doi:10.1108/09593840510615888

Day, G. S., & Reibstein, D. J. (1997). *Wharton on dynamic competitive strategy*. New York: John Wiley & Sons.

De Freitas, S. (2006). *Learning in immersive worlds: A review of game-based learning*. Bristol, UK: Joint Information Systems Committee (JISC) E-Learning Programme. Retrieved from http://www.jisc.ac.uk/whatwedo/ programmes/elearning_innovation /eli_outcomes/ GamingReport.aspx.

de Internacionalización de la Empresaa, E. P. (1994b)... *Información Comercial Española, 725*(Enero), 127–143.

Dean, D., Mengüç, B., & Myers, C. (2000). Revisiting Firms Characteristics, Strategy and Export Performance Relationship. *Industrial Marketing Management, 29*, 461–477. doi:10.1016/S0019-8501(99)00085-1

Dede, C. (1996). The evolution of distance education: Emerging technologies and distributed learning. *American Journal of Distance Education, 10*(2), 4–36. doi:10.1080/08923649609526919

Dede, C. (2004). Enabling distributed-learning communities via emerging technologies. *Proceedings of the 2004 Conference of the Society for Information Technology in Teacher Education (SITE)*, Charlottesville, VA. 3-12.

Dedrick, J., Kraemer, K. L., & Tsai, T. (1999). *ACER: an IT Company Learning to Use Information Technology to Compete. IT in Business, Center for Research on Information Technology and Organization*. University of California.

Deloitte Research. (2000). *At the Dawn of E-Government*. New York: Deloitte Consulting.

DeLone, W., & McLean, E. (1992). Information Systems Success: The Quest for the Dependent Variable. *Information Systems Research, 3*(1), 60–95. doi:10.1287/ isre.3.1.60

DeLone, W., & McLean, E. (2003). The DeLone and McLean Model of Information Systems Success: A Ten-Year Update. *Journal of Management Information Systems, 19*(4), 9–30.

DeSanctis, G., & Monge, P. (1999). Introduction to the special issue: communication processes for virtual organizations. *Organization Science, 10*(6), 693–703. doi:10.1287/orsc.10.6.693

Devaraj, S., Fan, M., & Kohli, R. (2002). Antecedents of B2C channel satisfaction and preference: Validating e-commerce metrics. *Information Systems Research, 13*(3), 316–333. doi:10.1287/isre.13.3.316.77

Dey, A. K., & Abowd, G. D. (2000). *Towards a Better Understanding of Context and Context-Awareness.* In CHI 2000 Workshop on the What, Who, Where, When, and How of Context-Awareness.

Diamantopoulos, A., & Inglis, K. (1988). Identifying Differences Between High-and-Low Involvement Exporters. *International Marketing Review,* (Fall): 5, 52–60.

Dichtl, E., Köglmayr, H., & Müller, S. (1990). nternational orientation as a precondition for export success. *Journal of International Business Studies, 21*(1), 23–41. doi:10.1057/palgrave.jibs.8490325

Dittrich, K., Duysters, G., & Man, A.-P. d. (2007). Strategic repositioning by means of alliance networks: The case of IBM. *Research Policy, 36*, 1496–1511. doi:10.1016/j. respol.2007.07.002

Doke, E. R., & Swanson, N. E. (1995). Decision variables for selecting prototyping in information systems development: A Delphi study of MIS managers. *Information & Management, 29*, 173–182. doi:10.1016/0378-7206(95)00021-N

Domínguez, L., & Sequeira, C. (1993). Determinants of LDC Exporte's Performance: A Cross National Study. *Journal of International Business Studies. First Quarter, 24*, 19–40.

Donoso, V. (1989a). *Características y Estrategias de la Empresa Exportadora Española*. Madrid: Icex.

Donoso, V. (1989b). La Empresa Exportadora Española: Una Caracterización. *Papeles de Economía Española, 39*, 311–338.

Donoso, V. (1992). Mercado único y empresa exportadora. *Información Comercial Española, 705*, 153–167.

Donoso, V. (1994). *Competitividad de la Empresa Exportadora Española*. Madrid: Icex.

Donoso, V. (1996). Obstáculos a la Internacionalización y Políticas Públicas de Promoción. El caso de España. *Papeles de Economía Española, 66*, 124–143.

Donoso, V. (1998a). *Competir en el Exterior. La empresa Española y los Mercados Internacionales*. Madrid: Icex.

Donoso, V. (1998b). La empresa española en el final de los noventa. *Economistas, 77*, 131–139.

Donoso, V. (2000). Modelización del comportamiento de la empresa exportadora española· . *Información Comercial Española, 788*, 35–58.

Donoso, V. (1993) Rasgos y Actitudes de la Empresa Exportadora Española. *Economistas, 55 Extr.,*134.143.

Donoso, V. (1995). La Internacionalización de la Empresa y el Apoyo Público.*Economistas, 64*, 194.204.

Donthu, N., & Kim, S. H. (1993). Implication of Firms Controllable Factors on Export Growth.*Journal of Global Marketing, 7*(1), 47–63. doi:10.1300/J042v07n01_04

Driffield, N., & Girma, S. (2002). *Regional Foreign Direct Investment and Wage Spillovers: Plant level Evidence from the Electronics Industry*. University of Nottingham.

Du De bin, (2001). *The Research on the Multinational R & D globalization Location Model.*Shanghai: Fudan University Press.

Dunmade, I. (2002). Indicators of sustainability: assessing the suitability of a foreign technology for a developing economy. *Technology in Society, 24*(4), 461–471. doi:10.1016/S0160-791X(02)00036-2

Dunning, J. (1988). The Eclectic Paradigm of International Production. *Journal of International Business Studies, 19*(1), 1–31. doi:10.1057/palgrave.jibs.8490372

Dunt, E., & Harper, I. (2002). E-Commerce and the Australian Economy. *The Economic Record, 78*(242), 327–342. doi:10.1111/1475-4932.00061

Durán, J. (1994). Factores de competitividad en los procesos de internacionalización de la empresa. *Información Comercial Española, 735*, 21–41.

Dyche, J. (2002). *The CRM handbook: A Business Guide to Customer Relationship Management*. Boston: Addison-Wesley.

Eijndhoven, J. C. M. V. (1997). Technology assessment: product or process. *Technological Forecasting and Social Change, 54*, 269–286. doi:10.1016/S0040-1625(96)00210-7

Eisenhardt, K. M. (1989). Building theories from case study research. *Academy of Management Review, 14*(4), 532–550.

eQNet (2011). *EU LLP eQNet (Quality Network for a European Learning Resource Exchange) project (2009 – 2012) web site*. Retrieved on June 28, 2011, from http://eqnet.eun.org/ web/ guest

Erickson, A. S., & Walsh, K. A. (2008). National security challenges and competition: Defense and space R&D in the Chinese strategic context. *Technology in Society, 30*, 349–361. doi:10.1016/j.techsoc.2008.04.001

Estallo, J. (2000). The new organizational structure and its virtual functioning. *International Advances in Economic Research, 6*(2), 241–255. doi:10.1007/BF02296105

Eteokleous, N., & Ktoridou, D. (2009). Investigating mobile devices integration in higher education in Cyprus: Faculty perspectives.*International Journal of Interactive Mobile Technologies, 3*(1), 38–48.

EUN. (2011). *European Schoolnet (EUN) web site*. Retrieved on June 28, 2011, from http://www.eun.org

European Commission. (2009). *European Innovation Scoreboard*. EIS.

European Commission. (2009). *Regional Innovation Scoreboard*. RIS.

Eusebio, R. (2004). Innovación Tecnológica y Resultado Exportador: Un análisis empírico aplicado al sector textil-confección español. *Revista Europea de Dirección y Economía de la Empresa, 12*(2), 73–88.

Evangelista, U. (1994). Export Performance and Its Determinants: Some Empirical Evidence from Australian Manufacturing Firms.*Advances in International Marketing, 44*(2), 219–235.

Evans, R. (2002). E-commerce, Competitiveness and Local and Regional Governance in Greater Manchester and Merseyside: A Preliminary Assessment. *Urban Studies (Edinburgh, Scotland), 39*(5-6), 947–975. doi:10.1080/00420980220128390

Export performance revisited(1994).*International Small Business Journal, 18*.

Fagerberg, J. (1988). International Competitiveness. *The Economic Journal*, *98*, 355–374. doi:10.2307/2233372

Fagin, R., Kumar, R., & Sivakumar, D. (2003). Comparing top k lists. *SIAM Journal on Discrete Mathematics*, *17*(1), 134–160. doi:10.1137/S0895480102412856

Fan, E. X. (2003). Technological spillovers from foreign direct investment-a survey. *Asian Development Review*, *20*(1), 34–56.

Fan, P., & Watanabe, C. (2006). Promoting industrial development through technology policy: Lessons from Japan and China. *Technology in Society*, *28*(3), 303–320. doi:10.1016/j.techsoc.2006.06.002

Farris, G. F. (2007). Research on innovation management and technology transfer in China. *The Journal of Technology Transfer*, *32*, 123–126. doi:10.1007/s10961-006-9003-1

Featherman, M. S., & Pavlou, P. A. (2002). Predicting E-services adoption: a perceived risk facets perspective. *Proceeding in the Eight Americas Conference on Information Systems*, 1034-1045.

Fenwick, I., & Amine, L. (1979). Export Performance and Export Policy: Evidence from de UK Clothing Industry. *The Journal of the Operational Research Society*, *30*(8), 747–755.

Fernandes, C. C. C. & Pinto, S. L. (2003). Sociedad de la Información en Brasil: balance y perspectivas. *Nueva Sociedad* (187),153-168

Fernandes, C. C. C. (2006). Governo Eletrônico. In: FUNDAP/CONSAD. *Avanços e Perspectivas da Gestão Pública nos Estados*. Foundation for Administrative Development / National Council of Federal State Management Secretaries, 135-167

Fernández, E., & Vázquez, C. (1994). *La internacionalización de la empresa. Documento de Trabajo nº 75/94*. Universidad de Oviedo.

Fillis, I. (2000).Being creative at the marketing /entrepreneurship interface: lessons from the art industry. *Journal of Research in Marketing and Entrepreneurship*.

Fingar, P., Kumar, H., & Sharma, T. (2000). *Enterprise E-Commerce*. Tampa, FL: Meghan-Kiffer Press.

Fishbein, M., & Ajzen, I. (1975). *Belief, attitude, intention, and behavior: An introduction to theory and research*. Reading, MA: Addison-Wesley.

Fontrodona, J., & Hernádez, J. (2001). *Les multinacionals industrials catalanes*. Departament d'Indústria, Comerç i Turisme, Generalitat de Catalunya.

Force, D. O. T. (2001). *Digital Opportunities for All: Meeting the Challenge*. Report of the Digital Opportunity Task Force (DOT Force). Retrieved from http://www.dotforce.org./ reports/ DOT_ Force_ Report_ V_ 5.0h.html#ac

Ford, D., & Leonidou, L. (1991). Research Development in International Marketing: A European Perspective. In Plaiwoda, S. (Ed.), *New Perspectives on International Marketing*. London: Routledge.

Fornell, C., & Larcker, D. F. (1981). Evaluating structural equation models with unbearable and measurement error. *JMR, Journal of Marketing Research*, *18*, 39–50. doi:10.2307/3151312

Fosfuri, A. (2000). Patent protection, imitation and the mode of technology transfer. *International Journal of Industrial Organization*, *18*, 1129–1149. doi:10.1016/S0167-7187(98)00056-3

Founrain, J. E. (2001). *Building the Virtual State: information technology and institutional change*. Washington, D.C: Brookings Institution Press.

Fountain, J. E. (2001). *Building the Virtual State: Information Technology and Institutional Change*. Washington, D.C.: Brookings.

Fraser, C., & Hite, R. (1990). Participation in the International Market Place by US Manufacturing Firms. *International Marketing Review*, *7*(5), 63–71. doi:10.1108/EUM0000000001536

Frey, B. A., Sass, M. S., & Arman, S. W. (2006). Mapping MLIS asynchronous discussions. *International Journal of Instructional Technology & Distance Learning*, *3*(1).

G8 Kyushu-Okinawa Summit. (2000). *Okinawa Charter on Global Information Society*. Retrieved from http://www.dotforce.org./ reports/ it1.html

Gabrielsson, J., & Wictor, I. (2004). International activities in small firms: Examining factors influencing the internationalization and export growth of small firms. *Canadian Journal of Administrative Sciences, 21*(1), 22–34.

Gao, X., Zhang, P., & Liu, X. (2007). Competing with MNEs: developing manufacturing capabilities or innovation capabilities. *The Journal of Technology Transfer, 32,* 87–107. doi:10.1007/s10961-006-9002-2

García, J., Álamo, F., & Suárez, S. (2002). Determinantes organizativos y directivos de la actividad exportadora: evidencia empírica en el sector vitivinícola español. *Cuadernos de Economía y Dirección de la Empresa, 13,* 519–544.

García-Crespo, A., Chamizo, J., Rivera, I., Mencke, M., Colomo-Palacios, R., & Gómez-Berbís, J. M. (2009). SPETA: Social pervasive e-Tourism advisor. *Telematics and Informatics, 26*(3), 306–315. doi:10.1016/j.tele.2008.11.008

García-Crespo, A., Colomo-Palacios, R., Gómez-Berbís, J. M., Chamizo, J., & Rivera, I. (2010). Intelligent Decision-Support Systems for e-Tourism: Using SPETA II as a Knowledge Management Platform for DMOs and e-Tourism Service Providers. *International Journal of Decision Support System Technology, 2*(1), 36–48. doi:10.4018/jdsst.2010101603

Gee, J. P. (2005). *Why are video games good for learning?* Retrieved from http://www.academiccolab.org/ resources/ documents/ MacArthur.pdf.

Gefen, D. (2002). Customer Loyalty in e-Commerce. *Journal of the Association for Information Systems, 3,* 27–51.

Gefen, D., Karahanna, E., & Straub, D. (2003a). Trust and TAM in online shopping: an integrated model. *Management Information Systems Quarterly, 27*(1), 51–90.

Gefen, D., Karahanna, E., & Straub, D. (2003b). Inexperience and experience with online stores: the importance of TAM and Trust. *IEEE Transactions on Engineering Management, 50*(3), 307–321. doi:10.1109/TEM.2003.817277

Gemunden, H. G. (1991). Success Factors of Export Marketing: A Meta-Analytic Critic of the Empirical Studies. In Paliwoda, S. J. (Ed.), *New Perspective on International Marketing.* London: Routledge.

Generalitat de Catalunya (1990-1999). *Informe anual de l'empresa catalane.* Departament d'Economia i Finances. Direcció General de Programació Econòmica.

Georghiou, L. (2003). *Foresight: Concept and Practice as a Tool for Decision Making.* Expert Papers, Technology Foresight Summit Budapest.

Georghiou, L., & Keenan, M. (2006). Evaluation of national foresight activities: assessing rationale, process and impact. *Technological Forecasting and Social Change, 73,* 761–777. doi:10.1016/j.techfore.2005.08.003

Georgiev, G. S. (2008). The Reformed CFIUS Regulatory Framework: Mediating Between Continued Openness to Foreign Investment and National Security. *Yale Journal on Regulation, 25.*

Giamouridis, A. (2006). Policy, Politics, and Social Inequality in the Educational System of Greece. *Journal of Modern Greek Studies, 24*(1), 1–21. doi:10.1353/mgs.2006.0004

Gil-Garcia, J.-R., & Pardo, T. (2006). Multi-Method approaches to understanding the complexity of e-government. *International Journal of Computers, Systems and Signals, 7(2).* Retrieved May 9 2010, from http://citeseerx.ist.psu.edu/ viewdoc/download? doi=10.1.1.102.3801&rep=rep1&type=pdf

Girma, S., & Gong, Y. D. (2008). FDI, linkages and the efficiency of state-owned enterprises in China. *The Journal of Development Studies, 44*(5), 728–749. doi:10.1080/00220380802009233

Girma, S., & Gorg, H. (2007). The role of the efficiency gap for spillovers from FDI: Evidence from the UK electronics and engineering sectors. *Open Economies Review, 18*(2), 215–232. doi:10.1007/s11079-007-9031-y

Gloor, P. (2006). *Swarm Creativity, Competitive advantage through collaborative innovation networks.* Oxford, UK: Oxford University Press.

Gloor, P. (2004). *Net.Creators. Unlocking the Swarm Creativity of Cyberteams through Collaborative Innovation Networks.* Retrieved from http://www.swarmcreativity.net/ html/book_swarmcrea.htm

Gold, A. H., Malhotra, A., & Segars, A. H. (2001). Knowledge management: an organization capabilities perspective. *Journal of Management Information Systems*, *18*(1), 185–214.

Golden, A. (2005). *Memorias de una Geisha*. Punto de Lectura.

Gonzalez, R. (2008). *Arquitecturas Intermedias de Adaptación de Contenidos Online para Lograr la Accesibilidad en Entornos Cambiantes Mediante Técnicas Emergentes*. Pontifical University of Salamanca.

Goodhue, D. L. (1995). Understanding user evaluations of information systems. *Management Science*, *41*(12), 1827–1844. doi:10.1287/mnsc.41.12.1827

Goodhue, D. L., & Thompson, R. L. (1995). Task-technology fit and individual performance. *Management Information Systems Quarterly*, *19*(2), 213–236. doi:10.2307/249689

Gordon, S. R., & Gordon, J. R. (1996). *Information Systems: A Management Approach*. New York: Harcourt Brace & Company.

Gough, H. G. (1979). A creative personality scale for the adjective check list. *Journal of Personality and Social Psychology*, *37*(8), 1398–1405. doi:10.1037/0022-3514.37.8.1398

Greene, W. (2003). *Distinguishing Between Heterogeneity and Inefficiency: Stochastic Frontier Analysis of the World Health Organization's Panel Data on National Health Care Systems*. Working Paper 03-10, Department of Economics, Stern School of Business, New York University, New York.

Griliches, Z. (1979). Issues in assessing the contribution of R&D to productivity growth. *The Bell Journal of Economics*, *10*, 92–116. doi:10.2307/3003321

Grimm, R. (2004). System Support for Pervasive Applications. *ACM Transactions on Computer Systems*, *22*(4), 421–486. doi:10.1145/1035582.1035584

Groenveld, P. (2007). Roadmapping Integrates Business and Technology. *Research-Technology Management*, *50*(6), 49–58.

Guan, J. C., Mok, C. K., Yam, R. C. M., Chin, K. S., & Pun, K. F. (2006). Technology transfer and innovation performance: Evidence from Chinese firms. *Technological Forecasting and Social Change*, *73*, 666–678. doi:10.1016/j.techfore.2005.05.009

Gupta, M. P. (2004). *Promise of E-Governance: Operational Challenges*. New Delhi: Tata McGraw-Hill Publishing Company Limited.

Gutiérrez de Gandarilla, A., & Heras, L. (2000). La proyección exterior de las empresas españolas: Una contratsación empírica de la teoría gradualista de la internacionalización. *Información Comercial Española*, *788*, 7–18.

Hair, F. Jr, Anderson, R. E., Tatham, R. L., & Black, W. C. (1998). *Multivariate data analysis* (5th ed.). Upper Saddle River, NJ: Prentice Hall.

Håkansson, H., & Johanson, J. (1988). Formal and Informal Cooperation Strategies in International Industrial Networks. In Contractor & P. Lorange (eds). *Cooperative Strategies in International Business*. (pp.369-379) Lanham, MD: Lexington Books, F.J.

Hamel, G. (1991). Competition from competence and interpartner learning within international strategic alliances. *Strategic Management Journal*, *12*(Special Issue), 83–103. doi:10.1002/smj.4250120908

Hamilton, R. T. (1993). Firm Level Determinants of Export Performance: A Meta Analisys. *International Marketing Review*, *10*(3), 26–34.

Hammer, M., & Champy, J. (1993). *Reengenharia. S. Paulo*. Campus.

Han, L., & Jin, Y. (2009). *A Review of Technology Acceptance Model in the E-commerce Environment*, 2009 International Conference on Management of e-Commerce and e-Government.

Harker, P. T., & Vargas, L. G. (1987). The theory of ratio scale estimation: Saaty's Analytic Hierarchy Process. *Management Science*, *33*(11), 383–403. doi:10.1287/mnsc.33.11.1383

Hatani, F. (2009). The logic of spillover interception: The impact of global supply chains in China. *Journal of World Business*, *44*(2), 158–166. doi:10.1016/j.jwb.2008.05.005

Hauge, T. E., Dolonen, J. A., & Smørdal, O. (2007). *Semantic interoperability of learning resource descriptions based on national curricula.* Presented at CMC 2007, Oslo.

Hawking, S. (1998). *A Brief History of Time: updated and expanded tenth anniversary edition.* New York: Bantam Books.

Hayter, R., & Edgington, D. (2004). Flying Geese in Asia: The Impacts of Japanese MNCs as a Source of Industrial Learning. *Tijdschrift voor Economische en Sociale Geografie, 95*, 3–26. doi:10.1111/j.0040-747X.2004.00290.x

He, W., & Lyles, M. A. (2008). China's outward foreign direct investment. *Business Horizons, 51*, 485–491. doi:10.1016/j.bushor.2008.06.006

Heeks, R. (2001). *Understanding e-Governance for Development.* i-Government Working Paper Series, 11

Helfer, L. R. (2004). Regime Shifting: The TRIPs Agreement and New Dynamics of International Intellectual Property Lawmaking. *Yale Journal of International Law, 29.*

Hemphill, T. A. (2006). US innovation policy: creating (and expanding) a national agenda for global competitiveness. *Innovation: Management, Policy, &. Practice, 10.*

Henderson, J. C., & Venkatraman, N. (1993). Strategic alignment: leveraging information technology for transforming organizations. *IBM Systems Journal, 32*(1), 4–16. doi:10.1147/sj.382.0472

Herman, T., Laner, J., Keough, D., & Towne, S. & Mayes, L. (2002). *Alaska Technology Providers, an unpublished report.* University of Alaska Fairbanks.

Higino, S. P. (2005). International trade, economic growth and intellectual property rights: A panel data study of developed and developing countries. *Journal of Development Economics, 78*, 529–547. doi:10.1016/j.jdeveco.2004.09.001

Hipkin, I. (2004). Determining technology strategy in developing countries. *Omega, 32*(3), 245–260. doi:10.1016/j.omega.2003.11.004

Hirsch, S., & Bijaoui, I. (1985). R&D Intensity and Export Performance: a Micro View. *Weltwirtschaftliches Archiv, 121*, 138–251. doi:10.1007/BF02705822

Hitt, M., & Kim, H. (1997). International Diversification: Effects of Innovation and Firm Performance in Product-Diversified Firms. *Academy of Management Journal, 40*(4), 767–798. doi:10.2307/256948

Hobday, M. (1994). Technological Learning in Singapore: A Test Case of Leapfrogging. *The Journal of Development Studies, 30*, 831–858. doi:10.1080/00220389408422340

Hobday, M., Rush, H., & Bessant, J. (2004). Approaching the innovation frontier in Korea: the transition phase to leadership. *Research Policy, 33*, 1433–1457. doi:10.1016/j.respol.2004.05.005

Hoekman, B. M., Maskus, K. E., & Saggi, K. (2005). Transfer of technology to developing countries: Unilateral and multilateral policy options. *World Development, 33*(10), 1587–1602. doi:10.1016/j.worlddev.2005.05.005

Holzinger, A., & Errath, M. (2007). Mobile computer Web-application design in medicine: some research based guidelines. *Universal Access in the Information Society, 6*(1), 31–41. doi:10.1007/s10209-007-0074-z

Horst, M., Kuttschreuter, M., & Gutteling, J. (2007). Perceived usefulness, personal experiences, risk perception and trust as determinants of adoption of e-government services in The Netherlands. *Computers in Human Behavior, 23*, 1838–1852. doi:10.1016/j.chb.2005.11.003

Howard, M., Vidgen, R., & Powell, P. (2003). Overcoming stakeholder barriers in the automotive industry: building to order with extra-organizational systems. *Journal of Information Technology, 18*(1), 27–43. doi:10.1080/0268396031000077431

Huang, S.-Y., Chang, C.-M., & Yu, T.-Y. (2006). Determinants of user acceptance of the e-Government services: The case of online tax filing and payment system. *Government Information Quarterly, 23*(1), 97–122. doi:10.1016/j.giq.2005.11.005

Huerta, E., & Labeaga, J. M. (1992). Análisis de la decisión de exportar: una aproximación con datos macroeconómicos. *Investigaciones Económicas, suplemento*, pp. 41-47.

Hui, T. K., Wanand, D., & Alvin, H. (2007). Tourists' satisfaction, recommendation and revisiting Singapore. *Tourism Management, 28*(4), 965–975. doi:10.1016/j.tourman.2006.08.008

Huizingh, E. K. R. E. (2002). Towards Successful E-business Strategies: A hierarchy of three management models. *Journal of Marketing Management, 18*(4), 721–747. doi:10.1362/0267257022780615

Hymer, S. H. (1970). The efficiency (contradictions) of Multinational corporations. *The American Economic Review, 60,* 441–448.

IMS CC. (2011). *IMS Common Cartridge specification alliance website.* Retrieved on June 28, 2011, from http://www.imsglobal.org/ commoncartridge.html

IMS CP. (2011). *IMS Content Packaging specification.* Retrieved on June 28, 2011, from http://www.imsglobal.org/ content/ packaging/ index.html

IMS LD. (2011). *IMS Learning Design specification.* Retrieved on June 28, 2011, from http://www.imsglobal.org/ learningdesign/ index.html

INE - Instituto Naciaonal De Estadística. (2006). Retrieved from http://www.ine.es, [01/07/2006]

INSPIRE. (2009). *EU LLP INSPIRE (Innovative Science Pedagogy in Research and Education) project (2008 – 2009) web site.* Retrieved on June 28, 2011, from http://inspire.eun.org/ index.php/ Main_Page

Internationalization and Market Entry Mode: A Review of Theories and Conceptual Framework. (1997). Management. *International Review (Steubenville, Ohio), 37*(2), 27–42.

Internationalization of the firm from an entrepreneurial perspective (2000). *Int. Stud. Manage. Organ, 30*(1), 3-92.

Iseminger, D. (2000). *Active Directory Service for Microsoft Windows 2000 Technical Reference.* Redmond: Microsoft Press.

ISO/IEC 14598-1:1999. (1999). *Information Technology – software product evaluation – part 1: general overview.* 1st ed., 1999-04-15.

ITCOLE. (2003). *EU FP5 IST ITCOLE (Innovative Technology for Collaborative Learning and Knowledge Building) project (2001 – 2003) web site.* Retrieved on June 28, 2011, from http://www.euro-cscl.org/ site/ itcole

iTEC (2011). *EU FP7 IST iTEC (Innovative Technologies for an Engaging Classroom) project (2010 – 2014) web site.* Retrieved on June 28, 2011, from http://itec.eun.org/ web/ guest/

Ives, B., & Learmonth, G. P. (1984). The information system as a compete it vie weapon. *Communications of the ACM, 27*(12), 1193–1201. doi:10.1145/2135.2137

Jaeger, P. T., & Matteson, M. (2009). e-Government and Technology Acceptance: the Case of the Implementation of Section 508 Guidelines for Websites. *Electronic. Journal of E-Government, 7*(1), 87–98.

Jaffe, A. B. (1986). Technological Opportunity and Spillovers of R&D: Evidence from Firms' Patents, Profits, and Market Value. *The American Economic Review, 76*(5), 984–1001.

Jaffe, E. D., Nebenzahl, I. D., & Schorr, I. (2005). Strategic Options of Home Country Firms Faced with MNC Entry. *Long Range Planning, 38,* 183–195. doi:10.1016/j.lrp.2004.11.013

Jain Palvia, S., & Sharma, S. (2007). E-Government and E-Governance: Definitions/Domain Framework and Status around the World. *5th International conference on e-governance,* 28-30 December, Hyderabad, India

Jain, A., & Patnayakuni, R. (2003). Public Expectations and Public Scrutiny: An agenda for research in the context of e-government. *Ninth Americas Conference on Information Systems.*

James, L. R., & Williams, L. J. (2000). The cross-level operator in regression, ANOVA, and contextual analysis. In K. J. Klein, S. W. J. Kozlowski, (eds.) *Multilevel Theory, Research, and Methods in Organizations: Foundations, Extensions, and New Directions,* 382-424. San Francisco: Jossey Bass.

Javorcik, B. S. (2003). *Search of Spillovers through Backward Linkages. World Bank WP.* Does Foreign Direct Investment Increase the Productivity of Domestic Firms.

Johanson, J., & Vahlne, J. E. (1977). The Internationalization Process of the Firm: A Model of Knowledge Development and Increasing Foreign Market Commitments. *Journal of International Business, 8*(1), 23–32. doi:10.1057/palgrave.jibs.8490676

Johanson, J., & Wiedersheim-Paul, F. (1975). The Internationalization of the Firm: Four Swedish Cases. *Journal of Management Studies*, *12*(2), 305–322. doi:10.1111/j.1467-6486.1975.tb00514.x

Johnson, G. (2006). Synchronous and asynchronous text-based cmc in educational contexts: A review of recent research. *TechTrends: Linking Research & Practice to Improve Learning*, *50*(4), 46–53.

Johnson, C., & Walworth, D. J. (2003). *Protecting U.S. intellectual property rights and the challenges of digital piracy*. U.S. International Trade Commission.

Johnson, R. A., & Wichern, D. W. (1992). *Applied Multivariate Statistical Analysis*. Upper Saddle River, NJ: Prentice Hall.

Johnson-George, C., & Swap, W. (1982). Measurement of Specific Interpersonal Trust: Construction and Validation of a Scale to Access Trust in a Specific Other. *Journal of Personality and Social Psychology*, *43*, 1306–1317. doi:10.1037/0022-3514.43.6.1306

Johnston, W. J. (1983). Exporting: Does Sales Volume Make a Difference? *Journal of International Business Studies*, (Spring/Summer): 147–153.

Joia, L. A. (2006). A Framework for Developing Regional E-Government Capacity- Building Networks. *The Massachusetts Institute of Technology Information Technologies and International Development*, *2*(4), 61–73. doi:10.1162/154475205775249328

Joint, P. (1982). An Empirical Study of Norwegian Export Behaviour. Czinkota, M. & Tesar, G. (Ed.), Export Management an International Context, pp. 55-69. New York: Praeger.

Jones, M.V. (1999). The internationalization of small high-technology firms. Journal of International Marketing. Journal of Marketing Theory and Practice, 8 (2), 8-17 & 7(4), pp. 15-41.

Joo, J. (2002). A business model and its development strategies for electronic tourism markets. *Information Systems Management*, *19*(5), 58–69. doi:10.1201/1078/43201.19.3.20020601/37171.8

Jordan, J., & Lowe, J. (2004). Protecting strategic knowledge: Insights from collaborative agreements in the aerospace sector. *Technology Analysis and Strategic Management*, *16*, 241–259. doi:10.1080/09537320410001682900

Joyal, A., & Deshaies, J. (1994). SMEs and International Competition. *Journal of Small Business Management*, *32*(3).

Kaleka, A., & Katsikeas, C. (1998). Souces of Competitive Advantage in Hight Performing Export Company. *Journal of World Business*, *33*(4), 378–393.

Karagozoglu, N. & Lindell, M. (1998). nternationalization of Small and Medium-Sized Technology-Based Firms: An Exploratory Study. *Journal of Small Business*, 44.59.

Karamanlis, K. (2009). The developmental vision in an upcoming word. *SEPE news*, 30, 6-9.

Kascarone, R., Paauwe, J., & Zupan, N. (2009). HR practices, interpersonal relations, and intrafirm knowledge transfer in knowledge-intensive firms: a social network perspective. *Human Resource Management*, *48*(4), 615–639. doi:10.1002/hrm.20301

Katsikeas, C. (1996). The export development process: an integrative review of empirical models. *Journal of International Business Studies*, *27*(3), 517–551. doi:10.1057/palgrave.jibs.8490846

Katsikeas, C., & Piercy, N. (1998). Identifying Managerial Influences on Exporting: Past Research and Future Directions. *Journal of International Marketing*, *6*(2), 74–102.

Katsikeas, C., Piercy, N., & Ioannidis, C. (1995). Determinants of Exports Performance in a European Context. *European Journal of Marketing*, *30*(6), 6–35. doi:10.1108/03090569610121656

Katsikeas, C., & Samiee, S. (2002). Marketing strategy determinants of export performance: a meta-analysis. *Journal of Business Research*, *55*, 51–67. doi:10.1016/S0148-2963(00)00133-8

Kazienko, P., Musiał, K., & Zgrzywa, A. (2009). Evaluation of Node Position Based on Email Communication. *Control and Cybernetics*, *38*(1), 67–86.

Kedia, B., & Chocar, J. (1986). Factors Inhibiting Export Performance of Firms: An Empirical Investigation. *Management International Review*, *26*(4), 33–44.

Keen, P., & Mackintosh, R. (2001). *The Freedom Economy: gaining the mCommerce edge in the era of the wireless Internet*. New York: McGraw-Hill.

Kendall, M. G. (1948). *Rank Correlation Methods*. Oxford, UK:Oxford

Kenteris, M., Gavalas, D., & Economou, D. (2009). An innovative mobile electronic tourist guide application. *Personal and Ubiquitous Computing*, *13*(2), 103–118. doi:10.1007/s00779-007-0191-y

Kim, P. (2009). Action research approach on mobile learning design for the underserved. *Educational Technology Research and Development*, *57*(3), 415–435. doi:10.1007/s11423-008-9109-2

Kinzie, M., & Joseph, D. (2008). Gender differences in game activity preferences of middle school children: Implications for educational game design. *Educational Technology Research and Development*, *56*(5/6), 643–663. doi:10.1007/s11423-007-9076-z

Kirpalani, V., & Mcintosh, N. (1980). International Marketing Effectiveness of Technology-Oriented Small Firm. *Journal of International Business Studies*, *11*(Spring), 81–90. doi:10.1057/palgrave.jibs.8490625

Kiyota, K., & Okazaki, T. (2005). *Foreign Technology Acquisition Policy and Firm Performance in Japan, 1957-1970: Macro-aspects of Industrial Policy*. CIRJE Discussion Papers.

Klein, S., Frazier, G. L., & Roth, V. J. (1990). A Transaction Cost Analysis Model of Channel Integration in International Market. *JMR, Journal of Marketing Research*, *272*, 196–208. doi:10.2307/3172846

Klein, K. J., Lim, B., Saltz, J. L., & Mayer, D. M. (2004). How do they get there? An examination of the antecedents of centrality in team networks. *Academy of Management Journal*, *47*, 952–963. doi:10.2307/20159634

Klein, K. J., Tosi, H., & Cannella, A. A. (1999). Multilevel theory building: Benefits, barriers, and new developments. *Academy of Management Review*, *24*(2), 243–248. doi:10.5465/AMR.1999.1893934

Kleinschmidt, E., & Cooper, R. G. (1984). A Typology of Export Strategies Applied to the Export Peformance of Industrial Firm. In *Kainak* (pp. 217–231). E, International Marketing Mangement.

Kluge, S., & Riley, L. (2008). Teaching in virtual worlds: Opportunities and challenges. *Issues in Informing Science and Information Technology*, *5*, 127–135.

Koch, C. (2000). Building coalitions in an era of technological change: virtual manufacturing and the role of unions, employees and management. *Journal of Organizational Change Management*, *13*(3), 275–288. doi:10.1108/09534810010330922

Koetter, M. (2006). Measurement Matters – Alternative Input Price Proxies for Bank Efficiency Analyses. *Journal of Financial Services Research*, *30*, 199–227.. doi:10.1007/s10693-006-0018-4

Koh, A. (1991). Relationships Among Organizational Charateristics, Marketing Strategy and Export Performance. *International Marketing Review*, *8*(3), 46–60. doi:10.1108/02651339110004906

Kohn, T. O. (1997). Small Firms as International Players. Small Business Economics, 9 (1), 45-51. In Krugman, P. (1991). Geography and Trade. Cambridge, MA: MIT Press.

Kojima, K. (2000). The "flying geese" model of Asian economic development: origin, theoretical extensions, and regional policy implications. *Journal of Asian Economics*, *11*, 375–401. doi:10.1016/S1049-0078(00)00067-1

Kokko, A. (1992). *Foreign direct investment, host country characteristics, and spillovers. Economic Research Institute, Stockholm School of Economics* [Ekonomiska forskningsinstitutet vid Handelshögsk.]. EFI.

Kolko, J. (1999). *The Death of Cities? The Death of Distance? Evidence from the Geography of Commercial Internet Usage.* Paper read at Cities in the Global Information Society: An International Perspective, November, at Newcastle upon Tyne, UK.

Korres, G. (1996). *Technical change and Productivity Growth: an empirical evidence from European countries*. London: Avebury-Ashgate.

Koufaris, M. (2002). Applying the Technology Acceptance Model and flow theory to online consumer behavior. *Information Systems Research, 13*(2), 205–223. doi:10.1287/isre.13.2.205.83

Koutouzis, E., Bithara, P., Kyranakis, S., Mavraki, M., & Verevi, A. (2008). Decentralizing Education in Greece: In search for a new role for the school leaders. *CCEAM 2008 Conference* April 20, 2009 from http://www.emasa.co.za/ files/full/H2.pdf

Kozlowski, S. W. J., & Klein, K. J. (2000). A multilevel approach to theory and research in organizations: Contextual, temporal and emergent processes. In K. J. Klein, S. W. J. Kozlowski, (eds). *Multilevel Theory, Research, and Methods in Organizations: Foundations, Extensions, and New Directions*, 3-90. San Francisco: Jossey Bass.

Kraemer, K., & Dedrick, J. (1997). Computing and public organizations. *Journal of Public Administration: Research and Theory, 7*(1).

Kraemer, K. L., & King, J. L. (1986). Computing and Public Organizations. *Public Administration Review*, (46): 488–496. doi:10.2307/975570

Kraemer, K. L., & King, J. L. (2005). Information technology and administrative reform: will e-government be different? *International Journal of Electronic Government Research, 2*(1).

Kraut, R., Steinfield, C., Chan, A., Butler, B., & Hoag, A. (1999). Coordination and virtualization: The role of electronic networks and personal relationships. *Organization Science, 10*(6), 722–740. doi:10.1287/orsc.10.6.722

Kravtsova, V., & Radosevic, S. (2009). Are Systems of Innovation In Eastern Europe Efficient? *Economics Working Paper No.101*, Centre for Comparative Economics, UCL School of Slavonic and East European Studies UCL SSEES, Centre for Comparative Economics.

Krippendorff, K. (2004). *Content Analysis: An Introduction to Its Methodology* (2nd ed.). Thousand Oaks, CA: Sage.

Ku, E. C. S., & Fan, Y. W. (2009). Knowledge sharing and customer relationship management in the travel service alliances. *Total Quality Management & Business Excellence, 20*(12), 1407–1421. doi:10.1080/14783360903248880

Kumar, N. (2002). Intellectual property rights, technology and economic development: experiences of Asian countries. *RIS Discussion Paper, 25*.

Kumcu, E., Hancar, T., & Kumcu, E. (1995). Managerial Percepcions of the Adequacy of Export Incentive Programmes: Implications for Export-Led Economics Developments Policy. *Journal of Business Research, 32*, 163–174. doi:10.1016/0148-2963(94)00038-G

Kurilovas, E., & Dagienė, V. (2009). Multiple Criteria Comparative Evaluation of e-Learning Systems and Components. *Informatica, 20*(4), 499–518.

Kurilovas, E., & Serikoviene, S. (2010). Learning Content and Software Evaluation and Personalisation Problems. *Informatics in Education, 9*(1), 91–114.

Kurilovas, E. (2009). Interoperability, Standards and Metadata for e-Learning. In G.A. Papadopoulos & C. Badica (Eds.). *Intelligent Distributed Computing III, Studies in Computational Intelligence, 237*, 121–130. Springer-Verlag Berlin Heidelberg.

Kurilovas, E. (2009). Learning Objects Reusability and Their Adaptation for Blended Learning. In: *Proceedings of the 5th International Conference on Networking and Services (ICNS 2009)*. April 20–25, 2009, Valencia, Spain, 542–547.

Kurilovas, E., & Dagiene, V. (2009). Learning objects and virtual learning environments technical evaluation criteria. *The Electronic Journal of e-Learning, 7(2)*, 127–136. Retrieved on June 28, 2011, from www.ejel.org

Kurilovas, E., & Dagiene, V. (2010). Multiple Criteria Evaluation of Quality and Optimisation of e-Learning System Components. *The Electronic Journal of e-Learning, 8(2)*, 141–150. Retrieved on June 28, 2011, from www.ejel.org.

Kurilovas, E., & Dagiene, V. (2010). eLearning in Lithuania – II. In: *e-Learning Practices. Cases on Challenges Facing e-Learning and National Development: Institutional Studies and Practices. Anadolu University, Eskisehir, Turkey*, 2010, Vol. 1, 463–484.

Kurilovas, E., & Serikoviene, S. (2010). Application of Scientific Approaches for Evaluation of Quality of Learning Objects in eQNet Project. In M.D. Lytras et al. (eds.). *WSKS 2010, Part I, CCIS 111*, 437–443. Heidelberg: Springer

Kurilovas, E., & Serikoviene, S. (2010). *Personalisation of Learning Objects and Environments for Informatics Science Education in Lithuania*. Proceedings of the 4th International Conference on Informatics in Secondary Schools: Evolution and Perspectives (ISSEP 2010). Zurich, Switzerland, January 13–16, 2010, 52–72.

Kurilovas, E., Bireniene, V., & Serikoviene, S. (2011). Methodology for Evaluating Quality and Reusability of Learning Objects. *The Electronic Journal of e-Learning, 9(1)*, 39–51. Retrieved on June 30, 2011, from www.ejel.org

LaCroix, S. J., & Konan, D. E. (2002). Intellectual property rights in china: the changing political economy of Chinese-American interests. *World Economy, 25*, 759–788. doi:10.1111/1467-9701.00462

Lai, M., Wang, H., & Zhu, S. (2009). Double-edged effects of the technology gap and technology spillovers: Evidence from the Chinese industrial sector. *China Economic Review, 20*, 414–424. doi:10.1016/j.chieco.2009.06.007

Lai, V. S., Wong, B. K., & Cheung, W. (2002). Group decision making in a multiple criteria environment: A case using the AHP in software selection. *European Journal of Operational Research, 137*, 134–144. doi:10.1016/S0377-2217(01)00084-4

Laine, A., & Kock, S. A. (n.d.). Process model of internationalization. New times demands new patterns. *University of Bath.*

Lajoie, S. P., Lavigne, N. C., Guerrera, C., & Munsie, S. D. (2001). Constructing Knowledge in the Context of BioWorld. *Instructional Science, 29*(2), 155–186. doi:10.1023/A:1003996000775

Lall, S., & Streenten, P. (1977). *Foreign Investment, Transnational and developing countries*. London: Macmillan.

Lall, S. (1992). Technological capabilities and industrialization. *World Development, 20*(2), 165–186. doi:10.1016/0305-750X(92)90097-F

Lan, P. (2000a). Changing Production Paradigm and the Transformation of Knowledge Existing Form. *International Journal of Technology Management, 20*(1/2), 44–57. doi:10.1504/IJTM.2000.002857

Lan, P. (2006). A New Vision of Innovation Management: Towards an Integrated Paradigm. *I. J. of Technology Marketing., 1*(4), 355–374. doi:10.1504/IJTMKT.2006.010732

Lan, P. (2000b). The Technology-component matrix: a tool for analyzing and managing knowledge. *International Journal of Technology Management, 20*(5/6/7/8), 670-683.

Lan, P. (2002). *E-Business Space for E-innovation.* Proceedings of the 3rd World Congress on Management of E-commerce (CD-Rom format).

Lau, E. (2004). Principaux enjeux de l'administration ılectronique dans les pays membres de l'OCDE. In *Revue Franqaise d'Administration Publique, 110* (pp. 225–244). Paris: Icole Nationale d'Administration.

Lave, J., & Wenger, E. (1991). *Situated learning: Legitimate peripheral participation*. Cambridge, UK: Cambridge University Press.

Leacock, T. L., & Nesbit, J. C. (2007). A Framework for Evaluating the Quality of Multimedia Learning Resources. *Journal of Educational Technology & Society, 10*(2), 44–59.

Lee, C., & Yang, Y. (1990). Impact of Export Market Expansion Strategy on Export Performance. *International Marketing Review, 7*(4), 41–51. doi:10.1108/02651339010000910

Lee, W., & Brasch, J. (1978). The Adoption of Export as an Innovative Strategy. *Journal of International Business Studies, 9*(1), 85–93. doi:10.1057/palgrave.jibs.8490653

Lee, K. (2005). Making a Technological Catch-up: Barriers and Opportunities. *Asian Journal of Technology Innovation, 13*, 97–131. doi:10.1080/19761597.2005.9668610

Lee, K., & Lim, C. (2001). Technological Regimes, Catching-up and Leapfrogging: the Findings from the Korean Industries. *Research Policy, 30*, 459–483. doi:10.1016/S0048-7333(00)00088-3

Lee, S., Kim, I., Rhee, S., & Trimi, S. (2006). The role of exogenous factors in technology acceptance: The case of object-oriented technology. *Information & Management*, *43*(4), 469–480. doi:10.1016/j.im.2005.11.004

Lee, W. Y. (2000). The Role of Science and Technology Policy in Korea's Industrial Development. In Kim, L., & Nelson, R. R. (Eds.), *Technology, Learning, & Innovation - Experiences of Newly Industrializing Economies* (pp. 269–280). Cambridge, UK: Cambridge University Press.

Lee, G. K., & Cole, R. E. (2000). *The Linux Kernel Development as a Model of Knowledge Development.* Working Paper, October 25, 2000, Haas School of Business, University of California, Berkeley.

Lehmann, K. (2004). *Innovation Diffusion Theory* Rogers & Bass Model DiscussionHumboldt-Universität Berlin, Wirtschaftswissenschaftliche Fakultät Institut für Entrepreneurship/ Innovationsmanagement Retrieved April 3, 2010, from http://www.grin.com/ e-book/80117/ innovation-diffusion-theory

Lei, Sheng, & Yong, Ma & Du De bin. (2008). Research on Reasonable Scale of Foreign R & D in China, Asiapacific. *Economic Review*, *4*, 27–35.

Lei, S. (2009). *Spatial Agglomeration and Knowledge Spillover of Foreign R&D in China.* Unpublished Doctoral Dissertation, East China Normal University.

Leinbach, T. (2001). Emergence of the Digital Economy and E-Commerce. In Leinbach, T. R., & Brunn, S. D. (Eds.), *Worlds of ecommerce: economic, geographical and social dimensions*. Chichester, UK: J. Wiley.

LeMill. (2011). *CALIBRATE LeMill 'learning toolbox'.* Retrieved on June 28, 2011, from http://lemill.org

Lemoine, F., & Unal-Kesenci, D. (2004). Assembly Trade and Technology Transfer: The Case of China. *World Development*, *32*(5), 829–850. doi:10.1016/j.worlddev.2004.01.001

Leonidou, L. (1998). Organizational Determinants od Exporting:Conceptual, Methodological and Empirical Insights. *Management International Review, Special Issue*, *1998*(1), 7–52.

Leonidou, L., & Morgan, N. (2000). Firm-Level Export Performance Assessment: Review, Evaluation and Development. *Journal of the Academy management. Science*, *28*(4), 493–511.

Levitan, E. (2010). *Higher education administrators' perceptions of the use of simulation games for adult learners.* Argosy University.

Levitt, T. (1983). The Globalization of Market. *Harvard Business Review*, *61*(May-June), 92–102.

Lim, N. (2003). Consumers' perceived risk: sources versus consequences. *Electronic Commerce Research and Applications*, *2*, 216–228. doi:10.1016/S1567-4223(03)00025-5

Lin, L. H., & Lu, I. Y. (2005). Adoption of virtual organization by Taiwanese electronics firms: An empirical study of organization structure innovation. *Journal of Organizational Change Management*, *18*(2), 184–200. doi:10.1108/09534810510589598

Liou, J. H. (2009). A novel decision rules approach for customer relationship management of the airline market. *Expert Systems with Applications*, *36*(3), 4374–4381. doi:10.1016/j.eswa.2008.05.002

Liu, X., Magjuka, R., Bonk, C., & Lee, S. (2007). Does sense of community matter? *Quarterly Review of Distance Education*, *8*(1), 9–24.

Liu, X., & Buck, T. (2007). Innovation performance and channels for international technology spillovers: Evidence from Chinese high-tech industries. *Research Policy*, *36*, 355–366. doi:10.1016/j.respol.2006.12.003

Liu, X., & Wang, C. (2003). Does Foreign Direct Investment Facilitate Technological Progress? Evidence from Chinese Industries. *Research Policy*, *32*, 945–953. doi:10.1016/S0048-7333(02)00094-X

Llonch, J. (2005).Internal Key factor in Export Performance: A Comparative Analysis in Italian and Spanish textile-Clothing Firms. *Journal of Fashion Marketing Management.*

Lloyd, J., & Turkeltaub, A. (2006). India and China are the Only Real Brics in the Wall. *Financial Times (North American Edition)*, (Dec): 4.

Lobel, M., Neubauer, M., & Swedburg, R. (2002). Elements of group interaction in a real-time synchronous online learning-by-doing classroom without F2F participation. *USDLA Journal, 16*(4).

Lohr, S. (2002). New Economy- The Intellectual Property Debate Takes a Page from 19th-Century America. *The New York Times,* (Oct. 14).

LOM. (2002). *IEEE LTCS Learning Object Metadata (LOM) Standard.* Retrieved on June 28, 2011, from http://ltsc.ieee.org/ wg12/ files/ LOM_ 1484_ 12_ 1_ v1_ Final_ Draft.pdf

Lorange, P., & Roos, J. (1992). *Strategic Alliances: Formation, Implementation and Evolution.* Cambridge, MA: Blackwell Publishers.

Los enfoques micro-organizativos de la internacionalización de la empresa: Una revisión y síntesis de la literatura(1999)., *Información Comercial Española,* 781, 117-127.

Loudon, A. (2001). *Webs of Innovation: the networked economy demands new ways to innovate.* London: Pearson Education Ltd.

Louter, P. J., Ouwerkerk, C., & Bakker, B. (1991). An Inquiry into Succesful Exporting. *European Journal of Marketing, 25*(6), 7–23. doi:10.1108/03090569110001429

LRE Service Centre. (2011). *ASPECT LRE Service Centre web site.* Retrieved on June 28, 2011, from http://aspect-project.org/ node/ 52

LRE. (2011). *European Learning Resource Exchange service for schools web site.* Retrieved on June 28, 2011, from http://lreforschools.eun.org/

LSSIC - Ley Servicios de la Sociedad de la Información y de Comercio Electrónico. (2009). Retrieved from http://www.congreso.es/ public_oficiales/ L7/ CONG/ BOCG/ A/ A_068-13.PDF.

Lucas, H. C., & Baroudi, J. (1994). The role of information technology in organization design. *Journal of Management Information Systems, 10*(4), 9–24.

Luckraz, S. (2008). Process Spillovers and Growth. *Journal of Optimization Theory and Applications, 139*(2), 315–335. doi:10.1007/s10957-008-9425-z

Lundvall, B. A. (1992). *Introduction. National Systems of Innovation - Toward a Theory of Innovation and Interactive Learning.* London: Pinter.

Madsen, T. (1989). Successful Export Marketing Management: Some Empirical Evidence. *International Marketing Review, 6*(4), 41–57. doi:10.1108/EUM0000000001518

Maher, J. (1996). *Seeing Language in Sign: The Work of William C. Stokoe.* Washington, DC: Gallaudet University Press.

Malecki, E. J. (1991). *Technology and economic development: the dynamics of local regional and national change.* Essex, UK: Longman Scientific and Technical.

Malhotra, Y., & Galletta, D. (1999). Extending the Technology Acceptance Model to Account to Account for Social Influence: Theoretical Bases and Empirical Validation. In *Proceedings of the 32nd Hawaii International Conference on System Scie*nces.

Mansfield, E. (1968). *Economics of technological change.* New York.

Marche, S., & Mcniven, J. D. (2003). E-government and e-governance: the future isn't what it used to be. *Canadian Journal of Administrative Sciences, 20*(1), 74–86. doi:10.1111/j.1936-4490.2003.tb00306.x

Marchesi, A. (1999). *Psicología de la Comunidad Sorda.* Madrid, Spain: Fundación CNSE.

Margetts, H. (2003). Electronic Government: a revolution in public administration? In Peters, B. G., & Pierre, J. (Eds.), *Handbook of Public Administration.* London: Sage.

Marin, A., & Bell, M. (2006). Technology spillovers from foreign direct investment (FDI): The active role of MNC subsidiaries in Argentina in the 1990s. *The Journal of Development Studies, 42*(4), 678–697. doi:10.1080/00220380600682298

Markus, M. L., & Robey, D. (1988). Informational technology and organizational change: Causal structure in theory and research. *Management Science, 34*(5), 583–594. doi:10.1287/mnsc.34.5.583

Marshall, A. (1930). *Principles of Economics: an introductory tex"t. 1.890*, Principles of Economics. London:Macmillan and Co., First

Martin, B. R. (1995). Foresight in science and technology. *Technology Analysis and Strategic Management, 7*(2), 139–168. doi:10.1080/09537329508524202

Massialas, V. (1981). The Educational System of Greece. *Superintendent of Documents*, Washington, DC 20402: U.S, Government Printing Office.

Maswere, T., Dawson, R., & Edwards, J. (2006). Assessing the Levels of Knowledge Transfer within e-Commerce Websites of Tourist Organisations in Africa. *Electronic Journal of Knowledge Management, 4*(1), 59–66.

Matel, S., & Ball-Rokeach, S. J. (2001). Real and virtual social ties: Connections in the everyday lives of seven ethnic neighborhoods. *The American Behavioral Scientist, 45*(3), 550–564.

Maushak, N., & Ou, C. (2007r). Using synchronous communication to facilitate graduate students' online collaboration. *Quarterly Review of Distance Education, 8*(2), 161–16.

MC guinnes, N. & Little, B. (1981). The Influence of Product Characteristics on the Export Performance of New Industrial Products. *Journal of Marketing, 45,* spring, 110-122.

Mcauley (2000). *Modelling and measuring creativity at the interface.*

McCormick, R., Scrimshaw, P., Li, N., & Clifford, C. (2004). *CELEBRATE Evaluation report.* Retrieved on June 28, 2011, from http://celebrate.eun.org/ eun.org2/ eun/ Include_ to_ content/ celebrate/ file/ Deliverable7_ 2Evaluation Report02 Dec04.pdf

MCDM. (2011). *International Society on Multiple Criteria Decision Making website.* Retrieved on June 28, 2011, from http://www.mcdmsociety.org/

MCdougall, P. et al. (1994). Explaining the Formation of International New Ventures: The Limits of the Theories from International Business Research. *Journal of Business Venturing, 9,* 469–487. doi:10.1016/0883-9026(94)90017-5

McKenzie, R. (2001). *The Relationship-Based Enterprise: powering business success through customer relationship management.* Toronto: McGraw-Hill Ryerson.

McMillan, D. W., & Chavis, D. M. (1986). Sense of community: a definition and theory. *Journal of Community Psychology, 14*(1), 6–23. doi:10.1002/1520-6629(198601)14:1<6::AID-JCOP2290140103>3.0.CO;2-I

Meeusen, W., & van Den Broeck, J. (1977). Efficiency estimation from Cobb – Douglas Production Functions with Composed Error. *International Economic Review, 18*(2), 435–444.. doi:10.2307/2525757

Melin, L. (1992). Internationalization as a Strategy Process. *Strategic Management Journal, 13,* 99–118. doi:10.1002/smj.4250130908

Melle, M., & Raymond, J. (2001). Competitividad Internacional de las Pymes Industriales Españolas. *Ponencia presentatada al XI Congreso de ACED, Zaragoza,* 17-18 de setiembre de 2001.

MELT. (2010). *EU eContentplus programme's MELT (Metadata ecology for learning and teaching) project (2007 – 2010) website.* Retrieved on June 28, 2011, from http://melt-project.eun.org

Merino de Lucas, F. (1998). La salida al exterior de la Pyme manufacturera española. *Investigación Comercial Española, 773*(Septiembre-Octubre), 13–24.

Meyer, J. W., & Rowan, B. (1977). Institutionalized organizations: Formal structure as myth and ceremony. *American Journal of Sociology, 83*(2), 340–363. doi:10.1086/226550

Michalski, R., Palus, S., & Kazienko, P. (2011). *Matching Organizational Structure and Social Network Extracted from Email Communication.* BIS 2011, 14th International Conference on Business Information Systems. Lecture Notes in Business Information Processing LNBIP, Springer, Berlin Heidelberg.

Miesenbock, K. (1988). Small business and exporting: a literature review. *International Small Business Journal, 6*(2), 42–61. doi:10.1177/026624268800600204

Mimbela, J. (2009). *e-learning, bases teóricas.* Santa Cruz, Cajarmarca: Universidad Nacional Pedro Ruiz Gallo Lambayeque.

Mintzberg, H. (1979). *The Structuring of Organizations.* Englewood Cliffs, NJ: Prentice-Hall.

Mistree, D. (2007). Exploring e-governance. Salience, Trends and Challenges. *Mapping Sustainability*, 261-275

Moen (1999).The relationship between firm size, competitive advantages.

Mofleh, S., & Wanous, M. (1999). Understanding Factors Influencing Citizens Adoption of e-Government Services in the Developing World: Jordan as a Case Study. *Journal of Computer Science*, 7(2), 1–11.

Moodle. (2009). *Open-source community-based tools for learning.* Retrieved from http://www.moodle.org, [16/06/09]

Moon, J., & Lee, H. (1990). On the Internal Correlated of Export Stage Development: An Empirical Investigation in the Korean Electronics Industry. *International Marketing Review*, 7(5), 16–27. doi:10.1108/EUM0000000001532

Moon, J.-W., & Kim, Y.-G. (2001). Extending the TAM for a World-Wide-Web context. *Information & Management*, 38(4), 217–230. doi:10.1016/S0378-7206(00)00061-6

Moore, G. C., & Benbasat, I. (1991). Developing of an instrument to measure the perceptions of adopting an information technology innovation. *Information Systems Research*, 2(3), 192–222. doi:10.1287/isre.2.3.192

Moran, T. H. (1970). Multinational corporations and dependency: a dialogue for dependentistas and non-dependentistas. *International Organization*, 32, 79–100. doi:10.1017/S0020818300003878

Moreno, L. (1996). Actividad comercial en el exterior de las empresas manufactureras españolas, y estrategias de diferenciación de product. *Papeles de Economía Española*, 66, 107–123.

Moreno, L., & Rodríguez, D. (1998). Diferenciación de producto y actividad exportadora de las empresas manufactureras españolas, 1990-1996. *Investigación Comercial Española*, 773(Septiembre-Octubre), 25–35.

Moreno, R. (2007). Optimizing learning from animations by minimizing cognitive load: Cognitive and affective consequences of signaling and segmentation methods. *Applied Cognitive Psychology*, 21, 1–17..doi:10.1002/acp.1348

Movshuk, O. (2004). Restructuring, productivity and technical efficiency in China's iron and steel industry, 1988–2000, purch. *Journal of Asian Economics*, 15(1), 135–151.. doi:10.1016/j.asieco.2003.12.005

Müller, S. (1991). *Die psyche des managers als determinante des exporterfolges.* MP.

Murphy, E., & Manzanares, M. A. R. (2005). Reading between the lines: Understanding the role of latent content in the analysis of online asynchronous discussions. *International Journal of Instructional Technology & Distance Learning*, 2(6).

Musiał, K., & Juszczyszyn, K. (2008). A method for evaluating organizational structure on the basis of social network analysis. *Foundations of Control and Management Sciences*, 9, 97–108.

Musial, K., & Juszczyszyn, K. (2009). *Properties of Bridge Nodes in Social Networks, 1st International Conference on Computational Collective Intelligence - Semantic Web.* Social Networks & Multiagent Systems, Springer-Verlag, Lecture Notes in Artificial Intelligence 5796, 2009, pp. 357-364.

Musiał, K., Kazienko, P., & Bródka, P. (2009). *User Position Measures in Social Networks.* The third SNA-KDD Workshop on Social Network Mining and Analysis held in conjunction with The 13th ACM SIGKDD International Conference on Knowledge Discovery and Data Mining, KDD 2009, June 28, 2009, Paris France, ACM Press, Article no. 6.

Nagaoka, S. (2009). Does strong patent protection facilitate international technology transfer? Some evidence from licensing contracts of Japanese firms. *The Journal of Technology Transfer*, 34(2), 128–144. doi:10.1007/s10961-007-9071-x

Nakos, G., Brouthers, K., & Brouthers, L. (1998). The Impact of Firm and Managerial Characteristics on Small and Medium. Sized Greek Firm's Export Performance. *Journal of Global Marketing*, 11(4), 23–47. doi:10.1300/J042v11n04_03

Namiki, N. (1994). A Taxonomic Analysis of Export Marketing Strategy: An Exploratory Study of US Exporters of Electronic Products. *Journal of Global Marketing*, 8(1), 27–50. doi:10.1300/J042v08n01_03

Naor, J. (1987). Firm and Managment Characteristic as Discriminators of Export Marketing Activity. *Journal of Business Research*, *15*(3), 221–235. doi:10.1016/0148-2963(87)90025-7

Narin, F., & Frame, J. D. (1989). The growth of Japanese science and technology. *Science*, *245*, 600–605. doi:10.1126/science.245.4918.600

Nassimbeni, G. (2001). Technology, Innovation Capacity, and the Export Attitude of Small Manufaturing Firms: A Logit/Tobit Model. *Research Policy*, *30*, 245–262. doi:10.1016/S0048-7333(99)00114-6

Nelson, R. R. (2007). The changing institutional requirements for technological and economic catch up. *International Journal of Technological Learning. Innovation and Development*, *1*(1), 4–12.

Nelson, R. (1993). *National innovation systems: a comparative analysis*. Oxford University Press.

Nemet, G. F. (2009). Demand-pull, technology-push, and government-led incentives for non-incremental technical change. *Research Policy*, *38*, 700–709. doi:10.1016/j.respol.2009.01.004

Neter, J., Kutner, M. H., Nachtsheim, C. J., & Wasserman, W. (1999). *Applied Linear Regression Models*. New York: McGraw-Hill.

Nevin, J. R. (1981). International Determinant of Export Marketing Behaviour: An Empirical Investigation. *JMR, Journal of Marketing Research*, *18*(1), 114–119. doi:10.2307/3151322

Nieto, M., & Quevedo, P. (2005). Absorptive capacity, technological opportunity, knowledge spillovers, and innovative effort. *Technovation*, *25*, 1141–1157. doi:10.1016/j.technovation.2004.05.001

Nill, J., & Kemp, R. (2009). Evolutionary approaches for sustainable innovation policies: From niche to paradigm. *Research Policy*, *38*, 668–680. doi:10.1016/j.respol.2009.01.011

Nipper, S. (1989). Third generation distance learning and computer conferencing. In Mason, R., & Kaye, A. (Eds.), *Mindweave: Communication, Computers and Distance Education*. Oxford, UK: Pergamon.

Novak, J. D., & Cañas, A. J. (2008). *The Theory Underlying Concept Maps and How to Construct Them. Technical Report IHMC CmapTools 2006-01 Rev 01-2008*. Florida Institute for Human and Machine Cognition.

O'Neil, J., Byrne, A., Liddle, M., Talley, E., & Hoyos, C. (2002). *Profiles of Users, an unpublished report*. University of Alaska Fairbanks.

Observatory for the Greek Information Society. (2009). *Measurment of eEurope/i2010. Indicators for Greece 2008* Findings. Retrieved October 10 2009, from htt://www.observatory.gr

OECD. (2000). *Measuring the ICT Sector, Organisation for Economic Cooperation and Development*. Paris: OECD.

OECD. (2001a). *Basic research: statistical issues. OECD/NESTI Document DSTI/EAS/STP/NESTI(2001)38*. Paris: OECD.

OECD. (2002a). *Frascati Manual. Proposed standards practice for surveys on research and experimental development*. Paris: OECD.

OECD. (2002b). *Public funding of R&D - trends and changes. OECD Document DSTI/STP(2002)3/REV1 prepared by the ad hoc working group on «Steering and Funding of Research Institutions»*. Paris: OECD.

OECD. (1998). *Information Technology as an Instrument of Public Management Reform: a Study of Five OECD Countries*. Paris: Organization for Economic Co-operation and Development

OECD. (2001). *The New Economy: Beyond the Hype-Final Report on the OECD Growth Project, Executive Summary*. Meeting of the OECD Council at Ministerial Level 2001. Organisation for Economic Cooperation and Development (OECD). Retrieved from http://www.oecd.org/ pdf/ D00018000/ M00018624.pdf

OECD. (2003). *The E-Government Imperative*. E-Government Studies. Paris: Organization for Economic Co-operation and Development

Okediji, R. (2008). WIPO-WTO Relations and the Future of Global Intellectual Property Norms. *Netherlands Yearbook of International Law, 39*.

Oliveira, F. H. P., Jayme, F. G., & Lemos, M. B. (2006). Increasing returns to scale and international diffusion of technology: An empirical study for Brazil (1976-2000). *World Development, 34*(1), 75–88. doi:10.1016/j.worlddev.2005.07.011

Oliver, M. (2000). An introduction to the evaluation of learning technology. *Journal of Educational Technology & Society, 3*(4), 20–30.

Ondrejka, C. (2007). Education unleashed: participatory culture, education, and innovation in second life. *The John D. and Catherine T. MacArthur Foundation Series on DigitalMedia and Learning*, 229-251.

ONU. (2006). Convención De Derechos De Las Personas Con Discapacidad. Ed. ONU.

Ounaies, H. Z., Jamoussi, Y., & Ben Ghezala, H. H. (2009). Evaluation framework based on fuzzy measured method in adaptive learning system. *Themes in Science and Technology Education, 1*(1), 49–58.

Ouzts, K. (2006). Sense of community in online courses. *Quarterly Review of Distance Education, 7*(3), 285–296.

Özgenera, Ş., & İrazb, R. (2006). Customer relationship management in small–medium enterprises: The case of Turkish tourism industry. *Tourism Management, 27*(6), 1356–1363. doi:10.1016/j.tourman.2005.06.011

Paas, F., Renkl, A., & Sweller, J. (2004). Cognitive Load Theory: Instructional Implications of the Interaction between Information Structures and Cognitive Architecture. Instructional Science, 2 (1-2). New York: Springer.

Padden, C., & Humhries, T. (1988). *Deaf in America: Voices from a culture*. Cambridge, MA: Hardvard University Press.

Palmer, A. (2005). The internet challenge for destination marketing. In Morgan, N., Pritchard, A., & Pride, R. (Eds.), *Destination Branding: Creating the unique destination proposition* (pp. 128–140). Oxford, UK: Elsevier.

Panagis, Y., Sakkopoulos, E., Tsakalidis, A., Tzimas, G., Sirmakessis, S., & Lytras, M. D. (2008). Techniques for mining the design of e-government services to enhance end-user experience. *Int. J. Electronic Democracy, 1*(1), 32–50. doi:10.1504/IJED.2008.021277

Pandejpong, T., & Kocaoglu, D. F. (2003). *Strategic Decision: Process for Technology Selection in the Petrochemical Industry*. Paper presented at the Portland International Conference on Management of Engineering and Technology.

Panko, R. R. (2001). *Business Data Communications and Networking* (3rd ed.). Upper Saddle River, NJ: Prentice Hall PTR.

Papandreou, G. (2009).e-governance for the citizen. *SEPE news*, 30,12-15.

Park, W. G., & Lippoldt, D. C. (2008). Technology Transfer and the Economic Implications of the Strengthening of Intellectual Property Rights in Developing Countries. *OECD Trade Policy Working Papers*.

Parkhurst, S., & Parkhurst, D. (2000). *Un sistema completo para escribir y leer las Lenguas de Signos*. Madrid: PROEL.

Pashtan, A., Blattler, R., Heusser, A., & Scheuermann, P. (2003). *CATIS: A Context-Aware Tourist Information System*. In Proceedings of IMC 2003, 4th International Workshop of Mobile Computing, Rostock, Germany

Patel, H., & Jacobson, D. (2008). Factors Influencing Citizen Adoption of E-Government: A Review and Critical Assessment In Golden W, Acton T, Conboy K, van der Heijden H, Tuunainen VK (eds.), *16th European Conference on Information Systems* (pp.1058-1069), Galway, Ireland.

Paulsson, F., & Naeve, A. (2006). *Establishing technical quality criteria for learning objects*. Retrieved on June 28, 2011, from http://www.frepa.org/ wp/ wp-content/ files/ Paulsson- Establ- Tech- Qual_ finalv1.pdf

Pavlou, P. A. (2003). Consumer Acceptance of Electronic Commerce: Integrating Trust and Risk with the Technology Acceptance Model. *International Journal of Electronic Commerce, 7*(3), 69–103.

Pedersen, T., & Petersen, B. (1998). Explaining gradually increasing resource commitment to a foreign market. *International Business Review, 7*, 483–501. doi:10.1016/ S0969-5931(98)00012-2

Pena-Schaff, J. B., & Nicholls, C. (2004). Analyzing student interactions and meaning constructions in computer bulletin board discussions. *Computers & Education, 42,* 243–265. doi:10.1016/j.compedu.2003.08.003

Petricka, I. J., & Echols, A. E. (2004). Technology roadmapping in review: A tool for making sustainable new product development "decisions". *Technological Forecasting and Social Change, 71,* 81–100. doi:10.1016/S0040-1625(03)00064-7

Petty, R. E., & Cacioppo, J. T. (1981). *Attitudes and Persuasion: Classic and Contemporary Approaches.* Dubuque, Iowa: Wm. C. Brown Company Publishers.

Phaal, R., Farrukh, C., & Probert, D. (2004). Technology road mapping - A planning framework for evolution and revolution. *Technological Forecasting and Social Change, 71,* 5–26. doi:10.1016/S0040-1625(03)00072-6

Piccoli, G., O'Connor, P., Capaccioli, C., & Álvarez, R. (2003). Customer relationship management a driver for change in the structure of the US lodging industry. *The Cornell Hotel and Restaurant Administration Quarterly, 44*(4), 61–73.

Piercy, N. (1981). Company Internationalization: Active and Reactive Exporting. *European Journal of Marketing, 15*(3), 26–40. doi:10.1108/EUM0000000004876

Pla, J. (2000). *La Estrategia Internacional de la Empresa Española.* Fundació Universitària Vall d'Albaida.

Platt, L., & Wilson, G. (1999). Technology development and the poor marginalized: context, intervention and participation. *Technovation,* (19): 393–401. doi:10.1016/S0166-4972(99)00030-9

PNAGE (2004). *Diagnóstico Geral das Administrações Públicas Estaduais.* Ministry of Planning, Budget and Management, 2004

Ponnusawmy, H., & Santally, M. I. (2008). Promoting (quality) participation in online forums: A study of the use of forums in two online modules at the University of Mauritius. *International Journal of Instructional Technology & Distance Learning, 5*(4).

Porter, M. E. (1990). *The Competitive Advantages of Nation.* New York: The Free Press. Universidad de Stirling, Escocia.

Porter, A. (2004). Technology futures analysis: Toward integration of the field and new methods. *Technology Futures Analysis Working Group. Technological Forecasting and Social Change, 71,* 287–303. doi:10.1016/j.techfore.2003.11.004

Porter, M. E. (1987). From competitive advantage to corporate strategy. *Harvard Business Review, 65*(3), 43–59.

PWC. (2002). *Estudo de Benchmarking Global em e-Government.* Price Waterhouse & Coopers.

Rabino, S. (1980). An Examination of Barriers to Exporting Encountered by Small Manufacturing Companies. *Managment International Review, 20*(1), 67–73.

Rayens, M. K., & Hahn, E. J. (2000). Building consensus using the policy Delphi method. *Policy, Politics & Nursing Practice, 4,* 308–315. doi:10.1177/152715440000100409

Rayport, J., & Jaworski, B. (2001). *E-Commerce.* Boston: McGraw-Hill/Irwin.

Redish, E. F. (1999). *Building a science of teaching physics [online].* Millikan Award Lecture (1998). Available http://www.physics.umd.edu/rgroups/ripe/papers/millikan.htm

Reid, S. (1981). The Decision-Maker and Export Entry and Expansion. *Journal of International Business Studies, 12*(2), 101–112. doi:10.1057/palgrave.jibs.8490581

Reigeluth, C. M., & Nelson, L. M. (1997). A new paradigm of ISD? In R. C. Branch & B. B. Minor (eds.). *Educational media and technology yearbook, 22,* 24–35. Englewood, Co: Libraries Unlimited.

Reynolds, J. B. (2002). Export Controls and Economic Sanctions. *The International lawyer 36*(3).

Rialp, A. (1997). *Las fases iniciales del proceso de internacionalización de las empresas industriales catalanas: una aproximación empírica. Tesis doctoral.* Universidad Autónoma de Barcelona.

Rialp, J. (1996). El papel de los acuerdos de cooperación en los procesos de internacionalización de la empresa española: un anàlisis empírico. *Papeles de Economía Española, 66,* 248–266.

Rialp, J. (2001). Conceptual Framework on SME's Internationalisation: Past, Present and Future Trend of Research. In *f* Rodríguez, D. (1999).Relación entre innovación y exportaciones de las empresas: Un estudio empírico. *Papeles de Economía Española, 81,* 167–180.

Rinne, M. (2004). Technology roadmaps: Infrastructure for innovation. *Technological Forecasting and Social Change, 71,* 67–80. doi:10.1016/j.techfore.2003.10.002

Robinson, L. (2009). A summary of Diffusion of Innovations. Retrieved May 5 2010, from http://www.enablingchange. com.au /Summary_Diffusion_Theory.pdf

Rocha, A., Pereira, G., & Baldez, J. (2004). A sign matching technique to support searches in sign language texts. Workshop on the Representation and Processing of Sign Languages, (LREC), Lisboa, Portugal.

Rock, M., Murphy, J. T., Rasiah, R., van Seters, P., & Managi, S. (2009). A hard slog, not a leap frog: Globalization and sustainability transitions in developing Asia. *Technological Forecasting and Social Change, 76*(2), 241–254. doi:10.1016/j.techfore.2007.11.014

Rodríguez, D. (1999). Diversificación y tamaño en las empresas industriales españolas. *Papeles de Economía Española, 78/79,* 236–249.

Rodrik, D., Subramanian, A., & Trebbi, F. (2004). Institutions rule: The primacy of institutions over geography and integration in economic development. *Journal of Economic Growth, 9*(2), 131–165. doi:10.1023/B:JOEG.0000031425.72248.85

Rogers, E. M. (1995). *Diffusion of innovations* (4th ed.). New York: Free Press.

Romer, P. M. (1986). Increasing returns and long-run growth. *The Journal of Political Economy, 94*(5), 1002–1037. doi:10.1086/261420

Root, F. (1994). Entry Strategies for International Market. Milan: Lexinton book Mc.

Profitable Export Marketing Practices. (1987). An Exploratory Inquiry. In Rosson, P., & Reid, S. (Eds.), *Managing export entry and expansion.* New York: Praeger.

Rosson, P., & Ford, D. (1982). Manufacturer-Overseas Distributor Relations and Export Performance. *Journal of International Business Studies,* (Fall): 57–72. doi:10.1057/palgrave.jibs.8490550

Rotchanakitumnuai, S. (2008). Measuring e-government service value with the E-GOVSQUAL-RISK model. *Business Process Management Journal, 14*(5), 724–737. doi:10.1108/14637150810903075

Rovai, A. P., & Wighting, M. J. (2005). Feelings of alienation and community among higher education students in a virtual classroom. *The Internet and Higher Education, 8,* 97–110. doi:10.1016/j.iheduc.2005.03.001

Rowe, G., & Wright, G. (1999). The Delphi techniques as a forecasting tool: Issues and analysis. *International Journal of Forecasting, 15,* 353–375. doi:10.1016/S0169-2070(99)00018-7

Rowe, R., Creamer, G., Hershkop, S., & Stolfo, S. J. (2007). *Automated Social Hierarchy Detection through Email Network Analysis.* Proceedings of the 9th WebKDD and 1st SNA-KDD 2007 workshop on Web mining and social network analysis, pp. 109-117

Rui, L. (2004). *Multinational R & D investment and leapforward development of technology in China.* Beijing: Economic Science Press.

Rui, H., & Yip, G. S. (2008). Foreign acquisitions by Chinese firms: A strategic intent perspective. *Journal of World Business, 43,* 213–226. doi:10.1016/j.jwb.2007.11.006

Russo, T. C., & Benson, S. (2005). Learning with invisible others: Perceptions of online presence and their relationship to cognitive and affective learning. *Journal of Educational Technology & Society, 8*(1), 54–62.

Ryans, A. (1988). Marketing Strategy Factors and Market Share Achievement in Japan. *Journal of International Business Studies, 19*(3), 389–409. doi:10.1057/palgrave.jibs.8490393

Rynning, M., & Andersen, O. (1994). Structural and Behavioral Predictors of Exports Adoption: A Norwegian Study. *Journal of International Marketing, 2*(1), 73–89.

Saade, R., & Bahli, B. (2005). The impact of cognitive absorption on perceived usefulness and perceived ease of use in on-line learning: an extension of the technology acceptance model. *Information & Management, 42*(2), 317–327. doi:10.1016/j.im.2003.12.013

Saaty, T. (1980). *The Analytical Hierarchy Process: Planning, Priority Setting, Resource Allocation.* New York: McGraw-Hill.

Saliola, F., & Zanfei, A. (2009). Multinational firms, global value chains and the organization of knowledge transfer. *Research Policy, 38*(2), 369–381. doi:10.1016/j.respol.2008.11.003

Salo, A., & Salmenkaita, J.-P. (2002). Embedded foresight in RTD programs. *International Journal of Technology. Policy and Management, 2*(2), 167–193.

Samiee, S., & Anckar, P. (1998). Currency choice in industrial pricing: A cross-national evaluation. *Journal of Marketing, 62*(3), 112–127. doi:10.2307/1251747

Samiee, S., & Walters, P. G. P. (1990). Influence of Firm size on Export Planning and Performance. *Journal of Business Research, 20*(2), 325–342.

Samina, K., & will, M. (2004). Innovating through acquisition and internal development: A quarter-century of boundary evolution at Johnson & Johnson. *Long Range Planning, 37*(6), 525–547. doi:10.1016/j.lrp.2004.09.008

Sanchez, R. & Mahoney, J. T. (1996). Modularity, flexibility, and knowledge management in product and organization design. *Strategic Management Journal, 17*(Winter Special Issue), 63-76.

Sang, S., Lee, J.-D., & Lee, J. (2009). E-government adoption in ASEAN: the case of Cambodia. *Internet Research, 19*(5), 517–534. doi:10.1108/10662240910998869

Saur, R. (1997). *A tecnologia da informação na reforma do estado. Ciência da Informação, 26(1).* Jan/Apr.

Scanlon, J. (2007). Getting serious about gaming. *Business Week Online, 8-14,* 1–4.

Schaupp, L. C., & Carter, L. (2008). The impact of trust, risk and optimism bias on E-file adoption. *Information Systems Frontiers.* doi:.doi:10.1007/s10796-008-9138-8

Schilit, B. N., & Heimer, M. M. (1994). Disseminating Active Map Information to Mobile Hosts. *IEEE Network, 8*(5), 22–32. doi:10.1109/65.313011

Schiller, J., & Voisard, A. (2004). *Location-based services.* Amsterdam: Elsevier.

Schlegelmilch, E. (1987). Profile Analyses of Non-Exporters Versus Exporters Grouped by Export Involvement. *Marketing International Research, 27*(1), 38–49.

SCORM. (2011). *Shareable Content Object Reference Model.* Retrieved on June 28, 2011, from http://xml.coverpages.org/ scorm.html

Scott, J. (2000). *Social network analysis: A handbook* (2nd ed.). London: Sage.

Sharma, D., & Johanson, J. (1987). Technical Consultancy in Internationalization. *International Marketing Review, 4*(4), 20–29. doi:10.1108/eb008339

Shen, R., Wang, M., & Pan, X. (2008). Increasing interactivity in blended classrooms through a cutting-edge mobile learning system. *British Journal of Educational Technology, 39*(6), 1073–1086. doi:10.1111/j.1467-8535.2007.00778.x

Shih, H. P. (2004). Extended technology acceptance model of Internet utilization behavior. *Information & Management, 41*(6), 719–729. doi:10.1016/j.im.2003.08.009

Shneiderman, B. (2002). *Leonardo's Laptop: Human Needs and the New Computing Technologies.* Boston: MIT Press.

Shroeder, R. (2008). Defining virtual worlds and virtual environments. *Journal of Virtual Worlds Research, 1*(1), 2–3.

Siemens, G. (2003). *Learning ecology, communities, and networks: extending the classroom.* Elearnspace.

Sigala, M. (2005). Integrating customer relationship management in hotel operations: managerial and operational implications. *Hospital Management, 24*(3), 391–413. doi:10.1016/j.ijhm.2004.08.008

SIGNWRITING. (2009). Read, Write, Type Sign Languages. Retrieved from http://www.signwriting.org, [10/05/2009]

Singh, M., Sarkar, P., Dissanayake, D., & Pittachayawan, S. (2008). Diffusions of e-government services in Australia: Citizens' perspectives In *16th European Conference on Information Systems* Golden W, Acton T, Conboy K, van der Heijden H, Tuunainen VK (eds.) (pp. 1227-1238), Galway, Ireland.

Singh, V. (2007). Full Circle of Governance: How to Leverage Age Old Organic Structure of Governance. Paper presented at *5th International Conference on e-governance. 28-30 December 2007* Hyderabad, India Retrieved November 28, 2009, from http://www.iceg.net/2007/books /3/2_281_3.pdf

Sivan, E. (1986). Motivation in social constructivist theory. *Educational Psychologist, 21*(3), 209. doi:10.1207/s15326985ep2103_4

Slagter van Tryon, P., & Bishop, J. M. (2006, Spring). Identifying e-mmediacy strategies for web-based instruction. *Quarterly Review of Distance Education, 7*(1), 49–62.

Small firm internationalization: an investigative survey and future research directions(2001). *Management Decision, 39*(9), 767-783.

Snellen, I. (2000) Public Service in an Information Society. In: Peters, B. G. and Savoie, D. *Governance in the Twenty-first Century*: Revitalizing the Public Service. Montreal & Kingston: McGill-Queen's University Press

Spearman, C. (1904. (1987). The proof and measurement of association between two things. *The American Journal of Psychology, 15*, 72–101. doi:10.2307/1412159

Stagg, J. C. (2007). Scrutinizing Foreign Investment: How Much Congressional Involvement Is Too Much. *Iowa Law Review, 93*, 325.

Stein, D. S., Wanstreet, C. E., Engle, C. L., Glazer, H. R., Harns, R. A., Johnston, S. M., et al. (2006). *From personal meaning to shared understanding: The nature of discussion in a community of inquiry*. Midwest Research-to-Practice Conference in Adult, Continuing, and Community Education 2006.

Stoneman, P. (1987). *The economic analysis of technology policy*. Oxford, UK: Oxford University Press.

Stoneman, P. (1995). *Handbook of the Economics of Innovations and technological change*. Oxford, UK: Blackwell.

Styles, C., & Ambler, T. (1994). Export Performance Measures in Australia and the United Kingdom. *Journal of International Marketing, 6*(3), 12–36.

Suárez Ortega, S., Alamo Vera, F., & García Falcón, J. (2002). Determinantes organizativos y directivos de la actividad exportadora: evidencia empírica en el sector vitivinícola español. *Cuadernos de Economía y Dirección de la Empresa, 13*, 519–543.

Sweller, J. (2009). *Cognitive Load Theory.* Retrieved from http://tip.psychology.org/ sweller.html, [13/09/2009]

Taha, R. A., Choi, B. C., Chuengparsitporn, P., Cutar, A., Gu, Q., & Phan, K. (2007). *Application of Hierarchical Decision Modeling for Selection of Laptop*. Paper presented at the Portland International Conference on Management of Engineering and Technology.

Tassabehji, R., & Elliman, T. (2006).Generating citizen trust in e-government using a trust verification agent: a research note. *European and Mediterranean Conference on Information Systems* (EMCIS) 2006, July 6-7 2006, Costa Blanca, Alicante, Spain. Retrieved November 12, 2009, from http://www.iseing.org/ emcis/EMCIS2006/Proceedings/Contributions/ EGISE/eGISE4.pdf

Taylor, S., & Todd, P. (1995a). Assessing IT usage: The role of prior experience. *Management Information Systems Quarterly, 19*(4), 561–570. doi:10.2307/249633

Taylor, S., & Todd, P. (1995b). Understanding Information Technology usage: A test of competing models. *Information Systems Research, 6*(2), 144–176. doi:10.1287/isre.6.2.144

Teo, T., Srivastava, S., & Jiang, L. (2008). Trust and Electronic Government Success: An Empirical Study. *Journal of Management Information Systems, 25*(3), 99–131. doi:10.2753/MIS0742-1222250303

Tesar, G. (1977). The Export Behaviour of Smaller Sized Winsconsin Manufacturin Firm. *Journal of International Business Studies, 8*(1), 93–98. doi:10.1057/palgrave.jibs.8490783

The Impact of Size on Internationalization. (1993)... *Journal of Small Business Management,* (Octubre): 50–56.

The Mechanism of Internationalization. (1990)... *International Marketing Review, 7*(4), 11–24.

Thomas, H., Pollock, T., & Gorman, P. (1999). Global strategic analyses: frameworks and approaches. *The Academy of Management Executive, 13*(1), 70–82. doi:10.5465/AME.1999.1567340

Thomas, M. & Araujo, L. (1986). Theories of Export Behaviour: A Critical Analysis. *European Journal of Marketing, 19* (2), \42-52.

Thompson, R. L., Higgins, C. A., & Howell, J. M. (1991). Personal computing: Toward a conceptual model of utilization. *Management Information Systems Quarterly, 15*(1), 125–143. doi:10.2307/249443

On the Internationalization Process of Firms. (1990). In Thorelli, B., & Cavusgil, S. T. (Eds.), *International Market Strategy* (pp. 3–32). Oxford, UK: Pergamon Press.

Tian, X. (2010). Managing FDI technology spillovers: A challenge to TNCs in emerging markets. *Journal of World Business, 45*(3), 276–284. doi:10.1016/j.jwb.2009.09.001

Tidd, J., & Izumimoto, Y. (2002). Knowledge exchange and learning through international joint ventures. *Technovation, 22*, 137–145. doi:10.1016/S0166-4972(01)00006-2

Timmer, M. O'Mahony, M. & van Ark, B. (2008). T*he EU KLEMS Growth and Productivity Accounts: An Overview.* University of Groningen & University of Birmingham.

Tommaso, P. (1997). Multinational enterprises and technological spillovers: An evolutionary model. *Journal of Evolutionary Economics, 7*, 169–192. doi:10.1007/s001910050040

Topic Mapper. (2008). *CALIBRATE Topic Mapper application web site.* Retrieved on June 28, 2011, from http://www.tovek.cz/ produkty/ topicmapper.html

Topritzhofer, E., & Moser, R. (1979). Exploratorische LOGIT Analysen zur Empirischen Identifikation von Determinanten der Export Tüchigkeit von Unternehmen. *Zeitschrift für Betriebswirtschaft, 49*(10), 873–890.

Torkkeli, M., & Tuominen, M. (2002). The contribution of technology selection to core competencies. *International Journal of Production Economics, 77*(3), 271–284. doi:10.1016/S0925-5273(01)00227-4

Torres, S. (2008). *Curso de Bimodal. Sistemas Aumentativos de Comunicación.* Universidad de Málaga. Retrieved from http://campusvirtual.uma.es/ sac/ _contenidos/, [11/04/2009]

Tran, T. A., & Daim, T. (2008). A taxonomic review of methods and tools applied in technology assessment. *Technological Forecasting and Social Change, 75*, 1396–1405. doi:10.1016/j.techfore.2008.04.004

Tuominen, A., & Ahlqvist, T. (2010). Is the transport system becoming ubiquitous? Socio-technical roadmapping as a tool for integrating the development of transport policies and intelligent transport systems and services in Finland. *Technological Forecasting and Social Change, 77*, 120–134. doi:10.1016/j.techfore.2009.06.001

Tuominen, M., Rajala, A., & Moller, K. (2004). How does adaptability drive firm innovativeness? *Journal of Business Research, 57*(5), 495–506. doi:10.1016/S0148-2963(02)00316-8

UKP-POST. (1999). *Electronic Government - Information Technologies and the Citizen.* London: United Kingdom Parliament - Parliamentary Office of Science and Technology.

Un, C. A., & Cuervo-Cazurra, A. (2008). Do subsidiaries of foreign MNEs invest more in R&D than domestic firms? *Research Policy, 37*, 1812–1828. doi:10.1016/j.respol.2008.07.006

UN/DPEPA-ASPA. (2002). *Benchmarking E-government: A Global Perspective.* York: United Nations / Division for Public Economics and Public Administration - American Society for Public Administration. N.

UNCTAD. V. (2008). *World Investment Report.* United Nations Conference on Trade and Development New York and Geneva.

United Nations. (2008). UN e-government survey 2008 From E-Government to connected governance, Retrieved April 23, 2009 from http://unpan1.un.org/intradoc /groups/ public/ documents/UN/ UNPAN028607.pdf

United Nations. (2010). United Nations e-government survey 2010. Retrieved June 10, 2010 http://www2.unpan.org/ egovkb/ global_reports /10report.htm

Uzzell, B., Wornath, J., & Graves, J. & Ferris, D. (2002). A*n Analysis of Alaska's Community Websites, an unpublished report.* University of Alaska Fairbanks.

Vaidya, O. S., & Kumar, S. (2006). Analytic hierarchy process: An overview of applications. *European Journal of Operational Research, 169*(1), 1–29. doi:10.1016/j.ejor.2004.04.028

ValNet. (2004). *EU FP4 IST ValNet (European SchoolNet Validation Network) project (2000 – 2004) partners community web site.* Retrieved on June 28, 2011, from http://www.valnet.eun.org

Valos, M., & Baker, M. (1996). Developing an Australian model of export marketing performance determinants. *Marketing Intelligence & Planning, 14*(3), 11–20. doi:10.1108/02634509610117311

Van Assche, F. (2007). Linking Learning Resources to Curricula by using Competencies. *CEUR Workshop Proceedings of the 1ˢᵗ International Workshop on Learning Object Discovery & Exchange (LODE'07) within the 2ⁿᵈ European Conference on Technology Enhanced Learning (EC–TEL07).* Sissi, Crete, Greece, 17–20 September, 2007. Vol. 311, 80–91.

Vargo, J., Nesbit, J. C., Belfer, K., & Archambault, A. (2003). Learning object evaluation: Computer mediated collaboration and inter–rater reliability. *International Journal of Computers and Applications, 25*(3), 198–205.

Variables Associated with Export Profitability. (1982)... *Journal of International Business Studies, 13*(2), 39–56. doi:10.1057/palgrave.jibs.8490549

Venkatesh, V., & Davis, F. (2000). A theoretical extension of the technology acceptance model: Four longitudinal field studies. *Management Science, 46*(2), 186–204. doi:10.1287/mnsc.46.2.186.11926

Venkatesh, V., Morris, M., Davis, G., & Davis, F. (2003). User Acceptance of Information Technology: Toward a Unified View. *Management Information Systems Quarterly, 27*, 425–479.

Ventajas Comerciales y Competitividad: Aspectos Comerciales y Empíricos (1992*). Cuadernos del ICE*, 705, Mayo.

Vergara, S.(2005). *Métodos de pesquisa em administração.* S. Paulo: Atlas

Vijayasarath, L. (2004). Predicting consumer intentions to use on-line shopping: the case for an augmented technology acceptance model. *Information & Management, 41*(6), 747–762. doi:10.1016/j.im.2003.08.011

Viotti, E. B. (2002). National Learning Systems: A new approach on technological change in late industrializing economies and evidences from the cases of Brazil and Korea (R.O.). *Technological Forecasting and Social Change, 69*, 653–680. doi:10.1016/S0040-1625(01)00167-6

Von Hippel, E. (2001). Innovation by User Communities: Learning from Open-Source Software. *MIT Sloan Management Review, 42*(2), 82–86.

Vrana, V., Zafiropoulos, K., & Karavasilis, I. (2007). Quality Evaluation of local government website. A case of a primary education administration. Paper presented at *10th Toulon-Verona conference*, 3-4 September 2007, Thessaloniki.

Vygotsky, S. L. (1978). *Mind in society: The development of higher psychological process.* Cambridge, MA: Harvard University Press.

W3C - World Wide Web Consortium, (2005). Web Accesibility Initiative. Retrieved from http://www.w3c.es/traducciones/ es/ wai/ intro/ accessibility, [01/08/2009]

W3C (2011). *World Wide Web Consortium Web content accessibility guidelines.* Retrieved on June 28, 2011, from http://www.w3.org/ TR/ WAI- WEBCONTENT/

Wang, Y., & Blomstrom, M. (1992). Foreign investment and technology transfer: a simple model. *European Economic Review, 36*, 137–155. doi:10.1016/0014-2921(92)90021-N

Wang Chun Fa. (2003). *The historical evolution of national innovation systems and development trend in Major Developed Countries.* Beijing: Economic Science Press.

Wang, A. Y., & Newlin, M. H. (2001). Online Lectures: Benefits for the virtual classroom. *T.H.E. Journal, 29*(1), 17-24, Retrieved July 19, 2004 from http://www.thejournal.com/ magazine/vault/A3562.cfm.

Wangpipatwong, S., Chutimaskul, W., & Papasratorn, B. (2008). Understanding Citizen's Continuance Intention to Use e-Government Website: a Composite View of Technology Acceptance Model and Computer Self-Efficacy. *The Electronic. Journal of E-Government, 6*(1), 55–64.

Warkentin, M., Gefen, D., Pavlou, P. A., & Rose, G. (2002). Encouraging Citizen Adoption of eGovernment by Building Trust. *Electronic Markets*, *12*(3), 157–162. doi:10.1080/101967802320245929

Wasserman, S., & Faust, K. (1994). *Social network analysis: Methods and applications*. New York: Cambridge University Press.

Watanabe, C., Matsumoto, K., & Hur, J. Y. (2004). Technological diversification and assimilation of spillover technology: Canon's scenario for sustainable growth. *Technological Forecasting and Social Change*, *71*(9), 941–959. doi:10.1016/S0040-1625(03)00069-6

Waters, J., & Gasson, S. (2007). *Distributed knowledge construction in an online community of inquiry.* Proceedings of the 40th Hawaii International Conferences on System Sciences 2007.

Watson, R. T., Akselsen, S., Monod, E., & Pitt, L. F. (2004). The Open Tourism Consortium: Laying The Foundations for the Future of Tourism. *European Management Journal*, *22*(3), 315–326. doi:10.1016/j.emj.2004.04.014

WCAG1 - Web Content Accessibility Guidelines 1.0, (1999). Pautas de Accesibilidad al Contenido en la Web 1.0. Recomendación W3C de 5 de mayo de 1999. Retrieved from http://www.w3.org/ TR/ WCAG10/, [01/08/2009]

WCAG2 - Web Content Accessibility Guidelines 2.0, (2009). W3C Candidate Recommendation 30 April 2009. Retrieved from http://www.w3.org/ TR/ WCAG20/, [01/08/2009]

Weinberger, A., & Fischer, F. (2006). A framework to analyze argumentative knowledge construction in computer-supported collaborative learning. *Computers & Education*, *46*, 71–95. doi:10.1016/j.compedu.2005.04.003

Welch, L. S., & Loustarinen, R. (1988). nternationalization: Evolution of a Concept. *Journal of General Management*, *14*(2), 34–55.

Weller, M. (2007). The distance from isolation: Why communities are the logical conclusion in e-learning. *Computers & Education*, *49*, 148–159. doi:10.1016/j.compedu.2005.04.015

Wenger, E. (1998). *Communities of practice: Learning, meaning and identity*. New York: Cambridge University Press.

Westhead, P. (1995). Exporting and No-Exporting Small Firms in Great Britain: A Matched Pairs Comparison. *International Journal of Entrepreneurial Behaviour Research*, *1*(2), 6–36. doi:10.1108/13552559510090604

White, D. R. (2004). Network Analysis and Social Dynamics. *Cybernetics and Systems*, *35*, 173–192. doi:10.1080/01969720490426858

Wiebe J., Wilson T., Cardie C. (2005). Annotating Expressions of Opinions and Emotions in Language. *Language Resources and Evaluation, 1*(2). (2005), pp. 0-0.

Wiedersheim-Paul, F., Olson, H. C., & Welch, L. S. (1978). Pre-Export Activity: the First Step in Internationalization. *Journal of International Business Studies*, *9*(1), 47–58. doi:10.1057/palgrave.jibs.8490650

Wiley, D. A. (2000). *Connecting learning objects to instructional design theory: A definition, a metaphor, and a taxonomy*. Utah State University. Retrieved on June 28, 2011, from http://www.reusability.org/ read/

Williams, P. (2009). *Assessing Mobile Learning Effectiveness and Acceptance*. George Washington University.

Woodward, J. (1970). *Industrial Organization: Behaviour and Control*. London: Oxford University Press.

Wu, I.-L., & Chen, J.-L. (2005). An extension of Trust and TAM model with TPB in the initial adoption ofonline tax: An empirical study. *International Journal of Human-Computer Studies*, *62*, 784–808. doi:10.1016/j.ijhcs.2005.03.003

Yamada, M., & Akahori, K. (2007, February). Social presence in synchronous CMC based language learning: How does it affect the productive performance and consciousness of learning objectives? *Computer Assisted Language Learning, 20*(1), 37–65. doi:10.1080/09588220601118503

Yaprak, A. (1985). An Empirical Study of the Differences Between Small Exporting and No-Exporting Us Firm. *International marketing Review, spring, 2,* 72-83.

Yasunaga, Y., Watanabe, M., & Korenaga, M. (2009). Application of technology roadmaps to governmental innovation policy for promoting technology convergence. *Technological Forecasting and Social Change, 76,* 61–79. doi:10.1016/j.techfore.2008.06.004

Yi, M., Jackson, J., Park, J., & Probst, J. (2005). Understanding information technology acceptance by individual professionals: Toward an integrative view. *Information & Management, 43*(3), 350–363. doi:10.1016/j.im.2005.08.006

Yin, R. K. (2001). *Estudo de caso – planejamento e métodos*. Porto Alegre: Bookman.

Ying, Zhu & Du De bin. (2005). Organization patterns and evolution of R&D globalization of multinational corporations. *Science and Technology Management Research, 25*(8), 56–60.

Yoffie, D. B., & Cusumano, M. A. (1999). Judo Strategy: the competitive dynamics of internet time. *Harvard Business Review, 77*(1), 71–81.

Yun, J.-H. J. (2007). The Development of Technological Capability and the Transformation of Inward FDI in Korea from 1962 to 2000. *Innovation and Technology in Korea*, 33-54.

Zafiropoulos, K., Karavasilis, I., & Vrana, V. (2010). (to appear). Exploring E-governance by Primary and Secondary Education Teachers in Greece. *International Journal of Electronic Democracy*.

Zain, M., Che Rose, R., Abdullah, I., & Masrom, M. (2005). The relationship between information technology acceptance and organizational agility in Malaysia. *Information & Management, 42*(6), 829–839. doi:10.1016/j.im.2004.09.001

Zavadskas, E. K., & Turskis, Z. (2010). A new additive ratio assessment (ARAS) method in multicriteria decision-making. *Technological and Economic Development of Economy, 16*(2), 159–172. doi:10.3846/tede.2010.10

Zhang Li Li & Cheng De Yong. (1992). Extent analysis and synthetic decision. In: *Support Systems for Decision and Negotiation Processes, Preprints of the /FAC/IFORS/ IIASA/TIMS Workshop, Vol. 2. System Research Institute, Warsaw*, 633-640.

Zhou, Y. (2008). Synchronizing Export Orientation with Import Substitution: Creating Competitive Indigenous High-Tech Companies in China. *World Development, 36*(11), 2353–2370. doi:10.1016/j.worlddev.2007.11.013

Zhu, E., & Baylen, D. (2005). From learning community to community learning: pedagogy, technology and interactivity. *Educational Media International, 42*(3), 251–268. doi:10.1080/09523980500161395

Zook, M. (2000). *The web of production: the economic geography of commercial Internet content production in the United States.* Environment & Planning A, March, 411(16)

Zou, S., & Stan, S. (1998). The Determinants of Export Performance: A Review of the Empirical Literature Between 1987 and 1997. *International Marketing Review, 15*(5), 333–356. doi:10.1108/02651339810236290

Zurita, G., & Nussbaum, M. (2004). A constructivist mobile learning environment supported by a wireless handheld network. *Journal of Computer Assisted Learning, 20*(4), 235–243. doi:10.1111/j.1365-2729.2004.00089.x

About the Contributors

Ahmet Cakir is Director of the ERGONOMIC Institute for Occupational and Social Sciences Research Co., Ltd., Berlin, and the Editor-in-Chief of the journal *Behaviour and Information Technology*. He is the Convenor of the ISO-Standardization Committee dealing with computer input devices and workplace organisation. Ahmet Cakir is also the chairman of the German Standardisation Committee on ergonomics in informatics. His research interests focus on computer ergonomics, human reliability and health and safety. He has served as an expert member to the German Nuclear Safety Commission, health and safety authorities, commissions of the German Parliament, and Federal Ministries. Dr. Cakir has published numerous books, research reports, academic papers in refereed journals, and conference proceedings. He has organised and chaired more than 20 national congresses, and two international congresses of the series Working With Visual Displays. Together with Tom Stewart and David Hart, he has written the textbook *The VDT Manual* that has been published in five languages.

Patricia Ordóñez de Pablos is a Professor in the Department of Business Administration and Accountability in the Faculty of Economics of the University of Oviedo, Spain. Her teaching and research interests focus on the areas of strategic management, knowledge management, intellectual capital measuring and reporting, organisational learning and human resources management. In recent years she started a new stream of research: Asia. She serves as Editor in Chief of *International Journal of Asian Business and Information Management*. She serves as Executive Editor of the *International Journal of Learning and Intellectual Capital* and Associate Editor of *Behaviour and Information Technology*.

* * *

Adel S. Aldosary is a professor and chairmen of two departments: City and Regional Planning Department and Architecture in King Fahd University of Petroleum & Minerals (KFUPM), Saudi Arabia. He is an active member of several editorial boards and many scientific and professional councils (e.g., Eastern Province Tourism Council). He is currently in charge of many national projects, and the Director of the National Atlas of Saudi Arabia (KFUPM Centre). He has served as an advisor to many organizations and officials including the Minister of Higher Education, the Tourism Ministry, the Dammam Mayor's Office and SK Telecom, Saudi Arabia's latest economic city developer.

B. Cristina Pelayo G-Bustelo is a Lecturer in the Computer Science Department of the university of Oviedo. Ph.D. from the University of Oviedo in Computer Engineering. Her research interests include Object-Oriented technology, Web Engineering, eGovernment, Modeling Software with BPM, DSL and MDA.

Leong Chan is a doctoral student in the Department of Engineering and Technology Management at Portland State University, USA. He holds a Master of Science degree from the same department. His current research interests are in the areas of technology transfer, technology foresight, R&D management and innovation policy.

Yap Kueh Chin did his PhD at Georgia University in Science Education. He did his masters at Surrey University and his bachelors degree and diploma in education at University of Malaya. He has widely taught and consulted in the field of Science Education. His research interests include alternative conceptions in science, multiple representations in science and integration of ICT in science teaching and learning. He has published his research findings in leading journals and at international conferences and also received research awards.

Ricardo Colomo-Palacios is an Associate Professor at the Computer Science Department of the Universidad Carlos III de Madrid. His research interests include applied research in Information Systems, Software Project Management, People in Software Projects and Social and Semantic Web. He received his PhD in Computer Science from the Universidad Politécnica of Madrid (2005). He also holds a MBA from the Instituto de Empresa (2002). He has been working as software engineer, project manager and software engineering consultant in several companies including Spanish IT leader INDRA. He is also an Editorial Board Member and Associate Editor for several international journals and conferences and Editor in Chief of International Journal of Human Capital and Information Technology Professionals.

Angel García-Crespo is the Head of the SofLab Group at the Computer Science Department in the Universidad Carlos III de Madrid and the Head of the Institute for promotion of Innovation Pedro Juan de Lastanosa. He holds a PhD in Industrial Engineering from the Universidad Politécnica de Madrid (Award from the Instituto J.A. Artigas to the best thesis) and received an Executive MBA from the Instituto de Empresa. Professor García-Crespo has led and actively contributed to large European Projects of the FP V and VI, and also in many business cooperations. He is the author of more than a hundred publications in conferences, journals and books, both Spanish and international.

Ruben González Crespo is a research manager in accessibility and usability in web environments for people with severe disabilities. BS in Computer Management from the Polithecnical University of Madrid and Computer Engineering from the Pontifical University of Salamanca. Master in Project Management from the same university. PhD from the Pontifical University of Salamanca in 2008 and PhD Extraordinary Award given by the UPSA where is professor at the School of Computing (Madrid Campus) since 2005. Currently is the Director of the Master in Project Management, is professor of doctoral programs organized by the University and Master's programs in GIS, Software Engineering and Security.

Tugrul Daim is an Associate Professor and PhD Program Director in the Department of Engineering and Technology Management at Portland State University. Prior to joining PSU, he had worked at Intel Corporation for over a decade in varying management roles. His recent focus has been in the energy sector where he has been helping regional agencies develop technology roadmaps for their future investments. He is also a visiting professor with the Northern Institute of Technology at Technical University of Hamburg, Harburg. He has been recently appointed as Extraordinary Professor at the Graduate School of Technology Management at University of Pretoria. He has published over 100 refereed papers in journals and conference proceedings. His papers appeared in Technological Forecasting and Social Change, Technovation, Technology Analysis and Strategic Management, Computers and Industrial Engineering, Energy, Energy Policy and many others. He has coauthored four books of readings and several proceedings. He is the Editor-in-Chief of International Journal of Innovation and Technology Management and North American Editor of Technological Forecasting and Social Change. He received his BS in Mechanical Engineering from Bogazici University in Turkey, MS in Mechanical Engineering from Lehigh University in Pennsylvania, MS in Engineering Management from Portland State University, and PhD in Systems Science: Engineering Management from Portland State University in Portland Oregon.

Rossano Eusebio is Associate Professor of Marketing and Advertising at the Autonomous University of Barcelona (Spain), BA in Commerce (University of Turin –Italy) and Business (Autonomous University of Barcelona), MIM (ESC-France) and PhD (Autonomous University of Barcelona -Spain). Sub-Director of the Masters Programme in Marketing, Commerce and Distribution of the Autonomous University of Barcelona. In his professional career it has taken part in numerous research projects and consultancy for multinational companies of consumption and services (Danone and General Electric between others). We emphasize the launch of the hotel chain "Si Dorme" and the research works for Barberà del Vallès's hall and for the Chamber of Commerce of Terrassa and COPCA's. He is co-author of marketing cases textbook. Recent paper study the internationalization process of the Spanish and Italian manufacturing firm and marketing decision in the international context, marketing organization and measurement of marketing performance.

Ciro Campos Christo Fernandes is a Public Manager at the Brazilian Ministry of Planning, Budget and Management and a researcher at the *e:lab* – Research Laboratory on e-Government and e-Business at the Brazilian School of Public and Business Administration at Getulio Vargas Foundation. He holds a B.Sc. in Economics from Minas Gerais Federal University, and an MBA and DBA from the Brazilian School of Public and Business Administration at Getulio Vargas Foundation. His research interests lie on IT for Development, Information Systems Resistance, e-Government and Procurement in the Public Administration.

Luiz Antonio Joia is an Associate Professor and Principal of the *e:lab* – Research Laboratory on e-Government and e-Business at the Brazilian School of Public and Business Administration at Getulio Vargas Foundation. He is also an Adjunct Professor at Rio de Janeiro State University. He holds a B.Sc. in Civil Engineering from the Military Institute of Engineering, Brazil, and an M.Sc. in Civil Engineering and a D.Sc. in Production Engineering from the Federal University of Rio de Janeiro. He also holds an M.Sc. in Management Studies from the Oxford University, U.K. He was a World Bank consultant in Educational Technology and is an invited member of the Technical Board of the Working Group WG 8.5 (Informatics in the Public Administration) of the IFIP (International Federation for Information Processing). His research interests lie on IT for Development, Information Systems Resistance, e-Government, e-Business, Strategic Use of IT, Intellectual Capital, and Actor-Network Theory.

Lluís Jovell is Associate Professor of International Economic at the Autonomous University of Barcelona (Spain), BA in Economics and Commercial Sciences and studies in Law (University of Barcelona), Master in Applied Economics (Autonomous University of Barcelona) and Phd in Administration and Business Management (Ramon Llull University). He was a sub-director of the Business Management School (Autonomous University of Barcelona at Sabadell) during 5 years.Founder and Director of the Masters Programme in Marketing, Commerce and Distribution of the Autonomous University of Barcelona (since 1999). Director of Citius Programme (Autonomous University of Barcelona and Autonomous University of Madrid) and member of its academic commission. Member of the Academic Commission of the Postgraduate University Institute of Madrid and Director of the Master in Commercial Direction and Marketing. Director of different UAB Masters and trainings programme blended in company in International Business Management, Marketing and Retailing. He has taken part in numerous research projects and consultancy for multinational companies. Recent papers include works on applied economic and Innovation technology, effects of the innovation in the export performance. Member of the *Editorial Review Board* of the *International Journal of Asian Business and Information Management (IJABIM)*. Member of the Scientific Committee of the International Applied Economics Congress.

Xi Li (Jacky) is Associate Professor of Faculty of International Tourism, Macau University of Science and Technology. Dr. Li's research interests are Destination Management and Event Management. Since 2000, Dr. Li has participated in over 20 research projects as the team member and published over 30 academic papers in refereed journals and conference proceedings.

Ioannis Karavasilis is the Administrator of Administration of Primary Education of Serres, Greece. He is a teacher and he holds a master degree in administration of education. Currently he is PhD student in the Department of International and European Studies, University of Macedonia. He is the author of one book and has published many articles. His research interests include e-governance practices, TQM and reform of education.

Przemysław Kazienko received his MSc and PhD degrees in computer science with honours, both from Wrocław University of Technology, Poland, in 1991 and 2000, respectively. He obtained his habilitation degree from Silesian University of Technology, Poland, in 2009. Recently, he serves as a professor of Wroclaw University of Technology at the Institute of Informatics, Poland. He was also a Research Fellow at Intelligent Systems Research Centre, British Telecom, UK in 2008. For several years, he held the position of the deputy director for development at Institute of Applied Informatics. He was a co-chair of international workshops RAAWS'05, RAAWS'06, MMAML'10 and a Guest Editor of New Generation Computing and International Journal of Computer Science & Applications. He regularly serves as a member of international programme committees and the reviewer for scientific conferences and prestige international journals. He is a member of Editorial Board of International Journal of Knowledge Society Research. He has authored over 100 scholarly and research articles on a variety of areas related to social networks, social network analysis, knowledge management, collaborative systems, multiple model classification, data mining, recommender systems, Information Retrieval, data security, and XML. He also initialized and led over 20 projects chiefly in cooperation with commercial companies, including large international corporations.

Aikaterini Kokkinou holds a first-class Ph.D. Degree from the University of Aegean, a first-class Master of Science Degree in Business Analysis and Finance from the University of Leicester, a first-class Graduate Degree in Economic Sciences from the University of Crete, as well as a first-class Graduate Degree in Public Administration from the National School of Public Administration, Greece. During the last 5 years, Dr. Aikaterini Kokkinou worked for the Public Debt Management Agency, Ministry of Finance, Greece. She is currently a researcher in the Department of Economics, University of Glasgow, United Kingdom.

George M. Korres holds a doctorate in Economic Sciences (Economics of Innovation) from University of London (QMW) and an M.Sc from Essex University. He is currently a visiting fellow at the University of Newcastle, Centre of Urban and Regional Development Studies (CURDS) and an associate professor at the University of the Aegean, Department of Geography. Over the last 12 years, during both his academic and professional career, he has gained an in depth experience in the fields of economics, business and politics in the area of European Economics and Innovation Systems. His main areas of interest and specialisation include: European Integration, Social Policy and Social Inclusion, Economic and Innovation Policies, EU enlargement and the Euro-Mediterranean partnership

Ping Lan received his Ph.D from the University of Strathclyde, UK in 1995 and is currently the director of MBA program and a Professor in Business Management at University of Alaska Fairbanks (UAF) USA. Prior to joining UAF, Dr. Lan worked in Canada, Australia, Thailand, Britain and China as an academic, a journalist, and an entrepreneur. Dr. Lan has been published widely; his articles have appeared in *International Journal of Technology Management, International Journal of E-business, Asia Pacific Business Review, Regional Studies, Transnational Corporations, Journal of Euromarketing, Technovation, International Journal of Information Technology Management, International Journal of Technology Marketing* among others and more. His current teaching and research interests include technology/innovation management, and change management.

Kumar Laxman graduated with a PhD in instructional design and technology from Macquarie University, Australia. His other qualifications include a masters degree in educational technology from the National Institute of Education (Singapore), a bachelors degree in civil engineering from the National University of Singapore and a postgraduate diploma in education from the National Institute of Education (Singapore). He is knowledgeable in the field of instructional design and learning technologies, having published widely in reputable journals and presented at numerous international conferences. He has also independently carried out high quality research in learner-centric instructional design and technology and achieved cutting-edge research outcomes.

Aliana M W Leong is the Dean of the Faculty of International Tourism and the Director of School of Continuing Studies in Macau University of Science and Technology. Her research interests are Tourism Management and Adult Education. Aliana has published 3 monographs, edited 3 books and published over 80 papers in refereed journals, books, international and regional conferences proceedings in Europe, East Asia, China, and America. She is also the editor of the Journal of Macau Adult Education. As a chief investigator, Aliana has conducted over ten research projects funded by public institutions and Macau foundation in the recent five years.

Liang-Hung Lin is currently an Associate Professor in Department of International Business, National Kaohsiung University of Applied Sciences (Taiwan). Dr. Lin is interested in the fields of technology management and organizational innovation. He ever published academic papers in the *Journal of Business Ethics*, *Journal of Organizational Change Management*, *International Journal of Human Resource Management*, *International Journal of Technology Management* and *Total Quality Management and Business Excellence*.

Juan Manuel Cueva Lovelle is a Mining Engineer from Oviedo Mining Engineers Technical School in 1983 (Oviedo University, Spain). Ph. D. from Madrid Polytechnic University, Spain (1990). From 1985 he is a Professor at the Languages and Computers Systems Area in Oviedo University (Spain). ACM and IEEE voting member. His research interests include Object-Oriented technology, Language Processors, Human-Computer Interface, Web Engineering, Modeling Software with BPM, DSL and MDA.

Marcos Ruano Mayoral is a consultant at EGEOIT, Spain. Formerly he was a Research Assistant of the Computer Science Department at Universidad Carlos III de Madrid. He holds a BSc in Computer Systems from Universidad de Valladolid and a MSc in Computer Science from Universidad Carlos III de Madrid. He has been involved in several research projects as information management engineer and software consultant.

Radosław Michalski is a PhD student at the Institute of Informatics, Wroclaw University of Technology, Poland. He received his MSc in computer science from the Wroclaw University of Technology. His scientific interests include social network analysis and the problemsof trust between users in complex networks. He also holds IT manager position by a private manufacturing company.

Kh. Md. Nahiduzzaman is a faculty at the Department of City and Regional Planning in King Fahd University of Petroleum and Minerals (KFUPM), Saudi Arabia. He is a member of several professional organizations, such as Western Regional Science Association (WRSA), USA, European Network for Housing Research (ENHR), Bangladesh Institute of Planners (BIP), etc. He has extensive research and teaching experience in a number of countries, including Saudi Arabia, Sweden, Norway and Bangladesh. He is currently involved in a number of projects, funded by the university and national research financier, in the areas of 'third' place and sustainable development, GIS and photogrammetry application in sustainable planning, ICT influencing the city structure and planning strategies, and flood simulation modeling.

Sebastian Palus is a MSc student at the Computer Science faculty, Wroclaw University of Technology. He is interested in the complex social networks and their analysis. He is especially involved in social network approach to corporate management. Currently he is working on research and development project GRASP#, which is financed by Polish Ministry of Science and Higher Education.

Pedro Soto-Acosta is a Professor of Management at the University of Murcia (Spain). He holds a PhD in Management Information Systems (MISs) and a Master's degree in Technology Management from the University of Murcia. He received his BA in Accounting and Finance from the Manchester Metropolitan University (UK) and his BA in Business Administration from the University of Murcia. He attended Postgraduate Courses at Harvard University (USA). His work has been published in journals such as the European Journal of Information Systems, the International Journal of Information Management, the Information Systems Management, and the Journal of Enterprise Information Management, among others.

Vasiliki Vrana is a mathematician and holds a PhD in Computer Sciences, Aristotle University of Thessaloniki, Greece. She is an education consultant in secondary education and she teaches information systems at the Department of Business Administration, Technological Education Institute of Serres, Greece. Her research interests include the study of web 2.0, of IT in tourism and hospitality industries and e-governance. She has published one book and many articles in international and Greek journals.

Kostas Zafiropoulos is an Assistant Professor at the Department of International and European Studies, University of Macedonia. He holds a PhD in applied statistics and has published articles in international and Greek journals. He is the author of three books about marketing research and research methodology (in Greek). His research interests include sampling and data analysis and research methods.

Index

Symbols

3-D virtual worlds 30-31, 34

A

AA level 164, 167, 169
accessibility 17, 33, 138-139, 163-164, 167-170, 174-175, 189, 217, 240
Active Worlds 31
Adjusted Goodness of Fit Index (AGFI) 110
aesthetics 217
Agent-Based Search System (ABSS) 207
Alagoas 118, 126, 131, 133
Alaska Science & Technology Foundation (ASTF) 137, 140, 144, 149
American Competitiveness Initiative (ACI) 73, 92
American Sign Language (ASL) 166
Analytic Hierarchy Process (AHP) 87, 94-95, 98, 238-239
Annotea 209
application profile (AP) 208, 210-211, 229, 240
ASPECT project 230, 232
Authoring technologies 137-138

B

B2C e-commerce 187, 191-192, 196
Brazilian states 118-120, 122, 126
Business to consumer (B2C) 113, 187-188, 191-192, 196

C

CALIBRATE project 201, 209, 218, 227-229
CELEBRATE project 201-202, 207-208
Central Business District (CBD) 187-189, 193, 197
city structure 187-189, 191, 193-196, 198
collaborative learning environments 25, 202

Committee on Foreign Investment in the United States (CFIUS) 74, 89, 94
Company and Activity Characteristics (CAC) 44
comparative fit index (CFI) 110
context-aware computing 18
context-aware systems 15-16, 18
Contextual Attention Metadata (CAM) 207
contextual tourist information 18
Convergence 5, 15, 86, 98, 101, 132, 137-138, 176-177, 179
Cook's distance 156
Creative Personality Scale (CPS) 155, 161
Cronbach's alpha 107
customer relationship management (CRM) 15-17, 19, 21, 23-24, 150, 161

D

Deaf Community 164-166, 173
Deaf Culture 164-165
deafness 163
Decontextualisation 216
Delphi method 7-8, 86-87, 93, 97
Destination Management Office (DMO) 18-19, 21-23
Diffusion of Innovation (DOI) 14, 22-24, 34-37, 48-57, 68-69, 91-100, 103, 105, 112-117, 134-135, 149-150, 160-162, 175, 186, 243
Direct Foreign Investment (DFI) 40
DOT Force 136, 138-139, 146, 149

E

e-governance 99-105, 107, 111-112, 114-117, 134
e-government 100-101, 103-104, 106, 110-123, 125-135, 134, 139, 146
e-government development index (EGDI) 101
e-government maturity level 118
eIntegration 138

e-learning 34, 37, 163-164, 166, 175, 200-201, 203, 207, 211, 241-242

electronic data interchange (EDI) 138, 153

electronic tourist guides 15, 23-24

emergent technologies 25, 33-34

eMessaging 138

enterprise level 70-72, 78, 81-82, 86, 89

eQNet project 221-222, 239, 242

eStrategy 139, 146-147

eTransaction 138

European Learning Resource Exchange (LRE) 200-205, 207-208, 211, 219, 221-222, 224-232, 236, 239-242

European Schoolnet (EUN) 201-205, 209, 211, 228, 233, 235, 240-243

evaluation of quality 200, 214-215, 238, 241-242

Exon-Florio Amendment (EFA) 73-74

Export Administration Act (EAA) 73

Export Administration Regulations (EAR) 73

Export Intensity 38, 42, 44-45, 47-49

Export Strategy (ES) 44, 50, 174-175

F

Foreign Direct Investment (FDI) 2-4, 13, 75-81, 88, 92-98, 177, 185

G

General Agreement on Tariffs and Trade (GATT) 77

General systems theory (GST) 154

Geographic Information Systems 18

goodness-of-fit index (GFI) 110

gross state product (GSP) 140-141

H

Hsinchu Science-based Industrial Park (HSIP) 155

I

IAnnotate 209

industrial R&D 1-3, 5-13

Innovation an Implementation Strategy (IIS) 44

Innovative Science Pedagogy in Research and Education (INSPIRE) 133, 201, 203-204, 228, 232-233, 235-236, 240-241

Innovative Technologies for an Engaging Classroom (iTEC) 201, 205-206, 238-239, 241

Inquiry-Based Science Education 234-235

Integration 11, 13, 15-18, 21, 26, 35, 49, 53, 58, 81, 85, 92, 97, 112, 119, 122, 125, 127-129, 131, 133, 139, 142, 152-156, 173-174, 176-177, 203, 206, 225-227, 231, 239

intellectual property rights (IPR) 76-79, 88, 94-96, 203-204, 216, 219

international industrial R&D center 1, 6-8, 10-12

Internationalization Process 38, 40, 42-43, 45, 49-50, 52, 55

International Marketing Strategy (IMS) 34, 44, 201, 203, 208, 211-212, 216, 223-224, 230-232, 241

international technology transfer 70-79, 81-82, 85-92, 96

interoperability 200-203, 207-209, 211-212, 214, 216-217, 240-241

ITCOLE School of Tomorrow project 202

L

land price 189, 193, 197

Learning Design (LD) 34-35, 207, 223-224, 241

learning object/objects (LOs) 50-51, 54-55, 200-205, 210-211, 213-240, 242-243

learning resource exchange (LRE) 200-205, 207-208, 211, 219, 221-222, 224-232, 236, 239-242

Learning Technology Standards Observatory (LTSO) 201, 211, 240

LeMill learning toolbox 203, 223

Lifelong Learning Programme (LLP) 201, 204, 241

location-based services (LBS) 15, 18, 22, 24

location technology 18

LOM standard 209

LoTour 15-22

M

Macroeconomic Model 40

Made in Alaska (MIA) 144

mass customization technology 152

massively multiplayer online first-person shooter games (MMOFPSs) 32

master production schedule (MPS) 154

Math Science and Technology (MST) 204, 232-236

metadata 204-205, 207-209, 211-213, 216, 226, 228-230, 240-242

Microsoft Active Directory 60

Minas Gerais 118, 126-127, 131, 133

Ministries of Education (MoE) 201-206, 208-209, 211-212, 228, 230, 235-236, 240

mobile computation 16-17

mobile computing 17, 23-24

mobile computing systems 17

mobile devices 15-18, 21-22, 33, 35
mobile tourism 15
model analysis 1
Multinational Companies (MNCs) 3-4, 6, 8, 10-12, 75, 78-81, 83, 88-90, 93-96
multiplayer online role play games (MMORPs) 31
multiple criteria decision making/analysis (MCDM/ MCDA) 214, 242
multi-user dungeons (MUDs) 31

N

national level 71-72, 86, 88, 179-180, 228
National System of Innovations 176
National Validation Moderator/Moderators (NVMs) 224, 227-228
non-normed fit index (NNFI) 110
non-profit organizations (NPOs) 139-140
normed fit index (NFI) 110

O

online learning environments 25-26
ontology 209-210

P

Paraná 118, 126-127, 131, 133
Pernambuco 118, 126, 128, 131, 133
Personal Computing Model 100
physical and social environment 187
physical movement 187, 192, 195-198
Prior Experience Model 100
productivity spillover 4
public administration 102, 111, 118-120, 127-129, 133-135, 164, 167

R

R&D resources 2, 6-7
research and development (R&D) 1-14, 35, 43-44, 48, 52, 73-75, 77-78, 80, 83, 86, 88, 93-94, 98, 139, 176-177, 181-182, 186, 200-201, 232
research technological development (RTD) 85, 97, 185
root-mean-square error of approximation (RMSEA) 110

S

São Paulo 118, 129, 132-134
satellite channels 191, 193-195

scientific constructivism 30
Second Life 31, 34, 36
Sequential Inquiry Interface (SQI) 207
severe disabilities 163
Sign Language 164-167, 169-170, 172-173, 175
Sign-Symbol-Sequence (SSS) 171
Signwriting 164-167, 169-175
Signwriting Markup Language for Scalable Vector Graphics (SWMLSVG) 164, 167, 169-174
Signwriting Markup Language (SWML) 167, 169-171, 173
Small and Medium Enterprise 38
Social Concept Networks (SCN) 58, 65
socially-mediated learning structures 25
social network analysis (SNA) 58-59, 61-62, 64, 66, 69
social network extraction 59
Spanish Sign Language 164, 166
spillover effect 3
Standard Vectorial Graphics (SVG) 167, 169, 171-174
strategy 1-2, 10, 16-17, 34, 38, 42-44, 47-48, 50, 53-56, 72, 74-77, 80-81, 83, 85, 88-90, 94, 118, 120-123, 126, 129-130, 132-134, 136, 138-139, 146, 148, 150, 152, 154, 159-160, 162, 177, 184, 203, 206, 212, 236, 240
Structural Equation Modeling (SEM) 99, 101, 110
synchronous communications 28-29

T

Task-Technology Fit Model 100
technological matrixing 152
Technology Acceptance Model (TAM) 99-100, 102, 114-117
technology assessment 75, 85-86, 93, 98
technology foresight 85-86, 93
technology gap 74-75, 83-85, 95, 185
technology level 70-72, 76, 80-81, 87, 90
technology roadmapping 85-86, 96
technology spillovers 4-5, 78-79, 95-97
the action cone 137, 139-140, 148
theory of reasoned action (TRA) 100, 102
Topic, Goal and Activity (TGA) 209-210
Topic Mapper application 208, 242
total factor productivity (TFP) 181
Trade-Related Aspects of Intellectual Property Rights (TRIPs) 58, 77, 94, 188, 192-193, 195, 197
transitional city 187, 198
Transnational Corporation (TNC) 4

transportation 9-10, 153, 187, 189-191, 197
travel well quality (tw) 221-222

U

Unified Theory of Acceptance and Use of Technology (UTAUT) 100, 112

V

ValNet project 224
variance inflation factor (VIF) 156
venture capital (VC) 11, 140, 179
Virtual Learning Environments (VLEs) 31, 206, 223, 226, 231, 237, 241
virtual movement 187, 198

Vocabulary Bank for Education (VBE) 211, 240

W

Web 2.0 206, 213, 225
Web Accessibility Initiative (WAI) 164, 169, 174
web simulations 29
World Intellectual Property Organization (WIPO) 76-77
World Trade Organization (WTO) 76-77

Z

Zone of Proximal Development (ZPD) 26